T0369567

JUST SECURITY SERIES

Series Editor
RYAN GOODMAN

Race and National Security

JUST SECURITY

Series Editor
Ryan Goodman
Anne and Joel Ehrenkranz Professor of Law at New York
University School of Law and co-editor-in-chief of Just Security

The *Just Security* book series from Oxford University Press tackles contemporary problems in international law and security that are of interest to a global community of scholars, policymakers, practitioners, and students. With each volume taking a particular thematic focus and gathering leading experts, the series aims to reflect on developments rigorously and critically in these areas of law, policy, and practice. Each volume will be accompanied by a series of shorter digital pieces in *Just Security's* online forum at www.justsecurity.org, which tie the discussion to breaking news and headlines.

This series has been made possible through the extraordinary efforts of many individuals, including *Just Security* Postgraduate Fellow Haley Anderson and Oxford University Press editors John Louth, Merel Alstein, Robert Cavooris, Imogen Hill, and Jacqueline Larabee.

Race and National Security

Edited by

MATIANGAI V.S. SIRLEAF

OXFORD
UNIVERSITY PRESS

Oxford University Press is a department of the University of Oxford.
It furthers the University's objective of excellence in research, scholarship,
and education by publishing worldwide. Oxford is a registered trade mark of
Oxford University Press in the UK and certain other countries.

Published in the United States of America by Oxford University Press
198 Madison Avenue, New York, NY 10016, United States of America.

© Oxford University Press 2023

CIP data is on file at the Library of Congress

ISBN 978–0–19–764823–0 (pbk.)
ISBN 978–0–19–775464–1 (hbk.).

DOI: 10.1093/oso/9780197754641.001.0001

Paperback printed by Marquis Book Printing, Canada
Hardback printed by Bridgeport National Bindery, Inc., United States of America

Note to Readers
This publication is designed to provide accurate and authoritative information in regard to the subject
matter covered. It is based upon sources believed to be accurate and reliable and is intended to be
current as of the time it was written. It is sold with the understanding that the publisher is not engaged
in rendering legal, accounting, or other professional services. If legal advice or other expert assistance is
required, the services of a competent professional person should be sought. Also, to confirm that the
information has not been affected or changed by recent developments, traditional legal research
techniques should be used, including checking primary sources where appropriate.

*(Based on the Declaration of Principles jointly adopted by a Committee of the
American Bar Association and a Committee of Publishers and Associations.)*

You may order this or any other Oxford University Press publication
by visiting the Oxford University Press website at www.oup.com.

For my light and my love.

Contents

V. COMPARATIVE AND INTERNATIONAL PERSPECTIVES ON RACE AND NATIONAL SECURITY

VI. CONCLUSION

Preface

The cover image of this volume depicts federal officers deploying tear gas and other non-fatal munitions at a crowd of about a thousand protesters in front of the Mark O. Hatfield U.S. Courthouse on Thursday, July 24, 2020 in Portland, Oregon. This photograph taken during the racial justice uprising, provokes and disrupts preconceived notions about conflict, the geographic locations where such uses of force are deployed, as well as who "should be" the targets of such overwhelming displays of force. It captures the blurred lines in the field and practice of national security. The image renders visible how institutions and practices of racialized violence at home are connected to border enforcement and the overseas military engagements of the American security state. It also forces us to consider the role of race and racism and how they function in subtle and unsubtle ways – to inform everything from who is the perceived threat, to who is being protected, to whose security is at risk, as well as whose security is imperiled.

This book builds on the *Racing National Security* online symposium, which was published in *Just Security* in 2020 during the racial justice uprising. Professor and *Just Security* Executive Editor Matiangai V.S. Sirleaf curated, edited, and brought that symposium to life. While race and national security have always been intertwined, none of the contributors to the symposium forecasted the issues we were writing about being made visible so starkly and broadcast on television screens around the world.

However, on January 6, 2021, militia groups led a violent attack on the U.S. Capitol. Subsequently, Attorney General Merrick B. Garland told senators that the greatest domestic threat facing the United States came from "racially or ethnically motivated violent extremists," based on a report by the U.S. intelligence community drafted under the auspices of the Office of Director of National Intelligence. In his prepared testimony, Mr. Garland told the Senate that the threat emanated specifically from "those who advocate for the superiority of the [W]hite race." Alongside the threat of [W]hite supremacist violence, a backlash against racial reckoning and transformation has emerged on several fronts including in the sphere of education. Indeed, since "January 2021, 44 states have introduced bills or taken other steps that would restrict teaching critical race theory or limit how teachers can discuss racism and sexism. . . . Eighteen states have imposed these bans and restrictions either through legislation or other avenues" in the United States, as documented by *Education Week* (February 27, 2023). These are perilous times. The urgency of this moment makes it even more vital to return to, and to more fully excavate the question of how race and racism relate to national security domestically, transnationally, and internationally.

MATIANGAI V.S. SIRLEAF

Acknowledgments

Many of the chapters in this book were first published online in *Just Security* for the *Racing National Security* symposium during the racial justice uprising of 2020. I would like to thank *Just Security* for allowing us to adapt earlier versions of essays into more in-depth and durable chapters for this book. I am especially grateful to all the participants in the Race and National Security Workshop held in January 2022. Several experts provided feedback on the contributions in this book, which proved to be incredibly insightful and have greatly enriched this project: Tendayi Achiume, Aziza Ahmed, José Alvarez, Chaz Arnett, Khaled Beydoun, Tess Bridgeman, Maxwell Chibundu, Peter Danchin, Randle DeFalco, Mark Graber, David Gray, Michael Greenberger, Jasmine Gonzales Rose, Leigh Goodmark, Rebecca Hamilton, Adil Haque, J. Benton Heath, Maryam Jamshidi, Darryl Li, Tayyab Mahmud, Zinaida Miller, William Moon, Fionnuala Ní Aoláin, Priscilla Ocen, Michael Pinard, Wadie E. Said, Natsu Taylor Saito, Shirin Sinnar, and Maureen Sweeney. My heartfelt thanks to the editorial team at the University of Maryland School of Law for helping me bring this volume to fruition. Without the diligent editorial and research assistance of Mary Atta-Dakwa, Jennifer Chapman, Fasika Delessa, Alexis Lovings, Halla McDermon, Tamia Morris, and Victoria Roman none of this would have been possible. I would also like to recognize the editors at Oxford University Press, especially Jacqueline Larabee, for bringing this book to the world. I am indebted to Ryan Goodman, the series editor, and Haley Anderson, *Just Security* Postgraduate Fellow, for their support of this project. Finally, an extra-special shout-out goes to the contributors to this book for their intellectual fortitude and for dedicating their time and talents to this project.

List of Contributors

Andrea Armstrong, Dr. Norman C. Francis Distinguished Professor of Law, Loyola University New Orleans College of Law

Aslı Bâli, Professor of Law, Yale Law School

Monica C. Bell, Professor of Law, Yale Law School; Associate Professor of Sociology, Yale University

Adelle Blackett, Professor of Law and Canada Research Chair in Transnational Labour Law and Development, McGill University

Noura Erakat, Associate Professor of Africana Studies and the Program in Criminal Justice, Rutgers University, New Brunswick

James Thuo Gathii, Professor of Law and Wing-Tat Lee Chair in International Law, Loyola University Chicago School of Law; 2022–2023 William H. Neukom Fellows Research Chair in Diversity and Law, American Bar Foundation

Margaret Hu, Professor of Law and Director of the Digital Democracy Lab, William & Mary Law School

Yuvraj Joshi, Assistant Professor, Brooklyn Law School; Fellow, Harvard Carr Center for Human Rights; Faculty Affiliate, UCLA Promise Institute for Human Rights

Rachel López, Director of the Andy and Gwen Stern Community Lawyering Clinic, Associate Professor of Law, Drexel University Kline School of Law

Catherine Powell, Eunice Carter Distinguished Research Scholar Professor of Law, Fordham University School of Law; Adjunct Senior Fellow, Council on Foreign Relations

Jaya Ramji-Nogales, Associate Dean for Research & I. Herman Stern Research Professor, Temple University School of Law

Aziz Rana, Provost's Distinguished Fellow in 2023–2024, and then the J. Donald Monan, SJ, Chair in Law and Government beginning in 2024 Boston College Law School

Matiangai V.S. Sirleaf, Nathan Patz Professor of Law, University of Maryland School of Law; Professor, Department of Epidemiology and Public Health, University of Maryland School of Medicine

I
INTRODUCTION

Confronting the Color Line
in National Security

Matiangai V.S. Sirleaf

*The problem of the 20th century is the problem of the color-
line . . . the question of how far differences of race . . . will here-
after be made the basis of denying to over half the world the right
of sharing to their utmost ability the opportunities and privileges of
modern civilization. – W.E.B. Du Bois[1]*

Introduction: Hidden in Plain Sight

Failing to see and engage with race[2] obscures the role of racism and White
supremacy in national security.[3] Indeed, the relative absence of race in national security is especially striking when one considers that the *Journal of
Race Development* founded in 1910 was the first academic journal in the
United States in the discipline. The *Journal of Race Development* was subsequently renamed the *Journal of International Relations*, and later became

---

[1] W.E.B. Du Bois, *To the Nations of the World, in* LIFT EVERY VOICE: AFRICAN AMERICAN ORATORY,
1787–1900, at 905, 906 (Philip S. Foner & Robert James Branham eds., 1998) (1900).
[2] This edited volume understands race as the socially constructed and contingent system of
meaning that is attached to aspects of morphology and ancestry. *See* IAN HANEY L. LÓPEZ, WHITE BY
LAW: THE LEGAL CONSTRUCTION OF RACE xxi, 10 (2006).
[3] Motivated by this, I created and curated an online series hosted by *Just Security*, which ran from
July 13 to August 7, 2020, entitled "Racing National Security." This print volume expands the shorter
online pieces to be more in-depth and enduring. It affords an opportunity for the original series
contributors to provide more developed treatment of race in national security. It also expands the
scope of topics and number of contributors to afford this important topic the book-length treatment it deserves. *See* Matiangai Sirleaf, *Racing National Security: Introduction to the Just Security
Symposium*, JUST SEC. (July 13, 2020), https://www.justsecurity.org/71373/racing-national-secur
ity-introduction-to-the-just-security-symposium/#:~:text=%E2%80%9CRacing%20National%20S
ecurity%2C%E2%80%9D%20draws,center%20in%20national%20security%20discussions.

Matiangai V.S. Sirleaf, *Confronting the Color Line in National Security* In: *Race and National Security.* Edited by: Matiangai
V.S. Sirleaf, Oxford University Press. © Oxford University Press 2023. DOI: 10.1093/oso/9780197754641.003.0001

Foreign Affairs in 1922. It is worth remembering how demarcations based on race and empire were explicitly part of the calculus of defining the field's initial contours.

Writing in 1915, W.E.B. Du Bois noted that:

the brutal truth is clearing: a [W]hite man is privileged to go to any land where advantage beckons and behave as he pleases; the [B]lack or colored man is being more and more confined to those parts of the world where life for climatic, historical, economic, and political reasons is most difficult to live and most easily dominated by Europe for Europe's gain.[4]

He continued: "[T]hese nations and races, composing as they do a vast majority of humanity, are going to endure this treatment just as long as they must and not a moment longer."[5]

In his 1925 article in *Foreign Affairs*, "Worlds of Color," Du Bois argued that the "colour problem and the labor problem" were "two sides of the same tangle."[6] In 1935, Du Bois concluded that conflicts, like the Italian and Ethiopian war, would exacerbate tensions along the "global colour line."[7] His scholarship and the work of others on race and race relations indicate how foundational a racial analysis is to understanding the world order. As Robert Vitalis has argued, during "the first decades of the 20th century in the United States, international relations meant race relations. . . . The problem of empire or imperialism, sometimes referred to as 'race subjection,' was what preoccupied the first self-identified professors of international relations."[8]

Resurfacing this history is critical for understanding the subfield and practice of national security today. International relations "was concerned not with the consequences of the anarchical structure of world order, as it is" currently understood, but as Vitalis argues, "with the dynamics of domination and dependency among the world's [purportedly] superior and inferior races. The first self-identified 'realists' sought the preservation of exclusivist national and Anglo-Saxon prerogatives in exploiting the raw materials, labor, and material wants" of subordinated races.[9] Vitalis goes on to observe that the first Black scholars "(and only them) in a deeply segregated

---

[4] W.E.B. Du Bois, *The African Roots of War*, ATLANTIC (May 1915), https://www.theatlantic.com/magazine/archive/1915/05/the-african-roots-of-war/528897/.

[5] *Id.*

[6] W.E.B. Du Bois, *Worlds of Color*, 3 FOREIGN AFFS. 423, 442 (1925).

[7] W.E.B. Du Bois, *Inter-Racial Implications of the Ethiopian Crisis: A Negro View*, 14 FOREIGN AFF. 82 (1935).

[8] ROBERT VITALIS, WHITE WORLD ORDER, BLACK POWER POLITICS: THE BIRTH OF AMERICAN INTERNATIONAL RELATIONS 1 (2015).

[9] *Id.* at 106.

academy challenged" conventional wisdom in the field.[10] The dominant actors in the field did not sufficiently engage with the scholarship and critical interventions of Du Bois and other contemporaries. The presumption of racial differences as natural and inevitable tended to background the ways in which race, racialization and racism functioned in international relations. Even after World War II, the primacy given to "security" in international relations and its role as an organizing concept was not divorced from race.

Today questions of race and racial justice are still hidden in plain sight. It is quite common for textbooks in contemporary national security and foreign relations law to not engage with race at all.[11] When a book on U.S. foreign relations law or national security law examines race, such discussions are typically relegated to a single chapter, if that.[12] Yet the lack of sustained treatment of race, which silos race as some special topic that is of marginal relevance to the discipline is deeply problematic. Presumably, the obscuring of race may be in part influenced by the state-centric nature of much of the discipline and practice. The state as the primary unit of inquiry may tend to shift attention from macro-structural processes that facilitate racial subordination and stratification transnationally. Moreover, the absence of a racial analysis from national security texts may occur due to the erroneous view that important matters of national security obviate the need for consideration of race. However, the tendency to background and decenter race in conventional work on national security given the origins of the field and ongoing practices in it is baffling.

This volume builds on the voices of those that have demanded that national security engage with the historical and ongoing effects of race and racism.[13]

---

[10] Id.

[11] When you survey recent textbooks many do not even have a single chapter dedicated to race. See, e.g., GEOFFREY S. CORN ET AL., NATIONAL SECURITY LAW AND THE CONSTITUTION (2d ed. 2021); NATIONAL SECURITY LAW, PROCEDURE, AND PRACTICE (Robert Ward & Rupert Jones eds., 2021); JOHN NORTON MOORE & ROBERT F. TURNER, NATIONAL SECURITY LAW (2d ed. 2005); CURTIS A. BRADLEY, ASHLEY DEEKS & JACK L. GOLDSMITH, FOREIGN RELATIONS LAW: CASES AND MATERIALS (7th ed. 2020); H.L. POHLMAN, U.S. NATIONAL SECURITY LAW: AN INTERNATIONAL PERSPECTIVE (2018); NATIONAL SECURITY LAW AND POLICY: A READER (Melanie Marlowe & Thomas Karako eds., forthcoming June 2023).

[12] See STEPHEN DYCUS ET AL., NATIONAL SECURITY LAW (7th ed. 2020) (dedicating one chapter out of its forty-one to covering the issues of profiling and travel bans).

[13] This volume is in conversation with several works. For instance, AYANNA YONEMURA, RACE, NATION, WAR: JAPANESE AMERICAN FORCED REMOVAL, PUBLIC POLICY AND NATIONAL SECURITY (2019), examines international post-9/11 policies by connecting them to U.S. violations of Japanese Americans' human rights during World War II and illustrating how ideas of race and masculinity shape national security reactions. While this book certainly examines race, it does so by zeroing in on Japanese internment and does not consider other ways in which racialized national security practices have manifested. Other works that the edited volume is in conversation with tend to focus on a subordinated group and explore the racialized nature of national security with respect to that

Several contemporary scholars have sought to bring issues of race from the periphery to the center in national security discussions. In 1998, Natsu Taylor Saito wrote in "Crossing the Border: The Interdependence of Foreign Policy and Racial Justice in the United States" that the ill-treatment of racial and ethnic minorities within the borders of the United States makes it easier to disregard the rights and humanity of those outside the border.[14] Further, in Ruth Gordon's "Racing U.S. Foreign Policy," she questioned how race affects lawmaking and decision making in foreign policy and international law.[15] Makau Matua's work has also drawn attention to how international law, like national law, is captive to racial biases and hierarchies.[16] Certainly, experts like Henry J. Richardson III have also examined the role of race in U.S. foreign interventions in "U.S. Hegemony, Race, and Oil in Deciding United Nations Security Council Resolution 1441 on Iraq."[17] Moreover, Tayyab Mahmud's scholarship unearthed how constructions of race shaped the colonial encounter and influenced the development of nationalism and a security apparatus aimed at upholding racial hierarchy.[18] As important as this scholarship has been, far too much of the work done on race, empire, colonialism, and national security have been limited to short form pieces, which makes it harder to see through lines and to draw connections between theoretical insights.[19]

---

group. These include works like NICOLE NGUYEN, SUSPECT COMMUNITIES: ANTI-MUSLIM RACISM AND THE DOMESTIC WAR ON TERROR (2019), which describes how the drive to bring liberal reforms to contemporary security regimes through "community-driven" and "ideologically ecumenical" programming has further institutionalized anti-Muslim racism in the United States, id. at 31, and SAHER SELOD, FOREVER SUSPECT: RACIALIZED SURVEILLANCE OF MUSLIM AMERICANS IN THE WAR ON TERROR (2018), which argues that Muslim Americans have experienced higher levels of racism in their everyday lives since 9/11 and the declaration of the "war on terror." While important, none of these contributions examine the multitude of experiences with race and national security that historically subordinated groups face.

[14] Natsu Taylor Saito, Crossing the Border: The Interdependence of Foreign Policy and Racial Justice in the United States, 1 YALE HUM. RTS. & DEV. L.J. 53 (1998).

[15] Ruth Gordon, Racing U.S. Foreign Policy, 17 NAT'L BLACK L.J. 1 (2003).

[16] Makau W. Mutua, Critical Race Theory and International Law: The View of an Insider-Outsider, 45 VILL. L. REV. 841 (2000).

[17] Henry J. Richardson III, U.S. Hegemony, Race, and Oil in Deciding United Nations Security Council Resolution 1441 on Iraq, 17 TEMP. INT'L & COMP. L.J. 27 (2003).

[18] See, e.g., Tayyab Mahmud, Colonialism and Modern Constructions of Race: A Preliminary Inquiry, 53 U. MIAMI L. REV. 1219 (1999).

[19] In marked contrast, in January of 2020, the UCLA Law Review held a symposium on Transnational Legal Discourse on Race and Empire. The organizers of the symposium Tendayi Achiume and Aslı Bâli sought to revive connections between and amongst Third World Approaches to International Law scholars and Critical Race Theory scholars in a collaboration aimed at shared issues of concern on race, empire, and international law. See E. Tendayi Achiume & Aslı Bâli, Race and Empire: Legal Theory Within, Through, and Across National Borders, 67 UCLA L. REV. 1386 (2021) (introducing the symposium issue).

Significantly, this volume clarifies how White supremacy informs and shapes the parameters of what "counts" as national security. While several works in other fields and related disciplines[20] have considered the role of race extensively, national security as a field is lagging in many respects. Moreover, work in the field of critical security studies, while laudable, tends to engage with race as a subset of other critiques.[21] The field of critical security studies was recently compelled to engage with race in a sustained way.[22] Further, in recent years, gender has received much-needed attention as a critical lens on national security.[23] This has resulted in essential work in gendering national security. This edited volume provides analogous book-length treatment for addressing the crucial topic of racing national security.

Race and National Security interrogates what it would mean for the field and concept of national security to take issues of race and racial justice seriously. This volume is groundbreaking because it brings domestic, transnational, comparative, and international law perspectives on race and national security in conversation with each other. Pieces that would not otherwise appear together do so in this volume, leading to important theoretical and policy insights for reforming and transforming national security. The volume is intersectional in its approach with several of the contributions engaging with race and religion, race and gender, as well as language, and other forms of positionality. By unearthing what is otherwise hidden in plain sight, this

[20] *See, e.g.*, RACE AND RACISM IN INTERNATIONAL RELATIONS: CONFRONTING THE GLOBAL COLOUR LINE (Alexander Anievas, Nivi Manchanda & Robbie Shilliam eds., 2015); *see also* DECOLONIZING INTERNATIONAL RELATIONS (Branwen Gruffydd Jones ed., 2006).

[21] COLUMBA PEOPLES & NICK VAUGHAN-WILLIAMS, CRITICAL SECURITY STUDIES: AN INTRODUCTION (3d ed. 2021).

[22] *See* Alison Howell & Melanie Richter-Montpetit, *Is Securitization Theory Racist?: Civilizationalism, Methodological Whiteness, and Antiblack Thought in the Copenhagen School*, 51 SEC. DIALOGUE 3 (2020) (discussing securitization theory's anti-Blackness and methodological Whiteness). Their article prompted responses from the architects of securitization theory accusing Howell and Richter-Montpetit of poor scholarship. *See* Ole Wæver & Barry Buzan, *Racism and Responsibility—The Critical Limits of Deepfake Methodology in Security Studies*, 51 SEC. DIALOGUE 386 (2020). *See also* Lene Hansen, *Are "Core" Feminist Critiques of Securitization Theory Racist?*, 51 SEC. DIALOGUE 378 (2020) (providing another rejoinder to Howell and Richter-Montpetit's work). The backlash to these responses led the journal *Security Dialogue* to create a scholarly forum on race and racism within critical security studies. *See* Mark Salter et al., *Race and Racism in Critical Security Studies*, 52 SEC. DIALOGUE 3 (2021) (discussing the controversy, fallout, the call for papers, and the publication of the forum as a special supplement).

[23] *See, e.g.*, JOANA COOK, A WOMAN'S PLACE: US COUNTERTERRORISM SINCE 9/11 (2020) (reviewing the role of women in U.S. counterterrorism in the wider Middle East and at home); THE GENDER IMPERATIVE: HUMAN SECURITY VS STATE SECURITY (Betty A. Reardon & Asha Han eds., 2018) (describing the gendered aspects of human security excluded from the realist militarism that dominates current security policy in most countries); GENDER, NATIONAL SECURITY, AND COUNTER-TERRORISM: HUMAN RIGHTS PERSPECTIVES (Margaret L. Satterthwaite & Jayne Huckerby eds., 2014) (integrating gender into a human rights analysis of counterterrorism).

volume demonstrates that foregrounding race, as Du Bois proposed, is a task that is necessary not only for the field and practice of national security but also the discipline of domestic and international law more generally.

Reconceptualizing National Security

Centering race as an analytical tool in this volume assists in counteracting the "color-blind" approach to national security of many practitioners, policymakers, scholars, and students of national security. Several contributions in this volume advocate forcefully for dispensing with the normalization of Whiteness in national security. For instance, James Thuo Gathii in chapter one, argues for overcoming the disciplinary silos that characterizes the study of national security law, which results in the obfuscation of the field's intimate relationship to race, colonial era doctrines, and imperialism.

What constitutes national security is deeply contested.[24] National security as traditionally conceived refers to protecting a nation from military attack and safeguarding its political security. Contributors to this volume expand significantly on the contours of national security. The sheer breadth and depth of the topics and vantage points covered challenge conventional knowledge about national security. For example, Monica C. Bell, in chapter four, pushes the boundaries of what the concept of security entails and highlights the importance of reframing and centering affected communities' vision of security. Additionally, Catherine Powell's analysis of systemic racism, poverty, and police brutality in chapter two broadens the lens of analysis beyond military security to encompass economic, physical, and human security in ways that pay acute attention to the security of racially subordinated groups.

Race and National Security seeks to fundamentally shift how national security is conceptualized by helping to redefine the field and practice. Several contributions in this volume challenge national security orthodoxy and disrupt accepted truths. For example, in chapter three, Aziz Rana contends that the myth of the field's civil libertarian origins ignores the extent to which there is no golden age to revive. He insists that arguments centered on what the framers would have wanted regarding checks and balances offer a limited

---

[24] J. Benton Heath, *Making Sense of Security*, 116 AM. J. INT'L L. 289, 313–15 (2022).

account of the reforms necessary for genuinely protecting basic rights as well as for pursuing anti-imperial change in the present. Rana insists that race and colonialism have structured national security decisions from everything including decisions to go to war, to intervening in foreign places and in determining when a threat exists.

Race as Structuring National Security

Unquestionably, one of the persistent ways that race manifests in national security law is in the determination of who and what counts as a "threat." Several chapters in this volume illustrate how ideas about race perpetuate and reinforce existing hierarchies. Rachel López, in chapter eleven, elucidates how the jurisdictional and substantive law that governs the International Criminal Court systematically results in Black guilt being heightened while White guilt is minimized. López's work explores how the well-documented stereotype of darker skin being associated with wrongdoing and criminality plays out in international criminal law, with several implications for national security law and practice. Additionally, in chapter six, Jaya Ramji-Nogales charts how immigration law in the United States constructs and perpetuates racist imaginaries of national security that locate the border on people of color, including and extending beyond migrants. Her piece explicitly engages with the concept of "foreignness" as a label that contains within it race, religion, and language. Ramji-Nogales elucidates how immigration law performs the work of racial, religious, and linguistic discrimination through distinctions facially based on nationality. She demonstrates the complicity of national security frameworks in constructing and amplifying "foreignness" as a basis of exclusion. By surfacing the role of race, both pieces do significant work in unraveling the power of racialized hierarchies and the harm that they inflict on people of color.

Numerous interventions in this book also explicitly engage with the period of national and global reckoning on race and transformation provoked by the racial justice uprising of 2020 and the ongoing backlash prompted by it in ways that other projects have not. The seemingly unrelenting onslaught of police violence against Black people in the United States has resulted in many lives lost, both seen and unseen. Once-familiar names and hashtags have since been replaced with new ones. The banal circumstances surrounding their deaths indicate the precariousness of Black lives. The very ease with which our lives can be disposed presents substantial questions for security. During the racial justice uprising of 2020, people across the globe joined together demanding full equality, accountability, and an end to police brutality and systemic racism.[25] In the United States, the response to the uprising and allies protesting racial subordination included substantial militarization with armored vehicles, curfews, tear gas, pepper spray, and rubber and wooden bullets.[26] The uprising illuminated how quickly and swiftly some states are willing to deploy the military and police forces to quell those agitating for racial justice.

Yet the intersection between race and national security has only been made even clearer, following January 6, 2021, with images of an armed insurrection at the U.S. Capitol incorporating explicit White supremacist elements splashed across television screens and the front pages of newspapers worldwide. Nana Osei-Opare argued well before the insurrection that mainstream discussions obfuscate "White terrorism" from national security such that seemingly only non-Western bodies are capable of terrorism.[27] Some commentators like Tina Patel have even questioned whether the security framing simply masks racism inherent in counterterrorism strategies.[28] Juxtaposing the drastically different police responses to January 6 and the uprising is instructive. The tepid and at times complicit responses of law enforcement to an insurgency were in marked contrast to their actions during the uprising. Against this background, it is crucial to interrogate the role of national security in efforts to enforce the racial status quo and uphold racial hierarchy.

---

[25] Damien Cave, Livia Albeck-Ripka & Iliana Magra, *Huge Crowds Around the Globe March in Solidarity Against Policy Brutality*, N.Y. TIMES (June 6, 2020), https://www.nytimes.com/2020/06/06/world/george-floyd-global-protests.html.

[26] Tom Nolan, *Militarization Has Fostered a Policing Culture that Sets Up Protesters as "The Enemy,"* RICE U: KINDER INST. FOR URB. RSCH. (June 10, 2020), https://kinder.rice.edu/urbanedge/2020/06/10/police-brutality-militarization-racism-protests [https://perma.cc/94RC-SF52]; Liz Szabo et al., *Fractured Skulls, Lost Eyes: Police Break Their Own Rules when Shooting Protesters with "Rubber Bullets,"* USA TODAY (Sept. 11, 2020), https://www.usatoday.com/in-depth/news/nation/2020/06/19/police-break-rules-shooting-protesters-rubber-bulletsless-lethal-projectiles/3211421001 [https://perma.cc/5WJC-GAFE].

[27] Nana Osei-Opare, *Terrorism and Racism, Twin Sisters?*, 39 UFAHAMU: A J. AFR. STUD. 33 (2016).

[28] Tina G. Patel, *It's Not About Security, It's About Racism: Counter-terror Strategies, Civilizing Processes and the Post-Race Fiction*, 3 PALGRAVE COMMC'NS. 17031, 17031 (2017).

Centering Subordinated Groups

Conventional works tend to exclude from the vaulted category of national security topics that directly pertain to the security of subordinated groups, such as domestic policing in the United States and systemic racism in U.S. foreign policy and foreign affairs. However, contributions in this volume refocus the frame of reference. For instance, in chapter seven, Margaret Hu forcefully argues that the unprecedented collection of biometric data of the Afghan people by and under the direction of the United States from 2001 to 2021 transformed into both a method for data colonization and resource extraction, as well as a vehicle for surveillance capitalism. Her interrogation of the racialized impact of biometric cybersurveillance renders visible an experiment of sociotechnical control and coercion in both foreign and domestic spheres. Hu cautions us that after beta testing of biometric and cybersurveillance technologies abroad, these technologies have migrated to the United States and have been revealed in instances of militarized policing, especially within communities of color.

Several contributions to this volume similarly demonstrate how national security law and its implementation may subtly and directly facilitate racial subordination nationally and globally. In chapter five, Andrea Armstrong's analysis of experiences of Black and Latine incarcerated women shows both the raced and gendered nature of the security state. Additionally, in chapter nine, Noura Erakat examines how Israel's shoot-to-kill policy is predicated on the racialization of Palestinians within the framework of national security law. Erakat then uses an internationalist approach, which situates Black subjugation in the United States in the context of global regimes of capital, violence, and governance, to help explain the militarized response to Black uprisings. Erakat's piece captivatingly utilizes the metaphor of the "shrinking civilian" and sheds light on how the racialization of Black and Palestinian people render them always already guilty. Through this reframing and focusing on the faces at the bottom of the well,[29] the contributions in this volume create a far more accurate understanding of how race manifests in national security domestically, transnationally, and globally.

---

[29] DERRICK BELL, FACES AT THE BOTTOM OF THE WELL: THE PERMANENCE OF RACISM (1993).

The Importance of Racial Justice

This book positions racial justice as fundamental to understanding national security as praxis and theory. Notably, many of the contributions in this volume highlight the significance of a racial justice framework over and above one solely focused on racial discrimination. In chapter eight, Aslı Bâli concludes that defunding the police will require a transformative vision for the sprawling security state, one that disrupts practices of racialized violence and advances a vision of racial justice at home and abroad.

Centering a racial justice approach shifts the focus from an absence of discrimination and inequities. Instead, the focus is on constructing intentional structures and supports to attain and sustain racially just outcomes through preemptive and preventive practices and procedures. Shifting the framework to racial justice is necessary because of the strong associations that tend to view racism as psychological. Frantz Fanon long ago pointed out the problematic tendency of considering racial discrimination as the product of a mental quirk.[30] Instead, *Race and National Security* explicitly turns the emphasis toward subverting White hegemonic power and dominance in national security. Yuvraj Joshi's contribution in chapter ten maintains that recent racial justice uprisings should shift U.S.-based discussions of transitional justice, from gazing outward toward the international community to attending to the legacies of slavery, segregation, and White supremacy at home. Further, Adelle Blackett's chapter twelve contends that in their quest for racial justice, African Americans and pan-Africanist leaders have repeatedly turned to international organizations like the United Nations and the International Labor Organization. Blackett unmasks how these organizations are falling short of their founding documents, which link international peace, security, and social justice. She suggests that instead of relying on ad hoc statements and past antiracist efforts, the United Nations should take action to redress anti-Black racism throughout the United Nations system to further racial justice efforts. This and other contributions adopt a racial justice framework, which requires consideration of macro-structural processes that facilitate racial subordination and stratification as opposed to focusing on discrete episodes of individual discrimination. *Race and National Security* recognizes not only the gravity of the historical moment that continues to unfold in the United States and elsewhere but also the opening and potential

[30] *See* Frantz Fanon, Toward the African Revolution 38 (Haakon Chevalier trans., 1969).

that it presents to spark and revitalize debate and policy changes on these crucial issues globally.

There are several limitations of the volume. First, more explicit engagement with intersectionality as an approach would have been generative especially on gender and class lines. Moreover, while various contributions draw distinctions and highlight the interconnections of anti-Black and anti-Muslim policies in national security, this and other work could benefit from deeper engagement with how Latine and Asian people experience national security. A further limitation of this volume is that it could have rendered Whiteness more visible in national security law by dedicating more treatment to the very real threats posed by violent White nationalist groups.[31] Additionally, this volume is American-centric. The reach of the American security apparatus is so vast that perhaps such acute attention to the American security-state is warranted. However, in so doing this volume does not sufficiently account for how race and national security function in other places and contexts.

My intention is that *Race and National Security* will become a foundational text to inform future research and developments in this important area. My hope is that this book will serve as a primer and useful entry point. Ideally, this volume will serve as a catalyst for remembering, exposing, and reimagining the role of race in national security.

Organization of the Book

The book is organized around four interventions. Part II of the book explores the question of *why race and national security at all*. In chapter one, James Thuo Gathii makes the case that foreign affairs, colonialism, imperialism, and race are and have always been closely and intimately connected. In chapter two, Catherine Powell cautions that due in part to a narrow and privileged conception of national security, racism remains a deadly virus. She argues for a more expansive understanding of security. In chapter three, Aziz Rana, maintains that ignoring the structuring role of race and colonialism is deep-rooted in understandings of American ideas and practices in foreign

---

[31] Eileen Sullivan & Katie Benner, *Top Law Enforcement Officials Say the Biggest Domestic Terror Threat Comes from White Supremacists*, N.Y. TIMES (May 12, 2021), https://www.nytimes.com/2021/05/12/us/politics/domestic-terror-white-supremacists.html.

interventions, war-making, and threat perceptions. All the chapters in this section indicate how integral a racial analysis is for understanding national security in theory and in practice.

Part III of the book excavates the limits of national security—by inquiring *what the scope of national security is and, as a corollary, whose national security*. One limitation in national security is that policymakers are seemingly more focused on spectacular and direct acts of violence than slow or structural violence.[32] Monica C. Bell, in chapter four, questions the prioritization of the *thin safety*, for example, that the police may contribute to instead of the *thick safety* that all people, including Black people, are seeking. In chapter five, Andrea Armstrong uses an intersectional analysis focusing on incarcerated women of color, which raises questions of "security for whom" and highlights how disrupting secrecy is critical for reimagining security. Her chapter draws important parallels between domestic and international carceral spaces and the gendered dynamics informing their operations. In chapter six, Jaya Ramji-Nogales delves deeper into the issue of whose national security. She breaks down how immigration law in the United States constructs and perpetuates racist imaginaries of national security that locate the border on people of color, which includes but is not limited to migrants. Examining several points in the historical development of the concept of national security in immigration law, this chapter illustrates the work that "foreignness" performs in defending White supremacy and justifying the unequal distribution of political and economic power. The contributions in this section of the book raise fundamental issues about the project of national security—its purpose, contours, and its audience and beneficiaries.

All the pieces in the fourth Part of the book investigate the "imperial boomerang effect," which is a term used to capture "the way in which empires use their colonies as *laboratories* for methods of counter-insurgency, social control and repression, methods which can then be brought back to the imperial metropolis and deployed against the marginalised, subjugated and subaltern within."[33] In chapter seven, Margaret Hu interrogates these issues by analyzing how surveillance technologies ostensibly deployed for

---

[32] *See* Johan Galtung, *Violence, Peace, and Peace Research*, 6 J. PEACE RSCH. 167, 171 (1967); *see also* ROB NIXON, SLOW VIOLENCE AND THE ENVIRONMENTALISM OF THE POOR 13 (2011).

[33] Connor Woodman, *The Imperial Boomerang: How Colonial Methods of Repression Migrate Back to the Metropolis*, VERSO BLOG (June 9, 2020), https://www.versobooks.com/blogs/4383-the-imperial-boomerang-how-colonial-methods-of-repression-migrate-back-to-the-metropolis.

national security purposes during the "war on terror" abroad have been redeployed domestically against antiracism activists. Her chapter concludes that the biometric surveillance technology that the United States perfected in Afghanistan during its occupation is a form of data colonization and surveillance capitalism. Hu's chapter warns that the risks of entrenching biometric surveillance testing and use will fall disproportionately on people of color internally and externally. In chapter eight, Aslı Bâli connects the dots between two important movements that both gained momentum during the racial justice uprising of 2020: calls to "defund the police" and demands to end the United State's endless wars abroad. This chapter examines how techniques, weapons, and personnel circulate between wars abroad and militarized policing at home. It exposes the linkages in the military-industrial-policing complex. In chapter nine, Noura Erakat uses the analytical framework offered by Black Palestinian solidarity to reveal the co-constitutive nature of racism and colonialism as it relates to the state violence of extrajudicial killings of unarmed Black people in the United States and unarmed Palestinians. This chapter traces the iterative development of police militarization and highlights how contemporary U.S. law enforcement trainings in Israel are among the most recent instantiations of this problematic trend. Erakat's contribution explicitly utilizes Aimé Césaire's "boomerang effect," wherein the effect of colonization dehumanizes both the colonizer and the colonized[34] to explain the militarized responses to Black and Palestinian existence and protests. The contributions reveal how national security methods of repression developed for "over there" migrate back to the metropolis to be implemented on those that are othered internally.

The fifth Part of the book begins necessary discussions on *what remedy and redress might entail when race and racial justice is centered in national security* by looking to comparative and international perspectives. In chapter ten, Yuvraj Joshi observes that the U.S. government has endorsed transitional justice approaches abroad while ignoring the need for it at home. This chapter demonstrates that the centuries-long oppression of Black Americans is precisely the kind of massive human rights violation that necessitates a systematic transitional justice response. In chapter eleven, Rachel López warns that international criminal law risks being not much more than an expression of racialized perceptions of wrongdoing. Both the field of national

---

[34] AIMÉ CÉSAIRE, DISCOURSE ON COLONIALISM 36 (Joan Pinkham trans., 2000).

security law and international criminal law could be portrayed as what López terms as an extension of international law's civilizing mission, which relies on stereotypes regarding the inherent violence and inferiority of those othered as people of color. In chapter twelve, Adelle Blackett turns our attention to redressing anti-Black racism throughout the United Nations system. Blackett recommends that a fitting place to initiate necessary internal work would be to name a Special Representative to the United Nations Secretary-General on People of African Descent, with a mandate to look closely and carefully at the United Nations' past, present, and future role in addressing anti-Black racism, while building proactive measures to ensure critical representation of people of African descent throughout the United Nations and its specialized agencies. These preliminary interventions by no means exhaust the world of possibilities for transformation and reform. Instead, they indicate that national security both as praxis and theory has a lot to learn from work in other fields, but also that it has a lot to gain from confronting race in national security.

Finally, the book concludes with my own ruminations on the tremendous possibilities and numerous theoretical and policy implications offered in the volume. The problems identified are so profound and integral that the utility of reforms that tinker around the edges of the apparatus of national security is suspect. Using an abolitionist framework, this chapter finds that the security state has deleterious consequences for communities internally and externally and must be abolished as currently constituted. The only way to limit the excesses of the security state is to reduce its footprint in the world. In other words, if there is less contact between the public and the security state apparatus, then there are fewer opportunities for the security state to brutalize and enact violence. Yet fundamentally re-envisioning national security is more than just reducing the size and scope of the security state.

The final chapter challenges some of the core assumptions of national security, including removing from government officials their continuous capacity to exercise largely unfettered discretionary violence. It puts forward an abolitionist vision of security, which imagines a world where the security state does not keep Black, Brown, and other marginalized peoples subordinated through threats of and actual arrest, detention, torture, incarceration, violence, and death. Utilizing an abolitionist framework also provides a lens to question the ability of the current approach to deal with the worst of the worst offenders. Abolitionists encourage us to use radical imagination to envision another world. This chapter asks what it would mean to reimagine national security and the reach of the security state. If scholars and policymakers are really committed to addressing race and racism in national security in theory and in practice and to centering the experiences of those terminally on the receiving end of racialized state violence, radical imagination may well be the only meaningful path forward for true national security.

II

WHY RACE AND NATIONAL SECURITY?

1

Beyond Color-Blind National Security Law

James Thuo Gathii

Introduction

The metaphor that best exemplifies the wide gulf between those who acknowledge and explicitly engage with the racialized nature of many national security issues in their work and those who do not is that of two ships passing in the night—completely unaware and oblivious of each other.[1] The first ship carries approaches that connect and make visible how national security legal and policy questions are often intimately connected to issues of race and identity. It is marginalized by the second ship, which is the mainstream and predominantly White national security policy and scholarly community. This second ship carries approaches that emphasize doctrinal dilemmas and theoretical quandaries—what I call "plain vanilla" or color-blind scholarship and practice. This book is one small step toward demarginalizing critical approaches to national security law and policy that trace the centrality of race in national security policy and discourse.

Far too often, discussions about law in general, and national security law and foreign affairs specifically, are color blind.[2] This chapter builds on prior scholarship linking the two areas of national security and foreign affairs while contributing to the nascent efforts sparked by the post-Floyd uprising against systemic racism to demarginalize race in national security law and foreign affairs. The importance of continuing these efforts is reflected by the fact that the renewed focus on systemic racism in the United States is already

---

[1] *See* James Gathii, *Burying Sovereignty All Over Again: A Brief Review of Don Herzog's* Sovereignty RIP, EJIL: TALK! (July 7, 2020), https://www.ejiltalk.org/burying-sovereignty-all-over-again-a-brief-review-of-don-herzogs-sovereignty-rip/.

[2] When Just Security convened its 2020 symposium on Racing National Security, where a prior draft of this chapter was published, I began by congratulating Just Security for adding two phenomenal scholars, Matiangai Sirleaf and E. Tendayi Achiume, to its editorial board. That series as well as this book project shows that editorial appointments can be key to opening up conversations that are not traditional in the area of national security and foreign affairs in spaces like Just Security and indeed in much of public international law.

James Thuo Gathii, *Beyond Color-Blind National Security Law* In: *Race and National Security*. Edited by: Matiangai V.S. Sirleaf, Oxford University Press. © Oxford University Press 2023. DOI: 10.1093/oso/9780197754641.003.0002

experiencing a sustained right-wing backlash, which seeks to nip in the bud efforts that are more systemically tracing the indelible footprint of race across many disciplines.[3]

For those of us who adopt a non-mainstream or critical approach to the study of international law and international relations,[4] it has always been clear that national security, foreign affairs, and race are closely and intimately connected.[5] Hopefully, the pigeonholes that segregate where and by whom each is discussed in policy, activist, and academic circles will continue to erode.[6]

This chapter is a general overview of the relationship between international law, race, and violence. It uses examples from international law and practices of colonialism, and their enduring legacy to date, to support my claim about the close links between national security, foreign affairs, and race. In the second section, I trace the relationship between international law, race, and violence by focusing on how African Americans and Third World intellectuals have traced this relationship in the context of antislavery and anticolonialism. The third section extends this discussion by looking in-depth at the 2004 *Rasul* case in the U.S. Supreme Court, as well as the habeas cases it cited brought against colonial authorities by anticolonial nationalists in commonwealth Africa.

---

[3] *See* Office of the U.N. High Commissioner on Human Rights, Statement on the Protests against Systemic Racism in the United States (June 5, 2020), https://www.ohchr.org/en/NewsEvents/Pages/DisplayNews.aspx?NewsID=25927&LangID=E.

[4] *See, e.g.,* Tilden J. LeMelle & George W. Shepherd Jr., *Race in the Future of International Relations,* 25 J. INT'L AFFS. 302 (1971); ERIC K. YAMAMOTO, LORRAINE J. BANNAI & MARGARET CHON, RACE, RIGHTS AND NATIONAL SECURITY: LAW AND THE JAPANESE AMERICAN INCARCERATION (3d ed. 2021).

[5] *See, e.g.,* Ileana Porras, *On Terrorism: Reflections on Violence and the Outlaw,* 1994 UTAH L. REV. 119 (1994), https://repository.law.miami.edu/cgi/viewcontent.cgi?article=1734&context=fac_artic les; Gil Gott, *A Tale of New Precedents: Japanese American Interment as Foreign Affairs Law,* 19 B.C. THIRD WORLD L.J. 179 (1998) , arguing that the "relationship between race and foreign affairs, or race and international relations, remains undertheorized, especially from a legal perspective," *id.* at 261. Gott further argues that "the mass killings by nuclear bombs dropped on civilian centers in Japan [during the Second World War] centers in Japan were directly conditioned by the racist dehumaniza-tion of Asian peoples generally, a product of domestic race 'relations' in the United States," *id.* at 201–02.) *See also* Sahar Aziz, *Race, Entrapment and Manufacturing "Homegrown Terrorism,"* 111 GEO. L.J. 381 (2023); Shirin Sinnar, *Hate Crimes, Terrorism, and the Framing of White Supremacist Violence,* 110 CAL. L. REV. 489 (2022).

[6] For an initiative seeking a "more diverse cohort of scholars to enter the field [of national security law], legal academia must make a conscious, concerted effort to welcome individuals who have tradi-tionally remained at the margins of national security discourse because of their critical perspectives, their demographics, and/or their professional experiences," *see* Maryam Jamshidi & Emily Berman, *Embracing Diversity and Critical Perspectives in National Security Law,* JUST SEC. (Oct. 30, 2020), https://www.justsecurity.org/73129/embracing-diversity-and-critical-perspectives-in-national-security-law/ .

International Law, Race, and Violence

African American and non-European scholars and policymakers have led the way in exposing the racial dimensions of national security, international law, and violence. These scholars and policymakers object to national security and foreign policy discussions that justify war and intervention on the pretext that Third World countries[7] are bedeviled by backwardness, violence, corruption, calamities, and disaster.[8] Yet so far, these conversations about its racial dimensions have remained at the periphery of mainstream national security and foreign policy discussions.

Consider the work of Henry J. Richardson III, who has traced,[9] like no other scholar of international law, how national security and foreign policy decision-making is deeply implicated in the legacy of the transatlantic slave trade, colonialism, post-colonial wars for self-determination, apartheid, and other conflicts to maintain control over access to resources of Third World nations by First World nations. Richardson uncovers the Black international law tradition to the early 17th century in colonial Brazil where rebellious Africans and African Americans organized the Republic of Palmares, lasting from 1605 to 1694, to the revolts against slavery in Haiti, and the early Black rebellions against slavery and the plantation system in the United States.[10] For Richardson, these resistance and freedom initiatives took a more global outlook in the 19th century as part of the struggles of Black communities in the United States against their subjugation.[11] Jeremy Levitt has traced the extensive engagements of Martin Luther King with African independence movements and leaders, including his attendance of Ghana's independence celebrations in 1957.[12] Historians like Carol Anderson, have traced in detail

---

[7] As I have argued elsewhere, the term "Third World" is not merely geographic, rather it is "an epistemic site of production and not merely a site of reception for international legal knowledge. Recognizing the Third World as a site of knowledge production and of the practice of international law disrupts the assumptions that international legal knowledge is exclusively produced in the West for consumption and governance of the Third World." James Thuo Gathii, *The Promise of International Law: A Third World View*, 36 AM. U. INT'L L. REV. 379 (2021).

[8] *See* Makau Mutua, *Savages, Victims, and Saviors: The Metaphor of Human Rights*, 42 HARV. INT'L L.J. 201 (2001).

[9] *See* James Thuo Gathii, *Henry J. Richardson III: The Father of Black Traditions of International Law*, 31 TEMP. INT'L & COMP. L.J. 325 (2017).

[10] *See generally* HENRY J. RICHARDSON III, THE ORIGINS OF AFRICAN-AMERICAN INTERESTS IN INTERNATIONAL LAW (2008).

[11] *Id.* at 441–70.

[12] Jeremy I. Levitt, *Beyond Borders: Martin Luther King Jr., Africa and Pan-Africanism*, 31 TEMP. INT'L & COMP. L.J. 301 (2017).

the symbiotic relationships that emerged between the civil rights movement in the United States and decolonization initiatives in Africa.[13]

African Americans exposed the deep connections between U.S. imperialism, race, and violence. This is best exemplified in African Americans' struggles in the movement for nuclear disarmament. For them, Black freedom struggles could not be separated from struggles for nuclear disarmament in the 1950s.[14] Black freedom struggles and debates within the United States were closely linked not only to nuclear disarmament but also to anticolonialism. African American antinuclear weapons internationalism was part of a wider African American commitment to global peace movements as well as anticolonialism. Indeed, African American leaders often linked peace, colonialism, and racial equality in this period.[15] For instance, Paul Robeson criticized the United States for supporting colonialism in Belgium Congo and apartheid in South Africa, because both countries were sources of uranium that the United States needed to build the atomic bomb.[16] It is important to emphasize that during this period, particularly in the Truman administration, the U.S. government closely collaborated with the racist White settler minority government in South Africa because of the significance uranium had to U.S. national security interests.[17] As a result, in the 1960s, the newly African independent states condemned and isolated South Africa for continuing its racist White minority rule. The U.S. government only nominally criticized the South African government for its racist policies. By contrast, African American leaders and groups led the clarion calls for ending apartheid and colonialism. Many African Americans protested the U.S. government's assistance to the apartheid regime in South

---

[13] Carol Anderson, *International Conscience, the Cold War, and Apartheid: The NAACP's Alliance with the Reverend Michael Scott for South West Africa's Liberation, 1946–1951*, 19 J. WORLD HIST. 297, 297–98, 301–02 (2008).

[14] *See* VINCENT J. INTONDI, AFRICAN AMERICANS AGAINST THE BOMB: NUCLEAR WEAPONS, COLONIALISM, AND THE BLACK FREEDOM MOVEMENT (2015).

[15] *See, e.g., id.* at 83 (discussing the first public statement of the Black Panther Party).

[16] *See, e.g.,* Acklyn R. Lynch, *Paul Robeson: His Dreams Know No Frontiers.* 45 J. NEGRO EDUC. 225, 230 (1976) (citing Paul Robeson Jr., Message Sent to Symposium on "Paul Robeson and the Struggle of the Working Class and the African-American People Against Imperialism," Berlin, Apr. 13–14, 1971 (1971)). In the United States, hundreds of uranium mines were opened in the American Southwest in the 1950s, especially on Navajo territory. Those sites were subsequently abandoned when the nuclear arms race slowed down resulting in widespread sickness and environmental destruction. *See* Rachel Porter, *The Toxic Legacy of Uranium Mining on Navajo Land: The Disproportionate Struggle of Indigenous Peoples and Water,* SAVE THE WATER (Mar. 18, 2019), https://savethewater.org/the-toxic-legacy-of-uranium-mining/?gclid=CjwKCAjwgr6TBhAGEiwA3aVuIbsXM0w8BUkXXxc2EFZ70c2ozsGbvxh9J75yyZxZ5UOCobQAyTJ6zhoCsjEQAvD_BwE.

[17] *See* THOMAS BORSTELMANN, APARTHEID'S RELUCTANT UNCLE: THE UNITED STATES AND SOUTHERN AFRICA IN THE EARLY COLD WAR (1993).

Africa both under the Military Assistance Act as well as through World Bank loans, since these monies were being used to secure uranium for building the atomic bomb.[18] Further, African American leaders argued these loans were being used to fund a racist government that terrorized Black South Africans who resisted racist rule. One vehicle through which African Americans like Paul Robeson and W.E.B. Du Bois advanced their anticolonial, antiracist, pacifist, and pan-African goals was the Council on African Affairs founded in 1942. However, the organization crumbled in the mid-1950s amidst the U.S. government's repression of its leadership in the era of Cold War liberalism and anti-communism.[19]

The critical point here is that African American protests against the U.S.'s military power do not merely date to Martin Luther King's critiques of the war in Vietnam in 1967 and 1968, but rather date back to at least a decade earlier. The National Association of Colored People (NAACP) opposed South Africa's efforts to continue its annexation of South West Africa after the United Nations terminated its mandate in 1946. W.E.B. Du Bois, then director of the NAACP's Special Research, argued that South Africa's "treatment of Africans and Indians and its demand of absorption of Southwest Africa" was "utterly indefensible."[20] It was the work of the NAACP, including its presentation to the United Nations' Fourth Committee about the situation in South West Africa in 1949, that opened the door for the United Nations to request the International Court of Justice for an advisory opinion on the status of South West Africa and South Africa's responsibilities under international law.[21] The dropping of the atomic bomb against Japan by the United States in World War II followed decades of anti-Asian racism. For example, in 1875, Congress passed the Chinese Exclusion Act to limit Chinese immigration into the United States.[22] It is notable that African Americans made common cause with the Japanese in the Japanese struggle against racism in the United States.[23] Fast forward to the Second World War period, the U.S.

---

[18] Anderson, *supra* note 13, at 297–98, 301–02.

[19] Tony Pecinovsky, *Conference Presentation 2021 Working Class Studies Association Conference Forging a Cross-Atlantic "Red-Black Alliance": W. Alphaeus Hunton and the Council on African Affairs*, 20 AM. COMMUNIST HIST. 131 (2021); *see also* Daren Salter, *Council on African Affairs (1942–1955)*, BLACK PAST (Mar. 4, 2007), https://www.blackpast.org/african-american-history/council-african-affairs-1942-1955/.

[20] *See* Anderson, *supra* note 13, at 302.

[21] *Id.* at 318.

[22] For more, *see*, Paul Finkelman, *Coping with a New "Yellow Peril": Japanese Immigration, the Gentleman's Agreement, and the Coming of World War II*, 117 W. VA. L. REV. 1409 (2015).

[23] Yuichiro Onishi, *The New Negro of the Pacific: How African Americans Forged Cross-Racial Solidarity with Japan 1917–1922*, 92 J. AFR. AM. HIST. 191, 195 (2007).

Supreme Court legitimized the racialized evacuation and imprisonment of Japanese Americans in the *Korematsu* case,[24] one of the most significant national security judicial decisions of the 20th century.[25] In his dissent, Justice Murphy rejected the majority's justification of the evacuation and imprisonment of people with Japanese ancestry on account of military necessity, and noted it as an example of the "ugly abyss of racism."[26] Cases like *Korematsu* decided in the post–World War II period came to define how the balance between wartime security and constitutional liberty, and in particular the authority of the president outside the United States to detain suspects without any process, was understood.[27] Those cases, which curtailed the rights of Japanese Americans and according to Justice Murphy's dissent legalized racism,[28] are conveniently ignored in most mainstream national security literature. Even when these cases are remembered, they are often cleansed of the fact that they rest on racist foundations.[29]

Additionally, the more than two decades war against terrorism that accelerated with the illegal invasion of Iraq in 2003 accentuated the image of "the Muslim" as a racialized threat.[30] This racist notion of "the Muslim" as a terrorist has continued unabated even after the U.S.' disastrous withdrawal of ground troops from Afghanistan in 2021. The massive surveillance apparatuses, the drone warfare—including targeted killings and assassinations—as well as all the accompanying violence of this war have wrought destabilization and untold suffering especially outside the Anglophone Atlantic.[31] The virulent Islamophobia and xenophobia in the United States and Europe against non-European immigration[32] is part of counterterrorism foreign policies that

[24] *See* Korematsu v. United States, 323 U.S. 214 (1944), *conviction vacated*, 584 F. Supp. 1406 (N.D. Cal. 1984).

[25] Natsu Taylor Saito, *Crossing the Border: The Interdependence of Foreign Policy and Racial Justice in the United States*, 1 YALE HUM. RTS. & DEV. L.J. 53, 54 (1998).

[26] *Korematsu*, 323 U.S. at 233 (Murphy, J., dissenting).

[27] For a symposium introduction examining these issues, *see* James T. Gathii, *Wartime Security and Constitutional Liberty*, 68 ALB. L. REV. 1113 (2005).

[28] Further, Justice Murphy argued in dissent that "this legalization of racism [and] [r]acial discrimination in any form and in any degree has no justifiable part whatever in our democratic way of life." *Korematsu*, 323 U.S. at 242. For a discussion of some of this literature ignoring race, *see* James Gathii, *Writing Race and Identity in a Global Context: What CRT and TWAIL Can Learn from Each Other*, 67 UCLA L. REV. 1610 (2021).

[29] For further analysis, *see* Sumi K. Cho, *Redeeming Whiteness in the Shadow of Internment: Earl Warren, Brown, and a Theory of Racial Redemption*, 19 B.C. THIRD WORLD L.J. 73 (1998). On the racial foundations of U.S. Constitutional Law, *see* Juan F. Perea, *Race and Constitutional Law Casebooks: Recognizing the Proslavery Constitution*, 110 MICH. L. REV. 1123 (2012)..

[30] *See* Porras, *supra* note 5.

[31] Darryl Li, *Captive Passages: Geographies of Blackness in Guatánamo Memoirs*, 30 TRANSFORMING ANTHROPOLOGY 20 (2022).

[32] *See* E. Tendayi Achiume, *Migration as Decolonization*, 71 STAN. L. REV. 1509 (2019).

have driven these governments' immigration and national security program that became consolidated since September 11, 2001.[33] I return to this theme at greater length in the second section following.

Other scholars have traced the relationship between international law, race, and violence. For example, Antony Anghie reminded us in his 2010 Grotius Address at the Annual Meeting of the American Society of International Law that Hugo Grotius, considered by many as one of, if not the most important, intellectual father of international law, is habitually misrepresented as a bringer of peace and justice in a Europe strewn with religious conflict and war.[34] To attain his vision of order—and thus European national security— Grotius, a White Dutch lawyer, justified slavery. He also recommended and legitimized war against non-Europeans resisting colonial conquest. Anghie concluded that the Grotian approach dominates mainstream international law scholarship. This literature uncritically characterizes Grotius as advocating peace, when he in fact appears to "advocate violence of an almost unrestrained sort."

Moreover, Anghie's classic book, *Imperialism, Sovereignty and the Making of International Law*,[35] traced[36] the hallmarks of those influenced by Grotius and the ways this has mobilized the dynamic of difference between Europeans and non-Europeans, including in the post–Second World War era of the United Nations and the often illegal interventions into non-European countries of the post–Cold War era.

The foundational "savage/victim/savior" metaphor, as Makau Mutua calls it,[37] justifies these interventions into non-European countries by powerful nations of the Global North. From this perspective, Ruth Gordon has argued, the U.S. dominance in multilateral institutions like the United Nations means that "the racial ideology of the United States is being reproduced internationally and directly determines the content of international norms."[38] Thus, the

---

[33] Asli Bâli & Aziz Rana, *Constitutionalism and the American Imperial Imagination*, 85 CHI. L. REV. 257, 261 (2018). For further analysis, especially with regard to the racialized and gendered nature of the wars in Syria and Iraq led by the United States, *see generally* NTINA TZOUVALA, CAPITALISM AS CIVILIZATION: A HISTORY OF INTERNATIONAL LAW (2020); *see also* Amna Akbar, *National Security's Broken Windows*, 62 UCLA L. REV. 834 (2015).

[34] *See generally* Antony Anghie, *International Law in a Time of Change: Should International Law Lead or Follow?*, 26 AM. U. INT'L L. REV. 1315 (2011) (expanded version of the Grotius Lecture delivered on March 24, 2010, at the 2010 American Society of International Law Conference).

[35] *See* ANTONY ANGHIE, IMPERIALISM, SOVEREIGNTY AND THE MAKING OF INTERNATIONAL LAW (2012).

[36] Anghie, *International Law in a Time of Change, supra* note 34, at 1322–23.

[37] *See* Mutua, *supra* note 8, at 20.

[38] Ruth Gordon, *Racing U.S. Foreign Policy*, 17 NAT'L BLACK L.J. 1, 22 (2003).

debates about the boundaries of violence in international law around issues of conquest, colonization, slavery, and self-determination are not simply issues of war and peace but also of different epistemic and racialized visions of international law that have to be surfaced and interrupted more often.[39]

In the era of decolonization, which sought to dismantle colonialism's racialized system of oppression and underdevelopment, Third World states and scholars viewed key international instruments as constituting a new international law that reversed the just war tradition influenced by Grotius used to repeatedly legitimize war against non-Europeans.[40] Third World states asserted that the 1970 "Declaration on Principles of International Law Concerning Friendly Relations and Co-Operation among States in Accordance with the Charter of the United Nations" outlawed both military intervention and economic and political coercion.[41] This declaration, according to Third World jurists of the period, traced its provenance to the prohibition of the threat or use of force in international relations in the United Nations Charter, which protected both the territorial integrity and political independence of states. The International Court of Justice's celebrated *Nicaragua v. United States* decision also came to represent this classic endorsement of the prohibition of the threat or use of force.[42]

Third World scholars, such as Georges Abi Saab,[43] argued that national liberation movements that sought to end racist, alien, and colonial rule were rights-holders on behalf of non-self-governing territories. This claim was recognized in 1973 in the United Nations General Assembly Resolution 3103, which resolved that the "struggle of peoples under colonial and alien domination and racist régimes for the implementation of their right to self-determination and independence is legitimate and in full accordance with the principles of international law."[44]

[39] *See* James Thuo Gathii, *Grotius Lecture at the 2020 Virtual Meeting of the American Society of International Law: The Promise of International Law: A Third-World View* (June 25, 2020) (text of speech available at https://papers.ssrn.com/sol3/papers.cfm?abstract_id=3635509).

[40] *See, e.g.*, U.O. Umozurike, *International Law and Self-Determination in Namibia*, 8 J. MOD. AFR. STUD. 585 (1970).

[41] G.A. Res. 26/25 (XXC), ¶ 1 (Oct. 24, 1970).

[42] Military and Paramilitary Activities in and against Nicaragua (Nicar. v. U.S.), Judgement, 1986 I.C.J. 14 (June 27), https://www.icj-cij.org/public/files/case-related/70/070-19860627-JUD-01-00-EN.pdf; Military and Paramilitary Activities in and Against Nicaragua (Nicar. v. U.S.), Judgment, 1984 I.C.J. 392 (Nov. 26), https://www.icj-cij.org/public/files/case-related/70/070-19841126-JUD-01-00-EN.pdf.

[43] *See* Georges Abi-Saab, *Wars of National Liberation in the Geneva Conventions and Protocols, in* 165 COLLECTED COURSES OF THE HAGUE ACADEMY OF INTERNATIONAL LAW (1979) 357 (1982).

[44] G.A. Res. 3103 (XXVIII), ¶ 1 (Dec. 12, 1973).

While many then newly independent states supported these emerging international legal principles in the era of decolonization, many also resorted to strong claims of sovereignty that repressed secessionist movements and opposition political movements. For example, Algeria, a leader of Third World anticolonial nationalism, exemplified this repression of internal political dissent.[45] Thus, while rejecting a colonial vision of national security, governments in many newly independent states themselves resorted to national security as a pretextual strategy to protect their territorial integrity and political survival. Many cited national security threats posed by coups to suspend bills of rights and in some cases entire constitutions.[46]

Thus, international and national security legal regimes have always been steeped in racial connotation, even if rarely acknowledging as much. This raises the question of what a different epistemic account of national security law, one that centers race might look like.[47] This chapter is one attempt to answer that question.

U.S. National Security Law and Colonialism: Rereading *Rasul v. Bush*

There are very few examples of policy-related work or scholarship in the national security area that are explicitly grounded in exploring its colonial underpinnings. The work of Ernesto Hernandez-Lopez, Natsu Taylor Saito, Amna Akbar, and Mary Dudziak are among the few examples that come to mind.[48] Yet close connections between U.S. national security law

---

[45] *See, e.g.*, JEFFREY JAMES BYRNE, MECCA OF REVOLUTION: ALGERIA, DECOLONIZATION, AND THE THIRD WORLD ORDER (2016). Notably, women played an important role in the Algerian revolution, *see* Danièle Djamila Amrane-Minne & Farida Abu-Haidar, *Women and Politics in Algeria from the War of Independence to Our Day*, 30 RSCH. AFR. LITERATURES 62 (1999).

[46] *See* Tayyab Mahmud, *Praetorianism & Common Law in Post-Colonial Settings: Judicial Responses to Constitutional Breakdowns in Pakistan*, 1993 UTAH L. REV. 1225 (1993).

[47] *See* Gathii, *Grotius Lecture*, *supra* note 39.

[48] *See* Ernesto Hernandez-Lopez, *Kiyemba, Guantanamo, and Immigration Law: An Extraterritorial Constitution in a Plenary Power World*, 2 U.C. IRVINE L. REV. 194 (2012); Saito, *supra* note 25; Mary L. Dudziak, *The Little Rock Crisis and Foreign Affairs: Race, Resistance, and the Image of American Democracy*, 70 S. CAL. L. REV.1641 (1997);; Amna Akbar & Rupal Oza, *Muslim Fundamentalism and Human Rights in an Age of Terror and Empire, in* GENDER, NATIONAL SECURITY AND COUNTER TERRORISM: HUMAN RIGHTS PERSPECTIVES 152 (Margaret L Satterwithe & Jayne C. Hukcerby eds., 2013). *See also* Aziz Z. Huq, *The Signaling Function of Religious Speech in Domestic Counterterrorism*, 89 TEX. L. REV. 833, 854–55 (2011); Sunaina Maira, *"Good" and "Bad" Muslim Citizens: Feminists, Terrorists, and U.S. Orientalisms*, 35 FEMINIST STUDS. 631, 637–39 (2009); Shirin Sinnar, *Questioning Law Enforcement: The First Amendment and Counterterrorism Interviews*, 77 BROOK. L. REV. 41, 51 (2011).

and colonialism do exist. One example of this typically unacknowledged connection is the Supreme Court's decision in *Rasul v. Bush*.[49] In *Rasul*, the Supreme Court had to decide whether the scope of the habeas writ extended extraterritorially—that is, "whether United States courts lack jurisdiction to consider challenges to the legality of the detention of foreign nationals captured abroad in connection with hostilities and incarcerated at the Guantanamo Bay Naval Base, Cuba."[50] To answer this question, the Court discussed "the historical reach of the writ of habeas corpus,"[51] drawing heavily upon British case law from colonial-era Africa.[52] Like *Rasul*, the question posed in those colonial era African cases was whether the writ of habeas extended over distant possessions. The framing of this question was informed by a racial premise—that non-European people living outside the heart of the British empire in distant lands were not eligible to benefit from the writ of habeas. On this account, the writ did not extend to them both on account of their identity as well as on account of their being outside of the metropole where only citizens enjoyed the benefits of the writ. Similarly, Theodore Woolsey, writing in 1899 about whether the writ of habeas extended to territories like Cuba, Puerto Rico, and the Philippines, answered in the negative.[53] My contention is that similar patterns of judicial accommodation of political branches of government can be seen in British case law: the *Insular Cases* and the *Rasul* line of cases. Moreover, these cases carry forward an assemblage of legal rules that rest on a paternalistic and racialized foundation as the debate around the recent Supreme Court case, *United States v. Vaello Madero*,[54] illustrates.[55]

---

[49] Rasul v. Bush, 542 U.S. 466 (2004).

[50] *Id.* at 470. The majority later rearticulated the issue in the following terms: "The question now before us is whether the habeas statute confers a right to judicial review of the legality of executive detention of aliens in a territory over which the United States exercises plenary and exclusive jurisdiction, but not "ultimate sovereignty." *Id.* at 475.

[51] *Id.* at 481.

[52] These authorities consisted of case law, particularly *Ex parte Mwenya* and *Ex parte Sekgome. See Rasul*, 542 U.S. at 481–82, 482 nn.11–14; *see also id.* at 500–05, 505 n.5 (Scalia, J., dissenting).

[53] *See* Theodore S. Woolsey, *The Government of Dependencies*, 13 ANNALS AM. ACAD. POL. & SOC. SCI. (SUPP. 12) 3, 6 (1899). Carl Landauer further argues that Woolsey was uncomfortable with the U.S.'s imperial expansion. *See* Carl Landauer, *The Ambivalences of Power: Launching the* American Journal of International Law *in an Era of Empire and Globalization*, 20 LEIDEN J. INT'L L. 325, 349 (2007).

[54] 142 S. Ct. 1539 (2022).

[55] In this case some Justices of the U.S. Supreme Court have argued in favor of overruling the Insular Cases not because they rest on racist foundations but because they were wrongly decided, *see* Adam Liptak, *Gorsuch Calls for Overruling of "Shameful" Cases on U.S. Territories*, N.Y. TIMES (May 2, 2022), https://www.nytimes.com/2022/05/02/us/politics/gorsuch-supreme-court-insular-cases. html#commentsContainer. *But see* Ediberto Román & Ernesto Sagás, *SCOTUS Declares U.S. Citizens*

In *Rasul*, the majority relied on Ex parte *Mwenya*,[56] a case involving sixty-one African activists and trade unionists[57] and members of the African National Congress who had been excluded from the Copper Belt in Northern Rhodesia (now Zimbabwe) by virtue of restriction orders issued under the Emergency Powers Regulations by the racist British colonial government. Arrested in 1957 and detained in isolation from home, they had been held incommunicado with no charge for at least three years when their habeas petition was finally determined.[58] These African activists and nationalists · challenged the repressive security system designed to clamp down organized resistance against legalized systems of land inequality, an industrial color bar and racial discrimination in public accommodations that systematically discriminated against Africans while favoring White settlers.[59] In this rare circumstance departing from a long line of precedents in a case decided in the decade that witnessed the independence of several African countries, the petitioners were successful in obtaining habeas writs. Therefore Ex parte *Mwenya* is the exception, rather than the rule, as one of the rare cases in which common law courts extended the writ extraterritorially.

Unless we look very closely, we can miss how the sustained historical exegesis between Justice Scalia and Justice Kennedy in leading habeas cases like *Rasul* heavily rely on English precedents relating to unincorporated territories. Reading these cases as Justice Scalia and Kennedy did, the overwhelming amount of policy and scholarly commentary missed the broader historical context in which the cases were being decided and the policymakers who were making and implementing the laws that triggered these habeas applications. The precedents used to decide important legal questions raised in these cases were developed in the context of British territorial possessions. What is more, these territorial possessions were regarded as not having been fully incorporated as British colonies. There is therefore a perfect analogy between cases from British possessions and colonies seeking habeas, on the one hand, and cases like *Rasul* brought by non-citizens held

in Puerto Rico Inferior, BLOOMBERG L. (May 2, 2022), https://news.bloomberglaw.com/us-law-week/scotus-declares-u-s-citizens-in-puerto-rico-inferior.

[56] [1959] 3 W.L.R. 767 (C.A.).
[57] *See* HC Deb (13 Mar. 1957) (566) cols. 1112–14.
[58] *See* HC Deb (15 May 1959) (605) cols. 1571, 1579, 1581, 1586, 1588–89.
[59] *See* RONALD WEITZER, TRANSFORMING SETTLER STATES: COMMUNAL CONFLICT AND INTERNAL SECURITY IN NORTHERN IRELAND AND ZIMBABWE 54–55 (1990).

outside the territorial United States many decades later in U.S. federal courts, on the other.

This example shows why we must often trace the connections between different colonies and pay closer attention to the continuities and discontinuities between them. In other words, locations that we often study separately may turn out to have abiding similarities. Studying them together produces new analytic and productive possibilities. For example, by intentionally reading the *Rasul* majority's reliance on Ex parte *Mwenya* and discussing them together, I try to illustrate the kind of analytic possibilities that can be produced. Looking only at the citation to Ex Parte *Mwenya* in the *Rasul* case without digging further, you would not know that it was a case decided in the twilight of colonial rule in Africa. Further, it is unlikely that you would know that it is one of the rare cases in which common law courts extended the writ of habeas extraterritorially.

King v. the Earl of Crewe: Ex parte *Sekgome*,[60] also cited by the *Rasul* majority in support of the writ's historical reach, is an example of the contrary proposition. That proposition is to the effect that the writ was unavailable outside the territories in which the Crown had not acquired territorial sovereignty even if the Crown exercised complete jurisdiction and control over such territories. In fact, Sir Edward Coke had long before reassured the Crown that common law courts would not meddle with anything done "beyond the seas."[61] These views expressed by Sir Edward Coke in 1628 have strong resonances to views of Langdell, who more than two and half decades later argued that "the Constitution of the United States as such does not extend beyond the limits of the States which are united by and under it."[62]

In a large sense, Langdell was echoing a claim well established under the common law for dealing with territories under the Crown's jurisdiction. The common law writ of habeas corpus was available in the dominions of the Crown in the absence of legislation.[63] However, Section 1 of the 1862 Habeas Corpus Act, made its issuance from England unavailable in territories under the Crown's foreign jurisdiction unless there was specific statutory

---

[60] [1910] 2 K.B. 577 (C.A.).

[61] *See* Daniel J. Hulsebosch, *The Ancient Constitution and the Expanding Empire: Sir Edward Coke's British Jurisprudence*, 21 L. & HIST. REV. 439, 477 (2003).

[62] *See* C.C. Langdell, *The Status of Our New Territories*, 12 HARV. L. REV. 365, 371 (1899).

[63] R v. Cowle [1759] 2 Burr 834 (K.B.) (Lord Mansfield held that writs such as habeas corpus "are not restrained by any clause in the constitution . . . [and] upon a proper case they may issue to every dominion of the crown of England"); *see also* WILLIAM S. CHURCH, A TREATISE OF THE WRIT OF HABEAS CORPUS 118 (1884) ("The general principle is, that the writ of habeas corpus may issue to every dominion of the crown of England, upon a proper cause being shown.").

authorization. This statutory limitation of the availability of the writ reversed the Queen's Bench decision of the previous year, *In re John Anderson*,[64] where the Queen's Bench had held that the writ could issue into any part of the Crown's dominions.[65]

In my view, the *Rasul* majority therefore performed a sleight of hand by citing Ex parte *Sekgome* to support their view of the historical reach of the writ. This is because Ex parte *Sekgome* was decided on exactly the contrary premise.[66] Thus, the Court's decision in *Rasul* is not faithful to the precedents—especially the deeply authoritarian and racist progeny of this case law at common law. The Supreme Court in *Rasul* did this to arrive at its conclusion on the historical reach of the writ. History did not support such a conclusion. The Court could have instead acknowledged this problematic legacy and found that it was creating a new interpretation on the reach of habeas, but it decided against that.

By ignoring the common law cases that clearly showed that the writ was never routinely available to non-European peoples in the colonies of the Crown, the *Rasul* majority avoided having to address the implication that when the United States acts abroad, particularly in its refusal to extend constitutional guarantees or jurisdiction to extraterritorial habeas petitions from persons within its custody, it acts without the constraints of the rule of law as Justice Harlan had feared in his dissent in *Hawaii v. Mankichi*.[67] It

---

[64] [1758] 30 L.J. 129 (Q.B.).

[65] *See* Norman Bentwich, *Habeas Corpus in the Empire*, 27 L.Q. REV. 454, 455 (1911).

[66] *See* Rasul v. Bush, 542 U.S. 466, 482 n.14 (2004).

[67] Territory of Hawaii v. Mankichi, 190 U.S. 197, 235–37, 238–41 (1903) (Harlan, J., dissenting). Justice Harlan went on to imagine the consequences of the Court's extension of certain rights but not others to residents of unincorporated territories:

> [It] would place Congress above the Constitution. It would mean that the benefit of the constitutional provisions designed for the protection of life and liberty may be claimed by some of the people subject to the authority and jurisdiction of the United States, but cannot be claimed by others equally subject to its authority and jurisdiction. It would mean that the will of Congress, not the Constitution, is the supreme law of the land for certain peoples and territories under our jurisdiction. It would mean that the United States may acquire territory be cession, conquest, or treaty, and that Congress may exercise sovereign dominion over it, outside of and in violation of the Constitution, and under regulations that could not be applied to the organized territories of the United States and their inhabitants. It would mean that, under the influence and guidance of commercialism and the supposed necessities of trade, this country had left the old ways of the fathers, as defined by a written constitution, and entered upon a new way, in following which the American people will lose sight of, or become indifferent to, principles which had been supposed to be essential to real liberty. It would mean that, if the principles now announced should become firmly established, the time may not be far distant when, under the exactions of trade and commerce, and to gratify an ambition to become the dominant political power in all the earth, the United States will acquire territories in every direction, which are inhabited by human beings, over which territories, to be

also avoided a discussion that would have portrayed a historical pattern of denying habeas to foreigners simply because they are foreigners and were held outside the territorial sovereignty of the colonial and imperial powers, like the British Crown under colonial rule and the United States in relation to its unincorporated territories. Unincorporated territories are a technique used by colonizing powers to disclaim responsibility for "extraterritorial" territories and justify denying those that live within them rights available within the metropolitan territory of the colonizing power. Such a discriminatory governance system was rejected by the dissenters in *Downes v. Bidwell*, where they argued that this imperial era jurisprudence "would substitute for the present system of republican government a system of domination over distant provinces in the exercise of unrestricted power."[68]

In re Ning Yi-Ching,[69] like Ex parte *Sekgome*, is another paradigmatic habeas British case. Tientsin was considered by the court to be a foreign country since the British government had only obtained a lease over it from the Chinese government, and the British government only had to administer justice to its citizens, not Chinese citizens in Tientsin. *In re Ning Yi-Ching* is also instructive to the extent that though Tientsin was part of China, it was in the de facto control of Japan. The Crown therefore argued that its interests in Tientsin as represented by the British Consul-General in Tientsin were of an advisory nature, although the prisoners who brought the habeas petition in the case were in a British prison under the control of the chairman of the British Municipal Council. Thus, it is really a case involving overlapping layers of authority: the prisoners were under British imprisonment notwithstanding the court's finding that Tientsin was a foreign country.

called "dependencies" or "outlying possessions," we will exercise absolute dominion, and whose inhabitants will be regarded as "subjects" or "dependent peoples," to be controlled as Congress may see fit, not as the Constitution requires nor as the people governed may wish. Thus will be engrafted upon our republican institutions, controlled by the supreme law of a written Constitution, a colonial system entirely foreign to the genius of our government and abhorrent to the principles that underlie and pervade the Constitution. It will then come about that we will have two governments over the peoples subject to the jurisdiction of the United States, – one, existing under a written Constitution, creating a government with authority to exercise only powers expressly granted and such as are necessary and appropriate to carry into effect those so granted; the other, existing outside of the written Constitution, in virtue of an unwritten law, to be declared from time to time by Congress, which is itself only a creature of that instrument. *Id.* at 239–40 (Harlan, J., dissenting).

[68] Downes v. Bidwell, 182 U.S. 244, 373 (1901) (Fuller, C.J., dissenting).
[69] 56 T. L. R. 3 (Vacation Ct. 1939).

Ex parte *Mwenya* had its strange twists as well. Justice Scalia correctly asserted that Ex parte *Mwenya* proceeded on the premise that Northern Rhodesia was a protectorate and as such a foreign country. However, both the Ex parte *Mwenya* court and Scalia ignored the fact that in 1923, Northern Rhodesia became a colony. As such, it was like Ex parte *Sekgome*, a case involving an alien not outside the territory of the Crown since colonies were considered to be within the territory of the crown by virtue of the acquisitive act of a proclamation of colony status. Ex parte *Mwenya* was nevertheless a case in which the writ was issued even though the court proceeded on the premise it was a protectorate, therefore, emphasizing its departure from the long line of cases in which habeas under similar circumstances was denied. Moreover, as the late Thomas Franck reminded us,[70] Ex parte *Mwenya* "affords another example of a situation in which courts should not refuse to abdicate from the determination of international law issues."[71]

Relying on *Rasul* and the closely related cases, *Rumsfeld v. Padilla*[72] and *Hamdi v. Rumsfeld*[73]—together, the "June 28 trilogy"[74]—Steve Vladeck has argued that "the Supreme Court went to war—and the judges won."[75] According to Vladeck, "the decisions in hindsight represented only modest setbacks" for the George W. Bush administration's post-9/11 detention program at Guantanamo Bay.[76] In *Padilla*, the Court avoided addressing the merits of the president's authority to militarily detain Jose Padilla,[77] an alleged "enemy combatant" and al-Qaeda conspirator.[78] Rather, the Court

---

[70] *See, e.g.*, Dennis Havesi, *Thomas Franck, Who Advised Countries on Law, Dies at 77*, N.Y. TIMES (May 29, 2009), https://www.nytimes.com/2009/05/30/nyregion/30franck.html?ref=obituaries.

[71] Thomas M. Franck, *The Courts, the State Department and National Policy: A Criterion for Judicial Abdication*, 44 MINN. L. REV. 1101, 1110 (1960). Franck describes the phenomenon of judicial "abdication by accommodation" in the following passage:

> Even in areas in which the balance of powers was constitutionally contrived by a grant of co-ordinate jurisdiction, the judicial and political branches have occasionally accommodated each other by abdicating from the exercise of a shared power. . . . [T]he courts, by characterizing disputes as political, have also abdicated from certain issues in deference to the political process. This technique of accommodation by abdication is probably not pre-conditioned so much by the traditional decision-making processes of the political and judicial branches as by a desire to avoid the protracted conflict which may result from a trespass by one branch of government into the *sanctum sanctorum* of another branch. *Id.* at 1102–03.

[72] 542 U.S. 426 (2004). Please note that *Padilla* preceded *Rasul* in order of publication.

[73] 542 U.S. 507 (2004).

[74] *See* Steve Vladeck, *The Supreme Court Goes to War: Hamdi, Padilla, and Rasul at 10*, JUST SEC. (June 27, 2014), https://www.justsecurity.org/12260/supreme-court-war/.

[75] *Id.*

[76] *Id.*

[77] *Padilla*, 542 U.S. at 430.

[78] *Id.*

limited its inquiry to whether the U.S. District Court for the Southern District of New York could properly exercise jurisdiction over Padilla's habeas petition.[79] The Court answered in the negative, reasoning that Padilla should have brought the petition in the District of South Carolina,[80] which had personal jurisdiction over Padilla's immediate custodian, Commander Marr.[81]

Likewise, *Hamdi* required that a citizen-detainee seeking to challenge "enemy combatant" classification to receive both the notification of the classification's factual basis and a fair opportunity to rebut such assertions before a neutral decision maker,[82] but the Court also held that the executive has authority to detain citizens qualifying as "enemy combatants."[83] On the basis of the latter holding, Vladeck concluded that "the Bush Administration won on the key detention authority question."[84]

Moreover, Vladeck infers that, in response to the Bush administration's efforts to exclude courts from reviewing such detentions, the Court fixated on asserting its power to decide such cases,[85] while otherwise abstaining from review on the merits.[86] A later case in the *Rasul* line, *Hamdan v. Rumsfeld*,[87] confirms Vladeck's observation that, "because the Court was no longer faced with the threat to judicial power raised by the specter of individuals who could neither be detained nor released, review was no longer warranted."[88] In *Hamdan*, the Court found it unnecessary to address the plaintiff's concerns regarding Congress's authority to restrict the Court's jurisdiction in habeas cases or his suggestion that "Congress has unconstitutionally suspended the writ of habeas corpus" altogether.[89] Rather, the Court focused on rejecting the government's argument that Congress statutorily divested the Court of jurisdiction over the appeal.[90]

Four years later, in *Boumediene*, the Court relied on the *Insular Cases* and *Rasul* (including its references to the British case law) to arrive at its holding

[79] *Id.* at 442.
[80] *Id.* at 451.
[81] *Id.* at 442.
[82] Hamdi v. Rumsfeld, 542 U.S. 507, 533 (2004).
[83] *Id.* at 516, 518.
[84] *See* Vladeck, *supra* note 74.
[85] *Id.*
[86] *See* Stephen I. Vladeck, *The Passive-Aggressive Virtues*, 111 COLUM. L. REV. SIDEBAR 122, 129 (2011); *see also* James Thuo Gathii, *Torture, Extraterritoriality, Terrorism and International Law*, 67 ALB. L. REV. 335 (2003) (coming to the same conclusion).
[87] 548 U.S. 557 (2006).
[88] *See* Vladeck, *The Passive-Aggressive Virtues*, *supra* note 86, at 130.
[89] *Hamdan*, 548 U.S. at 575.
[90] *See* Vladeck, *The Passive-Aggressive Virtues*, *supra* note 86, at 129.

that the Suspension Clause[91] "has full effect at Guantanamo Bay."[92] However, as Gerald L. Neuman argues, *Boumediene* effectively treated Guantanamo Bay, like Puerto Rico in *Downes*,[93] as "foreign in a domestic sense."[94] More specifically, by finding that Guantanamo is "technically outside the sovereign territory of the United States,"[95] but also that "[i]n every practical sense Guantanamo is not abroad,"[96] *Boumediene* treated Guantanamo as a "dual-status space."[97] Furthermore, Neuman observes that *Boumediene* "gave a sanitized account of the motivations for the *Insular Cases* doctrine, underplaying the racial element in U.S. colonialism, and overemphasizing the usefulness of the doctrine in temporary governance of a territory that would later be granted independence."[98]

The main takeaway from the foregoing analysis is that some of the key precedents for the U.S. Supreme Court, in cases like *Rasul*, are colonial-era cases that are predicated on racist justifications in at least two senses. First, because the construction of what is foreign and what is domestic overlaps substantially, if not entirely with, the colonial logic that justified conquest. But also, whether rights such as habeas extended extraterritorially to those foreign possessions. That central logic of what is domestic and foreign continues to frame how far and what rights should extend extraterritorially to places like Guantanamo. Second, because especially in cases like *Rasul*, the Supreme Court engaged in a very selective reading of the precedents that ignored the overwhelming weight of those precedents to the effect that the writ of habeas was unavailable extraterritorially especially when claimed by citizens of colonized territories.

This unfaithful reading of the precedents as well as the racialized underpinnings of the foreign/domestic binary has been ignored in the overwhelming policy and scholarly treatment of these cases. The fact the precedents from British colonial Africa and elsewhere centered around avoiding holding White colonial governors responsible for violating the

---

[91] U.S. CONST. art. I, § 9, cl. 2 ("The Privilege of the Writ of Habeas Corpus shall not be suspended, unless when in Cases of Rebellion or Invasion the public Safety may require it.").

[92] Boumediene v. Bush, 553 U.S. 723, 771 (2008).

[93] Downes v. Bidwell, 182 U.S. 244, 341–42 (White, J., concurring).

[94] *See* Gerald L. Neuman, *The Extraterritorial Constitution after* Boumediene v. Bush, 82 S. CAL. L. REV. 259, 270 (2009).

[95] *Boumediene*, 553 U.S. at 768.

[96] *Id.* at 769 (referencing *Rasul v. Bush*, 542 U.S. 466, 480 (2004) (Kennedy, J., concurring in judgment)).

[97] *See* Neuman, *supra* note 94, at 271.

[98] *Id.* at 270. *See also Boumediene*, 553 U.S. at 756–59.

rights of their non-White subjects illustrates the enduring legacy of racialized repression of people of color in both colonial era African protectorates and the U.S.' unincorporated territories. That is why, by focusing only on the outcomes of these cases, for example, whether or not the courts found habeas was available or not, fails to engage with the selective reading of common law habeas precedents that erase the consistent denials of the writ to non-White colonial subjects. This selective reading of the precedents in my view constitutes a silencing of issues of race.

In this chapter, I push back against this silencing, which is deeply embedded in commentary as well as habeas petitions made by non-White colonized subjects or by detainees held against their will in a "foreign" territory. The foreign/domestic binary was and continues to be predicated on the racist assumption that underpinned the *Insular Cases* and their progeny: that non-White colonial subjects, and therefore non-citizens, were incapable of having rights like habeas. These cases that invoke the foreign/domestic binary are also laden with explicitly racist ideas, such as the belief that non-White peoples were backward, ignorant, and unworthy of protections like habeas.[99]

Moreover, the precedents that the Supreme Court has invoked to decide important national security cases are also reflected in the current moment with state officials repressing protesters advocating for racial justice. The colonial-era arguments that justified repression of legitimate anticolonial and antiracist protests now characterize the backlash against critical race theory that is being recycled to repress similar movements and protests today.[100] That is why policymakers, scholars, and others must do much better to acknowledge and explicitly account for the racial and colonial logics that underpin the jurisprudence and practices of national security law and policy.

---

[99] A similar logic can be said to underlie the Supreme Court's decision in *Sale v. Haitian Centers Council*, 509 U.S. 155 (1993), where the Court found that an executive order issued by President George H.W. Bush requiring the return of Haitians illegally traveling by sea from Haiti to the United States before reaching its borders did not violate the Nationality Act of 1952 and Article 33 of the United Nations Protocol Relating to the Status of Refugees which protects individuals escaping potential prosecution from forced repatriation. Similarly, the potential use of the writ of habeas to get postconviction relief is heavily racialized in its applications and outcomes, *see* LeRoy Pernell, *Racial Justice and Federal Habeas Corpus as Postconviction Relief from State Convictions*, 69 MERCER L. REV. 453 (2018).

[100] Vivian E. Hamilton, *Reform, Retrench, Repeat: The Campaign Against Critical Race Theory, Through the Lens of Critical Race Theory*, 28 WM. & MARY J. WOMEN & L. 61 (2021); ; Kimberle Crenshaw, *The Panic over Critical Race Theory Is an Attempt to Whitewash U.S. History*, WASH. POST (July 2, 2021) https://www.washingtonpost.com/outlook/critical-race-theory-history/2021/07/02/e90bc94a-da75-11eb-9bbb-37c30dcf9363_story.html.

There is simply no credible justification—other than sustaining the dominance of a color-blind national security entrenched in White supremacy—to continue to separate streams of policy and scholarly discussions that facilitate the subordination of people of color. To overcome this legacy, a recent letter by national security scholars making the case for diversifying the field noted that for a "more diverse cohort of scholars to enter the field, legal academia must make a conscious, concerted effort to welcome individuals who have traditionally remained at the margins of national security discourse because of their critical perspectives, their demographics, and/or their professional experiences."[101]

Conclusion: A New Dawn or a Long Dusk?

Race has largely been absent in policy and academic discussions of national security and much of public international law,[102] yet it has been hiding in plain sight. We can see that many governments, including that of the United States, have deployed colonial era practices suppressing the protests against racist violence against Black people and other minority groups in the country. The labeling of Black Lives Matter protesters as "communists" in the United States today follows a very familiar pattern.[103] In the era of decolonization, the United States also tagged anticolonial movements with the Cold War label of "communists."[104]

I hope this book is the beginning of a more inclusive conversation about national security and foreign affairs and in other spaces in our discipline as well as in policy circles. Engaging in a discussion about race is productive not just for those who study national security from a critical lens and

---

[101] Maryam Jamshidi & Emily Berman, *Embracing Diversity and Critical Perspectives in National Security Law*, Just Sec. (June 30, 2020), https://www.justsecurity.org/73129/embracing-diversity-and-critical-perspectives-in-national-security-law/.

[102] James Thuo Gathii, *Studying Race in International Law Scholarship Using a Social Science Approach*, 22 Chi. J. Int'l L. 71 (2021).

[103] Cheryl Corley, *Black Lives Matter Fights Disinformation to Keep the Movement Strong*, NPR (May 25, 2021), https://www.npr.org/2021/05/25/999841030/black-lives-matter-fights-disinformation-to-keep-the-movement-strong; Bethany Allen Ebrahimian, *Right Wing Media Falsely Ties Black Lives Matter Movement to Beijing*, Axios (Oct. 20, 2020), https://www.axios.com/2020/10/20/right-wing-media-falsely-ties-black-lives-matter-movement-to-beijing; Kevin Roose, *No, a Black Lives Matter Co-Founder Didn't Partner with a Pro-Communist Chinese Group*, N.Y. Times (Sept. 18, 2020), https://www.nytimes.com/2020/09/18/technology/no-a-black-lives-matter-co-founder-didnt-partner-with-a-pro-communist-chinese-group.html.

[104] *See, e.g.*, Gerald Horne, *Race from Power: U.S. Foreign Policy and the General Crisis of "White Supremacy,"* 23 Diplomatic Hist. 437 (1999).

who incorporate race as an important element of their scholarship but also for those who do not consider race at all in their work, scholarly, policy, or otherwise.

Taking race into account is especially important for policymakers who provide advice to the political branches on foreign affairs. Providing color-blind advice that is decontextualized from considerations and implications relating to race and identity does not advance national security goals effectively. This is particularly important at a time when fewer Black individuals are working in the U.S. State Department than at any time in its history.[105] Of course, the responsibility for antiracism does not rest on the small cadre of people of color in government.[106] It is a responsibility that is and should be shared by all.

Perhaps this book means that scholars and policymakers who mostly attend separate conferences, publish in separate places, and rarely engage directly with each other's work will find this as one place where they can engage on these important issues. I hope this is a new dawn, but I must say that I am pinching myself, wondering whether this is a long dusk.

---

[105] *See* Christopher Richardson, *The State Department Was Designed to Keep African-Americans Out*, N.Y. TIMES (June 23, 2020), https://www.nytimes.com/2020/06/23/opinion/state-department-racism-diversity.html.

[106] *See* Robbie Gramer, *Fighting for U.S. Values Abroad, Black Diplomats Struggle with Challenges at Home*, FOREIGN POL'Y (June 11, 2020), https://foreignpolicy.com/2020/06/11/u-s-black-diplomats-state-department-george-floyd-protests-trump-pompeo-state-department-diversity-racial-injustice-police-violence-soft-power/.

2

Viral Convergence

Interconnected Pandemics as Portal to Racial Justice

Catherine Powell[*]

Introduction

As a moment of interconnected pandemics,[1] the era of COVID-19[2] has provided a new window into the pandemics of policing, poverty, and racism
around the globe. The fact that police officers killed George Floyd (and Eric
Garner and others) for a crime of poverty highlights the misguided ways that
the United States (and other nations) wrongly address economic insecurity
through the criminal law system rather than through more effective and
enduring solutions.[3] The 2020 uprisings over police brutality and George

---

[*] I want to start my contribution to this book collection by acknowledging its editor, Matiangai
Sirleaf, for her intellectual leadership and vision that paved the way for this scholarly exchange. As
part of the first group of Black scholars on the editorial board of the *American Journal of International
Law*, I have seen firsthand how, beyond representation, scholarly conversation is enriched by broadening the lens for analyzing international law and national security studies. I also want to thank
the other contributors and my research assistants, Fordham Law students, Alexis
Saulny and Tasha Brown, for superb research.

[1] Catherine Powell, *Color of Covid and Gender of Covid: Essential Workers, Not Disposable
People*, 33 YALE J.L. & FEMINISM 1 (2021); Catherine Powell, *"Virtual Convergence": Interconnected
Pandemics as Portal to Racial Justice*, JUST SEC. (Aug. 5, 2020), https://www.justsecurity.org/71742/
viral-justice-interconnected-pandemics-as-portal-to-racial-justice/ (published as part of the Racing
National Security online symposium).

[2] Biden allowed the coronavirus health emergency declaration to expire in May 2023 (as this book
goes to press). *Biden Ends COVID National Emergency After Congress Acts*, NPR (Apr. 11, 2023),
https://www.npr.org/2023/04/11/1169191865/biden-ends-covid-national-emergency. However, in
this chapter, I refer to the "era of COVID-19" as an ongoing phenomenon. As Harvard historian
Allan Brandt notes:

> We tend to think of pandemics and epidemics as episodic[.] . . . But we are living in the
> Covid-19 era, not the Covid-19 crisis. There will be a lot of changes that are substantial
> and persistent. We won't look back and say, 'That was a terrible time, but it's over.' We will
> be dealing with many of the ramifications of Covid-19 for decades, for decades.

Gina Kolata, *Past Pandemics Remind Us Covid Will Be an Era, Not a Crisis That Fades*, N.Y.
TIMES (Oct. 12, 2021), https://www.nytimes.com/2021/10/12/health/when-will-covid-end.html
(quoting Allan Brandt).

[3] *See* PETER EDELMAN, NOT A CRIME TO BE POOR: THE CRIMINALIZATION OF POVERTY IN
AMERICA (2017).

Catherine Powell, *Viral Convergence* In: *Race and National Security*. Edited by: Matiangai V.S. Sirleaf,
Oxford University Press. © Oxford University Press 2023. DOI: 10.1093/oso/9780197754641.003.0003

Floyd's murder by White police officer Derek Chauvin (who pinned his knee on Floyd's neck for eight minutes and forty-six seconds)[4] were widely viewed as paving the way for a racial reckoning and, yet, have also led to a widespread, profound backlash.

Van Jones interpreted the 2016 presidential election of Donald Trump as a powerful "Whitelash"[5] against Barack Obama's presidency and changing demographics. We are now experiencing yet another Whitelash. In fact, we can interpret the current rollback of voting rights, bans on books, and teaching about race in the classroom as a Whitelash against the 2020 protests and the ongoing calls for racial justice. Just as the January 6, 2021, insurrection demonstrated a revolt against Trump's electoral loss, it also reflected White anxiety in a moment of not only President Joe Biden's rise to power, but also Vice President Kamala Harris's ascension as the country's first woman (and African American) to assume the number two position in the White House. "White replacement theory"—the fear that White Americans will lose their majority status as America moves demographically toward becoming a majority minority country—has stoked distress over the "browning of America."[6]

Given this broader context and failure of the nation to engage in a genuine, sustained racial reckoning, national security observers must broaden the traditional lens for analysis beyond military security—and what Trump (and Richard Nixon in the 1970s) opportunistically call "law and order"—to encompass economic, physical, and human security. A more expansive understanding of "security" in turn calls for transformative change, beyond incremental reform.

When I worked in President Obama's White House National Security Council, I saw firsthand how, as a nation, we can reframe our security interests. President Obama took a step in this direction, recognizing, for example, that "[d]efending democracy and human rights is related to every

[4] Christina Carrega, *Derek Chauvin, Ex-Officer Accused of Killing George Floyd, Charged with Tax Evasion*, ABC NEWS (July 23, 2020, 3:09 PM), https://abcnews.go.com/US/derek-chauvin-officer-accused-killing-george-floyd-charged/story?id=71941032.

[5] Josiah Ryan, *"This was a whitelash": Van Jones' take on the election results*, CNN (Nov. 9, 2016, 9:16 AM), https://www.cnn.com/2016/11/09/politics/van-jones-results-disappointment-cnntv/index.html; *see also* TERRY SMITH, WHITELASH: UNMASKING WHITE GRIEVANCE AT THE BALLOT BOX 16 (2020) (exploring how White identity contributed to the 2016 election of President Trump by analogizing voting to a jury deliberation, in that like the jury, voting is a collective decision-making process undertaken on behalf of the democratic body politic, not on behalf of the individual voter).

[6] DaMareo Cooper, *How the White Replacement Theory Behind the Buffalo Shooting Also Fueled the January 6 Insurrection*, YAHOO NEWS (June 8, 2022), https://www.yahoo.com/video/white-replacement-theory-behind-buffalo-152511891.html.

enduring national interest."[7] Obama's foreign policy sought to promote economic and other forms of justice as cornerstones of U.S. national interests, as our national self-interests are more likely to thrive where we can help lift all boats in a secure and prosperous world with greater economic inclusion. Of course, the country was not perfect under Obama, and police violence has a long history in the United States, including during the Obama era, when Freddie Gray and Michael Brown were killed by police—the latter leading to the Ferguson uprising.

But in 2020, we witnessed even larger and more sustained protests—with global dimensions—sparked by the killings of George Floyd, Breonna Taylor (the EMT worker who was shot by police when she was "sleeping while Black"),[8] Ahmaud Arbery (who was attacked by a former police officer "jogging while Black"),[9] as well as many others. These protests seemed to call on America to move toward transformational change, by viewing the COVID-19 pandemic as a "portal," in the words of author Arundhati Roy, to a more just world.[10]

For years, we had been told that it was not possible to provide everyone with a guaranteed basic income, and yet, with COVID, governments around the world have done just that (or provided expanded unemployment benefits).[11] We had been told that it was not possible to ensure health access for all, and yet, governments around the globe have provided free coronavirus testing, vaccines, and other subsidized care. Notably too, calls to reverse Obamacare have subsided in the United States, at least for the moment (now that numerous individuals of all races have depended on Obamacare to survive the pandemic).[12] So, it turns out that transforming the law—and the

---

[7] WHITE HOUSE, NATIONAL SECURITY STRATEGY 19 (Feb. 2015), https://obamawhitehouse.archi ves.gov/sites/default/files/docs/2015_national_security_strategy_2.pdf.

[8] Amina Elahi, *"Sleeping While Black": Louisville Police Kill Unarmed Black Woman*, NPR (May 13, 2020, 6:33 PM), https://www.npr.org/2020/05/13/855705278/sleeping-while-black-louisville-pol ice-kill-unarmed-black-woman.

[9] Sam Louie, *Jogging While Black*, PSYCH. TODAY (May 14, 2020), https://www.psychologytoday. com/us/blog/minority-report/202005/jogging-while-black.

[10] Arundhati Roy, *The Pandemic Is a Portal*, FIN. TIMES (Apr. 3, 2020), https://www.ft.com/cont ent/10d8f5e8-74eb-11ea-95fe-fcd274e920ca; *see also Arundhati Roy: "The Pandemic Is a Portal,"* YES MAG. (Apr. 17, 2020), https://www.yesmagazine.org/video/coronavirus-pandemic-arundhati-roy.

[11] Sigal Samuel, *Everywhere Basic Income Has Been Tried, in One Map*, VOX (Oct. 20, 2020), https:// www.vox.com/future-perfect/2020/2/19/21112570/universal-basic-income-ubi-map. *See also* Ruha Benjamin, Viral Justice: Pandemics, Policing, and Portals, Harvard Kennedy School Carr Center for Human Rights Policy (Jul. 16, 2020) (as heard and paraphrased by the author) [hereinafter Benjamin, Viral Justice].

[12] SCOTUStalk Podcast, *Obamacare Back at the Court: Julie Rovner Joins SCOTUStalk to Preview the Newest ACA Challenge*, SCOTUSBLOG (Aug. 3, 2020), https://www.scotusblog.com/2020/08/aca-challenge-this-fall-with-julie-rovner-on-scotustalk/ (toward the end of Trump administration, even Trump's Justice Department had begun slow-rolling its support for the legal attack on the Affordable

march toward justice—was not impossible after all, though in many sectors, we are now observing significant retrenchment in voting rights, reproductive rights, and LGBTQIA+ rights. As Martin Luther King (and abolitionist Unitarian minister, Theodore Parker before him) intuited, bending the arc of the moral universe toward justice requires political will.[13] And political will depends on political activism by "We the People"—at home and abroad.

The Pandemic as a Portal to "Viral Justice"

We might view racism itself as a virus[14]—as a contagion that is sometimes invisible but can kill. Turning this insight on its head, Ruha Benjamin calls for "viral justice." Rather than view acts of racism as isolated incidents (or the acts of "a few bad apples"), Benjamin squarely confronts how

> [racism] is systemic, connected, constructed, productive. We say racism is socially constructed, but we fail to state the corollary: racism *constructs*. It's viral. If we were truly in this together, we would not be in this forever. [Racism] is not inevitable—it's a series of choices.[15]

To combat the virus of racism, Benjamin argues we must "recoup virality."[16] But more than a fleeting meme that goes viral, the virality of #BlackLivesMatter (or #MeToo and other social justice movements that go

---

Care Act in the Supreme Court, ensuring the Court would not address the merits of a challenge to the increasingly popular health program until after the 2020 election).

[13] Mychal Denzel Smith, *The Truth About "The Arc of the Moral Universe,"* HuffPost (Jan. 18, 2018), https://www.huffpost.com/entry/opinion-smith-obama-king_n_5a5903e0e4b04f3c55a252a4 ("'The arc of the moral universe is long, but it bends toward justice' is King's clever paraphrasing of a portion of a sermon delivered in 1853 by the abolitionist minister Theodore Parker").
[14] Iyiola Solanke, *Racial Discrimination Is Like Covid-19—A Virus We Can Tackle*, Yorkshire Post (July 9, 2020), https://www.yorkshirepost.co.uk/news/opinion/columnists/racial-discrimination-covid-19-virus-we-can-tackle-iyiola-solanke-2878306; Iyiola Solanke, *Tackling Discrimination as a Virus*, Microbiology Soc'y (July 6, 2020), https://microbiologysociety.org/blog/discrimination-as-a-virus.html; *Why Prejudice Should Be Treated Like a Virus*, CGTN: The Agenda (July 5, 2020, 8:47 PM), https://newseu.cgtn.com/news/2020-07-05/Why-prejudice-should-be-treated-like-a-virus-RPtFB8uly0/index.html; *see also* Ibram X. Kendi, How to Be an Antiracist 20 (2019).
[15] Benjamin, Viral Justice, *supra* note 11.
[16] *Id.*

global[17]) has moved beyond the performative to more meaningful calls for transformative change in our approach to public safety at all levels.

Small, individual acts of using a hashtag need not be superficial virtue signaling,[18] othering, or relying on celebrity popularism.[19] As Benjamin points out, "[s]mall is not superficial. Creating spaces to breathe is not superficial. The hashtag is a perfect example of the accumulation of many, connected individual acts. For us to each do better and demand better."[20] And yet, we must be mindful of what Zeynep Tüfekçi describes—in her brilliant treatment of modern protest—as "the power and fragility of networked protest" [21] as well as the raced terrain of internet (as Charlton McIlwain notes)[22] and technology (as Tendayi Achiume's United Nations report illustrates).[23]

Tracing the overlapping, yet distinct intellectual antecedents of Critical Race Theory (CRT) and Third World Approaches to International Law (TWAIL) suggests shared commitments and how we might recoup their critically significant shared tradition for developing a robust notion of "viral justice"[24] which might help reframe notions of security. What might Black intellectual thought teach us about reconceiving (and "racing") the notion of national "security?" Whose security? Security for what end?[25] To answer

---

[17] Catherine Powell, *How #MeToo Has Spread Like Wildfire Around the World*, NEWSWEEK (Dec. 15, 2017, 8:00 AM), https://www.newsweek.com/how-metoo-has-spread-wildfire-around-world-749171.

[18] Jamil Zaki & Mina Cikara, *Don't Be Afraid to Virtue Signal—It Can Be a Powerful Tool to Change People's Minds*, TIME (June 25, 2020, 10:19 AM), https://time.com/5859459/in-defense-of-virtue-signaling-2/.

[19] *But see _Kamari Clarke, The #BringBackOurGirlsCampaign and the Affective Turn to Hashtag Activism*, CORNELL U. (Oct. 27, 2017), https://events.cornell.edu/event/kamari_clarke_-_keynote_lecture_on_hashtag_activism (cautioning against the dangers of the hashtag activism of the #BringBackOurGirls transnational campaign on behalf of the Nigerian Chibok girls abducted by Boko Haram militants).

[20] Benjamin, Viral Justice, *supra* note 11; *see also* RUHA BENJAMIN, VIRAL JUSTICE: HOW WE GROW THE WORLD WE WANT (2022).

[21] ZEYNEP TÜFEKCI, TWITTER AND TEARGAS: THE POWER AND FRAGILITY OF NETWORKED PROTEST (2017); *see also* Zeynep Tüfekçi, TWITTER AND TEAR GAS: THE POWER AND FRAGILITY OF NETWORKED PROTEST, https://www.twitterandteargas.org/ (last visited May 2, 2022).

[22] Charlton McIlwain, *Racial Formation, Inequality and the Political Economy of Web Traffic*, 20 INFO., COMMC'N & SOC'Y 1073 (2016).

[23] Press Release, U.N. Human Rts. Council, Emerging Digital Technologies Entrench Racial Inequality, UN Expert Warns (July 15, 2020), https://www.ohchr.org/en/press-releases/2020/07/emerging-digital-technologies-entrench-racial-inequality-un-expert-warns.

[24] *See Viral Justice: Pandemics, Policing, and Portals with Ruha Benjamin*, HARV. KENNEDY SCH. CARR CTR., https://carrcenter.hks.harvard.edu/event/viral-justice-pandemics-policing-and-portals-ruha-benjamin (last visited June 29, 2022). As with the Négritude and Pan-Africanist intellectual movements from generations ago, the bridges between CRT and TWAIL can usefully be explored by scholars who bridge these fields. Such bridge building has led to novel insights—indeed, new paradigms of knowledge and political alliance.

[25] For parallel projects grappling with these questions in other contexts, *see, e.g.,* J. Benton Heath, *Making Sense of Security*, 116 AM. J. INT'L L. 289 (2021); Catherine Powell, *The War on Covid: Warfare*

these questions, it is helpful to look backward to draw on a rich intellectual tradition in determining how to move forward. Looking backward reveals ways in which Black thought leaders have consistently linked domestic civil rights to international human rights.

Origin Story: America's Raced and Colonial Founding

Since America was "raced" from its founding, our Constitution has never been truly color-blind,[26] and, as journalist Eugene Scott observes, "all politics are identity politics."[27] Reflecting back on America's founding, W.E.B. Du Bois, Paul Robeson, and Malcolm X saw the establishment of the nation as "a continuation of European projects of empire."[28] As Aziz Rana brilliantly notes, "the governing origin story obscured the real persistence of a colonial system in North America, organized around a fundamental racial dichotomy between settlers and non-settlers."[29] Tracing the work of Du Bois and others, Rana's work elegantly locates the United States alongside other White settler nations that divide insiders from subordinated outsiders—whether disposed Indigenous groups or racial and ethnic minorities.[30]

According to Rana, even though "the reality of American life was one of settler colonization, the anti-imperial narrative of the American Revolution meant that those ethnically included did not see themselves as colonizers."[31] According to this view, "the failure of U.S. constitutionalism to see the nation in colonial terms meant that [a]lthough dominant legal narratives in the 20th

---

and Its Discontents, UCLA L. REV. DISCOURSE (forthcoming 2023) (proposing shifting the warfare, security-based framing for addressing the pandemic to an ethics of care-based approach).

[26] Theodore R. Johnson, *How Conservatives Turned the "Color-Blind Constitution" Against Racial Progress*, ATLANTIC (Nov. 19, 2019), https://www.theatlantic.com/ideas/archive/2019/11/colorbl ind-constitution/602221/. *See also* Ian Millhiser, *What the Constitution Actually Says About Race, Explained*, Vox (Oct. 23, 2023), https://www.vox.com/policy-and-politics/23403021/supreme-court-affirmative-action-race-ketanji-brown-jackson-colorblind-originalism (noting Justice Ketanji Brown Jackson's discussion, (during the fall 2022 *Merrill v. Milligan* voting rights case oral argument) of how the passage of race-conscious civil rights legislation by the Reconstruction Congress demonstrates that the framers of the Fourteenth Amendment (the very same Congress) did not have a colorblind original understanding of the Equal Protection Clause in that Amendment).
[27] The Brian Lehrer Show, *Monday Morning Politics: Have BLM Protests Become White Spectacles?*, WNYC (July 27, 2020), https://www.wnyc.org/story/monday-morning-politics-2020-07-27/.
[28] Aziz Rana, *Freedom Struggles and the Limits of Constitutional Continuity*, 71 MD. L. REV. 1015, 1022 (2012).
[29] *Id.*
[30] Aziz Rana, *Colonialism and Constitutional Memory*, 5 U.C. IRVINE L. REV. 263 (2015).
[31] Rana, *Freedom Struggles, supra* note 29, at 1023.

century accepted the sinfulness of slavery, they essentially viewed the United States as an incomplete liberal society."[32]

In Du Bois's view, the failure to perceive the colonial nature of America's founding not only severed the linkage between. U.S. domestic civil rights and global anticolonial struggles, "it also downplayed the systematic forms of economic and political subordination that marked the pervasive experience of most Blacks [as well as most non-Whites generally]."[33] The problem for Du Bois, as historian Manning Marable writes, was that the mainstream civil rights movement failed to appreciate how "the Color Problem and the Labor Problem [are] two sides of the same human tangle."[34] Along similar lines, in his trenchant critique, Derrick Bell lambasted the prevailing mainstream civil rights/legal reformist focus mainly on ending formal segregation and emphasizing middle-class respectability.[35] Echoing Bell, Rana notes that this approach "emphasized social mobility for [B]lack elites and inclusion for some into arenas of corporate and political power, but it left prevailing socioeconomic hierarchies largely intact."[36]

Abolition and Suffrage: From Civil Rights to Human Rights and Intersectionality

Despite the failure of the connection between U.S. domestic civil rights reformers and global anticolonial struggles to take hold in the popular imagination, by the Civil War period, key Black intellectuals made this linkage in critical ways. Unsurprisingly, the antislavery movement is now recognized as one of the earliest *international* human rights movements, as Jenny Martinez illustrates.[37] Camille Gear Rich and I recently examined a gap in the literature

[32] *Id.*

[33] *Id.* at 1024.

[34] MANNING MARABLE, W.E.B. DU BOIS: BLACK RADICAL DEMOCRAT 107 (new updated ed., Routledge 2005) (1986).

[35] DERRICK BELL, FACES AT THE BOTTOM OF THE WELL: THE PERMANENCE OF RACISM (1993); *see also* Derrick A. Bell Jr., *Serving Two Masters: Integration Ideals and Client Interests in School Desegregation Litigation,* 85 YALE L.J. 470 (1976).

[36] Rana, *Freedom Struggles, supra* note 29, at 1024 (citing W.E.B. Du Bois, *Whither Now and Why, in* THE EDUCATION OF BLACK PEOPLE: TEN CRITIQUES 1906–1960, at 149, 149–58 (Herbert Aptheker ed., 1973) (warning civil rights leaders in 1960 about the limitations of liberal integration, particularly as a solution to the persistent economic marginalization experienced by the bulk of the Black community)).

[37] *See generally* Jenny S. Martinez, *Antislavery Courts and the Dawn of International Human Rights Law,* 117 YALE L.J. 550 (2008).

left open by Martinez, by examining the *domestic* dimensions of human rights as a framework for the abolition and suffrage movements—part and parcel of transnational, particularly transatlantic movements in both cases.[38]

In fact, Black intellectuals who were active in both the abolition and women's suffrage movements embraced a shared notion of human rights— one that Black women were central in articulating and embodying at the intersection of these two movements. This shared approach to the idea of rights and citizenship had to be more robust (than the more constrained formal liberal inclusion paradigm recognized by the status quo) as a way to move beyond the existing conception of rights that limited the right to vote to White men. The shared vision of rights was a human rights vision—broader than the prevailing civil and political rights framework of the Progressive Era (in which voting rights for Blacks were being rolled back, and women were still disenfranchised prior to the U.S. Constitution's 19th Amendment). As Gear Rich and I explained in our co-authored article, the human rights approach had to be capacious enough to cover those inhabiting the liminal space between subject and citizen and provide protection to "shadow populations"— then, women and Blacks—who had been stigmatized not only by the broader society, but also "even to each other as too incompetent or too untrustworthy to exercise the franchise."[39] This human rights vision, honed at the intersection of abolition and suffrage, became the basis for building bridges between Black voters of both sexes as well as between Black and White women.

Two Black leaders were especially important in articulating this human rights vision: suffragist Francis Ellen Watkins Harper and the abolitionist/ suffragist Frederick Douglass. Recognizing the potential for coalition building, Watkins Harper forcefully outlined the critical significance of an intersectional approach during Reconstruction, stating that "[w]e are all bound up together in one great bundle of humanity, and society cannot trample on the weakest and feeblest of its members without receiving the curse in its own soul"[40]—an insight importantly illuminated in historian Martha Jones's work.[41] Appealing to the ways that support for Black women

---

[38] *See generally* Catherine Powell & Camille Gear Rich, *The "Welfare Queen" Goes to the Polls: Race-Based Fractures in Gender Politics and Opportunities for Intersectional Coalitions*, 108 Geo. L.J. 105 (2020) (Nineteenth Amendment Edition).

[39] *Id.* at 105.

[40] Reva B. Siegel, *The Nineteenth Amendment and the Democratization of the Family*, 129 Yale L.J.F. 460 (2020).

[41] *See generally* Martha Jones, All Bound Up Together: The Woman Question in African American Public Culture, 1830–1900 (2009).

at the intersection of gender and race could benefit both White women (in securing suffrage) and Black men (in maintaining their voting rights) alike, as historian Rosalynn Terborg-Penn notes, a "coalition-building strategy was at work here, for African American women hoped that all three groups— Black women, Black men, and White women—could see the need to pull together in order to accomplish similar goals."[42]

Douglass also embraced a human rights vision grounded in the idea of intersectionality, even more explicitly invoking the terminology of "human rights." For example, in his autobiography, Douglass reflected on "a bold denunciation of slavery, and a powerful vindication of human rights."[43] In the context of women's suffrage, as Gear Rich and I note, Douglass stated those most directly affected—including women at various intersections of identity—should be placed at the center and heard in coalitional politics.[44]

The 1960s: Martin Luther King and Human Rights

Of course, the promise of Forty Acres and a Mule—which would have helped address the economic fragility of freed Black Americans following the Civil War—was abandoned as part of the greater backlash toward Reconstruction. However, President Franklin D. Roosevelt's famous "Four Freedoms" speech, and the adoption of the Universal Declaration of Human Rights (UDHR) and other human rights treaties in the aftermath of World War II, and eventually the civil rights era began to address this lacuna.

Toward the end of his life, Martin Luther King moved from civil rights to human rights, both with regard to his opposition to the Vietnam War, as well as in his linking of racial inequality and poverty. When King was assassinated in Memphis, he was in the midst of supporting local sanitation workers organizing for justice against poverty wages and conditions. In his 1967 book, *Where Do We Go from Here: Chaos or Community?*, King argues that with the rights Black Americans secured through the 1964 Civil Rights

---

[42] ROSALYN TERBORG-PENN, AFRICAN AMERICAN WOMEN IN THE STRUGGLE FOR THE VOTE, 1850-1920, at 9-10 (1998).

[43] NARRATIVE OF THE LIFE OF FREDRICK DOUGLASS, AN AMERICAN SLAVE, WRITTEN BY HIMSELF: A NEW CRITICAL EDITION BY ANGELA Y. DAVIS 150-51 (City Lights Books, 2010) (1845). He also spoke of being "awakened . . . on the subject of human rights." FREDERICK DOUGLASS, MY BONDAGE AND MY FREEDOM 274 (Miller, Orton & Mulligan, 1855). For further discussion of Douglass' embrace of the idea of human rights, *see* Powell & Rich, *supra* note 39, at 143 n.189.

[44] Powell & Rich, *supra* note 39, at 143-44.

and 1965 Voting Rights Acts, all Americans should come together to combat poverty and advance racial equality through initiatives such as a guaranteed basic income[45]—the idea Andrew Yang would advance years later in the 2020 Democratic presidential primary.[46] More recently, a global temporary guaranteed basic income has been promoted by the United Nations Development Program as a means of helping to protect the world's "poor and vulnerable" from the ravages of the ongoing COVID-19 pandemic.[47]

King's advocacy for economic security—even as the United States was fighting for more militaristic forms of national security in the Vietnam War—resonated with the linkage between civil rights and economic rights reflected in the UDHR. As historian Carol Anderson discusses in *Eyes Off the Prize: The United Nations and the African American Struggle for Human Rights, 1944–1955*, some civil rights leaders (including Du Bois) filed petitions with the United Nations challenging school segregation and other poverty conditions created by Jim Crow, charging in the United Nations petition that these practices and resulting conditions constituted "genocide."[48] However, with the Cold War and mistrust of anything that legitimized the notion of economic rights, such efforts to link race and poverty have been largely sidelined, even up through the current moment where "left-leaning" political figures who seek to make this linkage are branded as "socialists."

2020 and Beyond: Human Rights as a Site for Interest Convergence Theory

The global protests touched off by George Floyd's killing—and the expression of cruel indifference reflected by police officer Derek Chauvin as he pinned his knee on Floyd's neck—reflects resentment not only at American hypocrisy in failing to live up to its own ideals but also anger with homegrown racism and police brutality in sites around the world. Further, the demonstrations that spread across the globe following Floyd's murder illustrate opposition

---

[45] Martin Luther King Jr., Where Do We Go from Here: Chaos or Community? (1967).

[46] *The Freedom Dividend*, Yang 2020, https://web.archive.org/web/20210101194215/https://www.yang2020.com/what-is-freedom-dividend-faq/ (last visited May 2, 2022) (archived web page on the Wayback Machine).

[47] George Gray Molina & Eduardo Ortiz-Juarez, UNDP, Temporary Basic Income: Protecting Poor and Vulnerable People in Developing Countries (2020), https://www.undp.org/publications/temporary-basic-income-tbi.

[48] Carol Anderson, Eyes Off the Prize: The United Nations and the African American Struggle for Human Rights, 1944–1955, at 179 (2003).

toward the history of American imperialism generally and, to at least some extent at the time, the Trump administration specifically.

As Frederick Turner notes in his 1893 essay, *The Significance of the Frontier in American History*, as the U.S. western frontier closed, America had to expand beyond its borders and become imperialistic internationally.[49] But within its own borders, the country continued to engage in domestic imperialism by treating human bodies as frontiers for racialization and revisionism—where resource extraction took shape in a system of racial capitalism, as that term was coined and developed by Cedric Robinson.[50] The racialized body is itself a frontier of conquest.

This conquest operates in multiple sites, including (among others): the labor market, criminal justice system, immigration policy, and housing policy (as Trump, for example, tweeted to remind suburban voters that they would "no longer be bothered" by a fair housing rule he gutted).[51] A national context wherein White people, like Amy Cooper, enlist state violence by calling the police (even when Black people, like Christian Cooper, are merely engaged in mundane activities, such as "birding while Black")[52] evokes an eerie echo of Emmett Till, who was lynched at merely fourteen years old after being wrongfully accused of flirting with a White woman.

Building on the idea of "viral justice," we might capitalize on the ways this moment demonstrates Derrick Bell's insight regarding interest convergence.[53] According to Bell, meaningful racial justice can only be secured when the interests of oppressed racialized groups coincide (i.e., "converge") with the interests of Whites. For Bell, the Supreme Court's decision (and Justice Department's support for the result) in *Brown v. Board of Education* was, at least in part, motivated by an interest in improving the country's international image during the Cold War.[54]

---

[49] FREDERICK TURNER, THE SIGNIFICANCE OF THE FRONTIER IN AMERICAN HISTORY (1893).

[50] *See generally* CEDRIC J. ROBINSON, ON RACIAL CAPITALISM, BLACK INTERNATIONALISM, AND CULTURES OF RESISTANCE (H.L.T. Quan ed., 2019).

[51] Christina Wilkie, *Trump Tells Suburban Voters They Will "No Longer Be Bothered" by Low-Income Housing*, CNBC (July 29, 2020, 12:54 PM), https://www.cnbc.com/2020/07/29/trump-suburban-voters-will-no-longer-be-bothered-by-low-income-housing.html.

[52] Joan Walsh, *Birding While Black: Just the Latest Bad Reason for White People to Call Police*, THE NATION (May 26, 2020), https://www.thenation.com/article/society/amy-cooper-birding-police/.

[53] *See generally* Derrick A. Bell Jr., *Comment,* Brown v. Board of Education *and the Interest-Convergence Dilemma*, 93 HARV. L. REV. 518 (1980).

[54] *Id.* For additional support for this view, *see also* MARY L. DUDZIAK, COLD WAR CIVIL RIGHTS: RACE AND THE IMAGE OF AMERICAN DEMOCRACY (2011) and Mary L. Dudziak, *Desegregation as a Cold War Imperative*, 41 STAN. L. REV. 61 (1988).

Under the Trump administration, rather than "Making America Great Again"—with Trump's intolerant and derogatory remarks on Black Lives Matter protesters, Latine immigrants, the "China virus,"[55] and Native Americans (such as calling Elizabeth Warren "Pocahontas")[56]—Trump's clear goal had been to "Make America *Hate* Again." Elsewhere, I have written about how Trump's immigration policies drew on raced and gendered tropes of nationhood[57] as a means of normalizing human rights abuses—a point akin to Jaya Ramji-Nogales's insights on the "racialized border"[58] further developed in this volume.

However, by attacking so many marginalized groups at once, Trump spawned coalitions in the best tradition of Bell's interest convergence theory. Not only were the protests of summer 2020 multiracial, but they also often emphasized the intersectional identities of many affected by police violence, including Black women[59] such as Breonna Taylor and Black members of the LGBTQIA+ community.[60] White and Black allies, building bridges through grassroots networks, such as the "Wall of Moms"[61] (founded in Portland, before popping up nationally), stepped forward to support Black Lives Matter. This reflects the efforts of writers, such as Robin DiAngelo, in her best seller *White Fragility*, which called on Whites to do work within their own communities to address racism.[62]

At the same time, despite this momentum toward transformative change, in part because of backlash, President Biden's progress on racial justice has

[55] *Reports of Anti-Asian Assaults, Harassment and Hate Crimes Rise as Coronavirus Spreads*, ANTI-DEFAMATION LEAGUE (June 18, 2020), https://www.adl.org/blog/reports-of-anti-asian-assaults-harassment-and-hate-crimes-rise-as-coronavirus-spreads.

[56] *Pocahontas*, ELIZABETH WARREN, https://2020.elizabethwarren.com/pocahontas (last visited May 2, 2022).

[57] Catherine Powell, *Race, Gender, and Nation in an Age of Shifting Borders: The Unstable Prisms of Motherhood and Masculinity*, 24 UCLA J. INT'L L. & FOREIGN AFFS. 133 (2020).

[58] Jaya Ramji-Nogales, *Dispatches from a Racialized Border: The Invisible Threat*, JUST SEC. (July 27, 2020), https://www.justsecurity.org/71678/dispatches-from-a-racialized-border-the-invisible-threat/.

[59] Michele Goodwin, *The New Jane Crow: Women's Mass Incarceration*, JUST SEC. (July 20, 2020), https://www.justsecurity.org/71509/the-new-jane-crow-womens-mass-incarceration/.

[60] Lauren Holt, *Thousands Show Up for Black Trans People in Nationwide Protests*, CNN (June 15, 2020, 1:11 PM), https://www.cnn.com/2020/06/14/us/black-trans-protests/index.html.

[61] Dani Blum, *"The Moms Are Here": "Wall of Moms" Groups Mobilize Nationwide*, N.Y. TIMES (July 27, 2020), https://www.nytimes.com/2020/07/27/parenting/wall-of-moms-protests.html.

[62] ROBIN DIANGELO, WHITE FRAGILITY: WHY IT'S SO HARD FOR WHITE PEOPLE TO TALK ABOUT RACISM (2018); *but see* Jonathan Chait, *Is Anti-Racism Training Just Peddling White Supremacy?*, N.Y. MAG. (July 16, 2020), https://nymag.com/intelligencer/2020/07/antiracism-training-white-fragility-robin-diangelo-ibram-kendi.html; Danzy Senna, *Robin DiAngelo and the Problem with Anti-racist Self-Help*, ATLANTIC (Sept. 2021), https://www.theatlantic.com/magazine/archive/2021/09/martin-learning-in-public-diangelo-nice-racism/619497/.

been slow, and he has maintained certain aspects of Trump-era immigration policies and practices. On racial justice, while Biden nominated (and secured confirmation for) Ketanji Brown Jackson as the first Black woman Supreme Court Justice, he has failed to secure congressional approval for sorely needed voting rights legislation, including the Freedom to Vote Act (which would establish national election standards) and the John Lewis Voting Rights Advancement Act (which would reinstate a core provision of the Voting Rights Act).[63] Given state restrictions on voting rights,[64] the failure to secure voting rights protections at the federal level is a major blow for racial justice and, more broadly, the future of democracy.

In terms of economic justice, while Biden secured passage of the Inflation Reduction Act, which includes provisions on green jobs,[65] the final legislation dropped other key proposals involving the care economy.[66] Similar proposals were not adopted when Biden's earlier proposed Build Back Better legislation failed to secure passage.[67] While not framed in racial justice terms per se, the Build Back Better bill would have supported working families across the board, *inter alia*, supporting the care economy (disproportionately comprised of women of color) as well as the green economy.[68]

On the immigration front, while Biden raised the historically low annual refugee admissions ceiling from Trump's low admissions cap of 15,000 for fiscal year 2021 to 62,500, by the end of FY21 (which ended on September 30, 2021), the United States admitted only 11,411 refugees.[69] He eventually

---

[63] Kathryn Watson, *Biden Makes Push for Voting Bills and Says There Is "No Option" but to Kill the Filibuster*, CBS NEWS (Jan. 12, 2022), https://www.cbsnews.com/news/biden-voting-rights-speech-filibuster-atlanta/ (summarizing both bills and explaining that the John Lewis bill would reinstate the provision of the Voting Rights Act that the Supreme Court gutted in a 2013 decision, *Shelby County v. Holder*, 570 U.S. 529 (2013), which undermined a provision that required states with a history of racial discrimination to seek Justice Department approval before changing their election rules).

[64] For further discussion of the voter suppression bills and statutes, *see, e.g.*, *Vote Suppression*, BRENNAN CTR. FOR JUSTICE, https://www.brennancenter.org/issues/ensure-every-american-can-vote/vote-suppression; Powell & Rich, *supra* note 39 (providing overview of sources).

[65] Stefan Ellerbeck, *Here's How the Inflation Reduction Act is Impacting Green Job Creation*, WORLD ECON. F. (Mar. 14, 2023), https://www.weforum.org/agenda/2023/03/us-climate-bill-green-jobs/.

[66] See, e.g., Christopher Hickey, *Not the Year for Women and Parents: Child Care Provisions Were Cut From the Inflation Reduction Act. It's Not the First Time*, CNN (Aug. 12. 2022), https://www.cnn.com/2022/08/12/politics/inflation-reduction-children-families/index.html.

[67] Li Zhou, *What Happened to Build Back Better?*, VOX (MAR. 16, 2022, 2:30 PM), https://www.vox.com/2022/3/16/22955410/build-back-better-scenarios (analyzing different routes that congressional Democrats could take to pass the Biden administration's Build Back Better legislation in light of congressional Republicans' failure to support the legislation).

[68] *See* Powell, *Color of Covid and Gender of Covid, supra* note 1.

[69] Bill Frelick, *Biden Administration Falls Far Short of US Refugee Admissions Cap*, HUM. RTS. WATCH (Oct. 7, 2021, 8:53 AM), https://www.hrw.org/news/2021/10/07/biden-administration-falls-far-short-us-refugee-admissions-cap (noting that the Biden administration was "not even close to

raised the refugee admissions ceiling to 125,000 for FY22[70] and FY23.[71] Similarly, Biden was slow in reversing another Trump-era policy he vowed to end—Title 42—which had been the basis of Trump expelling more than one million migrants at the southern border. Finally, during his third year in office—and once the coronavirus public health emergency expired in May 2023—Biden lifted the Title 42 restrictions.[72] Further troubling was video footage during Biden's first year of the U.S. Border Patrol confronting Haitian refugees at the border swinging long reins, which was reminiscent of slave patrols policing the freedom of movement of Black slaves historically.[73]

In writing about the Color of COVID and Gender of COVID,[74] I've focused on how this moment of health and economic crisis impacts those at the intersection of different forms of oppression, but also creates opportunities for interest convergence. Ultimately, the human rights framework could provide a way for lawyers and advocates to bring these interests together, as a group of us did in preparing a "Human Rights at Home" policy blueprint transition paper we shared with President Obama's transition team[75]— providing a roadmap to reconceive civil rights in human rights terms.

---

hitting Trump's meager ceiling" and that "[m]ore than 51,000 places that could have been used to save lives and restore hope were lost forever").

[70] Michael D. Shear, *The Biden Administration Will Raise the Cap on Refugee Admissions to 125,000*, N.Y. TIMES (Sept. 20, 2021), https://www.nytimes.com/2021/09/20/us/politics/biden-refugee-cap.html (discussing 2022 cap).

[71] Presidential Determination No. 2022-25, Memorandum on Presidential Determination on Refugee Admissions for Fiscal Year 2023, 87 Fed. Reg. 60,547 (Sept. 27, 2022).

[72] *Biden Administration Ends Title 42. What Now?*, NPR (May 14, 2023), https://www.npr.org/2023/05/12/1175865631/biden-administration-ends-title-42-what-now.

[73] Jason Hoffman et al., *White House Says It's Seeking More Information on "Horrific" Footage of Border Patrol Agents Confronting Haitian Immigrants*, CNN (Sept. 21, 2021, 10:35 AM), https://www.cnn.com/2021/09/20/politics/border-patrol-haitian-immigrants-viral-video/index.html.

[74] Powell, *Color of Covid and Gender of Covid*, *supra* note 1; Catherine Powell, Opinion, *Color of Covid: The Racial Justice Paradox of Our New Stay-at-Home Economy*, CNN (Apr. 18, 2020, 9:13 AM), https://www.cnn.com/2020/04/10/opinions/covid-19-people-of-color-labor-market-disparities-powell/index.html (coining "Color of Covid," as acknowledged by Don Lemon and Van Jones in their CNN cable news miniseries, "The Color of Covid"); Catherine Powell, *The Color and Gender of Covid: Essential Workers, Not Disposable People*, THINK GLOB. HEALTH (June 4, 2020), https://www.thinkglobalhealth.org/article/color-and-gender-covid-essential-workers-not-disposable-people; Catherine Powell, Opinion, *A Year Later, the "Color of Covid" Still Matters*, CNN (Mar. 26, 2021, 10:37 AM), https://www.cnn.com/2021/03/26/opinions/color-of-covid-biden-administration-powell/index.html (critically analyzing the ongoing pandemics of race and gender inequality unmasked by COVID-19); Catherine Powell, *The Color of COVID After Biden's First 100 Days*, THINK GLOB. HEALTH (May 13, 2021), https://www.thinkglobalhealth.org/article/color-covid-after-bidens-first-100-days?utm_medium.

[75] CATHERINE POWELL, AM. CONST. SOC'Y, HUMAN RIGHTS AT HOME: A DOMESTIC POLICY BLUEPRINT FOR THE NEW ADMINISTRATION (Oct. 2008).

Not long before his death, civil rights leader and Congressman John Lewis characterized Trump's executive order replacing the administration's much-maligned family separation policy with one permitting the indefinite detention of children, an "assault not just on immigrant families but also on our country's legacy of affirmatively protecting *human rights*."[76] Congressman Lewis was not alone in invoking human rights. Activists are increasingly returning to the language and substance of human rights to draw interconnections among various movements at home and abroad. Hopefully, this return to the idea of human rights—including the indivisibility of rights and addressing harm at the intersection of identities—can pave the way for a "viral convergence" (combining the insights of Benjamin and Bell) of the racial and economic justice the United States so desperately needs. While the country will continue to experience periods of progress and retrenchment for rights, a human rights paradigm has the potential to develop broader, more robust movements to challenge periods of retrenchment. At the same time, the portal for a racial reckoning that appeared to open in 2020 has been swinging shut as a newly empowered conservative supermajority on the Supreme Court (entrenched in the Trump years) is rolling back hard-fought rights, and Republican-led initiatives to restrict voting rights are undermining political efforts toward change. We have been here before, and we must equip ourselves and those who come behind us for a longer battle.

---

[76] Press Release, Rep. John Lewis, Executive Order Fails to Address Moral Crisis, Congressman John Lewis (June 20, 2018) (emphasis added), https://web.archive.org/web/20200718154616/https://johnlewis.house.gov/media-center/press-releases/rep-lewis-executive-order-fails-address-moral-crisis (last visited May 2, 2022) (archived web page on the Wayback Machine).

3

National Security Law and the Originalist Myth

Aziz Rana

Introduction: The Narrative of the Golden Age

In 1973, Arthur Schlesinger Jr. published his landmark critique of national security excess in the age of Watergate and the Vietnam War, *The Imperial Presidency*.[1] Schlesinger, a Pulitzer Prize winning historian, political speechwriter, and John F. Kennedy adviser, had been a central Cold War intellectual architect. But now, he decried how the country had lost its way. Richard Nixon, for him, signified the subversion of a rights-respecting constitutional order in favor of an "imperial" and discretionary security state, one located primarily in the presidency and operating both at home and abroad in ways that violated classic American principles.

According to Schlesinger, the problem was that government officials had abandoned the country's original ideals. Schlesinger argued that the framers of the Federal Constitution, the nation's "Founding Fathers" were "exceptionally able and intelligent men, wiser on the whole than their posterity."[2] They had initiated a system premised on checks and balances, in which the liberty of all was safeguarded because power was "dispers[ed] . . . among three independent branches."[3] The problem, however, was that in the 20th century, political elites, individuals like Nixon, had treated the national security apparatus as their own playground and increasingly rejected that original vision. Presidents had usurped the war-making authority of the legislative branch while the state's national security infrastructure had grown exponentially and without meaningful legal constraints. All of this was in the service of

---

[1] *See* ARTHUR SCHLESINGER, THE IMPERIAL PRESIDENCY (1973).
[2] *Id.* at 13.
[3] *Id.* at 9.

Aziz Rana, *National Security Law and the Originalist Myth* In: *Race and National Security*. Edited by: Matiangai V.S. Sirleaf, Oxford University Press. © Oxford University Press 2023. DOI: 10.1093/oso/9780197754641.003.0004

near endless foreign interventions with limited connection to the country's actual national interests. In effect, the United States devolved from a republic into an empire. According to Schlesinger, the only solution to the imperial presidency was for there to be a return to founding ideals and a "reinvigoration of the written checks of the Constitution."[4] The "original intent" of the "Founding Fathers" had to infuse once more "the spirit of the American people."[5]

In the half-century since, Schlesinger's invocation of originalist principles and his declension narrative—or story of moral decline—have become ubiquitous ways for legal scholars and public commentators to critique rights abuses and power grabs in the national security context. Time and again, these abuses—as well as the specific military adventures they are connected to—are presented as a repudiation of 18th- and 19th-century American practices. A common framing of the overall history returns to the sense of collective civil libertarian descent from an ostensible high point in the past.[6]

This chapter offers a critical interrogation of the mainstream originalist reform narrative. By using the term "originalist," I am less interested in the technical scholarly debates about how best to interpret the text. Instead, I use the term to invoke a broader and pervasive legal and political culture, in which even liberal critics of the security state present their goals as part of a project of national restoration, or of returning to the constitutional values of deified framers. In the process, I argue that this originalist cultural myth— premised on civil libertarian and non-imperial national origins—ignores the extent to which there is no golden age or non-imperial past to revive. Such framings offer a limited account of the reforms necessary for genuine anti-imperial change in the present. And they ignore the structuring role of race and colonialism in deep-rooted American ideas of foreign intervention, warmaking, and threat.

The first section begins by detailing more concretely how the declension narrative conceives of empire, both as a foreign policy matter and as a constitutional one. The second section then explores the actual settler colonial

---

[4] *Id.* at 397.

[5] *Id.* at 13.

[6] Indeed, one can see the latter fact in the titles for civil libertarian critiques of the national security state. This includes texts I personally view as classics of the field, such as Jules Lobel, *Emergency Power, and the Decline of American Liberalism*, 98 YALE L.J. 1385 (1989); BRUCE ACKERMAN, THE DECLINE AND FALL OF THE AMERICAN REPUBLIC (2010). Lobel's article was among the first pieces of legal scholarship that truly moved me and helped to generate my own personal interest in engaging with the field of national security law.

past that this approach papers over. The third section further develops an alternative settler reading through an examination of a particular Supreme Court case, 1851's *Mitchell v. Harmony*. While the case is often depicted as proof of an earlier republican willingness by the courts to constrain executive power, I highlight the continuities in Chief Justice Taney's thinking between *Mitchell* and *Dred Scott v. Sandford*. The fourth section then turns to the persistence of this settler imagination—especially a governing duality between those worthy of rights and those subject to state power—in the shaping of 20- and 21-century notions of threat. Finally, by way of a conclusion, I suggest how rather than a separate domain of conversation, ongoing debates about American decolonization are essential to breaking free from the very trap of interventionism and security excess condemned by Schlesinger.

An Imperial Present, But a Republican Past?

The civil libertarian narrative of republican decline is framed around a specific understanding of what makes the American presidency "imperial" and, relatedly, what it means to discuss the American empire. Institutionally, the argument emphasizes the unilateral and unchecked nature of executive authority. And sociologically, it focuses on global military adventurism in the 20th century. In other words, under this reading, the United States, especially during and after the Cold War became consumed with global power. It abandoned George Washington's famed advice from his 1796 Farewell Address, namely, that so long as Americans avoided entanglement in European conflicts, they would be able to limit external threats and avoid military despotism. But rather than maintaining "a detached and distant situation,"[7] as Washington urged, the United States instead today projects power to an unfathomable degree, militarily present in nearly 80 percent of the world's countries.[8] In a context in which the United States intervenes continuously in the domestic politics of foreign states, it is unsurprising that the executive—as the locus of a centralized security apparatus—claims more and more power

[7] *The Papers of George Washington 1 April–21 September 1796*, 20 PRESIDENTIAL SERIES 703–22 (David R. Hoth & William M. Ferraro eds. 2019).
[8] *See* AZIZ RANA, THE TWO FACES OF AMERICAN FREEDOM 4 (2010).

for itself. Thus, returning to origins is both a call for a revived appreciation of checks and balances and for a smaller global footprint in keeping with the framers' advice.

These critiques both of presidential overreach and global interventionism are very well-taken. It is certainly the case that if the United States had a less aggressive international posture, it would be far easier to cabin the power of the national security state, including the president. Yet a striking feature of contemporary politics is how the declension narrative has itself been claimed by those like Donald Trump, in particular in his talk of "America First."

For Trump, the country, too, has lost its way, including through over-commitment abroad. However, for him, retreating behind the fortress of the border does not mean limiting or constraining the security apparatus. Although it requires avoiding unnecessary adventurism, it nonetheless entails a belligerent readiness to respond to whatever threats to the home-land may arise—especially from ethno-racial outsiders, such as Muslims or Mexicans. The approach is ethno-nationalist and bellicose and rests still on assumptions of an exceptional American right to intervene wherever and whenever necessary, even if with a smaller global footprint.

The ease with which the Trumpian right appropriates the declension narra-tive speaks to a constitutive problem with the overarching framing. The story of republican fall may criticize an "imperial" present of foreign meddling that diverges from the non-imperial past of republican self-limitation. But what it ignores is how, to a profound extent, 20-century American global domi-nance is rooted in a historic expansionist ethic. This ethic—present from the earliest days of colonization—long treated U.S. borders as provisional and continues to mark outsider communities as worthy only of conditional rights and of conditional sovereignty.

In a sense, the exhortation to return to origins offers a vision of American innocence that obscures this central fact. It fails to contend with the role of that earlier expansionist history in the shaping of contemporary practices. No doubt, the declension story provides a means for contesting particular se-curity excesses or for calling for global retreat. But in casting a nostalgic lens on the collective past, it avoids offering a clear-eyed basis for challenging an American imperial mindset with far deeper roots than global spread alone in the 20 century. The conventional reformist account thus allows space for a Trumpian right to then embrace returning to that past—precisely as a way of safeguarding a racial order perceived as under threat.

Reframing the American Republic as a Settler Empire

If the declension narrative misunderstands the driving dynamics of early American experience, how else should they be described? Simply put, the high tide of republican checks and balances, invoked by Schlesinger, was at one and the same time a period of sustained settler imperial development.[9] The U. S. was above all an outpost of Anglo-European rule in the non-European world—sharing many qualities in common with projects like the French in Algeria or the English in Ireland, Australia, and South Africa. In fact, American commentators often view aspects of national history to be uniquely homegrown, when in fact they are present to varying degrees in numerous other settler societies. Among others, these qualities include greater equality within the settler colony than in the imperial metropole or home country; a cultural sense of being "chosen" as a racial, ethnic, or religious community for a historical mission; a greater emphasis on militarism due to perceived threats from Indigenous and foreign populations; and, finally, a wariness of metropolitan social and political customs which are depicted at times as corrupt or decadent.[10]

But what made the American variation distinctively imperial concerns the essential role of continuous territorial conquest to internal economic and political development. Anglo-European settlers carried to North America a belief that the guiding ideological purpose of the national project was to make widely available to insiders a vision of freedom involving participatory political structures and broad access to land and property.[11] All of this underscored the extent to which settlers took for granted that their legal and political institutions were meant to do two things simultaneously. First, they were supposed to provide insiders with the emancipatory conditions

---

[9] *See id.*, for a comprehensive account of the idea of "settler empire" in American life. The basic descriptions of settler institutions and practices draw from this work.

[10] For more on historical examples and the common traits of transplanted settler communities, *see generally* EXCLUSIONARY EMPIRE: ENGLISH LIBERTY OVERSEAS, 1600–1900 (Jack P. Greene ed., 2010); LISA FORD, SETTLER SOVEREIGNTY: JURISDICTION AND INDIGENOUS PEOPLE IN AMERICA AND AUSTRALIA, 1788–1836 (2010); MICHAEL MANN, THE DARK SIDE OF DEMOCRACY: EXPLAINING ETHNIC CLEANSING (2004); LORENZO VERACINI, SETTLER COLONIALISM: A THEORETICAL OVERVIEW (2010); PATRICK WOLFE, TRACES OF HISTORY: ELEMENTARY STRUCTURES OF RACE (2016); Caroline Elkins & Susan Pedersen, *Settler Colonialism: A Concept and Its Uses, in* SETTLER COLONIALISM IN THE TWENTIETH CENTURY 1 (Caroline Elkins & Susan Pederson eds., 2005). For more on the specific limitations of traditional historical and theoretical scholarship on American political identity, *see e.g.*, JODI A. BYRD, TRANSIT OF EMPIRE: INDIGENOUS CRITIQUES OF COLONIALISM (2011); GLEN SEAN COULTHARD, RED SKIN, WHITE MASKS: REJECTING THE COLONIAL POLITICS OF RECOGNITION (2014).

[11] RANA, *supra* note 8, at 50–55.

of self-government and economic independence. And second, to support this overarching project, these institutions were designed to extract much-needed land and labor from Native and excluded groups, particularly enslaved African persons, and their descendants.[12]

This meant that Euro-Americans long presumed that the basic engine of internal republican freedom and economic prosperity was territorial growth and, therefore, Indigenous conquest. Indeed, conquest was often embraced as the key social experience cohering disparate European migrants into a single people. For the famed early 20-century historian Frederick Jackson Turner, "[m]ovement" was nothing less than the "dominant fact"[13] of the American experience, a point Teddy Roosevelt echoed even more emphatically when he declared, "[t]he winning of the West was the great epic feat in the history of our race."[14] Thus, republican checks and balances were very much only for those included as free citizens and rested on the sustained domination of excluded populations. Framers such as Washington may have wanted to avoid European entanglements, but they nonetheless still saw collective life as fundamentally built on claiming land and projecting power.

Over time, this imperial drive also made coterminous the categories of *settler* and of *White*. To succeed, the U.S. territorial project needed more settlers beyond those initially coming from England. Americans thus de-emphasized perceived differences among European communities, created easy naturalization procedures, and culturally promoted a composite White identity. Of course, this was not without its complications, as specific communities— such as Catholic populations (and the Irish in particular)—confronted various modes of informal and formal discrimination, especially at the workplace and often on grounds of questionable status as "White." Nonetheless, over time, "Whiteness" as a container from American membership produced a relatively inclusive approach to distinct European peoples—eventually whether Catholic or Protestant, French, German, or Irish.[15] But the focus on Whiteness also had the opposite effect for those on the outside looking in, hardening a sharp dichotomy between insiders and outsiders. Ideas of White supremacy became central to settler justifications for why it was appropriate to expropriate Native land or to control Black labor.

---

[12] For an overview of the ideologies of the American settler empire, *see id.* at 12–14.

[13] FREDERICK JACKSON TURNER, THE FRONTIER IN AMERICAN HISTORY 37 (1986).

[14] Theodore Roosevelt, *Manhood and Statehood, in* THE STRENUOUS LIFE: ESSAYS AND ADDRESSES 245, 254 (1902).

[15] *See generally* NOEL IGNATIEV, HOW THE IRISH BECAME WHITE (1995); RANA, *supra* note 8, at 116–17, 166–67.

Thus, for much of American history, such settler White supremacy generated a constitutional politics organized around two distinct and rigid accounts of sovereign authority—one for insiders of democratic consent and internal checks and another for outsiders of near limitless discretion. In fact, generations of settler insiders linked the very act of an energetic federal government to the project of empire building, a project that presupposed an unchecked imperial right deriving from British royal prerogative. Aggressive federal activity thus became synonymous with the internal application of a coercive power properly applied only to those outside the bounds of social inclusion, such as Indigenous peoples, Mexicans, and Black Americans. Under these circumstances, any internal appearance of the dreaded imperial prerogative was viewed as a dangerous threat to liberty and an attempt to reduce White settlers to the condition of outsiders—by treating *free* citizens as if they were colonial subjects. Particularly xenophobic, this dualist vision of political sovereignty upheld the necessity of empire and simultaneously remained ever vigilant about the possibility of imperial power seeping into White settler society.

Roger Taney's Constitution of Checks and Balances

Returning to a classic 19th-century case often treated as indicative of a lost republican heritage drives home this complicated historical relationship between internal constraint and external authority. As legal scholars like Jules Lobel highlight, 19th-century courts—in keeping with founding era assumptions—were often deeply suspicious of the capacity of executive officials to unilaterally determine both what constituted an emergency and what force was appropriate in response.[16] As a result, they created judicial tests that imposed striking constraints on military and presidential power.

One can see this in 1851's *Mitchell v. Harmony*, the pre–Civil War Supreme Court decision that provided perhaps the most extensive examination of the issue. The case concerned the seizure during the Mexican-American War of private property by a U.S. military colonel named David Mitchell.[17] There, Mitchell contended that he should not face liability because his actions were taken due to a military emergency, and, moreover, that he had secret

[16] *See generally* Lobel, *supra* note 6.
[17] Mitchell v. Harmony, 54 U.S. (13 How.) 115, 136 (1851).

information that the person whose property was seized planned to carry on illegal trade across enemy lines.[18] Today, these would be foreign wartime national security choices granted by courts a striking amount of deference.

But Taney essentially rejected Mitchell's claims and in his opinion for the Court presented a strong defense of the capacity of judges and even juries to hold executive officials accountable for constitutional rights violations, including abroad. For this reason, critics of the imperial presidency hold up the decision as a clear counterpoint to today's national security framework. Further burnishing the case's status, it was explicitly embraced by Justice Frank Murphy in his famed dissent in *Korematsu*, where he referred to the majority's holding on Japanese internment as "the legalization of racism" and held out *Mitchell* as offering the appropriate judicial test of what constitutes an emergency.[19]

Yet Taney's connection to *Mitchell* speaks to its double-sided implications, ignored by the traditional civil libertarian account. *Mitchell* is certainly an indicator of early American suspicions of broad deference to the security apparatus. In the opinion, Taney railed against governmental assertions of secrecy. According to the ruling, executive officials could not base claims merely on secret information and expect the court to accept their judgments. If Colonel Mitchell wanted to assert that the plaintiff planned on violating the law by trading with the enemy, "these rumors and suspicions" had to be backed up by publicly offered evidence.[20] As he declared, "[t]he fact that such an intention existed must be shown; and of that there is no evidence."[21]

Moreover, Taney articulated a remarkably narrow legal standard for emergency. In order to ensure that free citizens were not reduced to imperial subjects, Taney believed that courts should be especially reticent to expand the scope of executive power. For an emergency to exist, one that justified ceding discretionary authority to the president or to his military subordinates, the threat needed to be both "immediate and impending[,]"[22] approximating an armed attack or invasion. And, critically, what counted as "immediate and impending" could not be based purely on the executive branch actor's "honest judgment" of events.[23] It had to accord with what a "reasonable"[24] person would believe when placed in a similar informational

---

[18] *Id.* at 135.
[19] *See* United States v. Korematsu, 323 U.S. 214, 234, 242 (1944) (J. Murphy, dissenting).
[20] *Mitchell*, 54 U.S. at 133.
[21] *Id.*
[22] *Id.*
[23] *Id.*
[24] *Id.*

situation. It was therefore up to a jury of ordinary citizens to assess if this threshold had been met.[25] Thus, if officials sought to avoid liability, they would have to provide such a jury with all the relevant information—secret or otherwise—that might enhance the perceived reasonableness of their security decisions. In effect, Taney embraced the centrality of popular management of basic questions of war and peace and rejected the idea of an insulated security apparatus as final arbiters of how rights are safeguarded.[26]

Yet to make sense of the case it is also key to note the continuities between this decision and *Dred Scott v. Sandford* (1857). Today *Dred Scott* is remembered as the Supreme Court's reviled defense of slavery and racial subordination. Chief Justice Taney infamously wrote of the legal status of Black people: "They had for more than a century before been regarded as beings of an inferior order, and altogether unfit to associate with the [W]hite race, either in social or political relations; and so far inferior, that they had no rights which the [W]hite man was bound to respect."[27] At the same time, there was a second key aspect of the *Dred Scott* decision—the way in which such unchecked power went hand in hand with an assertion of constitutional protections for White frontier settlers, including protections of their slave-holding rights. Taney's majority opinion combined a vision of absolute sovereign power over Black Americans, whether formally free or enslaved, with a remarkable critique of the royal prerogative when directed internally at settlers. In the process, he articulated central components of the American settler empire: wariness of government, belief in the empire as a precondition for freedom, and a commitment to hardening the constitutional and racial divide marking collective life.

Similarly, in *Mitchell*, central to the case were *whose* rights Taney was vindicating. The initial plaintiff was Manuel Harmony, who although an immigrant born in Spain, was nonetheless a Euro-American naturalized citizen and New York–based merchant. In Taney's assessment, he was not that differently situated than the presumptive enslaver in *Dred Scott* and so the case could be generalized into a question of the rights owed to White settler members. In both contexts, the federal state was engaged in stripping insiders of property protections key to economic independence and thus to full participation in society. From Taney's perspective, each decision

[25] *Id.*
[26] For more on the case and its implications for debates around security and self-government, see Aziz Rana, *Who Decides on Security?*, 44 CONN. L. REV. 1417, 1445–51 (2012).
[27] Dred Scott v. Sandford, 60 U.S. 393, 407 (1857).

amounted to limiting the capacity of government officials to assert authority over individuals—whether enslavers or wartime merchants—that were supposed to be treated as free citizens. Critically, the problem with national security excess in *Mitchell* did not concern the underlying imperial conquest of Mexico—its legality or legitimacy. Rather, it entailed ensuring that a system of checks and balances toward racial insiders was sustained even as the polity engaged in broad territorial expansion and extreme force against outsiders.

The latter point was underscored by the lack of concern from Taney and others with how that same federal government engaged in property rights infringements after the war, but now directed at non-European Mexicans. For instance, Congress's California Land Settlement Act—the same year as Taney's decision in *Mitchell*—forced Mexicans to prove their land title in court. Since many, especially those who were not part of the Spanish elite, had no formal titles or the financial means for long-term litigation, they were either stripped of their property or forced to sell. The result was the nullification of most Mexican landholding and the transfer of property to White settlers, immigrant and native born.[28] In a sense, such expropriation was best understood, not as a constitutional violation, but instead as further facilitating insider freedom.

The Continuing Duality of American Institutions

There is no doubt a significant gulf between the world of 1796 or 1851 and the world of today. Especially given the defining 20th-century national experiences of World War II, the Cold War, and the successes of the civil rights movement, American institutions have clearly been shaped by commitments in favor of legal equality and against accounts of ethno-racial national identity. The official American story about the post–World War II international legal order and the country's role on the world stage also presumes that the United States is legally respectful of state sovereignty, regardless of the underlying racial makeup of the foreign nation.

Nonetheless, this structuring duality between those who enjoy checks and balances and those subject to extreme and discretionary violence continues to shape American national security practices. Indeed, one can see deep

[28] *See* FOREIGNERS IN THEIR NATIVE LAND: HISTORICAL ROOTS OF THE MEXICAN AMERICANS 156–57 (David J. Weber ed., 2004).

resonances in American foreign policy between the logic that structured settler expansion and the logic that undergirds contemporary assertions of power. These include an exceptionalist framework, in which officials still overwhelmingly present the American project as uniquely grounded in ideas of republican freedom—connected to a distinctive heritage of independence and constitutional founding. Such exceptionalism also goes hand in hand with claims regarding a special role on the world stage, where—just as with settler expansion—Americans enjoy a basic authority to step inside and outside of legal arrangements in fulfilling national destiny or security objectives. And, like the past, threats to these objectives primarily come from communities read as less culturally and politically attuned to free institutions. These threats create a Manichaean reality, in which unless the United States pacifies sites of disorder, domestic liberty is itself imperiled.

All of this creates a context in which national security abuse is not broadly dispersed across populations, but overwhelmingly falls on the same communities that were historically viewed as racially "unfit" for membership and self-governance. To the extent that the problem is presented as simply geostrategic overreach, that alone has little to say about why time and again the sites and populations viewed as "disordered" are those long associated with ethno-racial exclusion. Similarly, the institutional emphasis on presidentialism ignores how much of the security infrastructure that imposes racialized violence overseas or at home is a product of official consensus across the branches of government—judicial, executive, and congressional.

This effective replication of the old settler duality is driven home by reflecting on three key and overlapping domains of contemporary security violence: the carceral state, the post-9/11 "war on terror," and immigration. As recent racial justice protests highlight, the state's discretionary power when it comes to policing and incarceration are spectacularly and disproportionately visited on poor Black and Brown communities. Moreover, that power is exercised in a context in which "law and order" is very much a one-way street. In an obvious echo of the settler framework, while state apparatuses invoke threat as a way to impose coercive authority on marginalized communities, those very same communities enjoy limited capacity to hold police and other security officials accountable through rights rhetoric.

Similarly, the "war on terror" is critically shaped by the idea that the United States has a permanent right to intervene wherever officials perceive threats, in particular in Muslim-majority nation-states. For such polities, their internal capacity to make basic policy choices often ends up dependent on the willingness of local elites to first embrace U.S. strategic objectives. Moreover, while members of these communities—in the context of military occupation or targeted killings—find themselves subject to discretionary violence, they are nonetheless profoundly constrained in their ability to assert essential legal safeguards. Across a range of federal court cases in which plaintiffs describe extreme rights deprivations produced by the "war on terror," the repeated outcome has been a basic institutional unwillingness by American state officials to hold the security apparatus accountable for its acts of violence.

In the domain of immigration, rather than European co-ethnics, immigrants to the United States are now overwhelmingly non-White, the very individuals that settlers once rejected as full members. Instead of extending settler projects into the frontier or "periphery" as 19th-century Euro-American immigrants did, today's new arrivals in essence represent the movement of this periphery into the very center of metropolitan power. To a large extent, this movement was made possible by the elimination in 1965, during the height of the civil rights movement, of racially restrictive national origins quotas.

But while such policy shifts have challenged the country's racial identity, present-day immigrants have not enjoyed anything approaching the swift and full inclusion of their predecessors. Confronted by extensive social disabilities and facing the constant possibility of detention and forced removal, these immigrants' status at the edges of collective life offers a contemporary embodiment of the very political dependence that historically linked excluded communities to settler society. And as in the past, that dependence is sustained by a powerful discretionary prerogative in the form of militarized border policing that preserves the divide between insider privilege and outsider exclusion.

Each domain clearly highlights the fundamental inadequacy of invoking a mythic republican past as a way of constraining contemporary national security violence. At the same time, simply calling for retrenchment and a return to originalist values has no way of accounting for why past efforts at such retrenchment and at institutional re-balancing have failed repeatedly. Since Schlesinger wrote *The Imperial Presidency*, there have been multiple periods of global pullback—such as after both the Vietnam War and the Cold War—as well as persistent calls for reform across other sites of national security. Yet each moment of potential constraint has given way to further buildups.

What drives the tendency toward security state expansion? Such expansion is no doubt connected to a mid-20th-century vision of the United States as guarantor of the international order, such that the country has a claimed responsibility to address threats anywhere. This policymaking commitment to American primacy means that even as the United States attempts to disentangle from certain regions—the Middle East and Central Asia after wars in Iraq and Afghanistan—that shift is routinely joined to calls for a new "cold war" in another region, for instance, with China. One can see this even in support for Ukrainian resistance against Russian imperial aggression. Such support—filtered as it is through the existing national security framework—is not limited to providing defensive military assistance or principally concerned with seeking a peaceful resolution. Instead, it becomes tied to massive military sums and a general arms buildup across Europe, aimed increasingly at weakening geostrategic antagonists on a relatively peripheral battlefield (for Americans, at least).

The traditional declension story captures aspects of how the background assumptions of American international police power beget new cycles of yet further security state expansion and spending. But a key factor missing from that story concerns the intersection of long-standing racial logics with global political realities. Today's postcolonial and multiracial world—no longer contained within a European imperial system—is commonly depicted as marked by disordered Asian, African, and Latin American states and threatening non-White populations in movement. This has clear echoes of how the non-European world was conceived of in the 19th-century past. The sense of perpetual and racialized threat then creates profound internal incentives to pursue interventionist actions abroad or to impose draconian policing and border policies at home. It also affects judgments about moral concern, including which victims or impoverished communities are seen as worthy of large-scale humanitarian investment and inclusive refugee policies, an issue yet again raised by differential media and state treatment of suffering in Ukraine as opposed to in the Middle East or Africa.

The result in practice has been an American national security politics that even when retrenchment—say, a shift away from Vietnam or recently from Afghanistan—is pursued, it is nonetheless combined with a continued marshaling of near-limitless resources to protect the homeland from the next perceived external danger. In a sense, for all the handwringing about Trump's more explicitly racist rhetoric, policy outcomes in this way often mimic his logic of fortress defense.

Conclusion: National Security Reform
through Decolonization

Despite all of this, civil libertarian invocations of founding values in the national security arena remain commonplace. This is all the more note-worthy given the intensity of recent debates, through the *New York Times* 1619 Project and elsewhere, about race, colonialism, and American history. Indeed, outside of national security law, academic and popular conversation swirls around the extent to which the framers devised a pro-slavery compact or promoted American growth through sustained violence against Indigenous nations. Yet within the field's scholarly and policymaking circles, the primary way that mainstream critiques of security excess relate to the past is through the same story that appeals to a republican golden age, including by invoking cases whose actual meaning is often far more ambiguous. In this way, the field's dominant conversation about foreign policy, war-making, and threat appears strangely insulated from the broader national confrontation with American history—as if the state's exercise of coercive power against Black and Indigenous peoples was unrelated to debates about national security law or civil liberties, then or now.

Ultimately, any genuine project of national security reform requires more than reviving a fictive 18th century of checks and balances. It instead entails treating foreign interventionism as only one expression of a broader colonial imagination and infrastructure, present since the framing and never adequately uprooted. All of this underscores the need to engage with the same anticolonial imagination that circulated during the global era of decolonization but that has rarely been directed at the American security project itself. Alongside rejecting the presumptive legitimacy of the state's international police power, such a reformist approach includes ending the colonial status of all the existing territorial dependencies—in line with the genuine political desires of local and self-determining communities. It also revolves around everything from sharing sovereignty with Native peoples and land return to reparations, decriminalizing the border, transformative and structural reforms to intelligence and policing apparatuses, and providing judicial avenues for the remedy of past colonial crimes as well as contemporary national security ones.

These suggestions, only hinted at here, are certainly far afield from the topics that usually consume national security experts, especially when focused on technical legal debates about the means used to project American power: When is targeted killing acceptable? Where and for how long can detainees be held? But, in a sense, that disconnect speaks to the pervasive limitations of the ongoing debate. This debate—still about how to balance liberty and security—even when critical of particular security excesses, rarely confronts what it would mean to properly remove from government officials their continuous capacity to exercise discretionary violence. It often falls back into comforting American narratives about the basic goodness of collective arrangements and past practices, and rarely explores how today's modes of coercion replicate historic settler and racial assumptions. But, in the end, if scholars and policymakers are truly committed to providing rights, respect, and voice to those who have long been on the receiving end of state violence, such a colonial accounting is the only meaningful path.

III

RACE AND THE SCOPE
OF NATIONAL SECURITY

4

Black Security and the Conundrum of Policing

Monica C. Bell

Introduction

In the summer of 2020, we entered a new phase of the long police reform debate. There was a halting but broad recognition that the opaqueness of police
governance—especially with respect to spending,[1] staffing practices,[2] and
expansion of criminal codes and enforcement priorities[3]—had made some
places, especially Black and Brown urban communities, neighborhood-level
police states.[4] We were, perhaps for the first time, seriously interrogating
whether police should be able to function in these ways and, more fundamentally, questioning the role of police in producing public safety. With the
failure of Congress to pass the George Floyd Justice in Policing Act and with
murders, especially gun murders, rising across many American cities during
the COVID-19 pandemic, the political winds have since shifted away from
police reform and toward expanded police presence and power.[5] In cities

---

[1] Richard C. Auxier, *What Police Spending Data Can (and Cannot) Explain amid Calls to Defund
the Police*, URB. WIRE (July 9, 2020), https://www.urban.org/urban-wire/what-police-spending-
data-can-and-cannot-explain-amid-calls-defund-police.

[2] Simone Weichselbaum & Wendi C. Thomas, *More Cops. Is It the Answer to Fighting Crime?*, USA
TODAY (Feb. 12, 2019), https://www.usatoday.com/story/news/investigations/2019/02/13/marshall-
project-more-cops-dont-mean-less-crime-experts-say/2818056002/.

[3] *See, e.g.*, Tim Lynch, *Overcriminalization, in* CATO HANDBOOK FOR POLICYMAKERS (8th ed.
2017), https://www.cato.org/cato-handbook-policymakers/cato-handbook-policy-makers-8th-edit
ion-2017/17-overcriminalization#the-legal-minefield.

[4] *See* Joe Soss & Vesla Weaver, *Police Are Our Government: Politics, Political Science, and the Policing
of Race—Class Subjugated Communities*, 20 ANN. REV. POL. SCI. 565 (2017).

[5] *See, e.g.*, Jeff Asher, *Murder Rose by Almost 30% in 2020. It's Rising at a Slower Rate in 2021*, N.Y.
TIMES (Nov. 15, 2021), https://www.nytimes.com/2021/09/22/upshot/murder-rise-2020.html;
Felicia Sonmez & Mike DeBonis, *No Deal on Bill to Overhaul Policing in Aftermath of Protests over
Killing of Black Americans*, WASH. POST (Sept. 22, 2021), https://www.washingtonpost.com/powerp
ost/policing-george-floyd-congress-legislation/2021/09/22/36324a34-1bc9-11ec-a99a-5fea2b2da34
b_story.html; *see also* Chaz Arnett, *Race, Surveillance, Resistance*, 81 OHIO ST. L.J. 1103 (2020).

Monica C. Bell, *Black Security and the Conundrum of Policing* In: *Race and National Security*. Edited by: Matiangai V.S.
Sirleaf, Oxford University Press. © Oxford University Press 2023. DOI: 10.1093/oso/9780197754641.003.0005

like New York and San Francisco, these upticks have stoked political energy to reinvigorate "broken windows policing," or the deployment of police to surveil and intervene in petty crime—often targeting the unhoused population for offenses like public intoxication and urination—after several years of decreased support for those practices.[6]

Polarized narratives, one that places traditional policing at the heart of the project of building community security—and one that sees policing as perhaps an irreparably brutal force that should be minimized to create alternative governmental and community resources for safety—have put the political debate surrounding policing today on the highly fractured moral and political terrain. Yet what is continually lost in these conversations are the intricacies of the experiences, needs, and dreams of the people in communities most directly targeted by both private violence and state violence.

In this chapter, I draw upon qualitative research to explore what some Black people who live in dispossessed and criminalized urban neighborhoods believe, experience, and hope for with respect to policing and security. Through interviews, I have seen some of the complex fault lines at the heart of debates over police reform. These debates have sometimes centered on defunding, abolition, and other measures aimed at shrinking the footprint of policing in American life. More recently, governments have often and simultaneously resorted to the decades-old method of expanding police presence when there are upticks in crime. In both strategies, there is an inevitable response from skeptics: What about Black people's safety? The security of Black communities seems both reliant upon and threatened by the only public safety institution in which American governments at all levels consistently invest.

Crime, Policing, and the Paradox of Black Security

To the untrained eye, oft-maligned movement calls to defund the police and reinvest in alternatives are difficult to reconcile with simultaneous outcries for the government to respond to surging gun violence, which has hit Black urban communities especially forcefully. The complexity of this

---

[6] See, e.g., Katie Glueck & Ashley Southall, As Adams Toughens on Crime, Some Fear a Return to '90s Era Policing, N.Y. TIMES (Mar. 26, 2022), https://www.nytimes.com/2022/03/26/nyregion/broken-windows-eric-adams.html; Thomas Fuller, Shaila Dewan & Kellen Browning, San Francisco Mayor Declares State of Emergency to Fight City's "Nasty Streets", N.Y. TIMES (Dec. 17, 2021), https://www.nytimes.com/2021/12/17/us/san-francisco-state-of-emergency-crime.html.

perspective presents a conundrum for policymakers because it is so difficult to fit nuanced perspectives on Black security into slogans and straightforward policy proposals.

Policymakers must reckon with the fact that substantial social scientific research suggests that even as policing has been racially unjust and violent, some manifestations of policing have also prevented some crime.[7] Social scientific evidence supports the idea that investments in policing correlate with, and perhaps have a causal relationship with, reductions in violence. The Great Crime Decline of the 1990s, which seemed to persist at least until the COVID-19 pandemic, may have been partly attributable to policing tactics.[8] Some of those tactics include targeted deterrence or hot-spots policing using predictive algorithms to head off crime, as well as the controversial "broken windows" approach to policing, which prioritizes heavy policing of low-level offenses based on a theory that this preemptive approach prevents more serious offenses.[9]

But expanded policing on its own, like other causes that have gained attention over the years—abortion,[10] lead exposure,[11] seasonal fluctuations in heat levels,[12] the density of community organizations,[13] and more—does not and has never operated on its own to explain fluctuations in crime.[14] In contravention of the simplistic narrative that "more cops = less crime,"[15] it takes

[7] See, e.g., Aaron Chalfin & Justin McCrary, The Effect of Police on Crime: New Evidence from U.S. Cities, 1960–2010 (NBER, Working Paper 18815, 2013), https://www.nber.org/papers/w18815. Policing is also variable because of variations in departmental culture and personal characteristics of officers and police leaders. So policies or approaches that might appear similar on their face might have more or less crime prevention efficacy across different departments and individuals.

[8] See, e.g., Derek Thompson, Why America's Great Crime Decline Is Over, ATLANTIC (Mar. 24, 2021), https://www.theatlantic.com/ideas/archive/2021/03/is-americas-great-crime-decline-over/618381/.

[9] See George L. Kelling & James G. Wilson, Broken Windows: The Police and Neighborhood Safety, ATLANTIC (Mar. 1982), https://www.theatlantic.com/magazine/archive/1982/03/broken-windows/304465/; see also Robert J. Sampson & Stephen W. Raudenbush, Seeing Disorder: Neighborhood Stigma and the Social Construction of "Broken Windows," 67 SOC. PSYCH. Q. 319 (2004).

[10] John J. Donohue & Steven D. Levitt, The Impact of Legalized Abortion on Crime over the Last Two Decades (NBER, Working Paper 25863, 2019), http://www.nber.org/papers/w25863 (updating and extending 2001 analysis).

[11] Jessica Wolpaw Reyes, Environmental Policy as Social Policy? The Impact of Childhood Lead Exposure on Crime (NBER, Working Paper 13097, 2007), http://www.nber.org/papers/w13097.

[12] E.g., Kilian Heilmann, Matthew E. Kahn & Cheng Keat Tang, The Urban Crime and Heat Gradient in High and Low Poverty Areas, 197 J. PUB. ECON. 104408 (2021); Leah H. Schinasi & Ghassan B. Hamra, A Time Series Analysis of Associations between Daily Temperature and Crime Events in Philadelphia, Pennsylvania, 94 J. URB. HEALTH 892 (2017), https://dx.doi.org/10.1007%2Fs11524-017-0181-y; see also ERIC KLINENBERG, HEAT WAVE: A SOCIAL AUTOPSY OF DISASTER (2002).

[13] Patrick Sharkey, Gerard Torrats-Espinosa & Delaram Takyar, Community and the Crime Decline: The Causal Effect of Local Nonprofits on Violent Crime, 82 AM. SOCIO. REV. 1214, 1221 (2017).

[14] See, e.g., PATRICK SHARKEY, UNEASY PEACE (2018).

[15] One of many examples of this simplistic framing of the relationship between policing and crime can be found in Matthew Yglesias, The Case for Hiring More Police Officers, VOX (Feb. 13, 2019),

much more than increased policing alone to sustainably reduce violence. As social scientist Patrick Sharkey recently explained, "[s]o much research and journalism on violence gravitates toward single-cause explanations. And that's just misguided."[16] This debate over the causal relationship between policing and crime reduction is important for navigating the conundrum policymakers face: if it was possible to argue that policing historically has had *no* effect on crime, this would undermine political demands to increase the size of police budgets and forces during a COVID-era crime increase. Yet the evidence available presents a more complex picture, one in which policymakers are trading off between forms of safety and violence reduction.

This is because a parallel fact that policymakers must not ignore is that, at the same time that policing has contributed to crime reduction, it has also directly contributed to extensively documented devastating and multiple harms to Black communities.[17] As Bruce Western and Becky Pettit found nearly two decades ago, during the exponential growth of what came to be known as "mass incarceration," 60 percent of Black American men without high school diplomas born in the late 1960s spent time in prison.[18] Dorothy Roberts has argued that American cities' heavy reliance upon policing and the carceral system exacted devastating community-level harms upon Black communities, with substantial moral costs.[19] More recent scholarship, by social scientists such Ali Sewell, Joscha Legewie, and several others, has drawn precise causal links between exposure to harsh policing and wide-ranging harms to Black communities, such as poorer educational performance, greater anxiety, greater emergency room use, obesity, and higher blood pressure.[20] Moreover, the types of spatial and broad racial harms of policing,

---

https://www.vox.com/policy-and-politics/2019/2/13/18193661/hire-police-officers-crime-criminal-justice-reform-booker-harris.

[16] Thompson, *supra* note 8.

[17] *E.g.*, MICHELLE ALEXANDER, THE NEW JIM CROW: MASS INCARCERATION IN THE AGE OF COLORBLINDNESS (2010); TODD CLEAR, IMPRISONING COMMUNITIES (2007); BECKY PETTIT, INVISIBLE MEN: MASS INCARCERATION AND THE MYTH OF BLACK PROGRESS (2012); ANDREA RITCHIE, INVISIBLE NO MORE: POLICE VIOLENCE AGAINST BLACK WOMEN AND WOMEN OF COLOR (2017).

[18] Becky Pettit & Bruce Western, *Mass Imprisonment and the Life Course: Race and Class Inequality in U.S. Incarceration*, 69 AM. SOC. REV. 151 (2004). For more on the concept of "mass incarceration" vis-à-vis other concepts like "over incarceration," *see* Benjamin Levin, *The Consensus Myth in Criminal Justice Reform*, 117 MICH. L. REV. 259 (2018).

[19] Dorothy E. Roberts, *The Social and Moral Cost of Mass Incarceration in African American Communities*, 56 STAN. L. REV. 1271 (2004).

[20] *E.g.*, Amanda B. Geller et al., *Aggressive Policing and the Health of Young Urban Men*, 104 AM. J. PUB. HEALTH 2321 (2014); Erin M. Kerrison & Alyasah A. Sewell, *Negative Illness Feedbacks: High-Frisk Policing Reduces Civilian Reliance on ED Services*, 55 HEALTH SERVS. RSCH. 787 (2020); Joscha

incarceration, and related forms of penal control identified in previous decades persist today, even as rates of incarceration have slightly declined nationally.[21] Yet in a world more focused on the interpersonal violence that shows up in crime statistics than the slow, structural violence that does not,[22] policymakers, researchers, journalists, and members of the public tend to prioritize the *thin safety* that police may contribute to instead of the *thick safety* that all people, including Black Americans, are seeking. Thick safety demands social, economic, and physical conditions that produce the ability to protect self, family, and community from threats, including the threat of state violence. This distinction between thin safety and thick safety is not merely a domestic challenge; as other chapters in the volume explain, this bifurcation also appears in external and global conversations about national security.

Black Americans are not ignorant of these conundrums. Many Black Americans, including those who live in marginalized neighborhoods, report that they want police to be responsive to and present in their communities. They just want the police to "stop killing us."[23] I have heard many Black research participants share thoughts that are reminiscent of these polls, but with important caveats.

For example, Linda (pseudonym), a forty-six-year-old Black woman living in Washington, D.C., told me—with a jocular tone, sprinkled among numerous critiques of police bias and inefficacy: "I'd rather have [police] around here 24/7. It make me feel much safer, whether they're crooked or not. I wouldn't tell. They're in the uniforms. As long as they look like police, I'm alright, or security. I'm alright with any type of protection." Linda held

---

Legewie & Jeffrey Fagan, *Aggressive Policing and the Educational Performance of Minority Youth*, 84 AM. SOCIO. REV. 220 (2019); Abigail A. Sewell, *Illness Associations of Police Violence: Differential Relationships by Ethnoracial Composition*, 32 SOCIO. F. 975 (2017); Alyasah Ali Sewell et al., *Illness Spillovers of Lethal Police Violence: The Significance of Gendered Marginalization*, 44 ETHNIC & RACIAL STUD. 1089 (2020).

[21] John Gramlich, *America's Incarceration Rate Falls to Lowest Level Since 1995*, PEW RSCH. CTR. (Aug. 16, 2021), https://www.pewresearch.org/fact-tank/2021/08/16/americas-incarceration-rate-lowest-since-1995/.

[22] Rory Kramer & Brianna Remster, *The Slow Violence of Contemporary Policing*, 5 ANN. REV. CRIMINOLOGY 43 (2022).

[23] *See, e.g.*, Jay Caspian Kang, *"Our Demand Is Simple: Stop Killing Us,"* N.Y. TIMES MAG. (May 4, 2015), https://www.nytimes.com/2015/05/10/magazine/our-demand-is-simple-stop-killing-us.html; William Saletan, *Americans Don't Want to Defund the Police. Here's What They Do Want*, SLATE (Oct. 17, 2021), https://slate.com/news-and-politics/2021/10/police-reform-polls-white-black-crime.html.

out hope that the physical presence of police, "any type of protection," would protect her from interpersonal violence.

Yet her statement that "[i]t make me feel much safer, whether they're crooked or not" is hardly a strong endorsement of traditional policing. Linda presumed, as given, that police run the risk of being "crooked." Earlier in the interview, Linda complained about how much the police "suck" in her neighborhood. She also shared an unsettling story about her nephew's experience of physical police violence. Linda said she had a nephew who was committing some minor crime, "doing that bad stuff," at sixteen or seventeen. When he was twenty-three, he finally told his aunt about an experience he had back then, when he said that a police officer picked him up and put him in a van. According to the nephew, per Linda, another officer joined the one who picked him up and asked if he could "just take this nigger back there . . . I'll beat his ass and bring him back." Linda said this story almost made her cry. "They do that to our babies . . . the police do anything." Even on Linda's account, her nephew was ultimately not physically harmed; he was traumatized instead by the fear of physical attack. Neither Linda nor I have a way to corroborate this story. What is important is that, despite her horror at her nephew's terrifying story, Linda still said she wanted uniformed officers around her home for safety. In a poll that asks, "[i] f you have to choose, do you support or oppose increasing the number of police officers," there seems to be a reasonably good chance Linda would respond, "support."[24]

I have written about a similar phenomenon based on data from Cuyahoga County, Ohio, in my article, "Located Institutions: Neighborhood Frames, Residential Preferences, and the Case of Policing."[25] Of several examples, I describe the experiences of Michelle and Chris, both of whom reported seriously negative experiences with the police while also treating police as part of the American Dream, those who are supposed to "protect and serve." On one hand, Michelle, a twenty-three-year-old mother of two living on Cleveland's East Side, critiqued the police for not being "set up the right way." She complained that police "do anything just to pick with people, to spice up [lie about] people," and—unlike Linda in D.C.—was comparatively thrilled that police rarely patrolled her corner of the neighborhood.[26] Michelle

---

[24] Yglesias, *supra* note 15 (reporting the results of a January 2019 poll by Civis Analytics that asked, "Some members of your state legislature are proposing increasing the budget for the police force and hiring more police officers in high crime areas. If you have to choose, do you support or oppose increasing the number of police officers?").

[25] Monica C. Bell, *Located Institutions: Neighborhood Frames, Residential Preferences, and the Case of Policing*, 125 AM. J. SOC. 917 (2020).

[26] *Id.* at 948.

lamented the police shooting deaths of unarmed Black Clevelanders Malissa Williams and Timothy Russell in 2012, horrified by the number of officers who arrived on the scene and the lack of attention to whether Williams and Russell were armed. "Give somebody a chance first," Michelle demanded.

Yet even with her cynicism about police at both a broad and personal level, Michelle dreamed of moving to a neighborhood where she could rely on police to keep herself and her family safe, even though she had not experienced that before:

> If I know you're [police officers are] here, I know you're seeing a crime, and they ain't gonna be no more crime because they won't be around when they see a lot of police. When there's no police, they can get away with anything because nobody is watching you. So, no witnesses, nobody gets in trouble. That's how it is. Police stay around, I feel safe, I know my kids—my kids know what police is; I want them to know everything. They know how to call 911. They know all the emergency contact numbers.[27]

Despite all her criticisms of the police earlier in the interview, here we see Michelle, like Linda, dreaming of a safe place without crime, and of government officials who promote public safety through their presence and ability to deter and investigate crime. She wants her children to be able to access these safety resources as well. If an analyst focuses only on the latter part of Michelle's dreams of good policing in her ideal neighborhood, they miss her fundamental cultural and structural critique of policing in the world she inhabits today. Reducing her view to "supports police presence" misses her perspective entirely.

This bifurcation between experiences with traditional public safety approaches and ideals about security, brings into sharp relief how many Black people may experience police distrust and estrangement from the legal system while still desiring more and better policing. It is the paradox of Black security that yearns for an inclusive form of safety enjoyed by many Americans but that consistently, perhaps inevitably, slips from our grasp.[28]

---

[27] *Id.* at 949.

[28] For more on this paradoxical yearning for safety, *see* Monica C. Bell, *Safety, Friendship, and Dreams*, 54 HARV. C.R.-C.L. L. REV. 703 (2019).

The Tunnel Vision of Policing Research

For decades, research on crime and public safety has been focused heavily on policing, as if the sole pathway through which crime can be reduced and safety can be constructed is by improving what happens within police departments.[29] Yet social scientists may be misinterpreting their data on what security means to Black people, possibly overstating the centrality of policing to the safety-building project. Most of the research and polling data on policing were designed to probe policing so, unsurprisingly, their findings are about policing. The problem with this approach is that *security*, both objectively and subjectively, may not be solely or even primarily related to policing.

Consider, for example, Sandra (pseudonym), a forty-one-year-old Black woman who lives close to Linda in Washington, D.C. When I asked Sandra about the positive changes in her neighborhood, she replied:

> I see a whole lot of condos being built really really fast, and I think that's good. I got tired of seeing all Black people all the time. I want to be able to understand other people's cultures . . . I started seeing gardens and people that show interest and come to the community and motivate you and your kids. They have a One Stop where kids can go and play ball after school and earn stipends. I think that it's better than when we were coming up because there was nothing to do. We had to fight for summer jobs. We had to wait until school came back around until we could get our jobs back. I think it's changed for the better for my children and my children's children. It seems like it's going in the right direction. There's a lot more things to do instead of hanging out and being afraid to walk down the street. *More police presence is here, and you feel a little bit safer.* It could be better with the noise control sometimes. I understand on the weekend they're having parties and all that, but I never seen that when I was coming up. They have parties and it's all lit up . . . [T]hey rent the room and have block parties. We didn't have that. There wasn't no money, and if there was we didn't know about it. It's a lot of better options and food, shopping, and better quality of food. I'm just glad I have a chance to be a part of it.

---

[29] For expanded discussion of this point, *see* Monica C. Bell, *Next-Generation Policing Research: Three Propositions*, 35 J. ECON. PERSPS. 29 (2021).

A policing study would zero in on Sandra's comment about feeling safe in the presence of police, emphasized in the preceding quote: "More police presence is here, and you feel a bit safer." But Sandra's new sense of security in her redeveloping neighborhood has numerous components—economic integration, racial integration, greening, increased community engagement, activities for youth, employment opportunities for youth, social activities for adults, widely available healthy food.

While the proposals that would emerge from Sandra's response are to some extent the types of slow "root cause" investments that may take a generation to yield reductions in violence,[30] others, like youth summer employment and greening, can improve neighborhood safety and flourishing in a much shorter time frame. For example, several studies have found immediate reductions in violent crime among youth who are participating in summer work programs, especially if other factors in their life put them at risk of getting caught up in the penal system.[31] In addition, several studies have found that certain urban redevelopment efforts, such as the creation of green space in areas that were previously vacant lots, can reduce crime, depending on various situational factors.[32] In New York City, a bundle of efforts that

[30] *See* David M. Kennedy, *State Violence, Legitimacy, and the Path to True Public Safety*, NISKANEN CTR. (July 8, 2020), https://www.niskanencenter.org/state-violence-legitimacy-and-the-path-to-true-public-safety/ ("The perennial favorite alternative to policing and prisons is taking money away from the back end that is the criminal justice system to make investments in addressing 'root causes:' in family support, education, programs for young people, health care, economic development. We absolutely should do that . . . but the hard truth is that as a solution to policing, it's not nearly the panacea people want. At best, those changes are slow: Make things better for kids entering school today, and the impact on, say, violence won't be felt for a decade or more, when those kids enter their high-risk years.").

[31] Results on the effects of summer youth employment programs on property crime are more mixed. *See, e.g.*, Jonathan M.V. Davis & Sara B. Heller, *Rethinking the Benefits of Youth Employment Programs: The Heterogeneous Effects of Summer Jobs*, 102 REV. ECON. & STATS 664 (2020); Alexander Gelber, Adam Isen & Judd B. Kessler, *The Effects of Youth Employment: Evidence from New York City Lotteries*, 131 Q. J. ECON. 423 (2016); Alicia Sasser Modestino, *How Do Summer Youth Employment Programs Improve Criminal Justice Outcomes, and for Whom?*, 38 J. POL'Y ANALYSIS & MGMT. 600 (2019); Judd B. Kessler et al., *The Effects of Youth Employment on Crime: Evidence from New York City Lotteries* (NBER, Working Paper 28373, Jan. 2021), https://www.nber.org/papers/w28373. Importantly, these findings apply to summer youth employment programs, not youth employment during the school year which, depending on the number of hours worked, several studies have found to positively correlate with participation in criminalized activity. However, those associations tend to decline with additional controls, undermining the idea that there is a strong causal link between intense youth employment, on its own, and increased criminalized behavior. *See, e.g.*, Robert Apel et al., *Using State Child Labor Laws to Identify the Causal Effect of Youth Employment on Deviant Behavior and Academic Achievement*, 24 J. QUANTITATIVE CRIMINOLOGY 337 (2008).

[32] *See, e.g.*, John MacDonald et al., *Reducing Crime by Remediating Vacant Lots: The Moderating Effect of Nearby Land Uses*, J. EXPERIMENTAL CRIMINOLOGY (2021), https://doi.org/10.1007/s11292-020-09452-9; Sara Hadavi et al., *Resident-Led Vacant Lot Greening and Crime: Do Ownership and Visual Condition-Care Matter?*, 211 LANDSCAPE & URB. PLAN. 104096 (2021); Michelle Kondo et al.; *Effects of Greening and Community Reuse of Vacant Lots on Crime*, 53 URB. STUDS. 3279 (2016); Tania Schusler et al., *Examining the Association Between Tree Canopy, Parks and Crime in Chicago*, 170

included physical activity, public space (including lighting improvements), youth mentorship and employment, and more had been shown to reduce crime within New York City public housing projects before the pandemic surge in crime.[33] Thus, we see that Sandra's broad perspective on what it has taken for her formerly underresourced neighborhood to feel safe for her and to flourish falls in line with social scientific research. Reducing Sandra's thoughts about safety to one statement—"More police presence is here, and you feel a little bit safer"—gives a false sense of her vision for a safe and secure community. Yet policymakers, researchers, and journalists concerned about public safety routinely narrow their inquiries and interventions to police alone.

The Social Science of Black Security

Building security for Black America will require an expanded study of public safety writ large, both thin and thick. Thus, it demands moving beyond fluctuations in traditional variables, such as crime rates and opinions on the police, and toward variables that better account for individual and community flourishing. From this perspective, when a community's crime rates decrease, but residents feel more heavily under surveillance, segregated, or lose democratic power, the state cannot declare a safety victory.

Various researchers have sought to develop metrics that would better capture the full range of what it means for human beings to experience security. Psychologist Tyler VanderWeele's work is potentially instructive. VanderWeele has been developing measures for individual and community flourishing that might allow researchers to think more expansively about individual and community security. These metrics were not developed to study policing and therefore do not center the types of outcomes that tend to motivate traditional public safety officials. Instead, they may

LANDSCAPE & URB. PLAN. 309 (2018); *see also* Allegra M. McLeod, *Prison Abolition and Grounded Justice*, 62 UCLA L. REV. 1156, 1230–31 (2015) (situating greening and other urban redevelopment methods as forms of preventive justice that are compatible with theories of prison abolition). *But see* Dexter H. Locke et al., *Did Community Greening Reduce Crime? Evidence from New Haven, CT, 1996–2007*, 161 LANDSCAPE & URB. PLAN. 72 (2017) (finding a null relationship between greening and crime in one small city).

[33] SHEYLA A. DELGADO ET AL., JOHN JAY COLLEGE OF CRIMINAL JUSTICE RESEARCH & EVALUATION CTR., REPORTED CRIME IN MAP COMMUNITIES COMPARED WITH OTHER NYC AREA, MAP EVALUATION UPDATE 5 (2020).

assist policymakers in thinking more carefully about what security demands. VanderWeele's individual flourishing metrics are broad and include (1) life satisfaction, (2) mental and physical health, (3) whether people feel that what they do in life is worthwhile, (4) whether people feel that they behave virtuously, (5) how happy people are with their friendships and relationships, and (6) how financially and materially secure people are.[34] For communities, VanderWeele's flourishing metrics include (1) aggregate levels of individual flourishing; (2) the closeness, respect, trust, and mutuality of relationships in the community; (3) the sense that those in leadership truly care, have integrity, are competent, and have an inspirational vision for the community; (4) the community's resources for strengthening relationships, dealing with conflicts in a fair way, sustaining itself over time, and accomplishing its goals; (5) the sense of satisfaction, value, belonging, and welcome in the community; and (6) the feeling that the community has a shared purpose, contributes to the world, interconnectedness, and synergy or collective power and efficacy.[35]

VanderWeele's flourishing criteria might be a helpful place to start thinking about metrics that would better capture both the benefits of state responses to harm and the harms that tend to occur through traditional policing. Numerous research questions might flow from an agenda concerned with Black security and human flourishing, but here are some:

- How much access do Black people have to supportive people to disrupt and interject in moments where we are at risk of violence?
- What resources do Black people have to find ways to rebuild a sense of security once it has been violated?
- How free do Black people feel to move through neighborhoods of all varieties without encountering suspicion?
- How free do Black people have and feel to pursue leisure activities that bring us joy, such as birdwatching, running, and spending time with friends outdoors?
- How consonant are efforts ostensibly aimed at public safety with human dignity?[36]

---

[34] Tyler J. VanderWeele, *On the Promotion of Human Flourishing*, 114 PNAS 8148 (2017).

[35] Tyler J. VanderWeele, *Measures of Community Well-Being: A Template*, 2 INT'L J. CMTY. WELL-BEING 253 (2019).

[36] Scholars such as Jonathan Simon have been emphasizing human dignity as a core concern of a public safety agenda. JONATHAN SIMON, MASS INCARCERATION ON TRIAL: A REMARKABLE COURT DECISION AND THE FUTURE OF AMERICAN PRISONS (2014); *see also* Jonathan Simon, *Dignity and Its*

While survey or interview data would be the most obvious ways to examine most of these questions, there may also be objective or administrative data that might allow researchers to theorize certain of these outcomes. For example, voter turnout, attendance at community meetings, and other quantifiable metrics might be part of a bundle of decent proxies for assessing whether people in communities think leaders are proficient and beneficent or foster a sense of shared purpose.[37] The number of hours people spend at parks in the neighborhood could be a proxy for certain aspects of community resources. Frequency of and numbers attending neighborhood events, like block parties or festivals, might allow measurement of people's sense of belonging. There is much else that could be gleaned from other such available data, but researchers and policymakers must have their eyes trained toward the broader goal of non-oppressive security, with a richer understanding of what it means to be "safe," especially in communities trying to overcome the scourges of racial and economic oppression. To be sure, these types of metrics should be approached with caution: in a parallel to how officials use crime statistics to justify racially oppressive policing based on public safety, officials have sometimes relied on metrics and programs ostensibly focused on mental health and other public health outcomes to justify racial oppressive policing on the basis of national security.[38] Even if well-meaning, the use of alternative metrics and logics is never self-governing. It must be taken up with an overarching critical commitment to racial justice. In the policing of Black Americans, these types of well-being metrics could—with appropriate guardrails and critical engagement—provide an administrable baseline for expanded conceptions of security.

Social science expertise is valuable to policymakers because it helps them think carefully about what we have learned from the past and what potential consequences of certain types of policy interventions might be. Yet at times social scientists do a poor job of explaining their findings. Sometimes they

---

Discontents: Towards an Abolitionist Rethinking of Dignity, 18 EUROPEAN J. CRIMINOLOGY 33 (2021). In a recent manuscript, we explore dignity as a multipart operational criterion that policymakers can use to assess criminal system approaches and policies, such as law enforcement-assisted diversion. *See* Monica C. Bell et al., (unpublished manuscript) (on file with author).

[37] To be sure, no proxy would be indicative of a given metric on its own. For example, both voter turnout and community meeting participation can be constrained by time, resources, and other confounders. An ideal approach would include several objective and subjective measures.

[38] *See, e.g.,* Neil Krishan Aggarwal, *Questioning the Current Public Health Approach to Countering Violent Extremism,* 14 GLOB. PUB. HEALTH 309 (2018); M. Bilal Nasir, *Mad Kids, Good City: Counterterrorism, Mental Health, and the Resilient Muslim Subject,* 92 ANTHROPOLOGICAL Q. 817 (2019).

choose to highlight the flashiest takeaways from their research rather than the nuanced truth of their results. On other occasions, they fail to explain the limitations of their inquiries in ways that their audience can appreciate. Both types of errors inhibit policymakers and journalists from being able to meaningfully engage with the work, which is potentially detrimental to both policy and discourse.

In a recent article, "Next-Generation Policing Research: Three Propositions," I recount two major incidents within the last two years in which economists came under fire for failing to properly contextualize their findings and explain the limitations of their data analysis up front. In one high-profile incident, prominent but controversial economist Roland Fryer concluded that although there were racial disparities in handcuffing, pepper-spraying, and other nonlethal police force across ten cities, there was no racial disparity in the likelihood of being shot by police. However, the study had a serious, basic denominator problem: the study sampled only those who had been stopped by the police and did not account for those who had not been stopped by the police in the first place.[39] In another incident, a team of psychologists headed by David Johnson concluded that White police officers were not more likely to shoot non-White assailants than non-White officers, undermining arguments for police force diversification. But their data focused at an *aggregate* level on the number of White officers within an agency, not at the individual level. Thus, they did not have evidence that, as they reported, "White officers are not more likely to shoot minority civilians than non-White officers."[40] Troubled by how their work was being misused, Johnson and collaborators attempted to issue a correction but eventually retracted their article.[41] These are just two examples of how important social scientific findings about hot-button issues like policing can become misleading to policymakers, journalists, and the public, thereby threatening key vectors of change.

[39] *See* Bell, *Next-Generation Policing Research, supra* note 29, at 39.
[40] *Compare* David J. Johnson et al., *Officer Characteristics and Racial Disparities in Fatal Officer-Involved Shootings*, 116 PNAS 15877 (2019), *with* David J. Johnson et al., *Correction for Johnson et al., Officer Characteristics and Racial Disparities in Fatal Officer-Involved Shootings*, 117 PNAS 9127 (2020).
[41] David J. Johnson et al., *Retraction for Johnson et al., Officer Characteristics and Racial Disparities in Fatal Officer-Involved Shootings*, 117 PNAS 18130 (2020).

Social Science and the Work of Imagination

Even as social science could do a better job of accounting for interpretations and limitations, social science cannot answer more fundamental questions about the justice or moral rightness of approaches to security. Supporting the security of Black America means taking stock of historical and social scientific research without being unduly confined by its terms. This moment calls for expertise of many kinds. Social science is important for policymaking, but it is inherently backward-looking, a way to assess the worlds we have already inhabited. Empirical social scientists can only study approaches that have existed and ideas that have already been implemented.

Given this reality, it is obvious why research will generally show that people across many demographic groups still want the police in their neighborhoods: there has never been another widely available, well-funded, politically powerful institutionalized protective force against violence within this nation. Offering a choice between the devil one knows and an unknown, most people, at least initially, choose the devil they know.[42] It is similarly unsurprising that police presence deters violent crime when deployed in particular ways; again, there has never been a well-funded, institutionally embedded alternative with *primary control* over violence reduction.[43]

In this time of great change, we need practical solutions. Demands for pragmatism in this debate are often aimed at advocates for defunding or abolishing police, with many Democratic politicians concerned that relatively minor police reforms have been impossible, and the political fortunes of the party compromised because of the movement for police defunding.[44]

---

[42] This is not merely an idiom. Substantial social psychological research shows that adults and children often have cognitive biases that conflate descriptive thinking—the way things are—with prescriptive thinking—the way things ought to be. This tendency reinforces status quo thinking on matters of social inequality, likely including policing. *See* Steven O. Roberts, *Descriptive-to-Prescriptive (D2P) Reasoning: An Early Emerging Bias to Maintain the Status Quo*, EUROPEAN REV. SOC. PSYCH. (2021), https://doi.org/10.1080/10463283.2021.1963591 ("[A]dults and children often use beliefs about what is to make judgements about what should be—and they use beliefs about what is not to make judgements about what should not be . . . [This] reasoning plays a critical role in how children reason about social groups, biasing them to maintain the status quo"); *see also* Kimmo Eriksson, Pontus Strimling & Julie C. Coultas, *Bidirectional Associations Between Descriptive and Injunctive Norms*, 129 ORGANIZATIONAL BEHAV. & HUM. DECISION PROCESSES 59 (2015); Aaron C. Kay et al., *Inequality, Discrimination, and the Power of the Status Quo: Direct Evidence for a Motivation to See the Way Things Are as the Way They Should Be*, 97 J. PERSONALITY & SOC. PSYCH. 421 (2009).

[43] Patrick Sharkey, *Why Do We Need the Police?*, WASH. POST (June 12, 2021), https://www.washingtonpost.com/outlook/2020/06/12/defund-police-violent-crime/.

[44] *E.g.*, Julia Manchester, *Democrats Look to Shake Off "Defund the Police,"* HILL (Feb. 6, 2022), https://thehill.com/homenews/campaign/592920-democrats-look-to-shake-off-defund-the-police-as-crime-rises.

However, there is a deeper layer of concern one might have about a lack of pragmatism in the political discourse on race and policing, shaped by a focus on Black security. From the vantage point of Black security, the trickiest obstacle to a just set of systems for deterring and responding to the harms of violence is the policing-antiracism seesaw: on one end is support for "public safety," which is always encoded as status-quo policing, with all of its hierarchy and opacity. On the other end is antiracism. Depending on the nature of the political moment, policymakers and journalists lean from one side to the other. While crime rates may at times be the fulcrum, they are not always determinative of when the political winds will favor law-and-order discourse and when it will favor attention to racial oppression in the criminal system.[45] Indeed, while crime rose in 2021, police killings reached a record high. Yet the political discourse has moved on from Black security.

The United States has been in this space of retreat many times before. We were here in the late 1960s and early 1970s, when crime spiked and liberal political leaders traded off their commitments to civil rights and invested instead in the institutions and laws that yielded a racially disproportionate and oppressive system of incarceration.[46] We were here in the early 1990s, when a president who could rely on consistent Black support advocated for and signed a crime bill that deepened the prison boom and worsened racially disparate policing and punishment.[47] We are here again, when President Joe Biden, who owes his resurgence in the 2020 Democratic presidential primaries to Black voters in South Carolina, declared in his 2022 State of the Union address that, "[w]e should all agree the answer is not to defund the police; it's to fund the police. . . . Fund them with resources and training, they need to protect our communities."[48] Undoubtedly, many of the Black South

---

[45] Indeed, as sociologist Bruce Western showed years ago, changes in how the criminal system operates—arrest-related practices, sentence lengths, and prosecution of drug crimes—has historically been more predictive of increases in punishment than actual crime rates have been. BRUCE WESTERN, PUNISHMENT AND INEQUALITY IN AMERICA 34–51 (2006).

[46] See generally ELIZABETH HINTON, FROM THE WAR ON POVERTY TO THE WAR ON CRIME: THE MAKING OF MASS INCARCERATION IN AMERICA (2017). While the roots of mass incarceration run much deeper in America's past, the product of these roots in the form of mass incarceration began to increase exponentially in the early 1970s. See, e.g., JEREMY TRAVIS, BRUCE WESTERN & F. STEVENS REDBURN, THE GROWTH OF INCARCERATION IN THE UNITED STATES: EXPLORING CAUSES AND CONSEQUENCES 33 (2014).

[47] See generally DARYL A. CARTER, BROTHER BILL: PRESIDENT CLINTON AND THE POLITICS OF RACE AND CLASS (2016).

[48] Aaron Blake, Biden Tries to Nix "Defund the Police," Once and For All, WASH. POST (Mar. 2, 2022), https://www.washingtonpost.com/politics/2022/03/02/biden-nix-defund-police/; see also Anya van Wagtendonk, Biden Got Nearly Two-Thirds of the Black Vote in South Carolina, Vox (Mar. 1, 2020), https://www.vox.com/policy-and-politics/2020/3/1/21160030/biden-black-vote-south-carolina-results.

Carolinians who supported Biden would support his proposal to fund police with resources and training. Yet the seesaw problem remains: despite efforts from many sides to pour resources into training police officers to protect communities in ways that reduce policing's lethality, the best data available show that not only did police killings reach a record high in 2021, they also remain statistically unchanged since 2015.[49] Perhaps the deepest threat to Black security with respect to policing is that innovation will remain impossible because of locked-in political dynamics and failures of imagination.[50]

In times of rising violence and political turmoil, Black security is especially under threat. Right now, Black security is compromised by multiple forms of violence—*including* surging interpersonal physical harm, lost economic opportunity, assaults on political voice and the meaningful right to participate, the return to the mainstream of a narrative about crime, the criminal system, and the police—that is numb to the dehumanizing violence within those institutions. Many of those who supported deep change—even if not defunding—in the period immediately after George Floyd's murder may have been well-meaning but lukewarm supporters, in part because of the stranglehold of the idea that only policing can meet our security needs.

The failures of imagination surrounding Black security become even more starkly observable when examining the experiences of recent Black immigrants to the United States, who exist at the intersection of public safety and national security policing. In early 2022, protests erupted after a Grand Rapids, Michigan police officer shot twenty-six-year-old Patrick Lyoya in the back of the head during a difficult-to-justify traffic stop on April 4, 2022.[51] Lyoya, his parents, and other family members gained asylum in the United States in 2014 after leaving the Democratic Republic of the Congo, seeking safety after years of war and state persecution. Yet they encountered a parallel

---

[49] *See* Marisa Iati, Steven Rich & Jennifer Jenkins, *Fatal Police Shootings in 2021 Set Record Since The Post Began Tracking, Despite Public Outcry*, WASH. POST (Feb. 9, 2022), https://www.washingtonpost.com/investigations/2022/02/09/fatal-police-shootings-record-2021/.

[50] *See generally* Gwyneth McClendon, NYU School of Law, Russell Sage Foundation Visiting Scholar Presentation: Messaging for the Future: Inspiring Citizens to Imagine Structural Change (Mar. 23, 2022) (McClendon is an Associate Professor of Politics at the New York University Department of Politics).

[51] Niraj Warikoo, *Patrick Lyoya Escaped Violence and Persecution in Congo Only to Die in Michigan*, DETROIT FREE PRESS (Apr. 15, 2022), https://www.freep.com/story/news/local/michigan/2022/04/15/patrick-lyoya-refugee-congo-michigan/7324248001/; *see also* Bradley Massman, *Experts Say Grand Rapids Police Officer Could Have Avoided Fatally Shooting Patrick Lyoya*, MLIVE.COM (Apr. 15, 2022), https://www.mlive.com/news/grand-rapids/2022/04/experts-say-grand-rapids-police-officer-could-have-avoided-fatally-shooting-patrick-lyoya.html (describing experts' view that shooting Lyoya was unnecessary and a prediction that manslaughter charges will be deemed appropriate).

body of obstacles in the United States. As his mother, Dorcas Lyoya, described in her native Swahili, "in America the same thing has been following us."[52] This is a common category of experience for recent Black immigrants to America, who may be multiply policed through various intersecting marginalized statuses related to phenotype, racial identity, religion, immigration status, and other characteristics that position them as "suspicious" in the traditional U.S. public safety framework.[53] An imaginative vision of Black security will emerge from a collective, integrated understanding of how racially oppressive policing is a unifying but not homogenizing aspect of contemporary Blackness. It demands interventions that are aware of the shared pitfalls of contemporary police reform but also tailored for context and intersections that advocates and policymakers often overlook.

Political leftists and abolitionists often speak of their approach as "radical imagination."[54] By "radical imagination," they mean that their ideas are radical in a Left political sense and radical in their boldness and expansiveness. That language, though motivating to some advocates and activists, might seem frightening or unrealistic to others. Yet it is important to remember that there is magical thinking on all sides of this debate.

It takes imagination to envision a world without police and prisons (and I suspect that world will not come, though this may be a failure of my own capacity to dream). Yet it also takes a very bold imagination to believe that it is possible to stop unjustified, extrajudicial, and racialized police killings with mere training and resources. It is time to embrace new approaches to evidence production and consumption that take into account the complexity of Black security. It is time to approach policy with an eye toward serious structural interventions both within and beyond policing that consider the full scope of what it means to be secure. In both research and policy, we need approaches that are fit to the task of honoring and nurturing the security of Black people and Black communities.

[52] Warikoo, *supra* note 51.
[53] *See, e.g.*, Khaled A. Beydoun, *America, Islam, and Constitutionalism: Muslim American Poverty and the Mounting Police State*, 31 J.L. & RELIGION 279 (2016); ; B. Heidi Ellis et al., *"We All Have Stories": Black Muslim Immigrants' Experience with the Police*, 10 RACE & JUST. 341 (2020); Emmanuel Mauleón, *Black Twice: Policing Black Muslim Identities*, 65 UCLA L. REV. 1326 (2018).
[54] *See, e.g.*, Amna A. Akbar, *Toward a Radical Imagination of Law*, 93 N.Y.U. L. REV. 405 (2018).

5

Carceral Secrecy and (In)Security

Andrea Armstrong[*]

Introduction

In 2020, a whistleblower revealed that a doctor performed "excessive, invasive, and often unnecessary gynecological procedures" on women detained by U.S. Immigration Customs and Enforcement at Irwin County Detention Facility (ICDF) in Georgia.[1] Medical experts described the abuses, which included unnecessary surgeries, as "aggressive and unethical gynecological care,"[2] leaving some women temporarily or permanently infertile after treatment.[3] Over 60 percent of the women detained at ICDF are Mexican, with smaller shares from El Salvador, Jamaica, Honduras, and Guatemala.[4] The revelations prompted external investigations, revealing patterns of unconstitutional medical care since 2012.[5]

The abuses in ICDF are not singular or unique, nor do they present the full spectrum of harm endured by women and femmes of color while incarcerated. Examining the carceral experience through an intersectional lens[6] reveals how race and gender in combination create distinct risks for

[*] Sincere thanks to Lale Brown and Kenly Flanigan for their excellent research assistance and to Tamia Morris and Alexis Loving for their strong editorial assistance. This chapter also benefited from the insights, comments, and suggestions of Professors Maryam Jamshidi, Priscilla Ocen, and Matiangai Sirleaf.

[1] MEDICAL MISTREATMENT OF WOMEN IN ICE DETENTION: STAFF REPORT, PERMANENT SUBCOMM. ON INVESTIGATIONS, COMM. ON HOMELAND SECURITY AND GOV'T AFFAIRS, U.S. SENATE 4 (Nov. 15, 2022).

[2] *Id.* at 10.

[3] *Id.* at 10, 50, 58, & 62 (discussing the specific cases of former detainees: Cisneros Preciado (Depo-Provera shot); Castaneda-Reyes (D&C and LEEP); and Jane Doe #2 (removal of fallopian tube)).

[4] *Transfers of ICE Detainees from the Irwin County Detention Center*, TRAC IMMIGRATION, https://trac.syr.edu/immigration/detention/201509/IRWINGA/tran/ (last visited Jan. 13, 2023) (data is from 2016 or earlier).

[5] MEDICAL MISTREATMENT OF WOMEN IN ICE DETENTION, *supra* note 1 at 12–14, 42–43.

[6] *See* Kimberle Crenshaw, *Demarginalizing the Intersection of Race and Sex: A Black Feminist Critique of Antidiscrimination Doctrine, Feminist Theory and Antiracist Politics*, 1989 U. CHI. LEGAL F. 139 (1989) (discussing how traditional feminist and racial discrimination frameworks erase intersectional experiences of Black women).

Andrea Armstrong, *Carceral Secrecy and (In)Security* In: *Race and National Security*. Edited by: Matiangai V.S. Sirleaf, Oxford University Press. © Oxford University Press 2023. DOI: 10.1093/oso/9780197754641.003.0006

incarcerated women of color. As I discuss in more depth later in this chapter, incarcerated Black and Brown women and femmes experience sexual, physical, and mental abuse. The racialized and gendered nature of prisons, jails, and detention centers[7] facilitates and enables these abuses. Government invocations of security, operationalized through secrecy, not only mask the actual cost of "security" but also enhance the authority of carceral spaces to continue these abuses.

Conditions of confinement in the United States are not just harmful for women and femmes. People who have been incarcerated have shorter life expectancies immediately after release.[8] During their incarceration, regardless of the reason detained, they have a higher risk of death from violence and suicide.[9] Professor Sharon Dolovich includes "severe overcrowding," "unhygienic conditions," and "grossly inadequate healthcare" as typical features of American incarceration.[10] While incarceration is harmful for everyone involuntarily confined, the degree and type of abuses suffered by women and femmes of color, in some cases, is qualitatively different.[11]

This chapter first provides an overview of carceral spaces, including the disproportionate rates of incarceration for women and femmes of color. Second, I explore the idea of secrecy and its relationship to claims of security. I then turn to the hidden but racialized and gendered nature of carceral spaces through examining three areas—violence, discipline, and healthcare—where women and femmes of color experience harm. I conclude by suggesting that one of many tools to disrupt these abuses is to enhance the transparency of carceral spaces.

---

[7] *See* Angela Y. Davis, *Public Imprisonment and Private Violence: Reflections on the Hidden Punishment of Women*, 24 NEW ENG. J. ON CRIM. & CIV. CONFINEMENT 339 (1998).

[8] Evelyn Patterson, *The Dose-Response of Time Served in Prison on Mortality: New York State, 1989–2003*, 103 AM. J. PUB. HEALTH 523, 523–28 (2013).

[9] E. ANN CARSON, BUREAU OF JUST. STAT., U.S. DEP'T OF JUST., MORTALITY IN STATE AND FEDERAL PRISONS 2001–2019—STATISTICAL TABLES 3 (2021).

[10] Sharon Dolovich, *Foreword: Incarceration American-Style*, 3 HARV. L. & POL'Y REV. 237, 246 (2009).

[11] International law recognizes the unique needs of incarcerated women through the adoption of the U.N. Rules for the Treatment of Women Prisoners and Non-custodial Measures for Women Offenders (also known as the Bangkok Rules) in 2011, which complements, but is not replaced by, the U.N. Standard Minimum Rules for the Treatment of Prisoners (also known as the Nelson Mandela Rules) adopted in 2015. *See* G.A. Res. 65/229, U.N. Doc. A/RES/65/229 (Mar. 16, 2011); G.A. Res. 70/175, annex., U.N. Doc. A/RES/70/175 (Dec. 17, 2015).

Mapping the Carceral Footprint

The U.S. carceral enterprise is vast and varied. It includes several types of facilities, from state-operated prisons for people serving convictions, to local jails operated by elected sheriffs, to private work-release or immigration facilities. It includes different populations, confining youth and the elderly, people held pretrial or after conviction, as well as people with significant mental health and physical challenges. The legal authority to involuntarily confine a person may be civil, as with immigration detention, or criminal, for people accused or convicted of a crime. While there are no comprehensive lists of all carceral spaces nationwide, research by the Prison Policy Initiative indicates there are over 6,000 such spaces across the United States.[12] This includes approximately 2,850 local jails, 1,500 state prisons, 1,500 youth prisons and detention centers, and at least 186 immigration detention centers, 82 Native American country jails, and over a hundred federal prisons.[13]

This sprawling network of carceral spaces ensnares tens of millions of people annually. In 2021, there were approximately two million people behind bars in the United States. This includes over a million people held in state prisons, over half a million in local jails, with the rest being held in federal prisons, and youth and immigration detention centers.[14] Though carceral spaces, on average, hold a little more than half a percentage of the total United States population, with a national incarceration rate of 573 per 100,000, the impact of incarceration affects millions.[15] This is especially true in jails, which process millions of people annually, holding approximately 30 percent of the national incarcerated population behind bars on any given day. In 2019, local jails held more than 700,000 people on a given day but admitted over 10.3 million people during the same year.[16] Though the overall number of incarcerated people has declined since 2009 due to reforms in criminal law and procedure, "almost all of the decrease has been among men."[17]

---

[12] Wendy Sawyer & Peter Wagner, *Mass Incarceration: The Whole Pie 2022*, PRISON POL'Y INITIATIVE (Mar. 14, 2022), https://www.prisonpolicy.org/reports/pie2022.html.

[13] *Id.*

[14] *Id.*

[15] Based on a U.S. population of 332 million in 2021. *Quick Facts: United States Population Estimates, July 1, 2021 (V2021)*, U.S. CENSUS BUREAU, https://www.census.gov/quickfacts/fact/table/US/PST045221 (last visited Nov. 21, 2022).

[16] Zhen Zeng & Todd D. Minton, BUREAU OF JUSTICE STATISTICS, BULLETIN: JAIL INMATES IN 2019, NCJ 255608, 1 (Mar. 2021), https://bjs.ojp.gov/content/pub/pdf/ji19.pdf.

[17] Wendy Sawyer, *The Gender Divide: Tracking Women's State Prison Growth*, PRISON POL'Y INITIATIVE (Sept. 9, 2018), https://www.prisonpolicy.org/reports/women_overtime.html#statelevel.

Within the U.S. carceral system, there are approximately 200,000 women in prison on any given day. Since 1980, the incarceration rate for women has increased by more than 475 percent, double the rate of men.[18] Both Black and Latina[19] women are incarcerated at higher rates than White women.[20] The racial disparities in incarceration for women varies widely across states; in fifteen states, the incarceration rate for Black women is between "ten and thirty-five times greater than that of [W]hite women."[21] Similarly, for Latine women, the incarceration rate in eight states is between "four and seven times greater than those of [W]hite women."[22] While Black women are only 13 percent of the U.S. population, they are almost a third of the female prison population and almost half of the female jail population nationwide.[23] And though data is more limited, sample studies indicate that transgender women, particularly Black and Latine, also have disproportionately high incarceration rates.[24]

However, the impact of carceral conditions extends far beyond the number of women incarcerated—it extends to their children and to their communities in general. Five million children—7 percent of children nationwide—have experienced a parent's incarceration.[25] Nearly 80 percent of women in jails are mothers[26] and 3 percent of female jail admissions (approximately 55,000) are pregnant.[27] Children born to incarcerated mothers face increased

---

[18] SENTENCING PROJECT, FACT SHEET: INCARCERATED WOMEN AND GIRLS 1 (May 2022), https://www.sentencingproject.org/app/uploads/2022/11/Incarcerated-Women-and-Girls.pdf.

[19] This chapter uses Latina and Latine in the following manner: Latina is used if the data or material specifically applies only to cis-gender women of Latin American background; Latine is used if the discussion applies to both women and femmes of Latin American background.

[20] Table 2b. Rates of Incarceration Per 100,000 Women (Age 18–64), HUMAN RIGHTS WATCH PRESS BACKGROUNDER: RACE AND INCARCERATION IN THE UNITED STATES (Feb. 22, 2002), https://www.hrw.org/legacy/backgrounder/usa/race/pdf/table2b.pdf.

[21] HUMAN RIGHTS WATCH PRESS BACKGROUNDER: RACE AND INCARCERATION IN THE UNITED STATES (Feb. 22, 2002), https://www.hrw.org/legacy/backgrounder/usa/race/.

[22] Id.

[23] Talitha LeFlouria, Criminal Justice Reform Won't Work Until it Focuses on Black Women, WASH. Post (Feb. 12, 2021), https://www.washingtonpost.com/outlook/2021/02/12/criminal-justice-reform-wont-work-until-it-focuses-black-women/.

[24] Sarah Reisner et al., Racial/Ethnic Disparities in History of Incarceration, Experiences of Victimization, and Associated Health Indicators Among Transgender Women in the U.S., 54 WOMEN & HEALTH 750 (2014).

[25] Lindsey Cramer et al., Parent-Child Visiting Practices in Prisons and Jails a Synthesis of Research and Practice, URB. INST. 1 (Apr. 2017), https://www.urban.org/sites/default/files/publication/89601/parent-child_visiting_practices_in_prisons_and_jails.pdf.

[26] ELIZABETH SWAVOLA ET AL., VERA INST. OF JUST., OVERLOOKED: WOMEN AND JAILS IN AN ERA OF REFORM (2016), https://www.vera.org/downloads/publications/overlooked-women-and-jails-report-updated.pdf.

[27] Carolyn Sufrin et al., Pregnancy Prevalence and Outcomes in U.S. Jails, 135 OBSTETRICS & GYNECOLOGY 1177 (2020).

risks of early infant death[28] and, as they age, have higher probabilities of arrest, conviction, and incarceration.[29] Many incarcerated women are the sole caregivers for minor children,[30] but under the Adoption and Safe Family Act of 1997 (ASFA), an incarcerated mother's parental rights can be terminated if the child remains in foster care fifteen out of twenty-two months.[31]

Parenting as an incarcerated mother is difficult. Maintaining mother-child relationships entails high financial costs, including expensive transportation to geographically isolated facilities and the excessive cost of collect phone calls. Despite the well-documented benefits of in-person visitation, carceral spaces are increasingly adopting video visitation as the only visual method to connect with loved ones behind bars.[32] The overrepresentation of racial minorities within jails and prisons also means that the impact of this social and familial isolation is borne most heavily by racial minority groups.[33]

Carceral spaces, from clandestine military jails operated by the United States abroad to state and federal prisons to locally operated jails are worlds within themselves. While there may be differences in a person's conviction status or in the legal source for protection of individual rights,[34] a key characteristic in all carceral spaces is the ability to keep the interior secret by invoking security. People in these spaces are subject to rules and punishments beyond those established in state criminal laws.[35] They are also fully dependent on the facility for their own safety, prohibited from providing for their own security. These worlds are also shielded from public view, creating invisible fiefdoms that dot the national landscape.[36]

---

[28] CHRISTOPHER WILDEMAN, UNIV. OF MICHIGAN POPULATION STUDIES CTR., IMPRISONMENT AND INFANT MORTALITY 4 (May 2010), https://www.psc.isr.umich.edu/pubs/pdf/rr09-692.pdf.

[29] Lisa R. Muftic et al., *Impact of Maternal Incarceration on the Criminal Justice Involvement of Adult Offspring: A Research Note*, 53 J. RES. CRIM. & DELINQUENCY 98 (2016).

[30] SWAVOLA ET AL., *supra* note 26.

[31] 42 U.S.C. § 675(5)(E).

[32] Bernadette Rabuy & Peter Wagner, *Screening Out Family Time: The For-Profit Video Visitation Industry in Prisons and Jails*, PRISON POL'Y INITIATIVE 4 (Jan. 2015), https://static.prisonpolicy.org/visitation/ScreeningOutFamilyTime_January2015.pdf.

[33] *See* Holly Foster & John Hagan, *The Mass Incarceration of Parents in America: Issues of Race/Ethnicity, Collateral Damage to Children, and Prisoner Reentry*, 623 ANNALS AM. ACAD. POL. & SOC. SCI. 179 (2009).

[34] *Compare* HUMAN RIGHTS WATCH, QUESTIONS AND ANSWERS: U.S. DETAINEES DISAPPEARED INTO SECRET PRISONS: ILLEGAL UNDER DOMESTIC AND INTERNATIONAL LAW (Dec. 9, 2005), *with* Andrea Armstrong, *Unconvicted Incarcerated Labor*, 57 HARV. J. C.R. & C.L. L. REV. 1, 4–6 (2022).

[35] Armstrong, *supra* note 34.

[36] Andrea C. Armstrong, *No Prisoner Left Behind? Enhancing Public Transparency of Penal Institutions*, 25 STAN. L. & POL'Y REV. 435, 462–67 (2014) (discussing the lack of transparency of penal institutions).

Security and Secrecy

Carceral spaces are justified by some for protecting the security and safety of the general public.[37] For each woman behind bars, the U.S. Constitution requires the government to identify a legitimate reason for her confinement.[38] For women held in immigration detention, the standard reasons include the possibility of evading eventual deportation or a risk to public safety pending determination of their immigration status.[39] Women alleged, but not proven, to have committed a crime may be detained when they are unable to provide monetary security that assures their return to court or deters potential criminal activity before trial.[40] The confinement of women after conviction is undergirded, according to courts, by legitimate penological objectives including, among others, incapacitation and deterrence.[41] In short, the incarceration of these women, according to the government, produces safety and security for the nation.[42]

What constitutes "national security" is a deeply contested project. Historically, conceptions of national security focused on external (usually military) threats to state sovereignty, thus prompting the United Nations in 1994 to proffer the idea of "human security."[43] Laura Donohue, in arguing for a definition of national security that is centered on protecting national interests, chronicled how each "epoch" of national security discourse has also

---

[37] *See* TAE JOHNSON, U.S. IMMIGRATION & CUSTOMS ENFORCEMENT, INTERIM GUIDANCE: CIVIL IMMIGRATION ENFORCEMENT & REMOVAL PRIORITIES (Feb. 18, 2021), https://www.ice.gov/doclib/news/releases/2021/021821_civil-immigration-enforcement_interim-guidance.pdf   (discussing when custody is appropriate as a security concern).

[38] U.S. CONST. amend. V (Due Process Clause for federal deprivations of liberty); U.S. CONST. amend. XIV (Due Process Clause for state or local deprivations of liberty).

[39] JOHNSON, *supra* note 37.

[40] United States v. Salerno, 481 U.S. 739, 749–52 (1987).

[41] *See* Graham v. Florida, 560 U.S. 48, 71 (2010) (identifying legitimate penological justifications in review of life without parole sentences for youth).

[42] It is beyond the scope of this chapter but nevertheless worth noting that the types of behavior criminalized (and defenses allowed) also reflect racialized and gendered norms. *See, e.g.,* BETH E. RICHIE, COMPELLED TO CRIME: THE GENDER ENTRAPMENT OF BATTERED BLACK WOMEN (1996) (analyzing the role of gender and racial norms in criminalizing Black women); KAARYN GUSTAFSON, CHEATING WELFARE (2011) (criminalization of women through welfare). In addition, it is worth noting that the types of conduct for which women are incarcerated are predominantly nonviolent and thus the contribution to security achieved through their incarceration is worth questioning. *See, e.g.,* Kim Shayo Buchanan, *Impunity: Sexual Abuse in Women's Prisons,* 42 HARV. C.R.-C.L. L. REV. 45, 53 (2007) (describing the intersection of the racialized drug war and gender violence producing a subsequent steep rise in incarceration for Black and Latina women).

[43] Mahendra P. Lama, *Human v. National Security,* 11 GLOBAL-E (Apr. 17, 2018), https://globale journal.org/global-e/april-2018/human-vs-national-security; *Human Security Milestones & History,* U.N. TRUST FUND FOR HUM. SEC., https://www.un.org/humansecurity/human-security-milestones-and-history/ (last visited Dec. 20, 2022).

included internal or domestic threats to the state as well.[44] J. Benton Heath has proposed four different potential definitions of "national security" based on who defines a threat to national security and what means are available to address the threat.[45] The contributions to this edited volume—that excavate and center racial justice claims within national security discourse—are part of a broader reimagining of the meaning of "national security." Despite these varying and at times conflicting definitions of national security, for purposes of this chapter,[46] it is sufficient to understand that domestic security practices may be implicated within national security debates.

An additional revelation from these national security debates is attempts to expand the types of included threats, such as climate change,[47] through claims of "worthiness" of a "national security" response. Government claims of security are often accompanied by claims for enhanced governmental authority.[48] This is due, in part, to the urgency embedded within security frameworks.[49] The exigency of the threat, it could be argued, requires expanded power or authority to be meaningfully addressed. Such claims for expanded power often include additional economic resources to address the threat. Thus, attempts to expand or widen the frame are also a claim to expand the power of the state—politically, economically, and militarily—to address the harm.

Part of the government's claim of expanded authority is to keep secret or hide its activities. Within the national security field, scholars have repeatedly observed that security-advancing claims are often balanced against sacrifices in liberty.[50] And as Professor Maryam Jamshidi notes, the benefits of security and sacrifices expected do not accrue equally, with members of marginalized

[44] See Laura K. Donohue, The Limits of National Security, 48 AM. CRIM. L. REV. 1573, 1576–77 (2011).

[45] J. Benton Heath, Making Sense of Security, 116 AM. J. INT'L L. 289, 313–15 (2022).

[46] This approach is also implied within Professor Monica Bell's contribution to this volume on the content of security for Black community members.

[47] See Maryam Jamshidi, The Climate Crisis Is a Human Security, Not a National Security Issue, 93 S. CAL. L. REV. POSTSCRIPT 36, 36, 39 (2019) (arguing that expanding national security to include the climate crisis includes risks of expanding and "broadening and bolstering executive authority, reducing government transparency, increasing government secrecy, eroding civil liberties, and marginalizing disadvantaged groups").

[48] See Daniel A. Farber, Exceptional Circumstances: Immigration, Imports, the Coronavirus, and Climate Change as Emergencies, 71 HASTINGS L.J. 1143, 1145–46 (2020). Professor Farber also notes how some of these claims of emergencies or national security may in fact be "pretextual." See also Jamshidi, supra note 47, at 39 (". . . national security has become synonymous with increased executive branch power, and diminished judicial and Congressional authority, all of which has harmed American democracy and the rule of law").

[49] Heath, supra note 45, at 291.

[50] See Richard H. Ullman, Re-defining Security, 8 INT'L SECURITY 129 (1983).

groups losing on both sides of the equation.[51] Secrecy does important work within this context—it is simultaneously a tool to enact security as well as a tool to mask (disproportionate) insecurity.

The U.S. detention center in Guantanamo may be instructive in this regard. In May 2009, President Barack Obama declared "[r]ather than keeping us safer, the prison at Guantanamo has weakened American national security."[52] Scholars and lawyers have cataloged how the federal government created a secret prison, with secret interrogation techniques that produced secret evidence used against Muslim defendants in secret courts.[53] The brutal extraterritorial and extended detention of Muslims accused of terrorism against the United States, once made public, undermined U.S. moral authority and relationships with allies, while also serving as a "rallying cry for our enemies."[54] The secrecy surrounding conditions in the Guantanamo prison simultaneously enabled these abusive and allegedly security-making practices,[55] while also undermining U.S. national security and the security of Muslims in the United States.[56] And while increased transparency did not end all abuses at Guantanamo, it did increase the moral, legal, and financial costs for the government in maintaining the prison, which may be spurring its lingering demise.[57] The U.S. experience in Guantanamo illustrates how claims of security were foundational for expanded authority and secrecy.

This relationship between expansive authority (including the ability to keep secret) and the potential for abuse is magnified in carceral spaces where individual rights are diminished, and government authority is heightened. Prisons, jails, and detention centers are relatively unique spaces within the law. The U.S. Constitution operates differently within these spaces, where individual rights may be limited or curtailed solely due to the needs of the carceral institution.[58] Certain discrete rights are protected absolutely, such

[51] Maryam Jamshidi, *Whose Security Matters*, 116 AM. J. INT'L L. UNBOUND 236 (2022).

[52] Remarks by the President on National Security, White House Office of the Press Secretary (May 21, 2009), https://obamawhitehouse.archives.gov/the-press-office/remarks-President-national-security-5-21-09.

[53] *See generally* Julie Mertus & Lisa Davis, *Citizenship and Location in a World of Torture*, 10 N.Y. CITY L. REV. 411, 420 (2007); Neal Kumar Katyal, *Internal Separation of Powers: Checking Today's Most Dangerous Branch from Within*, 115 YALE L.J. 2314 (2006).

[54] Remarks by the President on National Security, *supra* note 52.

[55] *See* Clair MacDougall, *Guantánamo Is Still "a Black Hole of Secrecy,"* THE NATION (Jan. 11, 2022), https://www.thenation.com/article/society/guantanamo-anniversary-torture/.

[56] Wadie E. Said, *Law Enforcement in the American Security State*, 4 WISC. L. REV. 821 (2019).

[57] Alternatively, though it is risky to engage in hypothetical speculation, public awareness of the abuses within the prison may have prevented the expansion of the prison and hastened its depopulation.

[58] *See* Turner v. Safley, 482 U.S. 78, 93 (1987) (allowing prison limitations on First Amendment rights for personal correspondence between incarcerated people).

as the right not to be subject to intentional and explicit racial discrimination.[59] The right to freedom of religion is subject to both constitutional and statutory protection.[60] Under the Eighth Amendment, carceral spaces are prohibited from imposing cruel and unusual punishment, but jurisprudential doctrines have erected high barriers that often prevent liability, including proof of subjective knowledge.[61]

However, many other traditional constitutional rights are not similarly protected for incarcerated people. Most importantly for public visibility,[62] courts have allowed limitations on access to their family and communities,[63] to media,[64] to receiving mail[65] and publications,[66] and to courts.[67] Carceral spaces are also closed to the general public[68] and even elected members of the U.S. Congress.[69] Courts have also upheld internal policies that limit the ability of—or even penalize—incarcerated people to advocate for themselves through protests, organizing, or signing petitions behind bars.[70]

Simultaneous with the minimization of individual rights, courts extend exaggerated deference to the decisions of carceral officials.[71] This is partly a result of a judicial doctrine first announced in *Turner v. Safley*[72] in 1987 and partly the result of the way in which individual judges have interpreted that doctrine. In *Turner*, the Supreme Court lowered the standard it used

---

[59] Johnson v. California, 543 U.S. 499, 511 (2005) (applying strict scrutiny, the highest level of judicial review, to incarcerated plaintiff's claim of explicit racial segregation in housing assignments).

[60] U.S. CONST. amend. I; Religious Land Use and Institutionalized Persons Act (RLUIPA), 42 U.S.C. §§ 2000cc to 2000cc-5.

[61] Hope v. Pelzer, 536 U.S. 730, 738 (2002) (applying deliberate indifference, which requires subjective knowledge and disregard of a known and serious risk).

[62] *See, e.g.,* Ronald Kuby & William Kunstler, *Silencing the Oppressed: No Freedom of Speech for Those Behind the Walls,* 26 CREIGHTON L. REV. 1005, 1015–19 (1993) (surveying cases of diminished First Amendment rights for prisoners).

[63] *See, e.g.,* Overton v. Bazzetta, 539 U.S. 126 (2003).

[64] Pell v. Procunier, 417 U.S. 817, 819 (1974) (upholding prison rule limiting face-to-face interviews with members of the media).

[65] *See, e.g.,* Shaw v. Murphy, 532 U.S. 223 (2001).

[66] Thornburgh v. Abbott, 490 U.S. 401 (1989).

[67] *See, e.g.,* Lewis v. Casey, 518 U.S. 343 (1996).

[68] Adderly v. Florida, 385 U.S. 39 (1966).

[69] *See, e.g.,* Maggie Vespa & Nate Hanson, *"They're Basically in Limbo": Oregon Democrats Visit Federal Prison Where Immigrants are Held,* KGW8 (June 16, 2018), https://www.kgw.com/article/news/politics/amid-zero-tolerance-policy-oregon-democrats-to-visit-prison-where-immigrants-are-held/283-564962162; Lexi Lonas, *Gaetz, Greene and Gohmert Turned Away from Jail to Visit Jan. 6 Defendants,* THE HILL (July 29, 2021), https://thehill.com/homenews/house/565562-gop-reps-gaetz-green-and-gohmert-turned-away-from-jail-to-visit-jan-6/.

[70] Andrea C. Armstrong, *Racial Origins of Doctrines Limiting Prisoner Protest Speech,* 60 How. L.J. 221, 265 (2016).

[71] *See* Turner v. Safley, 482 U.S. 78, 93 (1987) (articulating deferential standard for constitutional challenges to conditions of confinement).

[72] *Id.* at 81–82.

to analyze prison rules from intermediate scrutiny[73] to the equivalent of rational basis.[74] The *Turner* decision has since been cited in thousands of prison litigation cases, including prominent U.S. Supreme Court cases *Thornburgh v. Abbott*,[75] *Beard v. Banks*,[76] and *Brown v. Plata*.[77] In practice, this deference means that courts rarely question decisions by carceral administrators particularly when carceral officials invoke the order, safety, or security of the facility as justification for their act.[78] In this regard, judicial deference to carceral administrators is eerily similar to the deference extended by courts in cases concerning national security.[79]

In addition, like military operations abroad, few carceral settings publish or analyze performance data or are subject to independent oversight. I have argued elsewhere how the broad swath of data available for school accountability pales in comparison to data currently collected, published, and analyzed for carceral spaces.[80] The lack of data, and more broadly of transparency, ultimately undermines public efforts for accountability.

An alternative form of accountability, independent oversight by governmental or nongovernmental bodies, is still a rarity. Professor Michele Deitch, who tracks oversight of prisons and jails nationwide, notes that though increasing, "relatively few jurisdictions have established independent agencies tasked with scrutinizing these institutions and addressing the problems they find."[81] The lack of data and independent oversight of carceral

---

[73] Procunier v. Martinez, 416 U.S. 396, 400, 409–09 (1974) (applying an intermediate scrutiny test to prison rules surrounding mail coming into and leaving the prison, relying on free people's First Amendment Right to free speech to avoid the issue of whether incarcerated people on their own hold robust freedom of speech guarantees).

[74] Jennifer A. Mannetta, *The Proper Approach to Prison Mail Regulations: Standards of Review*, 24 NEW ENG. J. ON CRIM. & CIV. CONFINEMENT 209, 215 (1998). In *Turner*, the Court held that a carceral regulation is reasonable when (1) it is rationally related to a legitimate government interest; (2) no "alternative means of exercising the right" exists; (3) the accommodation of the right will have a limited impact on guards, inmates, and "prison resources generally"; and (4) there are no reasonable alternatives to the regulation. Turner v. Safley, 482 U.S. 78, 89–91 (1987).

[75] 490 U.S. 401, 419 (1989).

[76] 548 U.S. 521, 527 (2006).

[77] 563 U.S. 493 (2011).

[78] *See* Bell v. Wolfish, 441 U.S. 520, 547 (1979) ("Prison administrators therefore should be accorded wide-ranging deference in the adoption and execution of policies and practices that in their judgment are needed to preserve internal order and discipline and to maintain institutional security.").

[79] *See* David E. Pozen, *The Mosaic Theory, National Security, and the Freedom of Information Act*, 115 YALE L.J. 628, 652–58 (2005) (discussing judicial deference to government claims invoking secrecy for terrorism related cases).

[80] Armstrong, *No Prisoner Left Behind?*, *supra* note 36 (proposing specific data points for collection).

[81] Michele Deitch, *But Who Oversees the Overseers?: The Status of Prison and Jail Oversight in the United States*, 47 AM. J. CRIM. L. 207, 215 (2020).

conditions, in combination with broad governmental authority in spaces of limited individual rights, obscures the interior of prisons, jails, and detention centers from the public gaze.

To describe carceral spaces as a secret is not to claim that the public knows nothing about how harmful these carceral spaces can be. Nor is it an argument to invade the privacy of the people confined. Instead, carceral secrecy exists at an organizational level and through limiting rights, access, performance data, review, and oversight, effectively shields the carceral space from accountability.

Prisons, jails, and detention centers have historically (and currently) been sites of exploitation,[82] medical experimentation,[83] degradation,[84] and torture.[85] To be clear, these abuses are unconstitutional, even within the framework of diminished individual rights previously described. While there are many reasons why carceral sites are continually sites of abuse, the lack of transparency is a potentially contributing factor.[86] What little we do know about conditions of confinement in the United States illustrates that the broad security carceral facilities claim to provide externally does not necessarily extend to those confined internally, particularly for Black and Latine women and femmes.

---

[82] See generally David Oshinsky, WORSE THAN SLAVERY: PARCHMAN FARM AND THE ORDEAL OF JIM CROW JUSTICE (1996) (examining the history of exploitation at Mississippi's Parchman State Penitentiary); Sophia Chase, Note, The Bloody Truth: Examining America's Blood Industry and Its Tort Liability Through the Arkansas Prison Plasma Scandal, 3 WM. & MARY BUS. L. REV. 597, 612 n.115, 614 (2012).

[83] See Greg Dober, Cheaper than Chimpanzees: Expanding the Use of Prisoners in Medical Experiments, PRISON LEGAL NEWS (Mar. 15, 2018), https://www.prisonlegalnews.org/news/2008/mar/15/cheaper-than-chimpanzees-expanding-the-use-of-prisoners-in-medical-experiments/; Keramet Reiter, Experimentation on Prisoners: Persistent Dilemmas in Rights and Regulations, 97 CAL. L. REV. 501, 501 (2009); Allen M. Hornblum, ACRES OF SKIN 163–83 (1998) (chronicling the story of Dr. Kligman's dioxin experiments at Holmesburg Prison); Julia Lutsky, Texas and Florida Prisoners Used in Medical Experiments, PRISON LEGAL NEWS (Apr. 15, 2001), https://www.prisonlegalnews.org/news/2001/apr/15/texas-and-florida-prisoners-used-in-medical-experiments/.

[84] Michael Kunzelman, "Alarming" Allegations in Lawsuit: Louisiana Prisoners Forced to Bark for Food, NOLA.COM (July 20, 2017), https://www.nola.com/article_ef70f608-a2a2-500a-bd2e-88c16fa08b67.html (describing prisoner treatment at the David Wade Correctional Center, including prisoners being stripped of clothes in winter and forced to bark for food).

[85] Amador v. Superintendent Dep't Correctional Srvcs., No. 03 Civ. 0650(KTD)(GWG), 2005 WL 2234050 (S.D.N.Y. Sept. 13, 2005) (detailing rampant sexual abuse at women's prisons in New York State).

[86] Armstrong, No Prisoner Left Behind?, supra note 36, at 462–67 (discussing the lack of transparency of penal institutions).

Three Distinct Harms for Incarcerated Women of Color

The distinct harms incarcerated women and femmes of color experience arise from both overt and covert causes. Racial bias and discrimination outside carceral spaces does not suddenly stop at the prison gate, nor do societal gender norms that regard women and femmes inferior. At the same time, as a structural matter, "prison systems and prison regimes have historically been designed for men—from the architecture of prisons to security procedures, to facilities for healthcare, family contact, work, and training."[87] The harms that accrue by virtue of their existence within a space (with its own rules and practices) may not be as readily visible but nonetheless exist.

Prisons, like other national security sites,[88] are often described as masculine spaces.[89] Carceral spaces—at the organizational level—are gendered and deploy U.S. cultural norms of masculinity, including dominance, to regulate and manage operations.[90] The "gender-based dominance hierarchy that prevails in men's facilities also shapes, constricts, and rationalizes behavior in women's prisons."[91] Within these spaces, individual behavior by women and men, staff and the incarcerated are shaped by "hegemonic masculinity" norms that prioritize dominance through power.

Carceral spaces are also highly racialized. Race, as a social construct, occurs within a societal context of power and "provides a template for the subordination and oppression of different social groups."[92] Explicit and implicit racial biases for Whiteness may infect prison discipline decisions.[93] Incarceration also compounds the harms of broader structural inequalities by race.

---

[87] WOMEN IN DETENTION, OFFICE OF THE HIGH COMMISSIONER FOR HUMAN RIGHTS (Sept. 2014), https://www.ohchr.org/sites/default/files/Documents/Issues/Women/WRGS/OnePagers/Women_and_Detention.pdf.

[88] Aluma Kepten, The "Supermen" Club: Organizational Secrecy and Masculine Identity in an Israeli National Security Organization, ARMED FORCES & SOC'Y 1, 5 (2022) ("War and national security are therefore considered to be pre- dominantly masculine territories, spheres where these discourses are constructed, reflected, and contrasted.").

[89] See generally DANA BRITTON, AT WORK IN THE IRON CAGE: THE PRISON AS GENDERED ORGANIZATION (2003); ; PRISON MASCULINITIES 3 (Don Sabo, Terry A. Kupers & Willie London eds., 2001).

[90] See Eamonn Carrabine & Brian Longhurst, Gender and Prison Organisation: Some Comments on Masculinities and Prison Management, 37 HOW. J. CRIM. JUST. 161 (1998); Sabo, Kupers & London, supra note 89, at 3.

[91] Terry A. Kupers, Gender and Domination in Prison, 39 W. NEW ENG. L. REV. 427, 434 (2017).

[92] MICHAEL OMI & HOWARD WINANT, RACIAL FORMATION IN THE UNITED STATES 108 (3d ed. 2018).

[93] Armstrong, Racial Origins of Doctrines, supra note 70.

Exposure to Violence

The conditions in prisons and jails fail to recognize the fundamental dignity of women and femmes and often create (and exacerbate) trauma in women and femmes held captive. Incarcerated women are more likely to experience sexual assault.[94] Three-fourths of reports of sexual assault by correctional staff were made by incarcerated women.[95] Women with prior histories of abuse, a common history for incarcerated women,[96] have a "heightened risk of sexual assault during incarceration."[97] While the U.S. Congress passed a federal law designed to prevent and detect sexual assault behind bars (the "Prison Rape Elimination Act") in 2003, a 2022 Senate investigation found persistent and continuing sexual assaults of women in two-thirds of federal prisons.[98] Transwomen are particularly at risk for sexual assault, with one California study indicating 58.5 percent of the 315 study participants had experienced sexual assault during incarceration.[99]

Race also plays a role in devaluing the claims of women of color who experience violence while incarcerated. One study of sexual assault violations in a state prison found that while differences in victimization of women by race were not statistically significant, race played a role in accountability. "Black women [were] less likely to have their report investigated [and] were less likely to receive a finding of 'substantiated,' meaning that most of their allegations did not have sufficient evidence to support them or that prison staff chose not to properly investigate a disproportionate amount of reports made by Black women."[100] At the same time, the most recent federal data on sexual assault behind bars fails to distinguish allegations of sexual violence by race.[101]

---

[94] Gina Fedock et al., *Incarcerated Women's Experiences of Staff-Perpetrated Rape: Racial Disparities and Justice Gaps in Institutional Responses*, 36 J. INTERPERSONAL VIOLENCE 8668, 8668 (2021).

[95] THE GROWTH OF INCARCERATION IN THE UNITED STATES: EXPLORING CAUSES AND CONSEQUENCES 225 (Jeremy Travis, Bruce Western & Steve Redburn eds., 2014).

[96] *See* SWAVOLA ET AL., *supra* note 26, at 11 (noting high percentages of prior sexual abuse and abuse by partners and caregivers); Buchanan, *supra* note 42, at 56 (noting high prevalence of prior abuse by incarcerated women).

[97] Travis, Western & Redburn, *supra* note 95, at 171.

[98] SEXUAL ABUSE OF FEMALE INMATES IN FEDERAL PRISONS, STAFF REPORT, PERMANENT SUBCOMM. ON INVESTIGATIONS, COMM. ON HOMELAND SECURITY AND GOV'T AFFAIRS, U.S. SENATE 1 (Dec. 13, 2022).

[99] Reisner et al., *supra* note 24, at 750 (citing Val Jenness 2009 study).

[100] Fedock et al., *supra* note 95, at 8668.

[101] LAURA M. MARUSCHAK & EMILY D. BUEHLER, BUREAU OF JUST. STAT., U.S. DEP'T OF JUST., SURVEY OF SEXUAL VICTIMIZATION IN ADULT CORRECTIONAL FACILITIES, 2012–2018—STATISTICAL TABLES (June 2021), https://bjs.ojp.gov/sites/g/files/xyckuh236/files/media/document/ssvacf121 8st.pdf.

Solitary Confinement

Solitary confinement is essentially a prison within a prison,[102] highly regulated, isolated, and restricted housing, which Cassandra Shaylor describes as "the ultimate expression of the regulation of the female body, often a racialized female body."[103] The conditions within solitary are severe:

> In the most-restrictive housing, people were held in their cells for at least 23 hours a day, with up to one hour of out-of-cell recreation, often held in a small caged area or a bare concrete space, sometimes with limited access to fresh air and direct sunlight. In some systems, barred indoor enclosures were used for recreation at times. Many cells were small, sparsely furnished, and lacked fresh air, and some had no windows or natural light. Opportunities for therapeutic programming or any form of productive activity were scarce.[104]

These conditions also produce severe results. According to the Canadian Supreme Court, the harms of solitary confinement include "anxiety, withdrawal, hypersensitivity, cognitive dysfunction, hallucinations, loss of control, irritability, aggression, rage, paranoia, hopelessness, a sense of impending emotional breakdown, self-mutilation, and suicidal ideation and behaviour."[105] Citing the severity of harms, the extended duration of the harm after release, and the indeterminacy of the amount of time spent in solitary, the Canadian Supreme Court found that solitary confinement violates their constitutional prohibition against cruel and unusual punishment.[106]

It is only since 2012 that the public has access to reliable data on solitary confinement in prisons, albeit from a nongovernmental source. According to a survey by the Correctional Leaders Association and the Arthur Liman Center for Public Interest Law at Yale Law School, which is currently the

---

[102] Craig Haney, *The Psychological Effects of Solitary Confinement: A Systematic Critique*, 47 CRIME & JUST. 365–66 (2018).

[103] Cassandra Shaylor, *"It's Like Living in a Black Hole": Women of Color and Solitary Confinement in the Prison Industrial Complex*, 24 NEW ENG. J. ON CRIM. & CIV. CONFINEMENT 385, 386 (1998).

[104] LÉON DIGARD, ELENA VANKO & SARAH SULLIVAN, VERA INSTITUTE OF JUSTICE, RETHINKING RESTRICTIVE HOUSING LESSONS FROM FIVE U.S. JAIL AND PRISON SYSTEMS (May 2018), https://storage.googleapis.com/vera-web-assets/downloads/Publications/rethinking-restrictive-housing/legacy_downloads/rethinking-restrictive-housing-report.pdf.

[105] British Columbia Civil Liberties Association v. Canada (Attorney General), 2018 BCSC 62 ¶ 247 (Jan. 17, 2018), https://www.bccourts.ca/jdb-txt/sc/18/00/2018BCSC0062.htm.

[106] *Id.* at ¶¶ 247–50.

only source for national statistics on restrictive housing in prisons, approximately twenty-five thousand people were held in solitary confinement within the federal system and thirty-five state systems in 2021.[107]As a share of the incarcerated populations of these state and federal systems, approximately 0.8 percent of incarcerated women were held in solitary confinement compared to 3.6 percent of incarcerated men.[108] For women in particular, solitary may result in maladaptive behaviors such as self-mutilation to assert some level of control over their surroundings.[109]

A 2018 study of solitary confinement in one large state highlights the differential rates for women by race. Placements in solitary confinement (for any reason) were highest among women of color (Black—15.9 percent, Native American—12.1 percent, Latinas—11.9 percent) compared to White women (8.3 percent).[110] The most-cited reason for solitary confinement placement for all genders and races was "routine operations," which includes "custody reclassification, lateral transfers, [and] inmate population adjustments."[111] Black women, however, were the largest share of the population placed in solitary housing for purposes of "security management" (5.5 percent), and White women represented the smallest share (2.1 percent).[112] Yet there is no reliable data on the use of solitary confinement in jails, where Black women in particular are disproportionately incarcerated.

The harms of solitary confinement also accrue external to the carceral space, impacting an incarcerated woman's community. In solitary confinement, communication and visitation are typically restricted.[113] Thus, children of incarcerated parents are deprived of contact with their mother. And the harms of solitary do not magically end when a woman is placed back into general population housing or even when released from the facility.[114] Instead, she carries that trauma with her, which may contribute to

---

[107] CORRECTIONAL LEADERS ASS'N & ARTHUR LIMAN CTR. FOR PUBLIC INTEREST LAW AT YALE LAW SCHOOL, REFORMING RESTRICTIVE HOUSING: THE 2021 SNAPSHOT OF RESTRICTIVE HOUSING viii (2022).
[108] Id.
[109] Joane Martel, Telling the Story: A Study in the Segregation of Women Prisoners, 28 SOC. JUST. 196, 203–04 (2001).
[110] MELINDA TASCA & JILLIAN TURANOVIC, EXAMINING RACE AND GENDER DISPARITIES IN RESTRICTIVE HOUSING PLACEMENTS 8 (2018), https://www.ojp.gov/pdffiles1/nij/grants/252062.pdf.
[111] Id. at 15.
[112] Id.
[113] Jessica Pupovac, Investigation: In U.S. Prisons, Women Punished More Often Than Men, NPR (Oct. 14, 2018), https://www.npr.org/2018/10/14/657341917/investigation-in-u-s-prisons-women-punished-more-often-than-men.
[114] Reassessing Solitary Confinement: The Human Rights, Fiscal, and Public Safety Consequences, Hearing Before the Subcomm. on Const., C.R. & Hum. Rts., S. Comm. on the Judiciary, 112th Cong. 20–22 (2012) (statement of Professor Craig Haney).

higher recidivism rates for people released directly from solitary back to community.[115]

Jails may also be more likely to utilize solitary confinement for routine operations, since jails—unlike most prisons—will house both male and female populations after arrest and pending trial and women, who are generally a smaller share of the jail population, must be housed separate from men. This data gap is yet another example of how the experiences of incarcerated women are kept secret from the public eye.

Inadequate Healthcare for Incarcerated Women

Imprisoned women, by virtue of both physiology and experiences, have unique healthcare needs that jails and prisons are ill-equipped to address, from gynecological exams to mammograms to mental health treatment for prior trauma.[116] Jails and prisons are constitutionally obligated to provide adequate healthcare for incarcerated people.[117] Yet the healthcare services within carceral spaces are not designed for women. All too often, their distinct needs are overshadowed by their limited share of the facility's population.

Much of the recent attention for healthcare for incarcerated women focuses on the experience of giving birth while incarcerated. At least thirty-seven states have passed laws prohibiting or limiting the use of restraints while an incarcerated woman is in active labor.[118] Shackling women during birth, according to professional medical associations, is dangerous for the health of both the laboring patient and the child.[119] Despite these newly enacted laws, a 2017 survey of perinatal nurses found that 82 percent of nurses reported shackling some or all of the time for incarcerated women giving birth.[120] The

---

[115] David Lovell, L. Clark Johnson & Kevin C. Cain, *Recidivism of Supermax Prisoners in Washington State*, 53 CRIME & DELINQUENCY 633 (2007).

[116] Nat'l Comm'n on Correctional Health Care, *Position Statement: Women's Health Care in Correctional Settings* (2020), https://www.ncchc.org/womens-health-care-in-correctional-settings-2020/.

[117] U.S. CONST. amend. VIII.

[118] Joe Hernandez, *More States Are Restricting the Shackling of Pregnant Inmates, but It Still Occurs*, NPR (Apr. 22, 2022), https://www.npr.org/2022/04/22/1093836514/shackle-pregnant-inmates-tennessee.

[119] *See, e.g.*, AMA, An "Act to Prohibit the Shackling of Pregnant Prisoners" Model State Legislation (2015) (providing background information and model legislative language).

[120] Lorie Goshin et al., *Perinatal Nurses' Experiences with and Knowledge of the Care of Incarcerated Women During Pregnancy and the Postpartum Period*, 48 J. OBSTETRIC, GYNECOLOGIC & NEONATAL NURSING 27, 30 (2019).

persistence of these practices is consistent with scholar Priscilla Ocen's observation that the shackling of pregnant women is rooted in race and gender norms extending as far back as chattel slavery.[121] Pregnancy also poses challenges for incarcerated women beyond the moment of childbirth.

Prisons and jails often fail to provide basic prenatal and postpartum care to pregnant women. Three-quarters of incarcerated women are within their prime childbearing years, namely, between the ages of eighteen and forty-four.[122] Nationally, the American College of Obstetricians and Gynecologists estimates that six to ten percent of imprisoned women are pregnant at intake and, due to the prevalence of prior medical and mental health conditions, often experience high-risk pregnancies.[123] In four states, three-quarters of births in prisons were marked by complications for either the mother or the infant child.[124] Incarcerated women have birthed live and stillborn babies alone in their cells without medical assistance or support.[125] Black women, in particular, experience higher rates of stillbirths than White women.[126]

Beyond pregnancy-related healthcare, incarcerated women also have different healthcare needs including prevention, diagnosis, and treatment for cervical and breast cancer and osteoporosis, among others.[127] While generally applicable standards of care would dictate periodic and routine screenings for these conditions, incarcerated women report they rarely, if ever, receive these tests while incarcerated.[128]

Structural and interpersonal violence against women generally[129] creates unique needs for incarcerated women and carceral mental healthcare. One study indicates pervasive prior abuse for women in jail, including sexual

[121] Priscilla Ocen, *Punishing Pregnancy: Race, Incarceration, and the Shackling of Pregnant Prisoners*, 100 CAL. L. REV. 1239, 1243 (2012).

[122] Jennifer Bronson & Carolyn Sufrin, *Pregnant Women in Prison and Jail Don't Count: Data Gaps on Maternal Health and Incarceration*, 134 PUB. HEALTH REPS. 57S, 58S (Supp. 2019).

[123] C.M. Kelsey et al., *An Examination of Care Practices of Pregnant Women Incarcerated in Jail Facilities in the United States*, 21 MATERNAL & CHILD HEALTH J. 1260, 1261 (2017).

[124] Bronson & Sufrin, *supra* note 122, at 58S.

[125] Memorandum in Support of Plaintiffs' Partial Motion for Summary Judgment on Liability at 2, 23–26, Woodward v. Lopinto, No. 18–04236 (E.D. La. Jan. 19, 2021).

[126] *What Is Stillbirth?*, CDC (Sept. 29, 2022), https://www.cdc.gov/ncbddd/stillbirth/facts.html.

[127] Flavia Bustrea, *Top Ten Issues for Women's Health*, WORLD HEALTH ORG. (Feb. 20, 2015), https://www.who.int/news-room/commentaries/detail/ten-top-issues-for-women%27s-health.

[128] *Screening Tests for Women*, HARV. HEALTH PUBL'G: HARV. MED. SCHOOL, https://www.hea lth.harvard.edu/topics/screening-tests-for-women (last visited Jan. 13, 2023); *USA: "Not Part of My Sentence": Violations of the Human Rights of Women in Custody*, AMNESTY INT'L (Mar. 26, 2011), https://www.amnestyusa.org/reports/usa-not-part-of-my-sentence-violations-of-the-human-rig hts-of-women-in-custody/.

[129] *See* Stephanie Montesanti & Wilfreda Thurston, *Mapping the Role of Structural and Interpersonal Violence in the Lives of Women: Implications for Public Health Interventions and Policy*, 15 BMC WOMEN'S HEALTH 100 (2015).

violence (86 percent, partner violence (77 percent), and caregiver abuse (60 percent).[130] Perhaps as a result, rates of serious psychological distress are higher among incarcerated women than incarcerated men and more women report a history of mental health problems.[131]

Racial biases may also structure how a jail or prison responds to mental health–related harm. A former director of medical and mental health services for Rikers jail described how "older [W]hite men were directed towards mental health services, while younger [B]lack and Hispanic men were directed to solitary confinement, and self-harm. I don't think that fact reflects different rates of mental illness, I think it demonstrates racial bias."[132] And despite greater attention to providing trauma-informed care for incarcerated women, only a few state departments of corrections have comprehensively incorporated trauma-informed care into their operations, such as use-of-force policies.[133]

The inability of carceral spaces to deliver gender appropriate healthcare creates a lasting effect. A recent study found that formerly incarcerated women of color carried greater health disadvantages than non-incarcerated women and all other formerly incarcerated men and women.[134] Racism and sexism combine, they argue, to produce long-lasting poor health outcomes for formerly incarcerated women of color, thus exacerbating existing inequalities.[135] At the same time, national health and justice agencies fail to collect reliable and continuing data on healthcare for incarcerated women.[136]

---

[130] SHANNON M. LYNCH ET AL., WOMEN'S PATHWAYS TO JAIL: THE ROLES AND INTERSECTIONS OF SERIOUS MENTAL ILLNESS AND TRAUMA, U.S. DEPARTMENT OF JUSTICE, OFFICE OF JUSTICE PROGRAMS, BUREAU OF JUSTICE ASSISTANCE 32 (2012), https://bja.ojp.gov/sites/g/files/xyckuh186/files/Publications/Women_Pathways_to_Jail.pdf.

[131] JENNIFER BRONSON & MARCUS BERZOFSKY, BUREAU OF JUSTICE STATISTICS, INDICATORS OF MENTAL HEALTH PROBLEMS REPORTED BY PRISONERS AND JAIL INMATES, 2011–12, NCJ 250612 (June 2017), https://bjs.ojp.gov/content/pub/pdf/imhprpji1112.pdf.

[132] Manuel Villa, *The Mental Health Crisis Facing Women in Prison*, MARSHALL PROJECT (June 22, 2017), https://www.themarshallproject.org/2017/06/22/the-mental-health-crisis-facing-women-in-prison.

[133] JANEEN BUCK WILLISON ET AL., EVALUATION OF IN-PRISON PROGRAMMING FOR INCARCERATED WOMEN: ADDRESSING TRAUMA AND PRIOR VICTIMIZATION (2021), https://www.ojp.gov/pdffiles1/nij/grants/256003.pdf.

[134] Kenzie Latham-Mintus et al., *Formerly Incarcerated Women of Color Face Worse Health in Later Life*, OUPBLOG (Sept. 2, 2022), https://blog.oup.com/2022/09/formerly-incarcerated-women-of-color-face-worse-health-in-later-life/.

[135] *Id.*

[136] Bronson & Sufrin, *supra* note 122, at 58S.

Conclusion

Conditions of incarceration in the United States impose extrajudicial harms under the guise of security. Carceral spaces are assumed to produce security for society through deterring future crime, incapacitating threats to safety, ensuring enforcement of immigration laws, and rehabilitating those who violated criminal laws. The vulnerabilities of Black and Latine incarcerated women and femmes within carceral spaces raises the question of who benefits from carceral conditions that facilitate violence, employ torturous methods, and fail to provide adequate healthcare.

The invocation of secrecy hides and obscures the intersectional impact of claimed security. An intersectional approach by race and gender reveals that harm exposure is concentrated in Black and Latine communities through the hyper incarceration of racial minorities and women and the racialized and gendered spaces in which they are confined. These same communities are simultaneously deprived of the claimed security benefits their incarceration allegedly provides. Reducing carceral secrecy will not end all carceral abuses against incarcerated women of color. As Kim Buchanan has argued in the context of sexual abuse, making the harms endured and the structures that facilitate those harms more visible can open conversations that shift "legal doctrine and social attitudes."[137] Disrupting carceral secrecy is one avenue towards embracing a broader and more just form of security.

---

[137] Buchanan, *supra* note 42, at 87.

6

This Border Called My Skin

Jaya Ramji-Nogales[*]

Introduction

We carry the border on our skin,[1] in our language, through our religion.[2] In the United States, these traits—racial, linguistic, religious—have become social markers that denote "foreignness," or out-group status from the community of citizens.[3] While discrimination explicitly based on race, religion, and, to a lesser extent, language is met with disapproval by many Americans and may be legally actionable, immigration law puts foreignness to work to enable invidious distinctions on exactly these grounds. At the same time, given its facial reliance on nationality, immigration law obscures the use of race, religion, and language as mechanisms of control. Immigration law plays a key role in embedding these invidious distinctions so deeply into the popular consciousness that even citizens of color are viewed as perpetual foreigners.[4] The concept of national security amplifies the power of foreignness to exclude. By tracing the evolution of the concept of national security in immigration law, this chapter illustrates the work that foreignness performs

[*] Many thanks to Matiangai Sirleaf, Fasika Delessa, and Victoria Roman. This chapter benefited from comments at the Race and National Security workshop hosted by Just Security and the University of Maryland School of Law. For thoughtful comments at that workshop, many thanks to Tendayi Achiume, Noura Erakat, James Gathii, Rachel López, Will Moon, Catherine Powell, Shirin Sinnar, Maureen Sweeney, Marley Weiss, and Heather Zimmerman. A special thank you to Sarah Kim for her excellent research assistance.
[1] This title is an homage to THIS BRIDGE CALLED MY BACK: WRITINGS BY RADICAL WOMEN OF COLOR (Cherríe Moraga & Gloria Anzaldúa eds., 1981).
[2] Jaya Ramji-Nogales, *Dispatches from a Racialized Border: The Invisible Threat*, JUST SEC. (July 27, 2020), https://www.justsecurity.org/71678/dispatches-from-a-racialized-border-the-invisible-threat/.
[3] *See also* Evelyn Rangel-Medina, *Citizenism: Racialized Discrimination by Design* (unpublished manuscript) (on file with author).
[4] Mae M. Ngai, *The Architecture of Race in American Immigration Law: A Reexamination of the Immigration Act of 1924*, 86 J. AM. HIST. 67, 70 (1999) (explaining that "[t]he racialization of [non-European immigrants'] national origins rendered them unalterably foreign and unassimilable to the nation").

Jaya Ramji-Nogales, *This Border Called My Skin* In: *Race and National Security*. Edited by: Matiangai V.S. Sirleaf, Oxford University Press. © Oxford University Press 2023. DOI: 10.1093/oso/9780197754641.003.0007

in defending White supremacy and justifying the unequal distribution of political and economic power. By recovering that history and surfacing the roles of foreignness and national security, this chapter aims to begin unraveling the power of these concepts and the harm that they inflict on people of color.[5] The chapter proceeds in three parts, beginning with an exploration of the concepts of race, religion, and language; examining the historical role of immigration law in constructing American understandings of foreignness and national security; and identifying the contemporary consequences and manifestations of this racist history.

Intersections

In the United States, the concepts of "foreignness" and national security are mutually constitutive, constructing each other and labeling people of color as existential threats to White supremacy based on their race, religion, and/ or language. Scholars such as Jennifer Chacón and Ian Haney Lopez have made convincing cases that immigration law has performed a central function in the production of race in the United States.[6] This chapter builds out in two directions from that literature, elucidating the relationship between race and immigration law. First, it describes the work that language and religion undertake alongside physical traits. Working together, these concepts create an expansive web of exclusion that I label "foreignness." It also foregrounds American conceptions of national security in the exclusionary work performed by immigration law both historically and contemporarily, examining the use of national security imaginaries to expand the reach of immigration law and the encoding of those imaginaries into immigration law and onto the skin of immigrants. These relationships—race, language, religion, immigration law, national security—are tangled and complicated, overlapping and overinclusive, creating inescapable stereotypes that ensnare immigrants of color and their descendants. This short chapter cannot do

---

[5] James Thuo Gathii, *Beyond Color-Blind National Security Law*, Just Sec. (Aug. 3, 2020), https:// www.justsecurity.org/71769/beyond-color-blind-national-security-law/.

[6] Jennifer Chacón, *Immigration and Race*, *in* The Oxford Handbook of Race and Law in the United States (Devon Carbado, Emily Houh & Khiara M. Bridges eds., 2022) (online publication); Ian Haney López, White by Law: The Legal Construction of Race (2006); *see also* Kevin R. Johnson, *Bringing Racial Justice to Immigration Law*, 116 Nw. U. L. Rev. Online 1 (2021).

justice to all of their manifestations but seeks to begin a conversation about their complexity and the damage they inflict.[7]

The exploration of these concepts must start with the challenging task of defining the key traits that constitute foreignness: race, religion, and language. This chapter offers basic definitions for these terms, each of which merits a book-length analysis. At the simplest level, race describes physical traits, religion describes spiritual beliefs, and language describes systems of communication. In contemporary American society, each trait is imbued with a range of "unstable and 'de-centered'" social meanings that are "constantly being transformed by political struggle."[8]

Of the three traits, race is perhaps most obviously a social construct. Michael Omi and Howard Winant explain that race, which involves a visual dimension, "signifies and symbolizes social conflicts and interests by referring to different types of human bodies."[9] Race acts through a range of different strategies and methods.[10] It can be put to work in service of exclusion, leveraging hatred as a political force but, in different hands, can enable solidarity in service of emancipation. Some leading immigrants' rights groups and social movements rely on race as an organizing principle to create community and encourage financial support. More nefariously, race is used by White supremacy as a mechanism of hierarchical social control. As explained further later, immigration law has played a key role in constructing race by designating certain groups, through the proxy of nationality, as permanently "foreign." Immigration law puts national security to work as a justification for that outsider status.

Religion might at first seem more clear-cut, as it involves an individual's choice of spiritual belief systems. As a social marker, however, religion is also

---

[7] There are of course many more intersectional identity factors, such as gender, at play, and other important forms of structural injustice, such as empire and settler colonialism, at work. Due to space constraints, this chapter focuses on race, religion, language, national security, and immigration law. For a thorough exploration of intersectional identity factors relevant to national security and immigration law, *see* Adrien Katherine Wing, Reno v. American-Arab Anti-Discrimination Committee: *A Critical Race Perspective*, 31 COLUM. HUM. RTS. L. REV. 561, 574–88 (2000). For thoughtful discussions of the role of empire, *see* E. Tendayi Achiume, *Racial Borders*, 10 GEO. L.J. 445 (2022), and of the role of settler colonialism, *see* NATSU TAYLOR SAITO, SETTLER COLONIALISM, RACE, AND THE LAW: WHY STRUCTURAL RACISM PERSISTS (2020).

[8] MICHAEL OMI & HOWARD WINANT, RACIAL FORMATION IN THE UNITED STATES 110 (3d ed. 2014)

[9] *Id.*

[10] Ian Haney López, *The Social Construction of Race: Some Observations on Illusion, Fabrication, and Choice*, 29 HARV. C.R.-C.L. L. REV. 1, 10 (1994) (describing race as "plastic, inconstant, and to some extent volitional").

"an unstable and fluid differentiating category."[11] Religion itself might capture those who actively practice through the performance of key rituals; it might expand to include those who are faithful but do not practice regularly; and it might encompass even nonbelievers who maintain a cultural affinity with the religion through family heritage. Religion can be a source of community for newcomers; many humanitarian agencies that provide support to immigrants are faith-based. Moreover, religion itself can be a basis for a claim to remain in the United States.[12]

In contemporary American society, however, non-Christian religions have become intertwined with racial traits that denote "foreignness." Muneer Ahmad explains that anti-Muslim racial profiling and violence by both individuals and the government have contributed to the construction of the category of "Muslim-looking."[13] These racial markers of Muslim identity encompass a broad range of people of color, including Arabs and South Asians who may or may not practice Islam or even hold Muslim heritage.[14] By denoting these individuals as "foreign" because of their presumed religion identified through racial traits, White supremacy has established another mechanism of social control. Immigration law can again deploy nationality-based distinctions and, in some cases, explicit religious preferences to consolidate this "foreign" label.[15] National security has been a particularly effective tool in designating religious out-groups.[16]

Of the three traits, language is the least theorized in legal scholarship on immigration law. Social psychologists and linguists have long identified

[11] SAHAR AZIZ, THE RACIAL MUSLIM: WHEN RACISM QUASHES RELIGIOUS FREEDOM 109 (2022). Professor Sahar Aziz identifies four factors that racialize Muslims: White Protestant supremacy, xenophobia resulting from forcible assimilation into Western European cultural norms, Orientalism, and American empire in Muslim-majority countries.

[12] For a particularly insightful examination of this process, see Jaeeun Kim, *Between Sacred Gift and Profane Exchange: Identity Craft and Relational Work in Asylum Claims-Making on Religious Grounds*, 51 THEORY & SOC'Y 303 (2022).

[13] Muneer I. Ahmad, *A Rage Shared by Law: Post-September 11 Racial Violence as Crimes of Passion*, 92 CALIF. L. REV. 1259, 1278 (2004) (the "gross overbreadth" of the "racial dimension of the construct allows it to capture not only Arab Muslims, but Arab Christians, Muslim non-Arabs (such as Pakistanis or Indonesians), non-Muslim South Asians (Sikhs, Hindus), and even Latinos and African Americans"); see also Khaled A. Beydoun, *Islamophobia: Toward a Legal Definition and Framework*, 116 COLUM. L. REV. ONLINE 108, 111 (2016).

[14] Ahmad, *supra* note 13, at 1278; see also Jaya Ramji-Nogales, *A Global Approach to Secret Evidence: How Human Rights Law Can Reform Our Immigration System*, 39 COLUM. HUM. RTS. L. REV. 287 (2008).

[15] Tally Kritzman-Amir & Jaya Ramji-Nogales, *Nationality Bans*, 2019 ILL. L. REV. 563.

[16] Ahmad, *supra* note 13, at 1279 (explaining the racist logics that associate "all Muslims with the terrorists who perpetrated the September 11 attacks").

language as a key trait in establishing social identity.[17] Language identity is
of course as complex and fluid as race and religion. Definitional challenges
abound, as a language group could include those who speak only the language in question, those who speak primarily that language, those who are
native speakers of the language, and those whose parents speak the language
but have limited or no proficiency. In some cases, language overlaps precisely
with nationality; in other cases, the relationship with nationality is over- or
underinclusive. Language can be a source of connection and community for
newcomers and citizens alike.

As with religion, language has become a racial marker; in some cases, language interacts with race traits to denote "foreignness," and in other cases,
language alone is a marker of "foreignness." The salience of language as
a method of social control is amplified in the United States because of the
domestic and global dominance of the English language. Speakers of other
languages are viewed as "disenfranchised," with the Spanish language in
particular "indicative of second-class citizenship, foreign even within our
borders."[18] The Arabic language interacts with religion such that Arab-
speakers are assumed to be Muslim, and vice versa.[19] Immigration law has
played a role in constructing language as a marker of "foreignness" through
literacy tests and other exclusionary measures. Once "foreignness" is established, language can be used to denote a threat to national security.[20]

In the context of immigration law and national security, social meanings
are attached to individuals based on their ancestry, appearance, language,
and religion, and used as a basis for exclusion.[21] This chapter seeks to explore
the construction, evolution, and perpetuation of that social meaning, namely,
"foreignness." Though it is hard to identify a beginning or an end to the cycle,
a key role is played by politicians who benefit from scapegoating immigrants.
These politicians leverage the national security frame to garner votes,
depicting migrants as perpetually foreign, a threat that must be contained

---

[17] Jette G. Hansen & Jun Liu, *Social Identity and Language: Theoretical and Methodological Issues*,
31 TESOL Q. 567, 568–70 (1997).
[18] Glenn S. Levine, *The Discourse of Foreignness in U.S. Language Education*, in TRANSFORMING
POSTSECONDARY FOREIGN LANGUAGE TEACHING IN THE UNITED STATES 55, 62 (Janet Swaffar & Per
Urlaub eds., 2014).
[19] *Id.* at 64.
[20] Ahmad, *supra* note 13, at 1278 (explaining the racist logics that equate "all Arabs and Muslims"
with terrorists, reasoning that rests on the equation of being Muslim with being a terrorist).
[21] Haney López, *The Social Construction of Race*, *supra* note 10, at 38 ("[S]ociety attaches specific
significance to our ancestry and appearance, and in that system of meanings lie the origins of our
race.").

through exclusion.[22] We see many variations on this theme, including claims that immigrants steal jobs, carry communicable diseases, commit violent crimes, and engage in terrorist acts—claims that are codified in the exclusion grounds of the Immigration and Nationality Act.[23] Though these claims are not borne out by empirical studies,[24] they are perpetuated through popular imaginaries as well as the law. The immigrant as a national security threat is demarcated in the public eye through the mechanism of "foreignness," constructed through race, language, and religion. These markers can be used to convince voters that national security threats can be minimized if only we as a society exclude "foreigners," defined by the expansive and malleable categories of physical characteristics, language, and religion. Conveniently, these markers can be tracked on to nationality groups, who can then be excluded through specific provisions of immigration law. The markers of "foreignness"—the borders called my skin—apply to all members of society who share them, locating citizens and noncitizens alike outside the national community and identifying them as threats to that community.

These are complex processes, and a great deal of work is being performed through them. Relying on "foreignness," migration status, nationality, and national security frameworks function together to obscure the role of race, religion, and language in decisions to exclude. While both law and social norms might condemn discrimination based on race and/or religion and possibly even language, distinctions based on migration status and even na-tionality can be viewed as acceptable in immigration law, especially where national security is a factor. Race, language, and religion link citizens to the undocumented, rendering entire groups of humans permanently foreign and threatening, regardless of their immigration status or potential for harm.[25] This obsessive focus on migrants and their descendants as national secu-rity threats enables particularly absurd outcomes in conjunction with more serious existential threats such as climate change, deadly pandemics, and

---

[22] Cas Mudde, *Three Decades Of Populist Radical Right Parties in Europe. So What?*, 52 EUR. J. POL. RES. 1, 13, 15–16 (2013).

[23] 8 U.S.C. § 1182.

[24] *See, e.g.*, Andri Chassamboulli & Giovanni Peri, *The Economic Effect of Immigration Policies: Analyzing and Simulating the U.S. Case* 798 (Nat'l Bur. of Econ. Research, Working Paper 25074, 2018), https://www.nber.org/papers/w25074; Alex Nowrasteh, *Terrorism and Immigration: A Risk Analysis*, 798 CATO INST. POL'Y ANALYSIS 1 (2016), https://www.cato.org/policy-analysis/terror ism-immigration-risk-analysis; Michael T. Light, Jingying He & Jason P. Robey, *Comparing Crime Rates Between Undocumented Immigrants, Legal Immigrants, and Native-born US Citizens in Texas*, 117 PNAS 32340 (2020), https://www.pnas.org/doi/pdf/10.1073/pnas.2014704117.

[25] Ngai, *supra* note 4, at 70.

White supremacist violence. In response to migrants of color being forced to leave their homes because of climate change, a border security frame depicts the migrants themselves as the threat. In contrast, an understanding based on the climate justice frame would more accurately capture the reasons those migrants are fleeing and identify climate change as the threat. In response to the COVID-19 pandemic, migrants of color, many of whom are essential workers in the medical field and beyond, have been treated as threats, justifying racially motivated violence against them.[26] While little expense has been spared in national security efforts to identify immigrants of color as terrorists and punish them, insufficient attention has been devoted to intelligence strategies to understand and dismantle White supremacist groups.[27]

Construction

Racism in immigration law in the guise of national security is not an aberration but, in the words of Natsu Taylor Saito, "a logical extension of all that [has] come before."[28] A historical perspective on the use of the national security frame in immigration law reveals its role in constructing "foreignness" in the United States, notably the use of race, language, and religion as bases for exclusion. The lens of history also demonstrates the shifting and expanding content of national security as a concept over time.

This chapter presents several selected historical case studies to illuminate these concepts and their construction.[29] History offers many more examples of the operation of racism in immigration law; this chapter focuses on the development of the immigration statute, highlighting case law interpreting the statute and policies executing the statute that are particularly instructive for an analysis of national security and "foreignness." This section starts in the late 1700s with the nation's first naturalization statute, through

---

[26] Luke Barr, *Hate Crimes Against Asians Rose 76% in 2020 Amid Pandemic, FBI Says*, ABC NEWS (Oct. 25, 2021), https://abcnews.go.com/US/hate-crimes-asians-rose-76-2020-amid-pandemic/story?id=80746198.

[27] Oona Hathaway, *COVID-19 Shows How the U.S. Got National Security Wrong*, JUST SEC. (Apr. 7, 2020), https://www.justsecurity.org/69563/covid-19-shows-how-the-u-s-got-national-security-wrong/.

[28] Natsu Taylor Saito, *Symbolism Under Siege: Japanese American Redress and the Racing of Arab Americans as Terrorists*, 8 ASIAN L.J. 1, 8 (2001).

[29] It is important to note that racism against immigrants of color has been consistent and continuous throughout U.S. history; the selection of case studies should not be read to suggest that these are the only incidents of violence and harm due to "foreignness."

which American immigration law first defined citizenship as a privilege of Whiteness. Through Asian exclusion, violence at the southern border and against Haitians at sea, and the demonization of Arab, Muslim, and South Asian immigrants, immigration law and its national security lens have worked in concert with race, language, and religion through the concept of "foreignness" to vilify and justify the marginalization and rejection of migrants and their descendants.

The foundations of racial citizenship and the national security frame were laid in immigration law as early as the 1790s. The Naturalization Act of 1790 dictated that only free White persons could obtain citizenship through naturalization.[30] From the start, citizenship in the United States was defined in racial terms; Whiteness was the criteria for belonging, and people of color were legally excluded from citizenship. It would be another eighty years before persons of African nativity and descent were allowed to naturalize, though many obstacles to the exercise of full citizenship rights remained.[31] Native Americans were granted citizenship in 1924, though their ability to enjoy citizenship rights on equal status with Whites was similarly "circumscribed."[32] For persons of "races indigenous to the Western Hemisphere" and Asians, it would take one hundred and fifty years before they were legally eligible for naturalization. This legal dispossession set the terms of "foreignness" from the early days of the nation; the naturalization laws were used as a mechanism of social control that designated people of color as outside of the social contract that was reserved for Whites.

From the national security side, the first federal immigration control laws, the Alien and Sedition Acts of 1798, depicted "foreigners" as a threat to national security.[33] Though these laws were never used to deport anyone, they set the conceptual foundations of immigration law through their reliance on national security rationales to disparage noncitizens.[34] The threat

---

[30] Naturalization Act of 1790, Pub, L. No. 1-3, 1 Stat. 103 (1790) (repealed and superseded by the Naturalization Act of 1795, Pub. L. No. 3-20, 1 Stat. 414 (1795)) ("[A]ny alien, . . . being a free [W]hite person . . . may be admitted to become a citizen.").

[31] *See, e.g.,* THE OXFORD HANDBOOK OF AFRICAN-AMERICAN CITIZENSHIP, 1865–PRESENT (Henry Louis Gates Jr. et al. eds., 2012).

[32] Ngai, *supra* note 4, at 71, 71 n.11.

[33] Alien Friends Act, ch. 58, 1 Stat. 570 (1798); Alien Enemies Act, ch. 66, 1 Stat. 577 (1798); Sedition Act, ch. 74, 1 Stat. 596 (1798).

[34] Kevin R. Johnson, *The Antiterrorism Act, the Immigration Reform Act, and Ideological Regulation in the Immigration Laws: Important Lessons for Citizens and Noncitizens,* 28 ST. MARY'S L.J. 833 (1997).

of deportation alone was an effective means of social control, though race was not yet involved in these laws, which were aimed at excluding citizens of France.

Nearly a century later, in 1882, racial hatred exploded into immigration law's infamous Chinese Exclusion Act.[35] In popular media at the time, the Chinese were designated as "foreign" through their physical traits and language and to a lesser extent their religion, and depicted as an invasive and barbarous national security threat.[36] Set in the context of widespread racism, the act's justification was scant, invoking the dog whistles of national security as defined by public order and an undefined economic threat: "[I]n the opinion of the Government of the United States the coming of Chinese laborers to this country endangers the good order of certain localities within the territory thereof."[37] The drafters of the act explicitly invoked White supremacy, classifying Chinese immigrants as "foreign" on largely racial grounds.[38] As Mae Ngai explains, the act simultaneously encodes and generates ideas about race and national security, incorporating racism and conceptions of national security into law and conveying an expressive message about the place of Chinese nationals and their descendants in American society.[39]

In *Chae Chan Ping*, the Supreme Court upheld the Chinese Exclusion Act, relying on "foreignness" and national security as justifications for their decision.[40] The Court explicitly invoked race alongside "customs," which presumably included religion and language, to explain the "impossibility" of Chinese assimilation.[41] This categorization of the Chinese as "foreign" underpinned the Supreme Court's depiction of the "Oriental invasion" as a "menace to our civilization."[42] In other words, it was the failure to assimilate that rendered the Chinese a menace to national security; the "vast hordes" were sufficient to establish a security threat even in the absence of state-sponsored

---

[35] ERIKA LEE, AT AMERICA'S GATES: CHINESE IMMIGRATION DURING THE EXCLUSION ERA, 1882–1943 (2003). Erika Lee's excellent book also discusses the gender and class dimensions of the Chinese Exclusion Act.

[36] *Id.* at 30–32.

[37] Chinese Exclusion Act, Pub. L. No. 47-126, 22 Stat. 58 (1882).

[38] *See, e.g.*, 13 CONG. REC. 1645 (1882) (Senator Henry M. Teller of Colorado, "The Caucasian race has a right, considering its superiority of intellectual force and mental vigor, to look down upon every other branch of the human family. . . . We are the superior race today. We are superior to the Chinese."); Erika Lee, *The Chinese Exclusion Example: Race, Immigration, and American Gatekeeping, 1882-1924*, 21 J. AM. ETHNIC HIST. 36, 37 (2002).

[39] Ngai, *supra* note 4, at 69.

[40] Chae Chan Ping v. United States, 130 U.S. 581, 606 (1889).

[41] *Id.* at 595.

[42] *Id.*

aggression.[43] Economics played a key role; the Supreme Court depicted the labor competition posed by the Chinese as a threat to national security "and possibly to the preservation of our civilization."[44] The labeling of the Chinese as "foreign" in law and media set the stage for racist violence against Chinese nationals across the country. From Los Angeles to Rock Springs, from San Francisco to Seattle, White mobs murdered Chinese nationals and destroyed their property.[45] The Chinese were unable to seek justice; as noncitizens, they were not entitled to testify in court.[46] The act was a crushingly effective example of social control.

The Immigration Act of 1917 expanded the scope of "foreignness" to cover all Asians and the scope of national security to include a broad array of conditions and situations.[47] In the wake of the Chinese Exclusion Act, politicians and public figures depicted immigrants from Japan, Korea, and India as another "Oriental invasion."[48] Newspapers urged readers to "step to the front once more and battle to hold the Pacific Coast for the [W]hite race."[49] These explicitly racist campaigns demonstrated the utility of "foreignness" and the malleability of national security as concepts. The Japanese were portrayed as a threat because they were purportedly tricky and unscrupulous, aggressive, and warlike, and ultimately "unassimilable."[50] In contrast, the Indians or "Hindu Hordes" were depicted as a dirty, diseased, cheap labor invasion; yet similar to the Japanese, they were viewed as "entirely foreign."[51] The 1917 Act codified these understandings of "foreignness" and national security into numerous new grounds for exclusion. Race was translated into nationality as the act excluded humans from an entire region, from Yemen and Saudi Arabia in the west, to China in the east, and from Mongolia and

[43] *Id.* at 606 ("To preserve its independence, and give security against foreign aggression and encroachment, is the highest duty of every nation, and to attain these ends nearly all other considerations are to be subordinated. It matters not in what form such aggression and encroachment come, whether from the foreign nation acting in its national character, or from vast hordes of its people crowding in upon us. . . . If, therefore, the government of the United States, through its legislative department, considers the presence of foreigners of a different race in this country, who will not assimilate with us, to be dangerous to its peace and security, their exclusion is not to be stayed because at the time there are no actual hostilities with the nation of which the foreigners are subjects.").

[44] *Id.* at 594–95.

[45] Kevin R. Johnson, *From Chinese Exclusion to Contemporary Systemic Racism in the Immigration Laws*, 97 IND. L.J. (2021).

[46] People v. Hall, 4 Cal. 399 (Cal. 1854).

[47] Act of February 5, 1917, Pub. L. No. 64-301, 39 Stat. 874 (1917).

[48] LEE, *The Chinese Exclusion Example, supra* note 35, at 44.

[49] *Id.*

[50] *Id.*

[51] *Id.* at 45.

Iran in the north, to the East Indies in the south, with few exceptions.[52] The act also cast a broad range of people as undesirable, and excludable for the benefit of the nation: immigrants with mental illness, living in poverty, with a "loathsome and dangerous" contagious disease; polygamists, prostitutes, and anarchists; those convicted of a crime involving moral turpitude; and contract laborers.[53] These categories, eerily resonant today, codified negative stereotypes about immigrants and created a powerful system of social control. Through racially designated "foreignness" and an expansive understanding of national security, Congress authorized the executive to exclude a broad range of individuals while at the same time creating a system of exceptions that enabled, for example, the entry of skilled laborers in a time of economic need.

Nearly half a century later, the federal government used the tools of "foreignness" and national security to deport even U.S. citizens of Mexican descent. In 1954, through Operation Wetback, the Border Patrol sought to deport as many undocumented Mexican nationals as possible.[54] This program was justified in terms of national security, by linking Mexican border crossers with communist infiltrators.[55] By manufacturing this security threat, the Border Patrol was able to command more federal dollars toward its deportation goals.[56] Identifying "Mexicans" through physical traits and language, the program was justified through rhetoric that painted border crossers as criminals and prostitutes alongside claims that the Border Patrol was protecting the interests of labor.[57] Building on the sweeping definition of national security of the 1917 Act, the Border Patrol put to work a theater of enforcement that branded Mexican Americans as foreigners in perpetuity. "Foreignness" was put to work to control Mexicans and Mexican Americans alike, and to grow the exclusionary power of the government.

These racist exclusion policies justified by national security interests were codified into law through the 1952 McCarran Act, which continues to be

---

[52] Act of February 5, 1917, *supra* note 47, at § 3.

[53] *Id.* The 1917 Act and other immigration laws of course excluded other nationalities, such as Eastern Europeans, Irish, and Italians, who would now be considered White. A full analysis of their experience would add further texture to the concept of "foreignness," but space limits unfortunately do not permit such a comprehensive examination in this chapter.

[54] HANEY LÓPEZ, WHITE BY LAW, *supra* note 6, at 27–28.

[55] Avi Astor, *Unauthorized Immigration, Securitization, and the Making of Operation Wetback*, 7 LATINO STUD. 5 (2009).

[56] *Id.*

[57] KELLY LYTLE HERNÁNDEZ, MIGRA! A HISTORY OF THE U.S. BORDER PATROL 173–75, 179–80, 187, 192 (2010).

deployed to exclude immigrants on dubious grounds. Section 212(f) of the Immigration and Nationality Act reads:

> Whenever the President finds that the entry of any aliens or of any class of aliens into the United States would be detrimental to the interests of the United States, he may by proclamation, and for such period as he shall deem necessary, suspend the entry of all aliens or any class of aliens as immigrants or nonimmigrants, or impose on the entry of aliens any restrictions he may deem to be appropriate.[58]

This clause expanded the definition of national security to incorporate anything that the president decides is harmful to the nation's interests. This extraordinarily capacious and unconstrained standard created a powerful mechanism of social control that could, and would, be used to exclude racial, religious, and linguistic "foreigners." While Senator McCarran intended this provision to be used against communists,[59] it was first applied to keep out refugees of color fleeing severe human rights violations.

In response to Haitians escaping murder, torture, and detention due to their political beliefs, the U.S. government erected a national security barricade on the high seas. In September 1981, to justify the interdiction of Haitians, President Ronald Reagan stated:

> [T]he continuing illegal migration by sea of large numbers of undocumented aliens into the southeastern United States [was] a serious national problem detrimental to the interests of the United States.[60]

In other words, in the view of the president, who was the authoritative decisional source on national security, the migrants themselves were now the threat, regardless of their individual identity.

Over ten years later, in May 1992, with detention camps at Guantanamo filled to capacity, President George H.W. Bush directed the Coast Guard to intercept vessels on the high seas and return passengers to Haiti without

---

[58] 8 U.S.C. § 1182(f).

[59] H. Richard Friman, *An "Untrammeled Right"? The McCarran Immigration Subcommittee and the Origins of Presidential Authority to Suspend and Restrict Alien Entry Under §1182(f)*, 31 J. Pol'y Hist. 433, 446–50 (2019) (Friman also explains that McCarran wanted to exclude Jewish refugees).

[60] Presidential Proclamation 4865: High Seas Interdiction of Illegal Aliens, 46 Fed. Reg. 48, 107 (Sept. 29, 1981).

consideration of their asylum claims.[61] President Bill Clinton continued this policy, which the U.S. Supreme Court upheld on national security grounds in *Sale v. Haitian Centers Council*:

> It is perfectly clear that 8 U.S.C. § 1182(f) grants the President ample power to establish a naval blockade that would simply deny illegal Haitian migrants the ability to disembark on our shores. Whether the President's chosen method of preventing the "attempted mass migration" of thousands of Haitians poses a greater risk of harm to Haitians who might otherwise face a long and dangerous return voyage is irrelevant to the scope of his authority to take action that neither the Convention nor the statute clearly prohibits.[62]

The contrast between the safety of Haitians and the imagined security threat they pose is striking, as is the role of race when viewed in light of the contemporaneous immigration policy that allowed Cubans who reached territorial waters to remain in the United States.[63] The sweep of presidential authority is breathtaking, enabling extraterritorial social control.

A few years later, with the immigration reforms of 1996, politicians shifted terrorism to the forefront as the predominant national security threat in the eyes of the American public, unmoored from both the actual risk of harm to Americans as well as the racial identity of perpetrators of terrorist acts. Though Americans viewed terrorism as a serious national security threat, at the time, more people in the United States drowned in toilets than were killed in terrorist incidents on U.S. soil.[64] The Anti-Terrorism and Effective Death Penalty Act and the Illegal Immigration Reform and Immigrant Responsibility Act created new forms of exclusion in response to the Oklahoma City bombings, which were of course perpetrated by a White male U.S. citizen named Timothy McVeigh yet somehow viewed through a national security lens deployed against racial, linguistic, and religious

---

[61] Exec. Order No. 12807, 57 Fed. Reg. 23,133 (May 24, 1992).

[62] Sale v. Haitian Ctrs. Council, 509 U.S. 155, 187–88 (1993).

[63] ANDORRA BRUNO, CONG. RSCH. SERV., R44714, U.S. POLICY ON CUBAN MIGRANTS: IN BRIEF 3 (2016), https://crsreports.congress.gov/product/pdf/R/R44714.

[64] John Mueller, *Simplicity and Spook: Terrorism and the Dynamics of Threat Exaggeration*, 6 INT'L STUD. PERSPS. 208, 220 (2005). Mueller explains that, including the September 11, 2001, attacks, the number of Americans killed by international terrorism since the 1960s is about the same number killed by lightning over the same time frame, and in nearly all years, the number of people who are killed worldwide by international terrorists is not much larger than the number of people who drown in bathtubs in the United States.

"foreigners": Arabs, Muslims, Middle Easterners, North Africans, and South Asians. This legislative response demonstrates one of the paradigmatic roles of White supremacy in the context of national security and immigration law. While the media and politicians treat White nationalist terrorists as aberrant individual actors, when it comes to racialized minorities, entire communities are labeled as threats to national security based on their race, religion, or language.

The federal government super-sized this national security frame in the wake of September 11, 2001, when federal law enforcement detained more than twelve hundred Muslim and Arab immigrants within weeks.[65] Racist actors responded to the government's message, as hate crimes against these groups spiked.[66] As Kevin Johnson and Bernard Trujillo explain, the "war on terror" came to dominate any policy debate relating to immigration, from the issuance of driver's licenses to regularization of the undocumented.[67] Grounds for exclusion relating to terrorism were expanded to an absurd extent through the USA PATRIOT Act of 2001 and the REAL ID Act of 2005.[68] In one example, a Salvadoran woman was kidnapped by guerrillas who forced her to watch her husband dig his own grave before they killed him. She was found to have provided "material support" to a terrorist organization because the guerrillas demanded that she cook and clean for them.[69] As a result of the application of this terrorism bar, she was found ineligible for asylum. Justified by national security grounded in the "foreignness" of particular racial, linguistic, and religious groups, Congress and the executive expanded the terrorist bars to exclude a broad range of immigrants of color. President Donald Trump leveraged this façade of national security concerns to gain voters and as a justification for his executive orders starting in 2017 that banned the entry of citizens of several majority Muslim countries.[70] The terrorist label has become particularly effective not only as a form of social control but also as a tool to expand political power.

[65] Shoba Sivaprasad Wadhia, *Is Immigration Law National Security Law?*, 66 EMORY L.J. 669 (2017).
[66] *Id.*
[67] Kevin Johnson & Bernard Trujillo, *Immigration Reform, National Security After September 11, and the Future of North American Integration*, 91 MINN. L. REV. 1369 (2007).
[68] USA PATRIOT Act, Pub. L. No. 107-56, 115 Stat. 272 (2001) (codified as amended in scattered sections of 8 U.S.C., 18 U.S.C., 31 U.S.C., 34 U.S.C., 49 U.S.C., 42 U.S.C., 50 U.S.C.); REAL ID Act of 2005, Pub. L. No. 109-13, 119 Stat. 302.
[69] Matter of A-C-M-, 27 I. & N. DEC. 303 (B.I.A. 2018).
[70] Kritzman-Amir & Ramji-Nogales, *supra* note 15.

Continuities

The historical violence deployed by immigration law against racial, linguistic, and religious "foreigners" in the name of national security continues in the contemporary era. Cruelty has become the currency of the day at the southwestern border. Politicians and the media depict families seeking to escape threats to their security as national security threats themselves. This racist logic enables federal government policies that force these vulnerable migrants to remain in squalid tent camps on the Mexican side of the border, where they lack access to basic hygiene, sustenance, and accommodations and are easy prey for cartels and gangs. While the occasional photograph of Haitian immigrants being chased with whips by mounted Border Patrol officers brings public attention to some of the harms being perpetrated in the name of national security against immigrants of color at the border, many systemic and less visible harms go unaccounted for, and countless other harms are backgrounded and go unnoticed. Immigration law constrains peoples' ability to move and to seek redress, and even their visibility.

The violence perpetrated by immigration law and its enforcement actors in the name of national security has constructed immigrants and Americans of immigrant descent as perpetual foreigners due to their race, language, and/or religion. Rather than a "nation of immigrants," people of color are a nation of foreigners, permanently excluded from full citizenship. This exclusion is exemplified by racist violence. The year 2020 saw the highest level of hate crimes for over a decade.[71] Hate crimes spiked against people of East Asian descent after March 2020.[72] Similarly, the year 2019 saw an eleven-year high in hate crimes against Latine populations in the United States.[73] These crimes include the August 2019 shooting massacre in El Paso that killed twenty-two Americans. Before the attack, the gunman had posted a White supremacist manifesto decrying the "Hispanic invasion of Texas" and explaining that his goal was to defend his "country from cultural and

---

[71] Christina Carrega & Priya Krishnakumar, *Hate Crime Reports in US Surge to the Highest Level in 12 Years, FBI Says*, CNN (Oct. 26, 2021), https://www.cnn.com/2021/08/30/us/fbi-report-hate-crimes-rose-2020/index.html.

[72] ASIAN AM. BAR ASS'N OF NEW YORK, A RISING TIDE OF HATE AND VIOLENCE AGAINST ASIAN AMERICANS IN NEW YORK DURING COVID-19: IMPACT, CAUSES, SOLUTIONS (2021), https://cdn.ymaws.com/www.aabany.org/resource/resmgr/press_releases/2021/A_Rising_Tide_of_Hate_and_Vi.pdf.

[73] Suzanne Gamboa, *Rise in Reports of Hate Crimes Against Latinos Pushes Overall Number to 11-year High*, NBC (Nov. 16, 2020), https://www.nbcnews.com/news/latino/rise-hate-crimes-against-latinos-pushes-overall-number-highest-over-n1247932.

ethnic replacement brought on by the invasion."[74] Drawing a clear link to hate crimes against other "foreigners," he hailed the Christchurch, New Zealand, mosque shooter, an anti-immigrant White supremacist who left fifty-one dead in March.[75] In 2016, hate crimes against Muslims and individuals of Middle Eastern and North African descent exceeded the level of hate crimes perpetrated in the wake of September 11.[76] One empirical study demonstrated that hate crimes are more likely to target Latine persons when politicians support anti-immigration policies that scapegoat whole communities. Another showed that Trump's tweets increased anti-Muslim hate crimes, likely by providing a source of social and political legitimacy for extreme viewpoints in the same way that racist immigration laws and policies could.[77] In a painful irony, "foreignness" itself is now viewed as a national security threat, while those categorized as "foreign" are threatened by xenophobic violence.

The Way Forward

In the words of Stacey Abrams, "Diversity is our superpower."[78] As a nation, we should celebrate racial, religious, and linguistic diversity, recognizing the beauty and benefits that our society gains from the heterogeneous array of immigrants who bring with them on their journey a wealth of perspectives and knowledge. Even with this goal in mind, given the weight of our history and the violence of the current political environment, the path forward can be difficult to visualize. What would it take to transform "foreignness" from a national security threat into a valuable asset?

[74] Press Release, *U.S. Attorney's Office for the Western District of Texas, Texas Man Charged with Federal Hate Crimes and Firearm Offenses Related to August 3, 2019, Mass-Shooting in El Paso* (Feb. 6, 2020), https://www.justice.gov/usao-wdtx/pr/texas-man-charged-federal-hate-crimes-and-firearm-offenses-related-august-3-2019-mass.

[75] Simon Romero, Manny Fernandez & Mariel Padilla, *Massacre at a Crowded Walmart in Texas Leaves 20 Dead*, N.Y. TIMES (Aug. 3, 2019), https://www.nytimes.com/2019/08/03/us/el-paso-shooting.html.

[76] German Lopez, *A New FBI Report Says Hate Crimes—Especially Against Muslims—Went Up in 2016*, Vox (Nov. 13, 2017), https://www.vox.com/identities/2017/11/13/16643448/fbi-hate-crimes-2016.

[77] Laura Dugan & Erica Chenoweth, *Threat, Emboldenment, or Both? The Effects of Political Power on Violent Hate Crimes*, 58 CRIMINOLOGY 714 (2020); Karsten Müller & Carlo Schwarz, *From Hashtag to Hate Crime: Twitter and Anti-Minority Sentiment*, AM. ECON. J.: APPLIED ECON. (forthcoming) (last revised July 24, 2020), https://papers.ssrn.com/sol3/papers.cfm?abstract_id=3149103.

[78] Stacey Abrams (@staceyabrams), TWITTER (May 1, 2022, 6:30 PM), https://twitter.com/staceyabrams/status/1520893326563569664.

An important first step in dismantling the harmful legacy of "foreign-ness" is to ensure that the history of racial, religious, and linguistic exclusion through immigration law and its national security lens is taught accurately. This chapter and other chapters in this volume offer a history that is rarely imparted in law or other graduate or professional schools, let alone grade or high schools. In order to dismantle the social norms that have constructed the racialized immigrant as a national security threat, Americans must understand the virulent racism and terroristic violence perpetrated against migrants of color throughout our history. It is only through recognition of this White supremacist violence, and the role of immigration law in codifying hatred, that the popular discourse can move in an antiracist direction. Contemporary attacks on the teaching of antiracist values in schools show that this will be an uphill battle. These tasks—identifying and describing the historical role of "foreignness" and national security and teaching that history accurately—and the struggle that ensues must fall on *all* Americans, not only migrants of color and their progeny. The media in particular have an important reparative role to play; both traditional media and social media companies must make a commitment to teach this history and to paint accurate and nuanced contemporary portraits of all racial, religious, and linguistic groups.

These efforts to dismantle "foreignness" must be accompanied by a concerted effort to redefine the vastly overbroad concept of national security and to replace fear-driven responses with evidence-based policies. Replying directly to messages of hate and fear, a range of Americans must make the case that migrants writ large do not pose a threat to national security and are in fact a core strength of our society. This message should come from experts in the national security realm, moral authorities from religious and educational institutions, neighbors, and friends. These stakeholders should encourage others to stop reacting in fear and instead act out of genuine concern for the human security needs of migrants and the role that the United States has played in creating their vulnerability. They must make the case that treating migrants callously does not make our nation more secure; instead, it makes our society less humane.

The final step is to undo the codification of anti-"foreignness" in immigration law. An immigration system grounded in fairness and equality would of course require radical transformation of current laws and policies, with an eye to both undoing historical harms and injecting humanity, dignity, and compassion throughout. All of these traits are in short supply in current political leadership, but if Americans were educated about the history of immigration law, that political tide could shift. If a broad range of Americans could take responsibility for pursuing these antiracist actions, an effective social movement could be born. Together, we could reclaim "foreignness," recognizing the historical harms that have been perpetrated in its name at the same time as we celebrate the beauty and benefits of our racial, religious, and linguistic diversity. Through such efforts, as a nation we can disconnect immigration law from an anti-immigrant national security frame, creating in its place a narrative that underscores human values and the positive impact that all migrants have on the security of our nation defined more broadly.

IV

RACE AND THE BOOMERANG EFFECT OF NATIONAL AND TRANSNATIONAL SECURITY

7

Militarized Biometric Data Colonialism

Margaret Hu

Introduction

Surveillance technologies deployed for counterterrorism and counterinsurgency purposes abroad have been migrating to the United States.[1] This migration necessitates a growing urgency to examine the rights-based impact of surveillance technologies deployed as part of U.S. military operations and nation-building projects[2] in the "war on terror." This includes a close examination of how the domestic migration of these technologies may affect all U.S. citizens generally and communities of color in particular. This chapter examines a subset of this larger inquiry: the nexus of race and national security policy through the lens of biometric data colonization[3] via biometric cybersurveillance. It concludes that one long-term impact of biometric-enabled warfare can be understood as a form of data colonialism.[4] This emerging practice of biometric data colonization encompasses the beta testing of new cybersurveillance tools through databasing and tracking digitized bodies for hypersurveillance.

---

[1] *See infra* section "Migration of Technology from Afghanistan and Iraq to the United States"; *see also* JULIA ANGWIN, DRAGNET NATION (2015); Margaret Hu, *The Ironic Privacy Act*, 96 WASH. U. L. REV. 1267 (2019); Margaret Hu, *Biometric Cyberintelligence and the Posse Comitatus Act*, 66 EMORY L.J. 697 (2017); Catherine Crump, *Surveillance Policy Making by Procurement*, 91 WASH. L. REV. 1595 (2016); Benjamin Powers, *Eyes over Baltimore: How Police Use Military Technology to Secretly Track You*, ROLLING STONE (Jan. 6, 2017), https://www.rollingstone.com/culture/culture-features/eyes-over-baltimore-how-police-use-military-technology-to-secretly-track-you-126885/; Katja Lindskov Jacobsen, *Biometric Data Flows and Unintended Consequences of Counterterrorism*, 103 INT'L REV. RED CROSS 619 (2021).

[2] *See, e.g., New Evidence that Biometric Data Systems Imperil Afghans: Taliban Now Control Systems with Sensitive Personal Information*, HUM. RTS. WATCH (Mar. 30, 2022), https://www.hrw.org/news/2022/03/30/new-evidence-biometric-data-systems-imperil-afghans.

[3] *See infra* section "Biometric-Enabled Warfare and Biometric Cybersurveillance as Experiment in Sociotechnical Control and Coercion."

[4] *See, e.g.,* Nick Couldry & Ulises A. Mejias, *Data Colonialism: Rethinking Big Data's Relation to the Contemporary Subject*, 20 TELEVISION & NEW MEDIA 336, 336–37 (2018).

Margaret Hu, *Militarized Biometric Data Colonialism* In: *Race and National Security.* Edited by: Matiangai V.S. Sirleaf, Oxford University Press. © Oxford University Press 2023. DOI: 10.1093/oso/9780197754641.003.0008

The first section of the chapter describes the domestic migration of sur-veillance technologies initially developed during the "war on terror" and deployed abroad after the terrorist attacks of September 11, 2001. These surveillance technologies were brought back to the homeland for routine investigations and used to surveil antiracism activists within the United States in ways that are alleged to have a disparate impact on communities of color. The second section focuses on biometric surveillance to illustrate how surveillance technologies initially deployed for national security purposes abroad have specifically affected communities of color through biometric data colonialism and surveillance capitalism. The third section interrogates how identifying the racialized impact of biometric cyberintelligence renders visible a form of sociotechnical control and coercion. The chapter concludes that a national security strategy of "population management"[5] in occupied countries such as Afghanistan ensures the future expansion and extraction capacities of biometric surveillance technology. This form of data coloniza-tion by the United States and other nations under biometric-enabled warfare risks entrenching biometric surveillance testing and use, especially within communities of color.

Migration of Technology from Afghanistan and Iraq to the United States

To contextualize the racialized impact of the stateside migration of counter-terrorism surveillance tools initially deployed abroad, this section reviews revelations stemming from a growing awareness of military-grade surveil-lance used during high-profile domestic antiracism protests. After 20 years of military operations and nation-building, when the final U.S. troops pulled out of Afghanistan in August 2021, there existed a robust dialogue in the United States on the increasing domestic use of military-grade surveillance technology. These technologies had been used overseas in military conflicts and for foreign intelligence operations, from the signal interception of cell phones to aerial surveillance as well as other forms of cybersurveillance and

---

[5] The 2011 U.S. Army Commander's Guide to Biometrics in Afghanistan specifically offers "a section titled 'Population Management[.]' " CTR. FOR ARMY LESSONS LEARNED, HANDBOOK: COMMANDER'S GUIDE TO BIOMETRICS IN AFGHANISTAN, No. 11–25, at 30–32 (Apr. 2011) (reproduced at *Identity Dominance: The U.S. Military's Biometric War in Afghanistan*, PUB. INTEL. (Apr. 21, 2014), https://pub licintelligence.net/identity-dominance).

have been seamlessly integrated into U.S. policing practices and within the programs of multiple federal agencies, including the FBI and the United States Department of Homeland Security (DHS).

Allegations of the deployment of militarized surveillance tools surfaced after protests for racial justice following both the 2013 acquittal of George Zimmerman of second-degree murder of Trayvon Martin,[6] as well as a multitude of deaths of other unarmed Black men and women at the hands of police, including Michael Brown,[7] Eric Garner,[8] and Tamir Rice[9] in 2014; Sandra Bland[10] and Freddie Gray[11] in 2015; and Breonna Taylor[12] and George Floyd[13] in 2020. Protesters, for example, alleged that local law enforcement and the FBI deployed militarized surveillance to target protesters and leaders of racial justice movements. Some of these allegations have been substantiated. These technologies have launched a national conversation surrounding whether local and domestic law enforcement should have access to militarized surveillance tools and whether these surveillance tools have been misused to monitor racial justice protesters and leaders of anti-racism movements.[14]

---

[6] Lizette Alvarez & Cara Buckley, *Zimmerman Is Acquitted in Trayvon Martin Killing*, N.Y. TIMES (July 13, 2013), https://www.nytimes.com/2013/07/14/us/george-zimmerman-verdict-trayvon-mar tin.html.

[7] *Timeline of Events in Shooting of Michael Brown in Ferguson*, ASSOCIATED PRESS (Aug. 9, 2019), https://apnews.com/article/shootings-police-us-news-st-louis-michael-brown-9aa3203369254 7699a3b61da8fd1fc62.

[8] Al Baker, J. David Goodman & Benjamin Mueller, *Beyond the Chokehold: The Path to Eric Garner's Death*, N.Y. TIMES (June 13, 2015), https://www.nytimes.com/2015/06/14/nyregion/eric-garner-police-chokehold-staten-island.html.

[9] Shaila Dewan & Richard A. Oppel Jr., *In Tamir Rice Case, Many Errors by Cleveland Police, Then a Fatal One*, N.Y. TIMES (Jan. 22, 2015), https://www.nytimes.com/2015/01/23/us/in-tamir-rice-shooting-in-cleveland-many-errors-by-police-then-a-fatal-one.html.

[10] Katie Rogers, *The Death of Sandra Bland: Questions and Answers*, N.Y. TIMES (July 23, 2015), https://www.nytimes.com/interactive/2015/07/23/us/23blandlisty.html.

[11] John Woodrow Cox, Lynh Bui & DeNeen L. Brown, *Who Was Freddie Gray? How Did He Die? And What Led to the Mistrial in Baltimore?*, WASH. POST (Dec. 16, 2015), https://www.washingtonp ost.com/local/who-was-freddie-gray-and-how-did-his-death-lead-to-a-mistrial-in-baltimore/ 2015/12/16/b08df7ce-a433-11e5-9c4e-be37f66848bb_story.html.

[12] Richard A. Oppel Jr., Derrick Bryson Taylor & Nicholas Bogel-Burroughs, *What to Know About Breonna Taylor's Death*, N.Y. TIMES (Apr. 26, 2021), https://www.nytimes.com/article/breonna-tay lor-police.html.

[13] Evan Hill et al., *How George Floyd Was Killed in Police Custody*, N.Y. TIMES (Jan 24, 2022) https:// www.nytimes.com/2020/05/31/us/george-floyd-investigation.html.

[14] *See, e.g.*, Brandon E. Patterson, *Homeland Security Is Tracking Black Lives Matter. Is That Legal?*, MOTHER JONES (July 30, 2015), https://www.motherjones.com/politics/2015/07/homeland-secur ity-surveillance-black-lives-matter/; Ali Winston, *Did the Police Spy on Black Lives Matter Protesters? The Answer May Soon Come Out*, N.Y. TIMES (Jan. 14, 2019), https://www.nytimes.com/2019/01/ 14/nyregion/nypd-black-lives-matter-surveillance.html; George Joseph & Murtaza Hussain, *FBI Tracked an Activist Involved with Black Lives Matter as They Traveled Across the U.S., Documents Show*, INTERCEPT (Mar. 19, 2018), https://theintercept.com/2018/03/19/black-lives-matter-fbi-surve

Specifically, in the two decades after the terrorist attacks of September 11, 2001, there has been increasing attention to how surveillance technologies originally deployed abroad for the "war on terror" have migrated to domestic U.S. policing strategies and tactics. Surveillance systems originally designed to identify and target terrorists are now deployed in U.S. cities to monitor antiracism protests, secure the U.S. border, and promote homeland security and criminal enforcement in the interior.[15] Significantly, the recent deployment of these emerging militarized surveillance technologies appears to be concentrated within communities of color. A growing number of experts have called for the cessation and prevention of systemic monitoring of people of color and civil rights leaders in the United States, a notable and important development, particularly given the established history of abuses.[16]

Antiracism protesters associated with Black Lives Matter (BLM) and BLM leaders, for example, have alleged targeted surveillance by local and federal law enforcement.[17] The BLM movement developed in the aftermath of George Zimmerman's acquittal of the killing of Trayvon Martin, an unarmed seventeen-year-old Black teenager, on February 26, 2012. Zimmerman, a neighborhood watch program volunteer in Sanford, Florida,[18] shot Martin but claimed self-defense, and the case quickly became the forefront of controversies surrounding "stand your ground" statutes.[19] Martin's killing—and

---

illance/; *see also* Justin Hansford, *The First Amendment Freedom of Assembly as a Racial Project*, 127 YALE L.J. F. 685 (2018); Chaz Arnett, *Race, Surveillance, Resistance*, 81 OHIO ST. L.J. 1103 (2020).

[15] Ali Watkins, *How the N.Y.P.D. Is Using Post-9/11 Tools on Everyday New Yorkers*, N.Y. TIMES (Sept. 8, 2021), https://www.nytimes.com/2021/09/08/nyregion/nypd-9-11-police-surveilla nce.html.

[16] *See, e.g.*, SIMONE BROWNE, DARK MATTERS: ON THE SURVEILLANCE OF BLACKNESS (2015); RUHA BENJAMIN, RACE AFTER TECHNOLOGY: ABOLITIONIST TOOLS FOR THE NEW JIM CODE (2019); Arnett, *supra* note 14; EXEC. OFF. OF THE PRESIDENT, BIG DATA: A REPORT ON ALGORITHMIC SYSTEMS, OPPORTUNITY, AND CIVIL RIGHTS 1, 5 (2016), https://obamawhitehouse.archives. gov/sites/default/ files/microsites/ostp/2016_0504_data_discrimination.pdf [https://perma.cc/ B42Y- GE3F]. For historical context of the systemic monitoring of civil rights leaders during the 1960s civil rights movement in the United States, *see generally* S. REP. No. 94-755 (1976) (Church Committee Report); *Senate Select Committee to Study Governmental Operations with Respect to Intelligence Activities*, U.S. SENATE, https://www.senate.gov/about/powers-procedures/investigati ons/church-committee.htm (last visited June 13, 2022); RUSSELL MILLER, PRIVACY AND POWER: A TRANSATLANTIC DIALOGUE IN THE SHADOW OF THE NSA-AFFAIR (2017).

[17] *See, e.g.*, Patterson, *supra* note 14; Winston, *supra* note 14; Joseph & Hussain, *supra* note 14; Orion Rummier, *NYT: Black Lives Matter Protests in over 15 Cities Were Under Surveillance by DHS*, AXIOS (June 19, 2020), https://www.axios.com/2020/06/20/black-lives-matter-protesters-surveille nce-dhs.

[18] Alvarez & Buckley, *supra* note 6.

[19] Glenn Kessler, *Was the "Stand Your Ground" Law the "Cause" of Trayvon Martin's Death?*, WASH. POST (Oct. 29, 2014), https://www.washingtonpost.com/news/fact-checker/wp/2014/10/29/was-the-stand-your-ground-law-the-cause-of-trayvon-martins-death/.

Zimmerman's 2013 acquittal—sparked national protests. Shortly thereafter, the BLM movement was founded on social media in July 2013 under the Twitter hashtag #BlackLivesMatter.[20]

In the late summer of 2014, BLM protesters rallied across the nation in the weeks after the deaths of two unarmed Black men. On July 17, forty-three-year-old Eric Garner died of a chokehold by a police officer in Staten Island, New York, declaring "I can't breathe" eleven times before his death.[21] Shortly thereafter, on August 9, an unarmed Black teenager, eighteen-year-old Michael Brown, was fatally shot by a local police officer in Ferguson, Missouri.[22] Thousands of protesters converged on Ferguson to demand racial justice. Immediately thereafter, approximately a year after BLM was founded, DHS began tracking followers of #BlackLivesMatter through social media surveillance. According to two documents released by DHS, both dated August 11, 2014, DHS began monitoring BLM through the Twitter and Vine apps to map and monitor protesters in Ferguson.[23] The FBI had also deployed surveillance flights to monitor protesters in Ferguson in the summer of 2014.[24]

Leaders and members of BLM later raised concerns that local law enforcement had used "Stingray" technology during antiracism protests in the fall and winter of 2014.[25] Stingray devices fall within the family of International Mobile Subscriber Identity (IMSI) catchers. The devices, through masquerading as a cell tower, can facilitate tracking and eavesdropping of mobile phones through tricking phones to connect to them and intercepting IMSI numbers, the unique number assigned to each cellular network user under the IMSI system. IMSI catchers were originally designed and used for foreign intelligence and military use as early as 1993[26] and were deployed heavily for counterinsurgency efforts in the "war on terror." They are now commonly

---

[20] Reis Thebault, *Trayvon Martin's Death Set Off a Movement that Shaped a Decade's Defining Moments*, WASH. POST (Feb. 25, 2022), https://www.washingtonpost.com/nation/2022/02/25/trayvon-martins-death-set-off-movement-that-shaped-decades-defining-moments/.

[21] Baker, Goodman & Mueller, *supra* note 8.

[22] Associated Press, *Timeline, supra* note 7.

[23] *See, e.g.*, Patterson, *supra* note 14.

[24] *Id.*

[25] *See, e.g., Activists Say Chicago Police Used "Stingray" Eavesdropping Technology During Protests*, CBS CHI. (Dec. 6, 2014), https://www.cbsnews.com/chicago/news/activists-say-chicago-police-used-stingray-eavesdropping-technology-during-protests/.

[26] SEAN NAYLOR, RELENTLESS STRIKE: THE SECRET HISTORY OF JOINT SPECIAL OPERATIONS COMMAND 263–64 (2015); Erich Eshelman, *Can You Hear Me Now? The Vulnerability of Cellular and Smartphone Use on the Battlefield* 14 (June 2020) (Master's Thesis, Naval Postgraduate School), https://apps.dtic.mil/sti/pdfs/AD1114556.pdf.

used by U.S. law enforcement to surveil and track cell phones.[27] Although investigations into the allegations of targeting antiracism protesters are ongoing,[28] the common use of IMSI catchers has become an increasingly common facet of U.S. policing, thus raising concern of their deployment to target activists protesting police brutality and racial inequality.[29]

Similarly, concerns have been raised that the FBI and local law enforcement conducted aerial surveillance flights over downtown Baltimore during antiracism protests over the death of Freddie Gray, a twenty-five-year-old Black man who died in police custody shortly after his arrest on April 12, 2015.[30] Media reporting revealed that the Freddie Gray protests led to the deployment of a persistent aerial surveillance system, originally deployed in Iraq and later used by domestic police departments for wide-scale surveillance.[31] In response to information requests, the FBI further revealed that it had tracked protesters for eighteen hours.[32] "The videos show people engaged in First Amendment-protected activities, people entering and exiting homes and other buildings, images of private back yards and roof decks, and other similar scenes and spaces. The videos sometimes track individual drivers as they traverse city streets."[33] Aerial surveillance has greatly advanced, integrating sophisticated imaging technology and data storage.[34] Aerial surveillance can be equipped with augmented reality system technology to superimpose information over video streams captured by the aircraft cameras and embed feeds into satellite imaging.[35]

By 2015, news reports documented how U.S. military and intelligence biometric surveillance technology—such as facial recognition technology, scanned fingerprints and irises, and DNA databasing—had become common

[27] *IMSI Catchers: Facilitating Indiscriminate Surveillance of Protesters*, PRIVACY INT'L (June 19, 2020), https://privacyinternational.org/news-analysis/3948/imsi-catchers-facilitating-indiscriminate-surveillance-protesters.
[28] Fruzsina Eördögh, *Evidence of "Stingray" Phone Surveillance by Police Mounts in Chicago*, CHRISTIAN SCI. MONITOR (Dec. 22, 2014), https://www.csmonitor.com/World/Passcode/2014/1222/Evidence-of-stingray-phone-surveillance-by-police-mounts-in-Chicago; Winston, *supra* note 14.
[29] *Stingray Tracking Devices: Who's Got Them?*, ACLU, https://www.aclu.org/map/stingray-tracking-devices-whos-got-them (last visited Sept. 14, 2022).
[30] *See* Monte Reel, *Secret Cameras Record Baltimore's Every Move from Above*, BLOOMBERG (Aug. 23, 2016), https://www.bloomberg.com/features/2016-baltimore-secret-surveillance/.
[31] *Id.*
[32] *Id.*; Nathan Freed Wessler & Naomi Dwork, *FBI Releases Secret Spy Plane Footage from Freddie Gray Protests*, ACLU (Aug. 4, 2016, 4:45 PM), https://www.aclu.org/blog/privacy-technology/surveillance-technologies/fbi-releases-secret-spy-plane-footage-freddie-gray.
[33] Wessler & Dwork, *supra* note 32.
[34] Reel, *supra* note 30.
[35] *Id.*

practice for local police surveillance.[36] Local law enforcement had adopted procedures similar to those adopted in Afghanistan, such as routinely using facial identification systems and biometric database screening technologies.[37] The FBI's use of militarized technologies such as aerial surveillance on protesters after the deaths of Michael Brown, Eric Garner, and Freddie Gray demonstrated how facial recognition technology could be used through real-time remote biometric identification systems within communities of color and as part of monitoring civil rights protests.

Unrestricted social media surveillance of BLM social media activity by DHS, commencing in 2014, as well as other increased border surveillance techniques, raised concern about the disparate policing impact of surveillance architecture on communities of color. The potentially concentrated deployment of military-grade surveillance technologies on antiracism protesters in the United States, as well as on immigrants through border security and what has been referred to the "extreme vetting" of migrants to the United States, provides a window into the interrelationships between race, national security, and surveillance, especially biometric cybersurveillance.[38]

Biometric Data Colonization and Surveillance Capitalism

Militarized biometric surveillance technology deployed abroad extensively during the "war on terror" has fully migrated to domestic use. Focusing on biometric surveillance illustrates how surveillance technologies initially deployed for national security purposes abroad have harmed communities of color through biometric data colonialism and surveillance capitalism. Data colonization literature has increasingly documented concerns surrounding the impact of biometric surveillance on communities of color in the United States, within occupied nations such as Afghanistan, and among vulnerable refugee and immigrant populations. The post-9/11 era ushered in the adoption of biometric surveillance tools for screening refugees and asylees globally, as well as for vetting migrants arriving in the United States and Europe. Western countries, for instance, have used DNA tests to

---

[36] *See, e.g.*, Timothy Williams, *Facial Recognition Software Moves from Overseas Wars to Local Police*, N.Y. TIMES (Aug. 12, 2015), https://www.nytimes.com/2015/08/13/us/facial-recognition-software-moves-from-overseas-wars-to-local-police.html.

[37] *Id.*

[38] *See, e.g.*, Margaret Hu, *Algorithmic Jim Crow*, 86 FORDHAM L. REV. 633 (2017); Margaret Hu, *Crimmigration-Counterterrorism*, 2017 WISC. L. REV. 955 (2017).

verify refugee claims such as familial relationships, ancestry, and country of origin.[39] Humanitarian aid distributed by the United Nations High Commissioner for Refugees now requires compliance with biometric identification requirements.[40] A foundational part of understanding data colonization, however, is distinguishing data colonialism from historical colonizing projects.

Different terms describe the mass collection of data within a global digital economy to underscore the era of data-driven capitalism it has created. The treatment of data as a resource that is captured and processed, exploiting humans for data as seen through lenses of historical colonialism, has been termed "data colonialism."[41] Data colonialism "combines predatory extractive practices of historical colonialism with the abstract quantification methods of computing."[42] The expansion of internet tracking in social media and the expansion of internet infrastructure in undeveloped areas fall under data colonialism. Within a discourse of what business scholar Shoshana Zuboff has coined "surveillance capitalism,"[43] and what law scholar Julie Cohen has referred to as "informational capitalism,"[44] data colonialism also identifies the goal of extracting and collecting data to be that of a capitalist profit motive and colonial legacy—one that captures and controls the datafication of all human life.[45]

From this view, the digital colonizers are represented by the "social quantification sector, corporations involved in capturing everyday social acts and translating them into quantifiable data which is analyzed and used for the generation of profit[,]" which includes Facebook, Google, and Baidu.[46] Colonization has expanded into all aspects of human life that can be digitally recorded, datafied, aggregated, and stored.[47] This data can then be

---

[39] *See, e.g.,* Trina Jones & Jessica L. Roberts, *Genetic Race? DNA Ancestry Tests, Racial Identity, and the Law,* 120 COLUM. L. REV. 1929 (2020).

[40] Songkhun Nillasithanukroh, *Rethinking the Use of Biometric Systems for Refugee Management,* CHI. POL'Y REV. (ONLINE) (Feb. 24, 2016), https://chicagopolicyreview.org/2016/02/24/rethinking-the-use-of-biometric-systems-for-refugee-management/.

[41] Couldry & Mejias, *supra* note 4, at 336–37.

[42] *Id.* at 336.

[43] SHOSHANNA ZUBOFF, THE AGE OF SURVEILLANCE CAPITALISM: THE FIGHT FOR A HUMAN FUTURE AT THE NEW FRONTIER OF POWER (2019).

[44] JULIE COHEN, BETWEEN TRUTH AND POWER: THE LEGAL CONSTRUCTIONS OF INFORMATIONAL CAPITALISM (2019).

[45] NICK COULDRY & ULISES A. MEJIAS, THE COSTS OF CONNECTION: HOW DATA IS COLONIZING HUMAN LIFE AND APPROPRIATING IT FOR CAPITALISM xi (2019).

[46] Couldry & Mejias, *supra* note 4, at 340–41.

[47] *See, e.g.,* Morgan Mouton & Ryan Burns, *(Digital) Neo-colonialism in the Smart City,* 55. REG'L STUD. 1890–1901 (2021), https://hal.archives-ouvertes.fr/hal-03236274; Kadija Ferryman, *The Dangers of Data Colonialism in Precision Public Health,* 12 GLOBAL POL'Y. 90 (Aug. 5, 2021), HTTPS://ONLINELIBRARY.WILEY.COM/DOI/FULL/10.1111/1758-5899.12953.

analyzed for insights, predictive risk, and security assessments. When communities are not yet datafied, digital colonizers expand their reach to increase the sensors and interactions from which data can be extracted.[48] Communication scholars Nick Couldry and Ulises Mejias identify the goal of data collection to extend beyond its initial collection purpose, such as consumer behavior for marketing purposes, or a piece of shared knowledge to develop the cure to a disease. Rather, they contend that the predictive power of mass data to enhance artificial intelligence (AI) technologies and machine learning enables social capture of all human behavior, moving beyond capitalist motives to governance objectives. AI and machine learning technology has expanded to be able to understand and influence data governance through digital dominance.[49]

The characteristics of data colonialism, with an uneven power dynamic and the benefit primarily vesting with the data extractor, has resulted in an expansion of exploitation through data capitalism. When data colonialism is exported, it is an outgrowth of "technocolonialism."[50] Data colonialism and digital colonialism have been theorized as "data as a form of capitalist expropriation[.]"[51] Technocolonialism, in academic research, has focused more on the historical colonialist relationships that are recreated through technology, especially in the humanitarian aid sphere. Technocolonialism, for example, can "analyze the convergence of digital developments with humanitarian structures and market forces and the extent to which they reinvigorate and rework colonial relationships of dependency."[52] Data colonialism observes how underdeveloped countries are used as regions where data collection can expand to grow the population from which information can be extracted.

Beyond national security contexts, biometric data colonialism occurs in humanitarian practices, where biometric databasing is seen as the solution to authentication and security issues, and as a method to advance the efficiency of relief distribution.[53] Both the United Nations' and the European

---

[48] COULDRY & MEJIAS, *supra* note 45, at 98–100.

[49] *Id.* at 126–28.

[50] HELEN TILLEY, AFRICA AS A LIVING LABORATORY: EMPIRE, DEVELOPMENT, AND THE PROBLEM OF SCIENTIFIC KNOWLEDGE, 1870–1950 (2011); *see also* Mirca Madianou, *Technocolonialism: Digital Innovation and Data Practices in the Humanitarian Response to Refugee Crises*, 5 SOC. MEDIA + SOC'Y (2019).

[51] Madianou, *supra* note 50, at 3.

[52] *Id.* at 2.

[53] Mirca Madianou, *Reproducing Colonial Legacies: Technocolonialism in Humanitarian Biometric Practices* (2020 Expert Workshop on Race, Technology and Borders Convened by UN Special Rapporteur E. Tendayi Achiume), https://www.ohchr.org/sites/default/files/Documents/Issues/Racism/SR/RaceBordersDigitalTechnologies/Mirca_Madianou.pdf.

Union's respective refugee databases manage biometrics for migrants as part of identity management programs.[54] These technologies were often introduced as pilot programs for future humanitarian use, which may be well-intentioned but carry the same types of inherent risks that are associated with potential data misuse and abuse that exist in other data collection systems.[55] However, biometric data systems are not just susceptible to misuse and abuse. Biometric technologies are fallible and can be embedded with discrimination.[56] Introducing these technologies before they reach sufficient maturity can incur unintended harm through algorithmic discrimination, for example, on communities from which they collect data.

Closely related to data colonialism is the theory of technocolonialism. Technocolonialism further observes how Africa has been used throughout history to test new forms of surveillance.[57] This continued past the colonial era into the neocolonial era, where surveillance technologies have first been applied in foreign countries for identity verification and security purposes.[58] Historian Helen Tilley has framed technocolonialism within the concept of a "living laboratory."[59] In a colonialist project, the living laboratory develops ways to extract knowledge or resources that can be exported to the home country. Tilley argues that colonial powers came to African populations with explicitly experimental technologies and goals, implicitly creating temporary laboratories in intervention contexts. This theory of a living laboratory illuminates why the data colonialism dynamic has raised conflict-of-interest concerns and allegations of racial discrimination. In one example, in 2019, the United Nations World Food Programme suspended food aid in Yemen because of opposition to biometric data collection, with biometric identification used to address low-level fraud.[60] This example illustrates how humanitarian relief such as food relief is made contingent on compliance with biometric tracking and collection systems. Although Tilley proposed the "living laboratory" concept to better understand technocolonial abuses in humanitarian relief in Africa, it can contextualize why biometric data

---

[54] *Id.*; Lauren Wilson et al., *A Systems Approach to Biometrics in the Military Domain*, 63 J. FORENSIC SCI. 1858–63 (2018).

[55] Madianou, *supra* note 50, at 3.

[56] *See, e.g.*, SHOSHANA AMIELLE MAGNET, WHEN BIOMETRICS FAIL: GENDER, RACE, AND THE TECHNOLOGY OF IDENTITY (2011); BROWNE, *supra* note 16.

[57] TILLEY, *supra* note 50, at 314; *see also id.* at 316–18.

[58] Thom Shanker, *To Track Militants, U.S. Has System That Never Forgets a Face*, N.Y. TIMES (July 14, 2011), https://www.nytimes.com/2011/07/14/world/asia/14identity.html.

[59] TILLEY, *supra* note 50.

[60] Madianou, *supra* note 53.

colonialism may be seen as technocolonial abuse in the post-9/11 era of militarized surveillance.

Tilley emphasizes that much of the competition for resources in Africa "occurred during a period when technologies of empire ... were employed as part of ever-expanding networks of power."[61] This approach results in stripping autonomy and informed consent from human subjects, who may be unaware of the assumptions or expectations placed on them. In a report for the International Review of the Red Cross, researcher Katja Jacobsen finds Tilley's living laboratory visible in the dynamic between Afghanistan and countries engaged in military or humanitarian efforts therein.[62] Focusing on the exploitative nature of intervention in Afghanistan, she notes that "[t]he issue of consent—often the absence of genuine consent—and arguably of the subsequent international legal obligation is an important consideration in relation to the making of biometric data in contemporary intervention contexts."[63]

In the digital age, data collection and processing occur on greater scales than before. Before the development of certain digital technologies, biometrics could not be taken and processed with the same immediacy, nor could data be tracked and recorded as efficiently. When these modern capacities are applied by nations like the United States to nations like Afghanistan, their outcomes can be viewed as coercive. This is especially true as humanitarian aid and security aid is tethered to a biometric surveillance architecture under the justification of securitization, where refugees are seen as a security threat, and the rationale of solutionism, which seeks to solve complex social problems using technology. Additionally, the ways biometric data collection and tracking tools may be perceived as methods for longer-term control under neoliberal frameworks[64] can be viewed in their test-bed stages as colonial in a "living laboratory" sense. This expands potential for the future misuse and abuse of data, especially when biometric surveillance and biometric-driven identity management systems are viewed as an experiment in beta testing technologies on underdeveloped nations.

---

[61] TILLEY, *supra* note 50, at 11.
[62] Jacobsen, *supra* note 1.
[63] *Id.* at 625.
[64] *See, e.g.,* COHEN, *supra* note 44.

Biometric-Enabled Warfare and Biometric Cybersurveillance as Experiment in Sociotechnical Control and Coercion

Sociotechnical inquiries consider the interplay between human and technological systems.[65] This section of this chapter turns its attention to the sociotechnical and data colonizing questions raised by the U.S. military's strategy of "identity dominance" in Afghanistan during its twenty-year military operation.[66] The concept of identity dominance stems from a biometric-enabled warfare rationale: that national security dominance and control in counterinsurgency postures depends on fully transparent identities. Biometric-enabled warfare arguably is a technological outgrowth of a data colonialism mindset. At the earliest stages of biometric data colonialism, Afghanistan witnessed the universal beta testing of cybersurveillance tools through the attempted data colonization of the digitized bodies of almost the entire Afghan population.[67]

The embrace of biometric cybersurveillance technologies—widespread collection of scanned fingerprints and irises, facial images, and in some instances, DNA—allowed for the U.S. military to coordinate biometric collection and sharing among the military, criminal, and civil functioning of the Afghan government. Biometric surveillance tools should also be understood as racialized technologies with empirically disparate accuracy. "Biometric technologies 'privilege [W]hiteness' (Browne, 2015) with significantly higher margins of error when measuring or verifying 'othered bodies' whether in terms of race, ethnicity, gender, class, disability or age (Magnet, 2011)."[68]

The dependence of the U.S. military and other federal agencies on tech corporations has led to additional concerns of a merger between a military-surveillance and industrial-corporate colonizing project. In recent years, more attention has been given to the use of technology by the United States and other Western powers in humanitarian and military settings. Guided by concerns for national security and a desire to solve various social problems,

---

[65] Shakir Mohamed, Marie-Therese Png & William Isaac, *Decolonial AI: Decolonial Theory as Sociotechnical Foresight in Artificial Intelligence*, 33 PHIL. & TECH. 659 (2020).

[66] *See, e.g.,* Jacobsen, *supra* note 1.

[67] *See, e.g.,* ANNIE JACOBSEN, FIRST PLATOON: A STORY OF MODERN WAR IN THE AGE OF IDENTITY DOMINANCE (2022); Margaret Hu, *The Taliban Reportedly Have Control of US Biometric Devices—A Lesson in Life-and-Death Consequences of Data Privacy*, CONVERSATION (Aug. 30, 2021), https://thec onversation.com/the-taliban-reportedly-have-control-of-us-biometric-devices-a-lesson-in-life-and-death-consequences-of-data-privacy-166465.

[68] Madianou, *supra* note 50, at 11.

national and international agencies often seek collaboration and support from private sector companies—allowing already complicated motivations to be further muddled by capitalist opportunity. A common criticism is that humanitarian aid can transform into a coercive dynamic—a means of cultivating dependence and recreating colonial relationships among the beneficiary countries.[69] These theories are helpful for contextualizing the discussion, but do not give as weighty a focus to the explicit military relationships that are often interwoven with the humanitarian ones. Using elements of technocolonialism theory in the humanitarian sphere, we can apply a more explicit national security framework to consider the biometric data colonialism ambitions in Afghanistan.

Colonialism is marked by power imbalances and resource extraction.[70] In civil conflict and humanitarian crises, the populations involved have an added layer of vulnerability. The United States, among other nations, researched a host of new applications of biometric technology in Afghanistan, purportedly for the ultimate benefit of the Afghan people. However, questions about risk, benefit, and consent remain unanswered. In conflicts like Afghanistan, the testing of new technology—biometric technology in particular—can be categorized as serving three distinct but overlapping themes: securitization, solutionism, and capitalism.

Considering securitization within a colonialist framework allows for keener interrogation of the consequences of biometric surveillance technology deployed first abroad and then stateside. During U.S. military operations in Afghanistan, biometric data and other data were collected with the aim to de-anonymize Taliban forces.[71] The Afghan biometrics program, formally established in 2009, shared information with the FBI.[72] This partnership—a domestic law enforcement agency actively involved in foreign data collection—was unusual. It is perhaps logical, however, within a view of militarized biometric data-gathering from a perspective of extraction. In a technocolonialist project, the living laboratory develops ways to extract knowledge or resources that can be exported to the home country.

[69] See, e.g., id.; Mark Duffield, The Symphony of the Damned: Racial Discourse, Complex Political Emergencies and Humanitarian Aid, 20 DISASTERS 173 (1996); Michael Stopford, Humanitarian Assistance in the Wake of the Persian Gulf War, 33 VA. J. INT'L L. (1993).

[70] Madianou, supra note 50.

[71] Shanker, supra note 58; Mission Afghanistan: Biometrics, FBI NEWS (Apr. 29, 2011), https://www.fbi.gov/news/stories/mission-afghanistan-biometrics; David Pendall & Cal Sieg, Biometric-enabled Intelligence in Regional Command—East, 72 JOINT FORCE Q. 69 (2014).

[72] Mission Afghanistan: Biometrics, supra note 71.

This framing may be present in the application of biometric technology in both warfare in foreign settings and day-to-day policing in domestic ones.[73] In Afghanistan, biometric surveillance eventually anchored all aspects of Afghan governance: biometric screening was integrated into voting access, welfare distribution, employment screening, and so on. Biometric surveillance transformed into an entire mode of governance.[74] This technology was largely experimental but was applied broadly within the United States after evidence of success in Afghanistan. Informed by the Snowden disclosures and other programs, including the Trump administration's use of biometric-driven identity management and social media surveillance for "extreme vetting" and the "Muslim ban," we can see how biometric and biographic data can be aggregated and transformed into a method of predictive policing.[75]

The U.S. military also embraced the concept of biometric surveillance—driven "population management" through the national security strategy of "identity dominance." Both population management and identity dominance, when viewed through the data colonialism frame, can be seen as integral to a data colonial project. When the Afghan government worked collaboratively with the U.S. military for almost two decades, the colonial ambitions were opaque. The Afghan government was purportedly given biometric surveillance tools to implement data collection and databasing for its own self-governing benefit. The beta testing of biometric surveillance technologies and other surveillance tools on occupied populations allowed data colonial and surveillance capitalist goals to flourish under the guise of securitization and governance efficiency.

Moreover, recent reports of the Taliban's abuse of the inherited biometric governance architecture now make clear the potential harms of biometric colonization technologies. In other words, the sudden withdrawal of the United States from Afghanistan enabled greater abuses under this architecture by the new Taliban government. It illustrated the potential for human rights abuses were always existent since the initial adoption of the biometric surveillance technologies.

The policing of communities of color has long relied on forms of biometric surveillance.[76] As these biometric surveillance techniques of policing

[73] Jacobsen, *supra* note 1.

[74] *Id.* at 631, 632.

[75] *See, e.g., Small Data Surveillance v. Big Data Cybersurveillance*, 42 PEPP. L. REV. 773 (2015); Hu, *Algorithmic Jim Crow, supra* note 38.

[76] *See, e.g.,* BROWNE, *supra* note 16; Hu, *Crimmigration-Counterterrorism, supra* note 38.

and identity management migrate from abroad to the homeland, it can be anticipated that abuses will likely proliferate in the United States. Not only should the technological impact of these techniques be assessed, but also their impact as a subjugating form of governance. Legal scholars Dorothy Roberts and Jeffrey Vagel observe that vigilance is especially appropriate in perceived moments of crises. "[W]e continue to see the instantiation of surveillance mechanisms in response to perceived public crises. These laws and practices were enacted seemingly to maintain public order generally, but disproportionately targeted minorities and the poor."[77] Understanding why and how justifications for the increased militarized surveillance of communities of color in the Unites States, such as in the wake of antiracism protests and social unrest, proliferate and run parallel with similar rationales for the adoption of biometric surveillance abroad in occupied nations, also within communities of color, opens the door to a range of questions on the nexus between race and national security.

Conclusion

The unprecedented collection of biometric data of the Afghan people by the United States during the military and nation-building operations from 2001 to 2021 transformed into a method for both data colonization and resource extraction, as well as a vehicle for surveillance capitalism. For almost two decades, the U.S. military coordinated and supervised the collection of scanned fingerprints, facial recognition images, DNA, and other biometric identifiers of the Afghan population.[78] Biometric data eventually formed the cornerstone of the Afghan government's "identity management" strategy, used for identity cards, election security, and other daily governance objectives.[79]

Deploying military-grade facial recognition technology and other advanced biometric technologies in the United States, originally designed for counterterrorism purposes, may be indicative of a troubling trend. Allegations of potential abuse of biometric technologies abroad by human

---

[77] Dorothy Roberts & Jeffrey Vagle, Opinion, *Racial Surveillance Has a Long History*, HILL (Jan. 4, 2016), http://thehill.com/opinion/op-ed/264710-racial-surveillance-has-a-long-history [https://perma.cc/R5WL-DQHG].

[78] *See, e.g.*, JACOBSEN, *supra* note 67; Hu, *supra* note 67; Report, HUMAN RIGHTS WATCH, *supra* note 2.

[79] Hu, *supra* note 67.

rights and immigrant rights advocates, and misuse of biometric and cybersurveillance tools against racial justice protesters domestically, raises concern that vulnerable communities and people of color are disproportionately used as laboratories to beta test these technologies. Militarized biometric data colonialization and the cybersurveillance of technocolonized bodies should be contemplated as one of the most significant long-term consequences of biometric-enabled warfare. Whether the identity dominance objectives of the U.S. military and private contractors were a consequence of technocolonial ambitions deserves future consideration and debate.

8

Extending the Logic of *Defund*
to America's Endless Wars

Aslı Bâli

Introduction

In the midst of the racial justice uprising of the summer of 2020, President Donald Trump characterized purported lawlessness in cities like Portland and Chicago as "worse than Afghanistan."[1] On this basis, he argued that federal officers should be sent into these and other cities over the objections of local officials.[2] Trump also characterized Black Lives Matter protesters as terrorists, while floating the possibility of designating Antifa as a terrorist organization.[3] These actions were all rightly and widely condemned.[4] Legal experts observed that the president did not have the authority to unilaterally designate Antifa or other domestic groups as terrorist organizations.[5] Similarly, Trump's treatment of the Department of Homeland Security (DHS) and other federal law enforcement agencies as paramilitary forces for

---

[1] Nick Miroff & Mark Berman, *Trump Threatens to Deploy Federal Agents to Chicago and Other U.S. Cities Led by Democrats*, WASH. POST (July 20, 2020), https://www.washingtonpost.com/natio nal/defending-portland-crackdown-trump-pledges-to-deploys-feds-to-chicago-and-other-us-cit ies-led-by-democrats/2020/07/20/fda42b8a-caaa-11ea-89ce-ac7d5e4a5a38_story.html.

[2] *Mayors of Major US Cities Reject Deployment of Federal Forces*, VOA NEWS (July 22, 2020), https://www.voanews.com/a/usa_race-america_mayors-major-us-cities-reject-deployment-fede ral-forces/6193218.html.

[3] Angela Dewan, *Trump Is Calling Protesters Who Disagree with Him Terrorists. That Puts Him in the Company of the World's Autocrats*, CNN (July 26, 2020), https://www.cnn.com/2020/07/25/ politics/us-protests-trump-terrorists-intl/index.html; *Antifa: Trump Says Group Will Be Designated "Terrorist Organization,"* BBC (May 31, 2020), https://www.bbc.com/news/world-us-canada- 52868295.

[4] Press Release, U.N. Human Rights Off. of the High Comm'r, UN Experts Decry US Rhetoric on Designation of Terrorist Groups (June 19, 2020), https://www.ohchr.org/EN/NewsEvents/Pages/ DisplayNews.aspx?NewsID=25980&LangID=E.

[5] Shirin Sinnar, *Invoking "Terrorism" Against Police Protestors*, JUST SEC. (June 3, 2020), https:// www.justsecurity.org/70549/invoking-terrorism-against-police-protestors/.

Aslı Bâli, *Extending the Logic of* Defund *to America's Endless Wars* In: *Race and National Security*. Edited by: Matiangai V.S. Sirleaf, Oxford University Press. © Oxford University Press 2023. DOI: 10.1093/oso/9780197754641.003.0009

him to deploy at his discretion against cities "run by Democrats"[6] produced substantial legal and political pushback (including lawsuits, a Department of Justice investigation, resistance from mayors, and criticism from former Republican DHS officials and legal scholars).[7]

The concerns raised during the summer of 2020 about the federal government laying siege to American cities have receded somewhat under President Joe Biden. In retrospect, Trump's willingness to deploy federal agents to violently repress political dissent may now be seen as an expression of his broader appetite for using violence to maintain control, including by inciting his followers to resist the peaceful transfer of power after he lost the 2020 presidential election.[8] Troublingly, that violence has resurfaced calls for new domestic terrorism criminal charges.[9] The threat from the rampaging mob at the Capitol was very real, but no new legal tools are needed to hold those responsible accountable.[10] An expanded domestic terrorism regime has every likelihood of being wielded against communities of color in precisely the ways Trump demanded in 2020. Rather than addressing the threat of White supremacist violence, the use of vague and overbroad categories like "domestic terrorism" invites the exercise of racialized discretion as to which communities constitute a threat.[11] Legitimate concerns about the January

---

[6] David Smith, *Trump Announces "Surge" of Federal Officers into Democratic-run Cities*, GUARDIAN (July 22, 2020), https://www.theguardian.com/us-news/2020/jul/22/donald-trump-federal-officers-police-surge-chicago.

[7] *Federal Court Issues Restraining Order on Federal Agents in Portland*, ACLU (July 23, 2020), https://www.aclu.org/press-releases/federal-court-issues-restraining-order-federal-agents-portl and (describing ACLU lawsuit to block Trump from using federal agents to attack protesters); Tom McCarthy, *DoJ to Investigate Federal Forces' Tactics in US Cities as Mayors Condemn Trump*, GUARDIAN (July 23, 2020), https://www.theguardian.com/us-news/2020/jul/23/us-doj-trump-fede ral-agents-trump-deployments (describing Department of Justice investigation of federal forces); *US: Growing Criticism for Trump's "Abuse of Power" in Portland*, AL JAZEERA (July 21, 2020), https:// www.aljazeera.com/news/2020/7/21/us-growing-criticism-for-trumps-abuse-of-power-in-portl and (describing criticism of Trump's threats by U.S. mayors and constitutional scholars); Greg Sargent, *Trump's Authoritarian Crackdown Is so Bad that Even Some in the GOP Are Blasting It*, WASH. POST (July 22, 2020), https://www.washingtonpost.com/opinions/2020/07/22/trumps-ugly-law-enforcement-crackdown-is-even-alienating-republicans/ (describing former Republican DHS officials criticizing Trump's moves); Emily Badger, *How Trump's Use of Federal Forces in Cities Differs from Past Presidents*, N.Y. TIMES (July 23, 2020), https://www.nytimes.com/2020/07/23/upshot/trump-portland.html (citing legal scholars criticizing Trump's tactics).

[8] *Capitol Riots: Did Trump's Words at Rally Incite Violence?*, BBC (Feb. 14, 2021), https://www.bbc.com/news/world-us-canada-55640437.

[9] Alex Emmons, *Capitol Hill Assault Revives Calls for Domestic Terrorism Law, But Civil Liberties Groups Are Wary*, INTERCEPT (Jan. 10, 2021), https://theintercept.com/2021/01/10/capitol-hill-riot-domestic-terrorism-legislation/.

[10] Shirin Sinnar, *Issue Brief, Rethinking our Counterterrorism Framework: How to Address Domestic Terrorism Twenty Years after 9/11*, AM. CONST. SOC'Y (Sept. 2021), https://www.acslaw.org/wp-cont ent/uploads/2021/09/Sinnar-ACS-Issue-Brief-Final.pdf.

[11] Amna Akbar, *Policing "Radicalization*," 3 U.C. IRVINE L. REV. 809 (2013).

6 insurrection should not divert national attention away from the urgent questions about abusive policing raised by racial justice protesters. This is all the more true given the striking—and widely remarked upon—difference between the hands-off policing of the insurrectionists and the brutal crackdown against racial justice protesters just six months earlier.[12] Discretionary and inevitably racialized threat assessments yield such disparities in lower profile contexts every day.[13]

The common thread between Trump's would-be terrorist designations of racial justice protesters in the summer of 2020 and his suggestion that American cities should be subjected to the same treatment as those in Afghanistan deserves sustained attention. What this through line reveals is more than the enormous dangers posed if Trump and his allies were to regain control of national security. Notwithstanding the exceptional vulgarity of Trump's words and deeds, in fact he could have achieved most of his goals using federal policing power precisely as other administrations have across party lines for decades. Trump's brutal instincts inadvertently made plain the deep connection between militarized domestic policing and America's wars abroad. Understanding this broader context—which long preceded Trump—allows for an analysis that connects arguments for reforming policing at home[14] to critiques of militarized border enforcement and demands to end this country's endless wars.[15] Turning our attention in this way to the interwoven logics of policing, border control, and militarism clarifies why calls to defund the police should be joined to a broader movement challenging the highly profitable military-industrial-policing complex that sustains the American security state.

---

[12] *See, e.g.,* Steve Inskeep, *How Police Handled Pro-Trump Mob Compared with Protesters for Black Racial Justice,* NPR (Jan. 7, 2021), https://www.npr.org/sections/insurrection-at-the-capitol/2021/01/07/954410419/how-the-u-s-capitol-mob-was-treated-differently-than-earlier-black-protesters.

[13] *See, e.g.,* Philip J. Levchak, *Stop-and-Frisk in New York City: Estimating Racial Disparities in Post-Stop Outcomes,* 73 J. CRIM. JUST. 1 (2021); Sharon LaFraniere & Andrew W. Lehren, *The Disproportionate Risks of Driving While Black,* N.Y. TIMES (Oct. 24, 2015), https://www.nytimes.com/2015/10/25/us/racial-disparity-traffic-stops-driving-black.html.

[14] Philip V. McHarris & Thenjiwe McHarris, *No More Money for the Police,* N.Y. TIMES (May 30, 2020), https://www.nytimes.com/2020/05/30/opinion/george-floyd-police-funding.html.

[15] Stephen Wertheim, *The Only Way to End "Endless Wars,"* N.Y. TIMES (Sept. 14, 2019), https://www.nytimes.com/2019/09/14/opinion/sunday/endless-war-america.html.

Pax Americana Comes Home

In comparing Chicago to Afghanistan, Trump borrowed from a well-worn American playbook on a purportedly lawless world.[16] Portraying large swathes of the world as plagued by anarchy and violence has long been a formula to legitimize the use of state violence in the name of pacification.[17] American interventions are often justified, to borrow President Barack Obama's words, on the grounds that "the instruments of war do have a role to play in preserving the peace."[18] So American forces are deployed abroad to restore order, end violence, and protect civilians in allegedly barbarous or failed states. These interventions, in turn, apply overwhelming force[19] together with counterinsurgency techniques[20] that often brutalize the civilians they purport to protect, all the while producing further violence.[21]

Moreover, battlefields abroad have all too often served as laboratories for counterinsurgency methods that are imported back into domestic policing.[22] The literal use of military hardware by domestic police is only the most visible expression of the degree to which American wars fuel militarization in law enforcement, with returning veterans recruited to police departments bringing their metaphor of the "jungle" to policing the urban poor.[23] The "boomerang effect" of military interventions is evident in domestic practices of militarized coercion including the rise of state surveillance, expanded use of drones, abusive practices in American prisons, and much more.[24] The

[16] *See, e.g.*, JOHN W. DOWER, THE VIOLENT AMERICAN CENTURY: WAR AND TERROR SINCE WORLD WAR II (2017).

[17] Mai Elliot, *The Terrible Violence of "Pacification,"* N.Y. TIMES (Jan. 18, 2018), https://www.nyti mes.com/2018/01/18/opinion/violence-pacification-vietnam-war.html (discussing pacification in the context of the Vietnam War).

[18] Press Release, The White House of President Barack Obama, Remarks by the President at the Acceptance of the Noble Peace Prize (Dec. 10, 2009), https://obamawhitehouse.archives.gov/the-press-office/remarks-president-acceptance-nobel-peace-prize.

[19] PHILIP ULRICH, OVERWHELMING FORCE—A PERSISTENT CONCEPT IN US MILITARY THINKING FROM VIETNAM TO OPERATION IRAQI FREEDOM, INSTITUTE FOR STRATEGY, ROYAL DUTCH DEFENSE COLLEGE (2013).

[20] *See, e.g.*, DEP'T OF THE ARMY, TACTICS IN COUNTERINSURGENCY, FMI No. 3-24.2 (Mar. 2009), https://irp.fas.org/doddir/army/fmi3-24-2.pdf.

[21] Michael A. Cohen, *Tossing the Afghan COIN*, NATION (Dec. 16, 2010), https://www.thenation.com/article/archive/tossing-afghan-coin/.

[22] John Zambri, *Counterinsurgency and Community Policing: More Alike than Meets the Eye*, SMALL WARS J. (July 8, 2014), https://smallwarsjournal.com/jrnl/art/counterinsurgency-and-community-policing-more-alike-than-meets-the-eye.

[23] Aisha M. Beliso-De Jesús, *The Jungle Academy: Molding White Supremacy in American Police Recruits*, 122 AM. ANTHROPOLOGIST 143, 145 (2020).

[24] The "boomerang effect" is how economists Christopher Coyne and Abigail Hall describe the ways that military tactics and technologies are re-imported into the United States from interventions overseas in ways that have accelerated the rise of a police state that threatens constitutional

mutually constitutive relationship between militarized policing at home and imperial interventions abroad has been ably chronicled by scholars[25] and journalists[26] studying America's wars from the Philippines[27] to Vietnam[28] to the "Global War on Terror" (GWoT).[29]

The pattern of circulating violence in which overseas military interventions provide opportunities to innovate, practice, and hone methods of social control and repression that are then imported back to the domestic context would be familiar to historians of European imperialism. For example, John Reynolds has ably documented the ways in which emergency governance—that is, the legal concept of a "state of emergency" and the exceptional and discretionary powers it enables—was a colonial legal technique that was absorbed into domestic practices, normalizing emergency repression as part of a constitutional repertoire and even a standard international law basis for derogating from human rights obligations.[30] In many ways, the very phrase "homeland security" reflects the domestic internalization of militarist logics presenting the nation as a territory to be secured from threat. In the aftermath of the September 11 attacks—the preeminent "emergency" of the post–Cold War period—President George W. Bush introduced the phrase in announcing his intention to create a "Department of Homeland Security" focused on securing the domestic realm against threats from without and within.[31] Having been inured to the phrase it is difficult to recall how dissonant it once seemed to Americans.[32] As one commentator noted, however:

protections and civil liberties. CHRISTOPHER J. COYNE & ABIGAIL R. HALL, TYRANNY COMES HOME: THE DOMESTIC FATE OF U.S. MILITARISM (2018).

[25] *See, e.g.,* STUART SCHRADER, BADGES WITHOUT BORDERS: HOW GLOBAL COUNTERINSURGENCY TRANSFORMED AMERICAN POLICING (2019).

[26] *See, e.g.,* Connor Woodman, *The Imperial Boomerang: How Colonial Methods of Repression Migrate Back to the Metropolis,* VERSO BLOG (June 9, 2020), https://www.versobooks.com/blogs/4383-the-imperial-boomerang-how-colonial-methods-of-repression-migrate-back-to-the-metropolis.

[27] Alfred McCoy, *Policing the Imperial Periphery: The Philippine-American War and the Origins of U.S. Global Surveillance,* 13 SURVEILLANCE & SOC'Y 4 (2015).

[28] Stuart Schrader, *"Tiger Cages" in Vietnam: How the Call for U.S. Prison Abolition Is a Global Issue,* U.C. PRESS BLOG (July 17, 2020), https://www.ucpress.edu/blog/51234/tiger-cages-in-vietnam-how-the-call-for-u-s-prison-abolition-is-a-global-issue/.

[29] Arthur Rizer & Joseph Hartman, *How the War on Terror Has Militarized the Police,* ATLANTIC (Nov. 7, 2011), https://www.theatlantic.com/national/archive/2011/11/how-the-war-on-terror-has-militarized-the-police/248047/.

[30] JOHN REYNOLDS, EMPIRE, EMERGENCY AND INTERNATIONAL LAW (2017).

[31] Press Release, The White House of President George W. Bush, President Releases National Strategy for Homeland Security (July 16, 2002), https://georgewbush-whitehouse.archives.gov/news/releases/2002/07/20020716-2.html.

[32] Elizabeth Becker, *Washington Talk; Prickly Roots of "Homeland Security,"* N.Y. TIMES (Aug. 31, 2002), https://www.nytimes.com/2002/08/31/us/washington-talk-prickly-roots-of-homeland-secur

There was something evocative about the term, combining a bit of military jargon with the idea in need of protection. This wasn't just America that was attacked, it was our *homeland*. We didn't simply need more security at airports, we needed homeland defense.[33]

The attendant blurring of the line between militarism and policing—and between domestic and overseas practices—has marked the forms of counter terrorism and border patrol overseen by DHS since it was formed.[34]

The intersection of the international realm and domestic policies at the borders of the nation offers a particularly sharp lens on the militarized and openly racial enforcement strategies that speak to continuities between policing and war-making. American elites have long justified U.S. military deployments as a necessary means of countering a violent and lawless world to shore up national security while providing a global system of "rule-based order."[35] Trump brought this logic to bear in an especially acute fashion at the border, depicting migrants as teeming and violent hordes against which the "homeland" required a literal wall (and even moat) of protection.[36] The racial logic of protecting fortress America from the non-White world was made explicit with Trump's menacing imagery of lawlessness at the border[37] and Central American "caravans" bent on invasion.[38] During the Trump years,

ity.html (canvassing views that the phrase has Germanic overtones and did not immediately get widespread acceptance).

[33] Philip Bump, *How "Homeland" Became a Part of Our American Lexicon*, WASH. POST (Sept. 11, 2014), https://www.washingtonpost.com/news/the-fix/wp/2014/09/11/how-homeland-became-part-of-our-american-lexicon/.

[34] For instance, the U.S. Congress's House Committee on Homeland Security routinely holds hearings that blur the line between domestic and foreign counterterrorism operations. *See, e.g., Homeland Security Beyond Our Borders: Examining the Status of Counterterrorism Coordination Overseas: Hearings before the Subcomm. on Border, Maritime and Global Counterterrorism of the Comm. on Homeland Security of the House of Representatives*, 110th Cong. 110–75 (2007).

[35] *See generally* Aslı Bâli & Aziz Rana, *Constitutionalism and the American Imperial Imagination*, 85 U. CHI. L. REV. 257 (2018).

[36] Michael D. Shear & Julie Hirschfield Davis, *Shoot Migrants' Legs, Build Alligator Moat: Behind Trump's Ideas for Border*, N.Y. TIMES (Oct. 1, 2019), https://www.nytimes.com/2019/10/01/us/polit ics/trump-border-wars.html (noting that Trump "often talked about fortifying a border wall with a water-filled trench, stocked with snakes or alligators, prompting aides to seek a cost estimate").

[37] Elliot Spagat, *Trump on the "Lawless" US Border with Mexico*, ASSOCIATED PRESS (Feb. 5, 2019), https://apnews.com/article/a7374e8333da459d972e411ec855edb6.

[38] Jay Willis, *Trump's Racist War on a "Migrant Caravan" Explained*, GQ (Oct. 23, 2018), https://www.gq.com/story/migrant-caravan-explained; Michael D. Shear & Thomas Gibbons-Neff, *Trump Sending 5,200 Troops to the Border in an Election-Season Response to Migrants*, N.Y. TIMES (Oct. 29, 2018), https://www.nytimes.com/2018/10/29/us/politics/border-security-troops-trump.html (noting that Trump characterized "a caravan of Central American migrants . . . as an 'invasion of our country'").

the continuities between border enforcement and militarism were made particularly visible, with over five thousand active-duty troops deployed to the border at one point.[39] The quiet at the Canadian border, which witnessed neither wall construction nor troop deployments, bears further witness to the racial character of American border enforcement. Once more, however, what Trump made plain were long-standing practices that preceded his administration and have continued since he left office. Border enforcement officials on horseback brandishing what appeared to be whips against Haitian migrants at the southern border were executing policies of the Biden administration.[40]

To take another example of the continuities between U.S. coercive practices at home and abroad, the history of "Special Weapons and Tactics" (SWAT) police units is instructive.[41] Both proponents[42] and critics[43] of SWAT units agree that they were developed in the 1960s and applied to domestic policing counterinsurgency methods used by American forces in Vietnam. Tellingly, the origins of SWAT in the United States can be traced to the Watts uprising[44] in 1965 in Los Angeles and the subsequent repression of the Black Panthers and the antiracist protest movements of the 1960s.[45] The early SWAT forces included a significant number of Korean and Vietnam war veterans, and to this day, these paramilitary forces often draw on veterans migrating to law enforcement.[46] As foreign wars bled into America's "war on drugs," the practice of storming homes in civilian areas overseas translated to no-knock search warrants,[47] authorizing SWAT operators to use techniques developed abroad

[39] Shear & Gibbons-Neff, *supra* note 38 (noting that "more than 5,000 active-duty military troops [were deployed] to the southern border" in advance of the 2018 election).

[40] Eileen Sullivan & Zolan Kanno-Youngs, *Images of Border Patrol's Treatment of Haitian Migrants Prompt Outrage*, N.Y. TIMES (Sept. 21, 2021), https://www.nytimes.com/2021/09/21/us/politics/haitians-border-patrol-photos.html.

[41] Peter B. Kraska, *Militarization and Policing—Its Relevance to 21st Century Police*, 1 POLICING 501 (2007).

[42] Dan Marcou, *Police History: How SWAT Got Its Start*, POLICE1 (Sept. 10, 2015), https://www.police1.com/police-history/articles/police-history-how-swat-got-its-start-A46mInV79ujHNIfW/.

[43] Julian Go, *The Racist Origins of U.S. Policing*, FOREIGN AFFS. (July 16, 2020), https://www.foreignaffairs.com/articles/united-states/2020-07-16/racist-origins-us-policing.

[44] GERALD HORNE, FIRE THIS TIME: THE WATTS UPRISING AND THE 1960S (1997).

[45] Matthew Fleischer, *50 Years Ago, LAPD Raided the Black Panthers. SWAT Teams have been Targeting Black Communities Ever Since*, L.A. TIMES (Dec. 8, 2019), https://www.latimes.com/opinion/story/2019-12-08/50-years-swat-black-panthers-militarized-policinglos-angeles.

[46] Simone Weichselbaum & Beth Schwartzapfel, *When Warriors Put on the Badge*, MARSHALL PROJECT (Mar. 30, 2017), https://www.themarshallproject.org/2017/03/30/when-warriors-put-on-the-badge.

[47] For a detailed discussion of such no-knock search warrants and their use, *see* Kevin Sack, *Forced Entry Warrant Drug Raid Interactive*, N.Y. TIMES (Mar. 18, 2017), https://www.nytimes.com/interactive/2017/03/18/us/forced-entry-warrant-drug-raid.html.

in residential areas within the United States.[48] Police officers executing a no-knock search warrant shot and killed Breonna Taylor after midnight while she slept in her home in Louisville.[49]

The militarized violence directed largely against communities of color at home, at the border and overseas reflects the imbricated logics of the police state at each of these levels. Yet the connections across these three levels are often obscured by geography while solidarity among affected communities can be difficult to sustain across the political divisions of national belonging. These too-often submerged continuities were brought to the surface and rendered visible for a time by racial justice protesters and their renewed focus on the SWAT tactics that killed Breonna Taylor. For the first time in a generation, voices were raised in protest not only of racialized domestic law enforcement but also against the ways that violent domination of people of color at the border and overseas—at the Wall and in the so-called "war on terror"—is "inextricably linked to the oppression of people of color at home."[50]

Racialized Counterterrorism

It is not only techniques,[51] weapons,[52] and personnel[53] that circulate between wars abroad and militarized policing at home. The

---

[48] In a disturbing indication of the popular currency of SWAT tactics, there is now a corresponding form of private harassment and persecution that has come to be termed "swatting." This version of "SWAT-ing" involves making a false report that a person is engaged in violent criminal activity in order to send police to an unsuspecting victim's home. The possibility that police responding to false reports might themselves use SWAT tactics against the victim only enhances the perversity of the ways in which these tactics circulate through official forms of violence deployed at home and abroad and then are reappropriated toward other violent ends. On "swatting," *see* Emma Whitman, *What Is Swatting?*, BUS. INSIDER (Jan. 14, 2021), https://www.businessinsider.com/what-is-swatting.

[49] Radley Balko, Opinion, *The No-Knock Warrant for Breonna Taylor was Illegal*, WASH. POST (June 3, 2020), https://www.washingtonpost.com/opinions/2020/06/03/no-knock-warrant-breonna-tay lor-was-illegal/.

[50] Shireen Al-Adeimi & Sarah Lazare, *How Our Bloated Military Strengthens the Police State*, IN THESE TIMES (June 17, 2020), https://inthesetimes.com/article/militarism-police-state-black-lives-matter-patriot-act-national-guard.

[51] ACLU, WAR COMES HOME: THE EXCESSIVE MILITARIZATION OF AMERICAN POLICING (June 2014), https://www.aclu.org/sites/default/files/field_document/jus14-warcomeshome-text-rel1.pdf.

[52] Michael Leo Owens, Tom Clark & Adam Glynn, *Where Do Police Departments Get Their Military-Style Gear?*, WASH. POST (July 20, 2020), https://www.washingtonpost.com/politics/2020/07/20/where-do-police-departments-get-their-military-style-gear-heres-what-we-dont-know/.

[53] Alireza Ahmadi, *How America's Wars in Asia Militarized the Police at Home*, DIPLOMAT (June 18, 2020), https://thediplomat.com/2020/06/how-americas-wars-in-asia-militarized-the-police-at-home/.

racialization[54] of targets of American state violence circulates across borders just as freely. The GWoT accelerated police militarization while furnishing a new enemy within. The GWoT's all-too-familiar category of racialized threat—the conflation of Arab, Muslim, or Middle Eastern identity with terrorism[55]—is so pervasive that anyone perceived to belong to this nebulous category is viewed as inherently suspect.[56] The specter of "sleeper cells" and internal enemies is used to employ some of the most extreme counterterrorism tactics—including surveillance,[57] detention[58] and even targeted killing[59]—against American citizens. As Atiya Husain has argued, "[i]n the GWoT counterinsurgency has become domestic practice."[60]

The idea that Muslim communities within the United States serve as threat incubators has produced an expansive apparatus of national security preventive policing[61] that mirrors the racial disparities[62] associated with American proactive policing more generally.[63] Where counterinsurgency methods counseled winning "hearts and minds" abroad by infiltrating communities, at home the "countering violent extremism" (CVE) program introduced by the Obama administration served much the same function.[64] Beginning from the premise that Muslim communities were vulnerable to becoming

[54] Stephen Mihm, *The Riots of the 1960s Led to the Rise in Militarization of Police*, BLOOMBERG (June 12, 2020), https://www.bloomberg.com/opinion/articles/2020-06-12/militarization-of-police-is-tied-to-1960s-riots-and-race.

[55] ARUN KUNDNANI, THE MUSLIMS ARE COMING!: ISLAMOPHOBIA EXTREMISM, AND THE DOMESTIC WAR ON TERROR (2014).

[56] *See generally* Jeanne Theoharis & Amna A. Akbar, *Islam on Trial*, BOS. REV. (Feb. 27, 2017), https://bostonreview.net/forum/amna-akbar-jeanne-theoharis-muslims-and-constitution/.

[57] DIALA SHAMAS & NERMEEN ARASTU, MUSLIM AM. CIVIL LIBERTIES COALITION, CREATING LAW ENFORCEMENT ACCOUNTABILITY & RESPONSIBILITY & ASIAN AM. LEGAL DEFENSE & EDUCATION FUND, MAPPING MUSLIMS: NYPD SPYING AND ITS IMPACT ON AMERICAN MUSLIMS (2013), https://www.law.cuny.edu/wp-content/uploads/page-assets/academics/clinics/immigration/clear/Mapping-Muslims.pdf.

[58] Carrie Johnson & Margot Williams, *"Guantanamo North": Inside Secretive U.S. Prisons*, NPR (Mar. 3, 2011), https://www.npr.org/2011/03/03/134168714/guantanamo-north-inside-u-s-secretive-prisons.

[59] Peter Finn & Greg Miller, *Anwar al-Awlaki's Family Speaks Out Against His, Son's Deaths*, WASH. POST (Oct. 17, 2011), https://www.washingtonpost.com/world/national-security/anwar-al-awlakis-family-speaks-out-against-his-sons-deaths/2011/10/17/gIQA8kFssL_story.html.

[60] Atiya Husain, *Terror and Abolition*, BOS. REV. (June 11, 2020), https://bostonreview.net/articles/atiya-husain-terror-and-abolition/.

[61] Wadie Said, *Forum Response*, BOS. REV. (Feb. 2017), https://bostonreview.net/forum_response/wadie-said-wadie-said-responds-amna-akbar-and-jeanne-theoharis/ (discussing the preventive approach to counterterrorism).

[62] Sarah Childress, *The Problem with "Broken Windows" Policing*, PBS (June 28, 2016), https://www.pbs.org/wgbh/frontline/article/the-problem-with-broken-windows-policing/.

[63] Justin Peters, *Loose Cigarettes Today, Civil Unrest Tomorrow*, SLATE (Dec. 5, 2014), https://slate.com/news-and-politics/2014/12/edward-banfield-the-racist-classist-origins-of-broken-windows-policing.html.

[64] Amna Akbar, *National Security's Broken Windows*, 62 UCLA L. REV. 834 (2015).

radicalized and embracing terrorism, CVE developed metrics of alleged radicalization and methods to prevent it. Though widely debunked,[65] these theories of radicalization have resulted in law enforcement infiltration of places
of worship,[66] schools and student organizations,[67] and other community
centers[68] with undercover agents and informants engaged in forms of preventive policing that in effect criminalize whole communities.[69]

Ordinary indicia of Muslim identity including cultural practices—from
dress, to grooming, to food and drink choices—religious beliefs, and family
ties are treated as evidence of radicalism.[70] Racist cultural stereotyping
is thereby passed off as legitimate counterterrorism intelligence. When a
Muslim American (or someone mistaken for one) is critical of America's
conduct of the "war on terror," views that should be protected by the First
Amendment are instead treated as evidence of radicalization.[71] Pro-
Palestinian speech and activism, too, is routinely conflated with terrorism.[72]
Moreover, all of these practices long predated the Trump administration and
have survived without disruption since Biden took office.[73] The degree to
which this racialization of Muslims transcends partisan politics, even in a
highly polarized context, speaks to the entrenched and pervasive character
of the paradigm of Muslim-as-threat.

Of course, these same scripts have inevitably radiated out to other racial
minorities and marginalized groups.[74] The counterterrorism frame now

---

[65] FAIZA PATEL, BRENNAN CTR., RETHINKING RADICALIZATION (Mar. 2011), https://www.brenna
ncenter.org/sites/default/files/legacy/RethinkingRadicalization.pdf.

[66] Paul Harris, *The Ex-FBI Informant with a Change of Heart: "There Is No Real Hunt. It's Fixed,"*
GUARDIAN (Mar. 20, 2012), https://www.theguardian.com/world/2012/mar/20/fbi-informant.

[67] John Christoffersen, *Monitoring of Muslim Students Sparks Outrage*, NBC4 NEW YORK (Feb. 21,
2012), https://www.nbcnewyork.com/news/local/muslim-surveillance-nypd-spy-counter-terror-
student/1972234/.

[68] Colin Moynihan, *Last Suit Accusing N.Y.P.D. of Spying on Muslims Is Settled*, N.Y. TIMES (Apr. 5,
2018), https://www.nytimes.com/2018/04/05/nyregion/last-suit-accusing-nypd-of-spying-on-musl
ims-is-settled.html.

[69] Sarah Beth Kaufman, *The Criminalization of Muslims in the United States, 2016*, 42 QUALITATIVE
SOCIO. 521 (2019).

[70] FAIZA PATEL & MEGHAN KOUSIIIK, BRENNAN CTR., COUNTERING VIOLENT EXTREMISM (2017),
https://www.brennancenter.org/sites/default/files/publications/Brennan%20Center%20CVE%20
Report.pdf.

[71] Amna Akbar, *Policing "Radicalization,"* 3 U.C. IRVINE L. REV. 809 (2013).

[72] Chip Gibbons, *FBI Opened Terrorism Investigations into Nonviolent Palestinian Solidarity Group,
Documents Reveal*, INTERCEPT (Apr. 5, 2020), https://theintercept.com/2020/04/05/israel-palestine-
fbi-terrorism-investigation/.

[73] *See, e.g.*, Radhika Sainath, *When It Comes to Palestine, Free Speech Rights Are Under Attack*,
JACOBIN (May 23, 2021), https://jacobinmag.com/2021/05/palestinian-israeli-conflict-occupation-
free-speech-palestine-exception.

[74] Lisa Stampnitzky, *Forum Response: Lisa Stampnitzky Responds to Amna Akbar and Jeanne
Theoharis*, Bos. REV. (Feb. 27, 2017), https://bostonreview.net/forum_response/lisa-stampnit

extends to so-called "Black Identity Extremists" (BIE);[75] what should be the protected speech of critics of systemic racism in the United States is instead treated as evidence of threatening radicalism, a basis for law enforcement targeting.[76] One study[77] of the policing of activism on social media shows the convergence of CVE and BIE (magnifying further the threats faced by Black Muslims).[78]

Nor is the criminalization of dissent[79] and targeting of activists based on race or ideology new to American policing.[80] The indictment of people of color for protest activity is a long-standing tradition of the U.S. policing and judicial apparatus, styling dissent as everything from disturbance of the peace to conspiracy.[81] As Ian Haney Lopez argued nearly a quarter century ago, these practices are the very definition of institutional racism.[82] The propensity to manufacture phantom menaces[83] emanating from minority communities is thus itself an expression of the systemic racism in policing that fueled the largest protests in the country's history in 2020.

zky-lisa-stampnitzky-responds-amna-akbar-and-jeanne/ (responding to Theoharis & Akbar, *supra* note 56).

[75] Maya Berry & Kai Wiggins, *Leaked Documents Contain Major Revelations About the FBI's Terrorism Classifications*, JUST SEC. (Sept. 11, 2019), https://www.justsecurity.org/66124/leaked-documents-contain-major-revelations-about-the-fbis-terrorism-classifications/.

[76] Shanelle Matthews & Malkia Cyril, *We Say Black Lives Matter. The FBI Says that Makes Us a Security Threat*, WASH. POST (Oct. 19, 2017), https://www.washingtonpost.com/news/posteveryth ing/wp/2017/10/19/we-say-black-lives-matter-the-fbi-says-that-makes-us-a-security-threat/.

[77] Sahar Aziz & Khaled Beydoun, *Fear of a Black and Brown Internet: Policing Online Activism*, 100 B.U. L. REV. 1153 (2020).

[78] Su'ad Abdul Khabeer, *Forum Response: Suad Abdul Khabeer Responds to Amna Akbar and Jeanne Theoharis*, BOS. REV. (Feb. 28, 2017), https://bostonreview.net/forum_response/suad-abdul-khab eer-suad-abdul-khabeer-responds-amna-akbar-and-jeanne/ (responding to Theoharis & Akbar, *supra* note 56). The experience of Black Muslim communities reflects the intersectional character of their identity and the degree to which the abuses to which they are subjected are the product of intersecting patterns of anti-Black and anti-Muslim racism. On patterns of intersectional discrimination, *see* Kimberle Crenshaw, *Mapping the Margins: Intersectionality, Identity Politics and Violence against Women of Color*, 43 STAN. L. REV. 1241, 1243 (1991).

[79] CHIP GIBBONS, DEFENDING RIGHTS AND DISSENT, STILL SPYING ON DISSENT: THE ENDURING PROBLEM OF FBI FIRST AMENDMENT ABUSE (2019), https://rightsanddissent.org/fbi-spying/.

[80] Michael German, *Manufacturing a "Black Separatist" Threat and Other Dubious Claims: Bias in Newly Released FBI Terrorism Training Materials*, ACLU (May 29, 2012), https://www.aclu.org/blog/ national-security/discriminatory-profiling/manufacturing-black-separatist-threat-and-other.

[81] Ian Haney Lopez, *Institutional Racism: Judicial Conduct and a New Theory of Racial Discrimination*, 109 YALE L.J. 1717, 1721 (1999) (describing the indictment of Mexican-American student protesters on charges "ranging from disturbing the peace to conspiracy").

[82] *Id.* at 1722 (explaining that he examines the cases brought against Mexican American protesters, and the composition of the grand juries assembled to hear these charges, in order to "address the nature of institutional racism").

[83] Andrew Rosenthal, *The FBI's Black Phantom Menace*, N.Y. TIMES (Oct. 19, 2017), https://www. nytimes.com/2017/10/19/opinion/columnists/fbi-blacks-civil-rights.html.

Ending America's Wars at Home and Abroad

The fact that protests against police brutality have consistently engendered further police brutality lays bare the recursive logic of America's wars at home and abroad. Violence breeds resistance that is met with further violence. The "war on crime," the "war on drugs," and the "war on terror"—together with militarized border policing—each produce their racialized targets and then continuously reinforce the internal racial logic of such targeting across America's wars.[84] For example, police surveillance of Muslim communities collapsed "barriers between foreign and domestic spying and import[ed] scripts from the war on crime into the war on terror."[85] Customs and Border Patrol "elite units"[86] were deployed to subjugate protesters in Portland in 2020. And the "war on terror's" global battlefield clearly came to encompass U.S. cities in the context of that year's racial justice uprising.[87]

Describing protesters and racial justice activists as terrorists—as the sitting president,[88] attorney general,[89] and agents of the FBI[90] all did in the summer of 2020—underscores again the links between domestic law enforcement and America's military engagements. Calls to defund the police[91] were at the center of protests in 2020 and continue to be debated since.[92] But defunding the police requires demilitarizing the American conception of law enforcement, which in turn requires fundamentally rethinking our foreign

[84] Wadie E. Said, *Law Enforcement in the American Security State*, 2019 WIS. L. REV. 819 (2019).

[85] Ramzi Kassem, *The Long Roots of the NYPD Spying Program*, NATION (June 14, 2012), https://www.thenation.com/article/archive/long-roots-nypd-spying-program/.

[86] Alicia A. Caldwell & Michelle Hackman, *Elite Border Patrol Unit Is Among Federal Agents Deployed to Portland*, WALL ST. J. (July 25, 2020), https://www.wsj.com/articles/elite-border-patrol-unit-is-among-federal-agents-deployed-to-portland-11595689780.

[87] Joshua Keating, *The War on Terror Comes Home*, SLATE (June 3, 2020), https://slate.com/news-and-politics/2020/06/war-on-terror-floyd-protests-military.html.

[88] Angela Dewan, *Trump Is Calling Protesters Who Disagree with Him Terrorists*, CNN (July 26, 2020), https://www.cnn.com/2020/07/25/politics/us-protests-trump-terrorists-intl/index.html.

[89] Press Release, Dep't of Justice, Attorney General William P. Barr's Statement on Riots and Domestic Terrorism (May 31, 2020), https://www.justice.gov/opa/pr/attorney-general-william-p-barrs-statement-riots-and-domestic-terrorism.

[90] Chris Brooks, *After Barr Ordered FBI to "Identify Criminal Organizers," Activists Were Intimidated at Home and at Work*, INTERCEPT (June 12, 2020), https://theintercept.com/2020/06/12/fbi-jttf-protests-activists-cookeville-tennessee/.

[91] Leila Fadel, *Protesters Call for Police to be Defunded. But What Does that Mean?*, NPR (June 22, 2020), https://www.npr.org/2020/06/22/881559687/protesters-call-for-police-to-be-defunded-but-what-does-that-mean.

[92] Nathan Schneider, *How Can We Honor Martin Luther King Jr.? Defund (While Respecting) the Police*, AMERICA (Jan. 17, 2022), https://www.americamagazine.org/politics-society/2022/01/17/mlk-defund-police-nathan-schneider-242208.

policy and commitment to a national security state.[93] What would it mean to connect the call for ending endless war to demands to demilitarize the border and defund the police?

Following decades of police reform—from body cameras to de-escalation and implicit bias training—that has generally failed to stem police violence, the movement to defund issued a transformative call to reimagine public safety and racial justice.[94] Divesting from the police entails addressing one of the principal sources of state-sanctioned violence against Black (and Brown) lives by questioning the relationship between armed enforcement and safety.

The Movement for Black Lives (M4BL) formulated their demands in ways that made clear that divestment from policing[95] also requires investment in education, health, and safety.[96] This approach is continuous with the earlier Black freedom struggle of the 1960s, with the Black Panther Party galvanized fifty years earlier to combat police brutality and demand, instead, investment in community programs, health clinics, legal aid, and education.[97] Communities today across the country are linking the defund campaign to demands for improved community services—from mental health and social workers to schools, housing, and hospitals.[98] Such a transformative vision of

[93] Aziz Rana, *Constitutionalism and the Foundations of the Security State*, 103 Calif. L. Rev. 335 (2015).

[94] Marbre Stahly-Butts et al., Law for Black Lives, Ctr. for Popular Democracy & BYP100, Freedom to Thrive: Reimagining Safety and Security in Our Communities (2017), https://populardemocracy.app.box.com/v/FreedomtoThrive.

[95] *The Time Has Come to Defund the Police*, M4BL, https://m4bl.org/defund-the-police/ (last visited June 22, 2022).

[96] *Invest-Divest*, M4BL, https://m4bl.org/policy-platforms/invest-divest/ (last visited June 22, 2022).

[97] On comparisons of the demands of the Black Panther Party and the Movement for Black Lives, *see, e.g.*, Peniel E. Joseph, *From the Black Panthers to Black Lives Matter, the Ongoing Fight to End Police Violence Against Black Americans*, Wash. Post (May 29, 2020), https://www.washingtonpost.com/nation/2020/05/29/black-panthers-black-lives-matter-ongoing-fight-end-police-violence-against-black-americans/; Colette Gaiter, *Black Panthers and Black Lives Matter—Parallels and Progress*, Conversation (Nov. 6, 2015), https://theconversation.com/black-panthers-and-black-lives-matter-parallels-and-progress-48313; Nivi Manchanda & Chris Rossdale, *Resisting Racial Militarism: War, Policing and the Black Panther Party*, 52 Sec. Dialogue 473 (2021).

[98] *See, e.g.*, Meera Jagannathan, *As Activists Call to Defund the Police, Mental Health Advocates Say "The Time Is Now' to Rethink Public Safety*, MarketWatch (June 19, 2020), https://www.marketwatch.com/story/long-before-defund-the-police-mental-health-advocates-have-been-redefining-public-safety-2020-06-11; Sharon Kwon, *It's Time to Defund the Police and Start Funding Social Workers*, HuffPost (June 11, 2020), https://www.huffpost.com/entry/defund-police-social-workers_n_5ee12d80c5b6d1ad2bd82777; Daarel Burnette II, *Schools or Police: In Some Cities, a Reckoning on Spending Priorities*, EducationWeek (June 18, 2020), https://www.edweek.org/leadership/schools-or-police-in-some-cities-a-reckoning-on-spending-priorities/2020/06; Sydney Brownstone, *In Activists' Demands to Defund Police, Calls to Fund Housing and Human Services*, Seattle Times (June 13, 2020), https://www.seattletimes.com/seattle-news/homeless/in-activists-demands-to-defund-police-calls-to-fund-housing-and-human-services/; Dennis Kosuth, *Chicago Unions Demand to Defund Police and Fund Health Care for All*, LaborNotes (July 7, 2020), https://labornotes.org/blogs/2020/07/chicago-unions-demand-defund-police-and-fund-health-care-all.

public safety has further implications for the criminal justice system, such as decriminalizing poverty by reforming drug policies and eliminating offenses that disproportionately impact the poor and unhoused.[99] Prison abolition is also a closely related demand.[100]

Arguments for "ending endless war" dovetail seamlessly with this M4BL invest-divest framework. Indeed, M4BL has issued a call to cut military expenditures and reallocate funds to domestic infrastructure and community well-being.[101] But the similarities go beyond shared demands to shift funding priorities. The call to end America's permanent war footing involves a transformative vision of its own: abandoning a posture of American military dominance.[102]

Rethinking U.S. military primacy is a necessary corollary to ending state-sanctioned violence at home because America's wars abroad sustain and feed into militarized and racialized domestic policing. Beyond the conveyor belt of equipment, training, and manpower that circulates between America's wars—within our borders and overseas—lie massive vested interests in what today is best understood as the military-industrial-*policing* complex. And this complex profits from and entrenches the very forms of racialized state violence that protesters oppose.[103]

The Political Economy of Defunding

The "military-industrial complex" is the phrase first used by then outgoing President Dwight Eisenhower to warn of the relationships that had developed in the wake of the Second World War between government and defense industries.[104] What Eisenhower highlighted was the growing danger

[99] *See, e.g.*, Aaron Ross Coleman, *Police Reform, Defunding and Abolition, Explained*, Vox (July 16, 2020), https://www.vox.com/21312191/police-reform-defunding-abolition-black-lives-matter-protests; Laura Pitter, *US Should Address Concerns Raised in UN Poverty Report*, Hum. Rts. Watch (July 17, 2018), https://www.hrw.org/news/2018/07/17/us-should-address-concerns-raised-un-poverty-report#.

[100] Rachel Kushner, *Is Prison Necessary? Ruth Wilson Gilmore Might Change Your Mind*, N.Y. Times Mag. (Apr. 17, 2019), https://www.nytimes.com/2019/04/17/magazine/prison-abolition-ruth-wilson-gilmore.html.

[101] Ben Ndugga-Kabuye & Rachel Gilmer, M4BL—A Cut in US Military Expenditures and a Reallocation of those Funds to Invest in Domestic Infrastructure (2020), https://m4bl.org/wp-content/uploads/2020/05/CutMilitaryExpendituresOnePager.pdf.

[102] Wertheim, *supra* note 15.

[103] Karena Rahall, *The Green to Blue Pipeline: Defense Contractors and the Police Industrial Complex*, 36 Cardozo L. Rev. 1785 (2015).

[104] *President Dwight D. Eisenhower's Farewell Address (1961)*, Nat'l Archives (Feb. 8, 2022), https://www.archives.gov/milestone-documents/president-dwight-d-eisenhowers-farewell-address.

that war-making was becoming a for-profit enterprise imperiling democratic processes. The continued need for lucrative multi-billion-dollar commissions for military equipment, personnel, and related services to funnel taxpayer funds to industry and industry support to political elites has only accelerated in the sixty years since that warning. The mutually beneficial relationship between war-planners and industry today extends to the many ways in which American primacy is tied not only to its global military footprint but also to its status as the world's largest arms supplier.[105] Expanding Eisenhower's formulation to account for the policing complex draws attention to the for-profit carceral system and law enforcement industries that are today the domestic complement to the lucrative defense industry and the political class that supports it.

Much has been written about the prison industrial complex, with mass incarceration producing a rural economic development strategy across the country dependent on building and expanding prisons purportedly to generate jobs in investment starved regions.[106] But the mass incarceration driving the expansion of a private, for-profit carceral system itself depends on funding streams that benefit law enforcement agencies and enable a brutal policing infrastructure that continually grows prison populations. In describing the policing and carceral logics that attend to the "war on drugs," one analyst writing in the late 1990s commented that a "confluence of special interests has given prison construction in the United States a seemingly unstoppable momentum," going on to explain that these interests are:

[C]omposed of politicians, both liberal and conservative, who have used the fear of crime to gain votes; impoverished rural areas where prisons have become a cornerstone of economic development; private companies that regard the roughly $35 billion spent each year on correction not as a burden on American taxpayers but as a lucrative market; and government officials whose fiefdoms have expanded along with the inmate population.[107]

---

[105] William Hartung, *We're #1: The U.S. Government Is the World's Largest Arms Dealer*, FORBES (Mar. 18, 2022), https://www.forbes.com/sites/williamhartung/2022/03/18/were-1-the-us-government-is-the-worlds-largest-arms-dealer/?sh=582cd1e55bb9.

[106] RYAN S. KING, MARC MAUER & TRACY HULING, THE SENTENCING PROJECT, BIG PRISONS, SMALL TOWNS: PRISON ECONOMICS IN RURAL AMERICA (Feb. 2003), https://www.sentencingproj ect.org/wp-content/uploads/2016/01/Big-Prisons-Small-Towns-Prison-Economics-in-Rural-Amer ica.pdf.

[107] Eric Schlosser, *The Prison-Industrial Complex*, ATLANTIC (Dec. 1998), https://www.theatlantic. com/magazine/archive/1998/12/the-prison-industrial-complex/304669/.

To this daunting list, the author might also have added law enforcement agencies that have used the same fears and perceived threats to augment local budgets and fuel the aggressive policing that inflates prison populations.

Counterterrorism is similarly big business that sustains budgets not only for the Department of Defense but also for agencies ranging from local police departments,[108] to border enforcement,[109] to the FBI Joint Terrorism Task Forces investigating protest leaders.[110] The government does not currently provide an accurate accounting of spending on counterterrorism, but research by the Stimson Center suggests that such funding in the fifteen years between 2002 and 2017 totaled nearly $3 trillion.[111] This figure includes "homeland security," the wars in Afghanistan, Iraq, and Syria, and domestic law enforcement tied to counterterrorism. As the Stimson report makes clear, in an age of budgetary caps in other areas, counterterrorism represents a "substantial component of total discretionary spending for programs across a wide range of areas."[112]

Government agencies compete for funding. When they are able to present themselves as essential to national security, they access more revenue. These priorities give law enforcement across the board a direct funding incentive to characterize minority communities and dissidents as threat incubators to establish the need for homeland security grants to their agencies.[113]

---

[108] MICHAEL PRICE, BRENNAN CTR. FOR JUSTICE, NATIONAL SECURITY AND LOCAL POLICE (2013), https://www.brennancenter.org/sites/default/files/publications/NationalSecurity_LocalPol ice_web.pdf.

[109] Muzaffar Chishti & Jessica Bolter, *As #DefundThePolice Movement Gains Steam, Immigration Enforcement Spending and Practices Attract Scrutiny*, MIGRATION INFO. SOURCE: MIGRATION POL'Y INST. (June 25, 2020), https://www.migrationpolicy.org/article/defundthepolice-movement-gains-steam-immigration-enforcement-spending-and-practices-attract.

[110] Brooks, *supra* note 90.

[111] AMY BELASCO ET AL., STIMSON CTR., STIMSON STUDY GROUP ON COUNTERTERRORISM SPENDING: PROTECTING AMERICA WHILE PROMOTING EFFICIENCIES AND ACCOUNTABILITY (2018), https://www.stimson.org/wp-content/files/file-attachments/CT_Spending_Report_0.pdf.

[112] *Id.* at 7.

[113] A 2010 study prepared by RAND's Safety and Justice program provides an overview of the homeland security and counterterrorism grant-making systems that present law enforcement agencies with opportunities for funding provided they can dedicate at least 25 percent of funding to "law enforcement terrorism prevention-oriented planning, organization, training, exercise and equipment activities, including those activities that support the development and operation of fusion centers." LOIS M. DAVIS ET AL., RAND, LONG-TERM EFFECTS OF LAW ENFORCEMENT'S POST-9/11 FOCUS ON COUNTERTERRORISM AND HOMELAND SECURITY xxvi (2010), https://www.rand.org/pubs/monographs/MG1031.html. Fusion centers, in turn, incorporate law enforcement agencies, private sector actors, and military personnel in counterterrorism activities in major urban areas deemed to be at substantial threat of terrorism-related criminal activity. On fusion centers, *see* MICHAEL GERMAN & JAY STANLEY, ACLU, WHAT'S WRONG WITH FUSION CENTERS? (2007), https://www.aclu.org/files/pdfs/privacy/fusioncenter_20071212.pdf.

Counterterrorism serves as a kind of racist gravy train.[114] Without addressing the revenue streams tied to counterterrorism at home and abroad, there can be no meaningful way to defund the police. As Sam Moyn and Stephen Wertheim have argued, a "militarized concept of America's world role . . . permeates Washington."[115] Defunding the police will require demilitarizing our understanding of American power and purpose.

Such demilitarization is no easy task where national identity is tied to a concept of American primacy and the prerogatives of hegemony are baked into a public conception of the country's role in the global order.[116] Yet one cannot understand the political economy of American militarism without addressing the defense budgets—and attendant government transfers to defense industries—that finance American global dominance. In 2022, the Biden administration requested $813 billion for national defense, including more than $773 billion for the Department of Defense alone.[117] When combined with separate ad hoc spending requests—such as the massive military appropriations for the Ukraine conflict, which alone accounted for more than $50 billion in the first hundred days of that war[118]—nuclear weapons maintenance, and other overseas defense spending, the total exceeded $1 trillion dollars annually as of 2017[119] and accounts for nearly half of all federal discretionary spending.[120] Taking note of the combined economic incentives produced by defense, counterterrorism and carceral spending helps make sense of the reasons that racialized violence remains so deeply entrenched in the American conception of "security."

---

[114] Tina G. Patel, *It's Not About Security, It's About Racism: Counter-Terror Strategies, Civilizing Processes and the Post-Race Fiction*, 3 PALGRAVE COMMC'NS 1 (2017).

[115] Samuel Moyn & Stephen Wertheim, *The Infinity War*, WASH. POST (Dec. 13, 2019), https://www.washingtonpost.com/outlook/2019/12/13/infinity-war/.

[116] Aziz Rana has argued along these lines that the effort to "giv[e] up on the symbolic and practical power of American primacy . . . is to run up against deep currents of national self-understanding and collective pride." Aziz Rana, *Left Internationalism in the Heart of Empire*, DISSENT (May 23, 2022), https://www.dissentmagazine.org/online_articles/left-internationalism-in-the-heart-of-empire.

[117] Paul Mcleary et al., *Biden Requests $813B for National Defense*, POLITICO (Mar. 28, 2022), https://www.politico.com/news/2022/03/28/biden-requests-largest-defense-budget-00020859.

[118] Jen Kirby, *The US Just Deepened Its Commitment to Ukraine by $40 Billion*, Vox (May 19, 2022), https://www.vox.com/23125706/ukraine-aid-russia-invasion-us-40-billion (noting that the $40 billion approved in May 2022 comes in addition to an earlier $13.6 billion in emergency assistance to Ukraine).

[119] For a breakdown of total spending on "defense" in any given year, beyond the official Pentagon budget, *see* William Hartung, *The Trillion-Dollar National Security Budget*, TOMDISPATCH (July 25, 2017), https://tomdispatch.com/william-hartung-the-trillion-dollar-national-security-budget/.

[120] *Federal Spending: Where Does the Money Go*, NAT'L PRIORITIES PROJECT, https://www.nationalpriorities.org/budget-basics/federal-budget-101/spending/ (last visited June 22, 2022) (providing a breakdown of mandatory and discretionary spending by the federal government in 2021).

Though President Biden campaigned on a platform that promised to ease ra-cial divisions[121] and "end forever wars," he has presided over further increases of more than five percent in the Pentagon's regular budget, not including ad-ditional appropriations for Ukraine and other conflicts.[122] Though the chaotic 2021 withdrawal from Afghanistan was touted as fulfilling Biden's campaign pledge, the administration's decision to redeploy troops to Somalia in 2022 shows that the logic of forever wars remains alive and well.[123] Most Americans likely have no idea that Somalia and any number of other shadow wars continue to be fought under the Biden administration with U.S. forces deployed to Africa, the Middle East, and Asia to engage in drone strikes or other uses of force in the absence of any declared war, justifying the ongoing ratchet upward of defense spending with untold and uncounted civilian casualties.[124]

In many ways, Biden's increased military spending echoes his approach to domestic law enforcement. Elected president with the support of Black voters in the wake of the 2020 racial justice uprising, Biden used his 2022 State of the Union speech to issue a pointed rejection of demands to defund the po-lice, calling instead for bipartisan support to "fund them, fund them, fund them."[125] Indeed, Biden's budget priorities from re-funding law enforcement at home to ballooning military budgets abroad reflect unwavering bipartisan support for financing the ever-expanding American national security state, which has been a feature of American politics since the mid-20th century, and has grown with each successive administration from Bush to Obama to Trump to the present.[126]

---

[121] Steve Inskeep, *Biden Vows to Ease Racial Divisions. Here's His Record*, NPR (Oct. 14, 2020), https://www.npr.org/2020/10/14/920385802/biden-vows-to-ease-racial-divisions-heres-his-record.

[122] Shannon Bugos, *Biden Approves $29 Billion Increase in Defense Budget*, ARMS CONTROL ASS'N (Apr. 2022), https://www.armscontrol.org/act/2022-04/news/biden-approves-29-billion-increase-defense-budget (noting that Biden requested increases in defense spending and Congress approved even larger appropriations than the administration requested). The Biden administration has also requested and secured over $54 billion additional funding for military aid to Ukraine as of May 2022. Bianca Pallaro & Alicia Parlapiano, *Four Ways to Understand the $54 Billion in U.S. Spending on Ukraine*, N.Y. TIMES (May 20, 2022), https://www.nytimes.com/interactive/2022/05/20/upshot/ukra ine-us-aid-size.html.

[123] Samar Al-Bulushi, *Biden's Promise to End Endless War Hits a Snag in Somalia*, RESPONSIBLE STATECRAFT (May 17, 2022), https://responsiblestatecraft.org/2022/05/17/bidens-promise-to-end-endless-war-hits-a-snag-in-somalia/.

[124] Oliver Eagleton, *Don't Ignore Biden's Shadow War*, NOVARA MEDIA (June 2, 2022), https://nova ramedia.com/2022/06/02/dont-ignore-bidens-shadow-war/?s=09 (noting that Biden has "expanded the lethal architecture" of using drone strikes and special forces to kill "countless enemies in unde-clared war zones").

[125] *"Fund the Police" Biden Says at State of the Union*, PBS NEWSHOUR (Mar. 1, 2022), https://www. pbs.org/newshour/politics/watch-fund-the-police-biden-says-at-state-of-the-union.

[126] For an account of the trajectory of defense budgets from Bush through Biden, *see* LAWRENCE J. KORB & KAVEH TOOFAN, CTR. FOR AM. PROGRESS, AN OPPORTUNITY FOR CHANGE: PRESIDENT

In the years since the calls to defund the police echoed across American cities, those demands have been met with skepticism among liberals. Some argue that the slogan alienates voters,[127] others worry that increases in crime might be attributed to (largely unrealized) police budget cuts.[128] But a deeper criticism has been that "defund the police" strikes at the heart of municipal coffers on which local communities rely.[129] This insight ties directly back to the idea of a military-industrial-policing complex in that it posits that local economies—and, by extension when it comes to defense, the national economy—depend on the for-profit dimensions of policing and militarism. In other words, movements to defund the police and to shrink the defense budgets fed by American warcraft have to reckon with the political economy implications of their demands.

On the political side of the equation, there can be no doubt that powerful and politically well-connected industries profit directly from aggressive policing, growing incarceration rates and massive military spending.[130] Any effort to defund the police or shrink defense budgets must address pork-barrel politics and corporate lobbying. Appropriations are driven by congressional priorities that, in turn, reflect campaign spending by industries that benefit from police budgets, carceral expansion, and military expenditures, not to speak of the revolving door between elected office and the lobbying industry enriched by these campaign dollars.[131] Congressional

BIDEN'S FIRST DEFENSE BUDGET PROPOSAL (Mar. 10, 2021), https://www.americanprogress.org/arti
cle/opportunity-change-president-bidens-first-defense-budget-proposal/.

[127] Njeri Mathis Rutledge, *Obama Is Right About "Defund the Police." A Terrible Slogan Makes It Hard to Win Change*, USA TODAY (Dec. 7, 2020), https://www.usatoday.com/story/opinion/2020/12/07/obama-is-right-defund-police-damages-reform-progress-column/3850652001/.

[128] Peter Nickeas et al., *Defund the Police Encounters Resistance as Violent Crime Spikes*, CNN (May 25, 2021), https://www.cnn.com/2021/05/25/us/defund-police-crime-spike/index.html; *see also* David Klepper & Gary Fields, *Homicides up, but "Defunding the Police" Not to Blame*, CHI. TRIB. (June 10, 2021), https://www.chicagotribune.com/nation-world/ct-aud-nw-crime-spike-police-funding-20210610-graeysr24zapbkvpsbhvlfiakm-story.html.

[129] Nolan McCaskill, *"Defund the Police" Faces Skepticism—Even in Deeply Liberal Cities*, POLITICO (June 19, 2020), https://www.politico.com/news/2020/06/19/defund-the-police-movement-faces-skepticism-328084 (noting that defunding demands pit activists against left-leaning politicians in fights over city budgets).

[130] *See, e.g.*, Stephen Losey, *This Is How the Biggest Arms Manufacturers Steer Millions to Influence US Policy*, MILITARY.COM (Mar. 7, 2021), https://www.military.com/daily-news/2021/03/07/how-biggest-arms-manufacturers-steer-millions-influence-us-policy.html; Michael Cohen, *How For-Profit Prisons Have Become the Biggest Lobby No One Is Talking About*, WASH. POST (Apr. 28, 2015), https://www.washingtonpost.com/posteverything/wp/2015/04/28/how-for-profit-prisons-have-become-the-biggest-lobby-no-one-is-talking-about/.

[131] Chris Cillizza, *The Revolving Door Between Congress and K Street Is Moving Faster Than Ever*, WASH. POST (Jan. 22, 2014), https://www.washingtonpost.com/news/the-fix/wp/2014/01/22/the-revolving-door-between-congress-and-k-street-is-moving-faster-than-ever/.

capture by special interest groups[132] representing arms manufacturers, security contractors, and prison corporations is undeniable[133] and explains a decades-long secular trend of increasing defense and policing budgets.[134] Detaching elected officials from the special interest lobbyists that profit from bloated security budgets requires broad reforms to campaign funding and establishing ethical rules limiting the availability of lucrative private sector career paths for elected officials and their staff.[135]

On the strictly economic side of the equation, there are separate concerns about the communities that depend on private prisons and military bases to sustain local economies. Here, new research casts a different light on long-standing claims about rural America's dependence on prison industries.[136] Studies also suggest that conventional ideas of military Keynesianism, treating defense spending as a sort of jobs program, need updating.[137] Contrary to claims that public and private prison development constitutes one of the few economic development strategies available to small towns experiencing postindustrial disinvestment, recent studies suggest little to no positive economic benefit from prisons to the local communities around them.[138] Some studies report little discernible difference between rural

---

[132] For a general analysis of such capture and strategies to resist it, *see* CTR. FOR AM. PROGRESS, FIGHTING SPECIAL INTEREST LOBBYIST POWER OVER PUBLIC POLICY (Sept. 27, 2017), https://www.americanprogress.org/article/fighting-special-interest-lobbyist-power-public-policy/.

[133] Kimberly Leonard, *20 Members of Congress Personally Invest in Top Weapons Contractors That'll Profit from the Just-Passed $40 Billion Ukraine Aid Package*, BUS. INSIDER (May 19, 2022), https://www.businessinsider.com/congress-war-profiteers-stock-lockheed-martin-raytheon-investm ent-2022-3.

[134] Emily Badger & Quoctrung Bui, *Cities Grew Safer. Police Budgets Kept Growing*, N.Y. TIMES (June 12, 2020), https://www.nytimes.com/interactive/2020/06/12/upshot/cities-grew-safer-police-budgets-kept-growing.html; Lawrence Korb, Laura Conley & Alex Rothman, *A Historical Perspective on Defense Budgets*, CTR. FOR AM. PROGRESS (July 6, 2011), https://www.americanprogress.org/arti cle/a-historical-perspective-on-defense-budgets/ (noting massive growth of defense spending after the end of the Cold War).

[135] For concrete policy recommendations on how to reduce military budgets through campaign finance and ethics reforms, *see* WILLIAM D. HARTUNG, QUINCY INST. FOR RESPONSIBLE STATECRAFT, PATHWAYS TO PENTAGON SPENDING REDUCTIONS: REMOVING THE OBSTACLES, QUINCY BRIEF NO. 21 (Mar. 2022), https://quincyinst.org/report/pathways-to-pentagon-spending-reductions-remov ing-the-obstacles/.

[136] On the increasing placement of prisons in rural America as an economic development strategy, *see* John M. Eason, *Why Prison Building Will Continue Booming in Rural America*, CONVERSATION (Mar. 12, 2017), https://theconversation.com/why-prison-building-will-continue-booming-in-rural-america-71920.

[137] For a discussion of military Keynesianism, and the political economy of U.S. militarism more generally, *see* James M. Cypher, *The Political Economy of Systemic U.S. Militarism*, 73 MONTHLY REV. 23 (2022), https://monthlyreview.org/2022/04/01/the-political-economy-of-systemic-u-s-militar ism-2/.

[138] Keri Blakinger, *Small Towns Used to See Prisons as a Boon. Now, Many Don't Want Them*, NBC NEWS (June 10, 2021), https://www.nbcnews.com/news/us-news/small-towns-used-see-prisons-boon-now-many-don-t-n1270147 (noting that in one small town, prisons are now seen as "more

counties hosting prisons and those that do not in terms of employment for local residents.[139] Others suggest an initial positive effect on median home values and income, that plateaus or declines over time.[140]

At the same time, there have been numerous examples of economic re-development and investment in the wake of prison closures, ranging from repurposing facilities for community-centered public services to developing waterfront condos and office buildings to generate economic growth.[141] Projects along these lines suggest important strategies for how calls for defunding can emphasize the "invest-divest" strategy of shifting budgets away from prisons and aggressive policing precisely toward the kinds of urban redevelopment from which some towns have benefited in the wake of prison closures.[142]

Similar insights also attend to concerns about closing military bases or reduced job growth among employers like Raytheon or Lockheed Martin, tied to government spending on weapons industries. One extended study documents the aftermath of military base closures and finds that immediate term job losses are offset in the medium term when elected officials and civic leaders enter into partnerships with interested businesses and nonprofits to convert former defense facilities into new development projects.[143] Showcasing the ways that redevelopment schemes can restore local econ-omies and deliver benefits to renters, homeowners, students, and civilian businesses (and their employees) underscores, again, that with careful

---

burden than boon, adding to the city's court costs while doing little to help the town's economy grow").

[139] RYAN S. KING, MARC MAUER & TRACY HULING, SENTENCING PROJECT, BIG PRISONS, SMALL TOWNS: PRISON ECONOMICS IN RURAL AMERICA (Feb. 2003), https://www.sentencingproject.org/wp-content/uploads/2016/01/Big-Prisons-Small-Towns-Prison-Economics-in-Rural-America.pdf; JACOB KANG-BROWN & RAM SUBRAMANIAM, VERA INST. OF JUST., OUT OF SIGHT: THE GROWTH OF JAILS IN RURAL AMERICA (June 2017), https://www.vera.org/downloads/publications/out-of-sight-growth-of-jails-rural-america.pdf.

[140] See, e.g., KANG-BROWN & SUBRAMANIAM, supra note 139; John M. Eason, Understanding the Effects of the U.S. Prison Boom on Rural Communities, 35 IRP FOCUS 14 (2019), https://www.irp.wisc.edu/resource/understanding-the-effects-of-the-u-s-prison-boom-on-rural-communities/.

[141] NICOLE D. PORTER, THE SENTENCING PROJECT, POLICY BRIEF, REPURPOSING: NEW BEGINNINGS FOR CLOSED PRISONS (Dec. 14, 2016), https://www.sentencingproject.org/publications/repurposing-new-beginnings-closed-prisons/.

[142] For a statement of the "invest-divest" strategy articulated by the Movement for Black Lives, see Invest-Divest, supra note 96.

[143] MICHAEL TOUCHTON & AMANDA J. ASHLEY, SALVAGING COMMUNITY: HOW AMERICAN CITIES REBUILD CLOSED MILITARY BASES (2019) (surveying 122 base closures and offering three in-depth case studies from California, showing that "effective governance is a major factor in successful redevelopment").

design invest-divest strategies can successfully offset short-term economic dislocation.

Yet reinvesting funds that are diverted from military budgets to civilian uses cannot be limited to redevelopment at home. The United States has waged destructive military campaigns globally—cutting a swathe of devastation across the Muslim-majority world from Libya to Afghanistan in the last two decades alone—that also impose obligations of repair and rebuilding. The war in Ukraine produced calls for exactly the kinds of reparations that should be required of countries that engage in destructive and unprovoked military interventions against smaller states. The United States has led Western condemnations of Russia's aggressive war against Ukraine, rightly holding Moscow accountable for the destruction that it has wrought.[144] The sanctions and asset freezes imposed on Russia by Western powers as punishment for the invasion of Ukraine are unprecedented against such a large and globally integrated economy.[145] Moreover, U.S. officials are seriously debating using Russian sovereign assets held in Western banks—and now frozen—to rebuild Ukraine.[146] Such a move would set a powerful example that a state invading a smaller nation and destroying its civilian infrastructure should be on the hook to pay for reconstruction with its sovereign funds.

The insight that an invading country owes a debt of reparation is welcome, coming from American commentators especially. Indeed, the United States owes no less to civilians living in Afghanistan, Iraq, and Libya than to deploy its own resources to pay for rebuilding civilian infrastructure that the

---

[144] *Fact Sheet: Joined by Allies and Partners, the United States Imposes Devastating Costs on Russia*, WHITE HOUSE (Feb. 24, 2022), https://www.whitehouse.gov/briefing-room/statements-releases/2022/02/24/fact-sheet-joined-by-allies-and-partners-the-united-states-imposes-devastating-costs-on-russia/.

[145] *US Announces Sanctions Cutting Russia off from Western Financial Institutions*, RADIO FREE EUROPE/RADIO LIBERTY (Feb. 22, 2022), https://www.rferl.org/a/russia-ukraine-western-reaction-putin-united-nations/31715724.html; *The "Unprecedented" Sanctions on Russia Could Make War Unsustainable*, NPR (Feb. 27, 2022), https://www.npr.org/2022/02/27/1083379242/the-unprecedented-sanctions-on-russia-could-make-war-unsustainable-expert-says; Alan Rappeport, *U.S. Escalates Sanctions with a Freeze on Russian Central Bank Assets*, N.Y. TIMES (Feb. 28, 2022), https://www.nytimes.com/2022/02/28/us/politics/us-sanctions-russia-central-bank.html.

[146] Alan Rappeport & David E. Sanger, *Seizing Russian Assets to Help Ukraine Sets Off White House Debate*, N.Y. TIMES (May 31, 2022), https://www.nytimes.com/2022/05/31/us/politics/russia-sanctions-central-bank-assets.html. The argument is not only that Russian assets might be used to rebuild but even to fund current defense needs in Ukraine. *See, e.g.*, Laurence Tribe & Jeremy Lewin, Opinion, *$100 Billion. Russia's Treasure in the U.S. Should be Turned Against Putin*, N.Y. TIMES (Apr. 15, 2022), https://www.nytimes.com/2022/04/15/opinion/russia-war-currency-reserves.html; *but see* Paul Stephan, *Giving Russian Assets to Ukraine—Freezing Is Not Seizing*, LAWFARE (Apr. 26, 2022), https://www.lawfareblog.com/giving-russian-assets-ukraine-freezing-not-seizing (arguing that constitutional and international law constraints limit the ability of the United States to seize Russian sovereign assets).

aerial bombardment of these countries destroyed—everything from roads and bridges to electricity, water, as well as sanitation systems, hospitals, and schools. Moreover, instead of using reconstruction as an opportunity to funnel tax dollars to American security contractors, manufacturers, and construction firms—the form of corporate welfare facilitated by past United States spending in Iraq and Afghanistan[147]—the funding should go to local businesses and contractors to rebuild their own devastated cities. Just as Moscow would not be allowed to use Ukraine reparations to bankroll its own industries, so too the United States must invest in rebuilding infrastructure by supporting local industries in countries laid waste by military interventionism.

Making a case for defunding the police and using budget differentials to invest in local communities has proven challenging over the last two years.[148] An argument to scale back military spending in order, at least in part, to honor overseas obligations to civilians devastated by American war-making is an even more difficult political lift, especially at a time of heightened polarization and jingoism. If self-interested demands to promote global vaccine equity to prevent new variants emerging in the Global South and circulating back to the United States gained little traction,[149] what prospect is there for a broader case to invest in far-flung communities devastated by U.S. airstrikes and drone programs? Still, given the porous borders between racialized violence at home and abroad, reforming brutal policing requires nothing less than tackling the broader security state and extending the logic of the defund platform—and its reinvestment priorities—to America's endless wars.

---

[147] On wasteful U.S. spending and misallocation of taxpayer dollars for "Afghanistan reconstruction," *see* SPECIAL INSPECTOR GENERAL FOR AFGHANISTAN RECONSTRUCTION, WHAT WE NEED TO LEARN: LESSONS FROM TWENTY YEARS OF AFGHANISTAN RECONSTRUCTION (Aug. 2021), https://www.sigar.mil/pdf/lessonslearned/SIGAR-21-46-LL.pdf; *see also* Derek Paulhus, *Waste, Greed and Fraud: The Business that Makes the World's Greatest Army*, HARV. POL. REV., https://iop.harvard.edu/get-involved/harvard-political-review/waste-greed-and-fraud-business-makes-world%E2%80%99s-greatest-army (last visited June 22, 2022).

[148] *See, e.g.*, Janae Bowens & John Seward, *Some Cities Working to "Re-fund" Police*, ABC7 NEWS (Nov. 19, 2021), https://wjla.com/news/nation-world/fact-check-team-some-cities-working-to-re-fund-police.

[149] *See, e.g.*, Stephanie Desmon, *Without Global Vaccinations Further Variants Ahead*, JOHNS HOPKINS U. HUB (Dec. 21, 2021), https://hub.jhu.edu/2021/12/21/global-vaccination-prevents-variants-durbin-moss/.

Dismantling America's Security State

The American security state encompasses everything from the domestic law enforcement and border policing apparatus of the DHS to the enormous defense budgets allocated to the Pentagon. The racial justice protests of 2020 gave new momentum to political organizing and advocacy focused on the highly visible domestic face of this sprawling security architecture. The uprising amplified demands that emerged from decades of Black-led mass struggle and organizing against the policing-and-prison-industrial prong of a broader complex. But equally, Trump's brutal response to the protests made visible relationships that are usually obscured from public view, between policing, border enforcement, and American militarism.

The clarity of Trump's coercive instincts brought millions to the streets and heightened the profile of the abolitionist movement aimed at ending incarceration and policing "in favor of a society grounded in collective care and social provision."[150] The activists articulating demands to "defund" understood that the causes of racial violence cannot be explained by abuses or excesses committed by particular officers, but lie instead in the institution of policing itself and the systems of criminal justice and incarceration connected to it. Moreover, the long-standing struggles against prisons and policing that came to the fore in 2020 had deep ties to movements to end violent border policing and immigration detention.[151] Trump's demands that the military intervene to suppress protests in American cities inadvertently illustrated how institutions and practices of racialized violence at home are connected to the aerial bombardment campaigns, extrajudicial (drone) killings, and indefinite detentions that are the hallmarks of the overseas military engagements of the American security state.

In the words of Portland Mayor Ted Wheeler, the actions of federal agents in that city in 2020 amounted to "urban warfare."[152] Policing at home and America's military engagements abroad are two faces of the same coin.

---

[150] Amna A. Akbar, *How Defund and Disband Became the Demands*, N.Y. REV. (June 15, 2020), https://www.nybooks.com/daily/2020/06/15/how-defund-and-disband-became-the-demands/.

[151] *See, e.g.*, Chishti & Bolter, *supra* note 109; Beth Hallowell, *How to Talk About Defunding ICE and CBP—And Investing in Communities*, AM. FRIENDS SERV. COMM. BLOG (Mar. 30, 2021), https://www.afsc.org/blogs/news-and-commentary/how-to-talk-about-defunding-ice-and-cbp-and-investing-communities; DETENTION WATCH NETWORK, DEFUND RACIST LAW ENFORCEMENT: POLICE, ICE AND CBP, https://www.detentionwatchnetwork.org/sites/default/files/Defund%20Police%2C%20ICE%2C%20%26%20CBP_DWN%20%26%20UWD_2020.pdf (last visited June 22, 2022).

[152] Mike Baker, *Federal Agents Envelop Portland Protest, and City's Mayor, in Tear Gas*, N.Y. TIMES (July 23, 2020), https://www.nytimes.com/2020/07/23/us/portland-protest-tear-gas-mayor.html.

Protests against police violence called out one important facet of the coercive apparatus of the state. And, in doing so, they drew attention to how the tactics, weapons, and training employed to suppress resistance abroad may also be deployed against protesters in America's cities.[153]

Dismantling the structures of racist policing at home requires recognizing this continuum of security state violence that connects domestic policing, border enforcement, and America's ever-expanding military footprint abroad.[154] In short, national debates about divestment from militarized policing must connect arguments about defunding the police to a transformative vision for the sprawling security state as a whole, one that disrupts practices of racialized violence and advances a vision of racial justice at home and abroad.[155] An advocacy strategy that connects investment in communities at home to global reparative justice is no doubt a daunting political challenge. But so long as America's security state comprises forms of racialized violence that connect the local to the global, opposition strategies, too, must address the deep connections between policing, border enforcement, and military deployments to do justice to the eloquent demands that radiated from Minneapolis across the world in 2020.

[153] Shirley Li, *The Evolution of Police Militarization in Ferguson and Beyond*, ATLANTIC (Aug. 2, 2014), https://www.theatlantic.com/national/archive/2014/08/the-evolution-of-police-militarization-in-ferguson-and-beyond/376107/.

[154] Paul K. MacDonald & Joseph M. Parent, *Trump Didn't Shrink U.S. Military Commitments Abroad—He Expanded Them*, FOREIGN AFFS. (Dec. 3, 2019); Jeremy Scahill, *Biden to Pentagon: Keep the War Machine Running*, INTERCEPT (Dec. 2, 2021), https://theintercept.com/2021/12/02/biden-military-deployment-global-footprint/.

[155] Aziz Rana, *Against National Security Citizenship*, BOS. REV. (Feb. 7, 2018), https://bostonreview.net/articles/aziz-rana-against-national-security-citizenship/.

9

Extrajudicial Executions from the United States to Palestine

Noura Erakat

Introduction

On June 23, 2020, an Israeli soldier shot dead Ahmad Erekat, my twenty-seven-year-old cousin, at a military checkpoint.[1] He was driving a Hyundai, which he rented to run errands for his sister's wedding. He had just picked up his mama from a salon and was driving from his village of Abu Dis, an East Jerusalem suburb cut off from the metropole by Israel's separation barrier, to Bethlehem, another Palestinian city. Dividing the two Palestinian areas is a notorious checkpoint known as the "Container," one of 705 road obstacles throughout the West Bank.[2] The checkpoints are an invention of the Oslo Peace Process, imagined as temporary and necessary features to facilitate the incremental transfer of authority from Israel to the Palestinians.[3] Instead, like Israel's settlements, the checkpoints have multiplied and evolved into a permanent feature of Palestinian life. The Container checkpoint separates two Palestinian areas, severely limiting the movement of Palestinians and undermining their potential for economic, social, and political development.

As the Israeli soldier waved for Ahmad to approach the kiosk, Ahmad's car seemed to veer out of control. Released video footage shows the car moving

[1] Letter from Al Haq et al. to U.N. Special Procedures, Joint Urgent Appeal to the United Nations Special Procedures on the Extrajudicial Execution and Wilful Killing of Ahmad Erekat by the Israeli Occupying Forces on 23 June 2020 (July 13, 2020), https://www.alhaq.org/cached_uploads/downl oad/2020/07/14/joint-urgent-appeal-to-un-special-procedures-on-the-killing-of-ahmad-erekat-final-1594706298.pdf.

[2] U.N. Off. for the Coordination of Humanitarian Aff., Over 700 Road Obstacles Control Palestinian Movement Within the West Bank, Humanitarian Bull. Occupied Palestinian Territory 11–17 (Sept. 2018), https://www.ochaopt.org/sites/default/files/hummon itor_september_2018.pdf.

[3] Rawan Damen, *The Price of Oslo*, Al Jazeera, https://interactive.aljazeera.com/aje/palestinere mix/the-price-of-oslo.html#/14.

Noura Erakat, *Extrajudicial Executions from the United States to Palestine* In: *Race and National Security*. Edited by: Matiangai V.S. Sirleaf, Oxford University Press. © Oxford University Press 2023. DOI: 10.1093/oso/9780197754641.003.0010

slowly at first and then jerking forward into the kiosk where four armed Israeli soldiers stood.[4] The impact of the collision knocks a soldier to the ground but causes no serious injuries; the soldier jumps back onto her feet in time to witness her fellow soldier shoot multiple rounds of live ammunition into Ahmad's unarmed body. Seemingly terrified by the accident, Ahmad attempts to get out of the car and to raise his arms above his head. The soldier shoots him before his elbows reach his ears. Ahmad then crumbled onto the asphalt where he writhed in pain and bled out for over an hour. An Israeli ambulance arrived on the scene within ten minutes to treat the Israeli soldier but refused to medically assist Ahmad. The soldiers also refused access to a Palestinian ambulance. Ahmad's father, Mustafa, arrived at the scene and begged to approach his son, but the Israeli officers instead forced Mustafa to watch his son bleed to death.

Israel's army spokesperson immediately declared Ahmad a "terrorist," the accident an attempted car-ramming, and Ahmad's killing a justified use of force.[5] The state has refused to conduct an investigation or permit an international one. It has refused to conduct an autopsy. It has refused to study the car's black box for malfunction or related *Consumer Reports* recounting numerous complaints of Hyundai vehicles losing control since 2012.[6] Moreover, the state has refused to interview Palestinian witnesses. It has also refused to consider that Ahmad, who was to be married that summer and who was preparing for his sister's wedding that day, had every reason to live.

Eight months after the fatal incident, Forensic Architecture, together with Al Haq, a research agency that studies human rights violations and a Palestinian human rights organization, completed an independent investigation of the incident. Using security videos, 3D imaging, and witness testimony, the organizations concluded that two soldiers shot Ahmad six times above the waist in two seconds, that Ahmad was likely decelerating his vehicle and attempting to course-correct away from the checkpoint booth. This investigation trumps all state's allegations and highlights its intransigent refusal to allow for a more thorough investigation. Significantly, it also reflects a broader context of a lack of accountability (i.e., failure to investigate

---

[4] Noura Erakat (@4noura), TWITTER (June 26, 2020, 1:55 PM), https://twitter.com/4noura/status/1276574917807439877?lang=en.

[5] Micky Rosenfeld (@MickyRosenfeld), TWITTER (June 23, 2020, 12:57 PM), https://twitter.com/MickyRosenfeld/status/1275473082786947074.

[6] Amy Martyn, *Deadly Car Crash Video Captures Possible Unintended Acceleration of Hyundai in Korea*, CONSUMER AFFS. (Nov. 10, 2016), https://www.consumeraffairs.com/news/deadly-car-crash-video-captures-possible-unintended-acceleration-of-hyundai-in-korea-111016.html.

incidents, denial of autopsies, refusal to release bodies for burial). Still and nonetheless, the narrative that Ahmad was a would-be terrorist persists.[7] Further, as a form of collective punishment, Israel continues to hold Ahmad's body hostage in the Greenberg Forensic Institute, an affiliate of Tel Aviv University, denying the family the dignity of burying their beloved son and beginning to heal what cannot possibly be healed.[8]

Upon the spread of Ahmad's story, I received dozens of calls and messages encouraging me to draw parallels between Ahmad's callous killing and the systematic killing of Black people with impunity in the United States: "They left him out to bleed with his parent watching like they did to Mike Brown." "They blamed him for his death like they did with Freddie Gray." "There's no accountability for his killing like there hasn't been for Breonna Taylor [or Tony McDade or Sandra Bland or Philando Castile or . . .]." "Tell them Palestinian lives matter."

Ahmad was killed during one of the most significant and ongoing uprisings in United States history. The recent Black Lives Matter demonstrations, precipitated by the confluence of COVID-19's disproportionate impact on Black communities, together with the grotesque killings of Black people— epitomized by the murder of George Floyd—centered concepts like defunding the police in a matter of weeks and catalyzed a generational shift in public consciousness regarding structural racism. Sympathetic friends and allies implored me to appeal to the fresh and fertile consciousness of indignant and antiracist Americans so that they could better understand the injustice of Ahmad's killing, indeed, the injustice of the Palestinian condition.

While I understood the impulse to use the parallels to illuminate the nature of the Palestinian question and have myself been a part of contemporary renewals of Black-Palestinian Solidarity, I hesitated to make the comparison publicly.[9] In part, I refrained because being in ethical solidarity means not inadvertently decentering the much-needed and overdue conversations about

---

[7] *The Extrajudicial Execution of Ahmad Erekat*, FORENSIC ARCHITECTURE, https://forensic-archi tecture.org/investigation/the-extrajudicial-execution-of-ahmad-erekat (last visited May 2, 2022).

[8] *Boycott and Cut All Ties with Tel Aviv University and the Greenberg Institute until Ahmed and Other Detained Palestinian Bodies Are Freed, Without Stipulation, to Their Families and Loved Ones for Burial*, AVAAZ, https://secure.avaaz.org/community_petitions/en/to_princeton_university_ cfaculty_universities_and__boycott_and_cut_ties_with_tel_aviv_university_the_greenberg_i nstitute_until_ahmed_and_ot/ (last updated July 1, 2020) (community petition begun by The B to "Princeton University, Columbia University, Swarthmore University, and all faculty, universities, and all honourable people around the world").

[9] Noura Erakat, *Geographies of Intimacy: Contemporary Renewals of Black-Palestinian Solidarity*, 72 AM. Q. 471 (2020).

anti-Black racism in the United States.[10] I also did not want to flatten the unique contexts that shaped Black and Palestinian lives into mere spectacles of violence. The differences between these two contexts are generative and precisely what have, historically and currently, animated transnational solidarity.

As many analysts have highlighted, solidarity does not mean sameness, and this is apt regarding Black-Palestinian solidarity. There are critical differences between the Black American freedom struggle and the Palestinian freedom struggle. The condition of Black unfreedom in the United States now spans some 350 years, including over a century of chattel slavery as well as its after-life since abolition. Generations of Black Americans have fought to dismantle de jure segregation and subordination, and some important civil rights have been achieved. The United States has failed to reckon with White supremacy as a central organizing principle of government that is predicated upon anti-Blackness and Native land expropriation.[11] The belated recognition of Black citizenship, the right to vote, and the symbolism of a Black president does not change this reality. In contrast, the Palestinian struggle for freedom is only a little over a century old, since 1917, when the British Empire designated the territory as a site of Jewish settlement. The native Palestinians, then 95 percent of the whole, who claimed sovereignty and sought self-determination, threatened Zionist settler sovereignty and have thus been marked for removal. Israel, with the support of British and American imperial patronage, steadily expanded its territorial takings in pursuit of its settler colonial ambitions. Sameness does not sustain Black-Palestinian solidarity and, yet, it has re-emerged as a powerful movement and analytical framework since the 2014 Gaza-Ferguson moment.[12]

Black-Palestinian solidarity helps pierce a formidable national security framework cloaking Palestinian life and reveals the racial nature of the Palestinian struggle. It also disrupts American exceptionalism, which insists that the United States is an imperfect democracy on the steady course of achieving its full potential and brings into acute view the anticolonial nature of the Black freedom struggle in the United States. Black Palestinian

---

[10] Kristian Davis Bailey, *How Palestine Advocates can Support Black Struggle*, ELECTR. INTIFADA (June 19, 2020), https://electronicintifada.net/content/how-palestine-advocates-can-support-black-struggle/30501.

[11] *See* Nikhil Pal Singh, *Universalizing Settler Liberty: An Interview with Aziz Rana*, JACOBIN (Aug. 4, 2014), https://www.jacobinmag.com/2014/08/the-legacies-of-settler-empire/.

[12] Kristian Davis Bailey, *Black-Palestinian Solidarity in the Ferguson—Gaza Era*, 67 AM. Q. 1017 (2015).

solidarity thus illuminates the co-constitutive nature of racism and colonialism and urges not only democratization of the colony but decolonization.

Black-Palestinian solidarity offers an analytical framework regarding
imperialism that helps deconstruct specific United States and Israeli policy
choices predicated on wholesale dehumanization along racialized lines.
Within this frame, we can examine how Israel's shoot-to-kill policy reflects a
racial regime designating Palestinians as always a threat and presumptively
guilty within the language of the law. It also centers an internationalist approach that situates Black subjugation within global regimes of capital, violence, and governance to help explain the militarized response to Black
uprisings and, particularly, the significance of U.S. law enforcement trainings
in Israel. I turn to these questions in the following sections.

Shoot-To-Kill: The Shrinking Civilian and
the Always-Already-Guilty

Today, Israel defends Ahmad's killing and claims the right to use similar
force again because it does not consider that Ahmad's car accident could
have been a human or mechanical error. Like nearly all other Palestinians,
he was considered always—"already-guilty." Ahmad was the twenty-third
Palestinian to be killed by Israeli forces in 2020 and the sixty-third to be held
hostage after death.[13] At the time of his killing, he was the latest casualty of
Israel's shoot-to-kill policy, which sanctions the extrajudicial execution of
Palestinians perceived as threats.[14] The policy is accompanied by a lack of
accountability, which underscores an environment of impunity for state violence. While the shoot-to-kill policy appears as an unchecked and lawless
use of force, Israel has attempted to justify it under the laws of armed conflict.

Beginning in 2000 during the Second Intifada (a militarized Palestinian
uprising against the Israeli occupation), Israel began to develop legal technologies that would allow it to use greater military force against the population it occupied. The legal advisers to the army innovated a new category

---

[13] U.N. OFF. FOR THE COORDINATION OF HUMANITARIAN AFFS., PROTECTION OF CIVILIANS
OCCUPIED PALESTINIAN TERRITORY REPORT, 14–27 JULY 2020 (July 30, 2020), https://www.ochaopt.
org/poc/14-27-july-2020.
[14] Harriet Agerholm, *Israeli Officials Back Shoot-to-Kill Policy of Palestinian Suspects, says Human
Rights Watch*, INDEPENDENT (Jan. 2, 2017, 4:39 PM) https://www.independent.co.uk/news/world/
middle-east/israel-shoot-to-kill-policy-palestinian-suspects-human-rights-watch-idf-soldiers-
west-bank-gaza-a7505486.html.

of armed conflict, "armed conflict short of war," that allowed the army to use military force against a population that could not legally fight back.[15] Deliberately evading available legal regulations offered by the First and Second Additional Protocols to the Geneva Conventions because of Israel's outstanding refusal to become a party to the treaties. The Israeli advisers argued that the conditions of resistance that they faced were sui generis, giving them the latitude to create new law where they insisted none existed.[16] The novel framework permitted Israel to use preventative force to extrajudicially execute suspected or would-be assailants in what would later become widely known as "targeted killings" in national security circles.

A cornerstone of Israel's legal technology has been what I call the "shrinking civilian": the steady and shrinking scope of Palestinians recognized as civilians entitled to immunity from attack.[17] The "shrinking civilian" framework has enabled Israeli law enforcement officers and soldiers to use excessive and disproportionate force against Palestinians as a matter of law and policy.

The "shrinking civilian" is predicated on the thorough racialization of Palestinians as innately dangerous subjects. Racial ideologies, reflecting settler-colonial desires to remove and replace the native population, render Palestinian bodies unwanted and sanction their killing with impunity. The native population is constructed as inherently "terrorist," presumed guilty by virtue of its refusal to disappear. Thus, Palestinians are racialized as dangerous not because of how they may individually harm Israelis but because their national existence challenges Israel's settler sovereignty (consider, for example, how the right of return of Palestinian refugees is constructed as an existential crisis for Israel).[18]

---

[15] NOURA ERAKAT, JUSTICE FOR SOME: LAW AND THE QUESTION OF PALESTINE 179–83 (2019); State of Israel to U.N. High Commissioner for Human Rights, *The Response of the Government of the State of Israel to the Report of the UN High Commissioners on Human Rights*, ¶ 28, ¶ 75 U.N. Doc. E/CN.4/2001/114 (Nov. 29, 2000) U.N. Econ. & Soc. Council, Comm. on Human Rights, *Report of the United National High Commissioner for Human Rights and Follow-up to the World Conference on Human Rights, Question of the Violation of Human Rights in the Occupied Arab Territories, Including Palestine*, U.N. Doc. E/CN.4/2001/133 (Feb. 23, 2001), https://digitallibrary.un.org/record/434 968?ln=en.

[16] *Protocols I and II additional to the Geneva Conventions*, INT'L COMM. RED CROSS (Jan. 1, 2009), https://www.icrc.org/en/doc/resources/documents/misc/additional-protocols-1977.htm.

[17] Noura Erakat, *The Sovereign Right to Kill: A Critical Appraisal of Israel's Shoot-to-Kill Policy in Gaza*, 19 INT'L CRIM. L. REV. 783 (2019).

[18] *Palestinian Refugees: The "Right of Return"—A Plot to Destroy the Jewish State*, JEWISH VIRTUAL LIBR., https://www.jewishvirtuallibrary.org/the-quot-right-of-return-quot-a-plot-to-destroy-the-jewish-state (last visited May 2, 2022).

While Israel has used security frameworks—drawn from law enforcement and armed hostilities paradigms—to justify its shoot-to-kill policy, Israel's right to kill is better understood as a form of settler-colonial eliminatory violence. This logic of collective punishment and violence as a defensive force even in cases where Palestinians have posed no military threat, undergirded Israel's military strategy in the founding years of the state and continues to shape its use of force in the present. Consider that upon its establishment, Israel adopted Mandatory Britain's emergency regulations and applied them to the Palestinians who remained in the new state. Upon a military commission finding that the Palestinians posed no threat, founding Prime Minister David Ben Gurion maintained that the martial law regime against the native population was necessary to expand Jewish-Zionist settlement.[19] The martial regime lasted for eighteen years, and the emergency regime is still in place.

The "shrinking civilian" was initially developed within an armed hostilities framework. It is constituted of several amendments to laws of armed conflict regarding distinction and proportionality. Notably, in a 2005 Israeli High Court decision, *Public Committee Against Torture in Israel v. the Government of Israel*, the judicial panel concluded that a civilian who takes up arms retains a continuous combat function as a result of membership, thus mitigating, if not eliminating, the temporal scope of imminence necessary to justify the use of lethal force. The impact has been to render greater numbers of Palestinians as legitimate targets in warfare even when they are idle, which has also expanded the scope of harm to surrounding civilians and civilian infrastructure in the language of the law.[20]

In September 2015, during the height of sporadic attacks by Palestinians using knives and other makeshift weapons, the Israeli government amended the rules of engagement regulating police force and further truncated who counts as a Palestinian civilian during peacetime. The amendments blurred the line between armed conflict, law enforcement, and the regulation of Palestinian existence and permitted officers to use lethal force as a measure of first resort against Palestinians for the sake of "prevent[ing] endangerment."[21] As a preventative measure, a Palestinian who "is about to throw a firebomb" or "about to shoot fireworks" or is "stone throwing using

---

[19] SHIRA ROBINSON, CITIZEN STRANGERS: PALESTINIANS AND THE BIRTH OF ISRAEL'S LIBERAL SETTLER STATE (2013).

[20] Erakat, *supra* note 17.

[21] *Extra-judicial Executions of Palestinians by Israel Police and Security Forces and the Failure to Investigate these Events*, ADALAH, https://www.adalah.org/uploads/uploads/Adalah_EJEs_Briefing_Paper_Updated_14Mar2017.pdf (last updated Mar. 14, 2017).

a slingshot" is presumably a legitimate target. Such a standard is, by definition, deferential to the subjective assessment of the shooting officer. Indeed, Adalah, the Legal Center for Arab Minority Rights, has shown that the Police Investigation Unit within the Israeli Ministry of Justice has refused to investigate nearly all complaints against the police.[22]

In 2016, following the relaxation of the rules of engagement, Israeli forces lethally shot ninety-seven Palestinians, including thirty-six children. Though Israel labeled the incidents as "alleged stabbings," the Palestinian Center for Human Rights found that in ninety-five out of the ninety-seven documented killings, there was evidence showing that the victims lacked the means to carry out a lethal attack.[23] In May 2016, the United Nations Committee Against Torture condemned Israel's revised rules of engagement as inconsistent with the Convention and other international standards.[24] In 2017, the Human Rights Council confirmed that Israel often used lethal force against Palestinians "on mere suspicion or as a precautionary measure."[25] Still, according to Human Rights Watch, senior Israeli officials not only condoned the policy but "have been encouraging Israeli soldiers and police to kill Palestinians they suspect of attacking Israelis even when they are no longer a threat."[26]

In 2018, the Israeli High Court of Justice had a chance to review Israel's shoot-to-kill policy as it was being used to suppress popular protests in the Gaza Strip, known as the "Great March of Return." As the death toll mounted and indicated the widespread use of indiscriminate lethal force by sniper fire—over 95 percent of casualties were shot above the waist, including in the back as they fled[27]—Israeli human rights organizations petitioned the High Court to restrain the military.[28] They argued that lethal force should be used as a last resort against the protests, which were civilian in nature.

[22] *Id.*

[23] PALESTINIAN CTR. FOR HUMAN RIGHTS, PCHR ANNUAL REPORT 2016 (2016), https://pchrgaza.org/en/wp-content/uploads/2017/06/PCHR-Annual_2016.pdf.

[24] Convention against Torture and Other Cruel, Inhuman or Degrading Treatment or Punishment, Dec. 10, 1984 1465 U.N.T.S. 85, 113; S. Treaty Doc. No. 100-20 (1988); 23 I.L.M. 1027 (1984).

[25] U.N. High Commissioner for Human Rights, *Implementation of Human Rights Council Resolutions S-9/1 and S-12/1*, UNGA, U.N. Doc. A/HRC/34/36 (Jan. 25, 2017).

[26] *Israel/Palestine: Some Officials Backing "Shoot-to-Kill,"* HUM. RTS. WATCH (Jan. 2, 2017, 12:00 AM), https://www.hrw.org/news/2017/01/02/israel/palestine-some-officials-backing-shoot-kill.

[27] Ahmad Nafi & Chloé Benoist, *Gaza: The Palestinians Who Died During the Great March of Return*, MIDDLE EAST EYE (Dec. 28, 2018, 1:35 PM), http://www.middleeasteye.net/news/gaza-palestinians-who-died-during-great-march-return?fbclid=IwAR3afQjnSqRjash5Lajs3ofD_ecN3O2qrUPnF6nfX5V9WqZhEUhSnCZHmo4.

[28] Yahil Shereshevsky, *HCJ 3003/18 Yesh Din—Volunteers for Human Rights v. Chief of General Staff, Israel Defense Forces (IDF)*, 113 AM. J. INT'L L. 361, 368 (2019).

The High Court accepted the government's arguments that the protests were organized by Hamas and constituted a "new tactic in the struggle against Israel."[29] It found that law enforcement and hostilities paradigms are interchangeable, and the appropriate use of force is subject to the discretion of military officers. Its finding of a security threat to Israel was largely hypothetical and based on the *possibility* of a threat emerging, thus permitting lethal use of force as a preventative measure. The Court's acceptance of the state's argument that Hamas led the protests overdetermined its conclusions and foreclosed the possibility of Palestinian civilian protests.

The Court conceded the participation of Palestinian civilians but only as a matter of exception. In effect, the Court expanded the scope of the "shrinking civilian," which has made otherwise disproportionate and excessive use of force permissible within the language of law. Between March and October 2018, Israel killed 217 Palestinians, including forty children, and injured 22,897; Palestinians killed one Israeli soldier.[30] Notably, only one soldier was convicted for killing an unarmed Palestinian boy and was sentenced to one month in military prison.[31]

"Black Is a Country": Black Internationalists Resist the U.S.'s "Internal Colony"

The enduring prevalence of extrajudicial executions of Black people in the United States has recently been a catalyzing force of mass protests since a deputized civilian killed Trayvon Martin in 2012. Martin was among 313 Black people killed by police, security guards, and vigilantes with impunity that year; his killing continued an American legacy.[32] The Malcolm X Grassroots Movement explains that such killings are "an integral part of the government's current overall strategy of containing the Black community

---

[29] *Id.*

[30] U.N. Off. for the Coordination of Humanitarian Affs., Humanitarian Snapshot: Casualties in the Context of Demonstrations and Hostilities in Gaza, 30 March–18 October 2018 (Oct. 18, 2018), https://www.ochaopt.org/content/humanitarian-snapshot-casualties-context-demonstrations-and-hostilities-gaza-30-march-18.

[31] David M. Halbfinger, *Israeli Soldier Gets One-Month Sentence over Killing of Gaza Teenager*, N.Y. Times (Oct. 30, 2019), https://www.nytimes.com/2019/10/30/world/middleeast/othman-helles-killing-israel-soldier.html.

[32] Operation Ghetto Storm, 2012 Annual Report on the Extrajudicial Killings of 313 Black People by Police, Security Guards and Vigilantes 3, 30 (updated ed. 2014), http://www.operationghettostorm.org/uploads/1/9/1/1/19110795/new_all_14_11_04.pdf.

in a state of perpetual colonial subjugation and exploitation."[33] Indeed, the Equal Justice Institute found that in the seventy-three years between 1877—the end of Reconstruction—and 1950, at least 4,084 Black people were lynched across twelve southern states alone.[34] The Institute explains that historically, "racial terror lynchings" were used as a form of collective punishment to enforce a rigid and hierarchal racial order aimed at preserving White supremacy. After the Second World War, police officers, originally mandated to kidnap runaway slaves (deemed "criminal" fugitives) and to quell slave rebellions, took on the primary role of enforcing that order.[35]

In its 1951 submission charging the United States with the crime of genocide, the Civil Rights Congress explained: "Once the classic method of lynching was the rope. Now it is the policeman's bullet."[36] Among the litany of incidents that the petition documents is the story of seventy-year-old Nicey Brown, who was beaten to death by a drunken police officer in Selma, Alabama, in 1945. The policeman's attorney appealed to the sensibilities of the all-White jury, warning them, "[i]f we convict this brave man who is upholding the banner of [W]hite supremacy by his actions, then we may as well give all our guns to the n—s and let them run the black belt."[37] The jury deliberated for a few minutes and then acquitted the officer.

This case was not about "qualified immunity"—the officer was drunk and off-duty when he bludgeoned Brown to death. Instead, it was about protecting the value of Whiteness, defined in an oppositional relationship to the devaluation of Blackness, as well as the negation and erasure of Indigenous sovereignty.[38] Defined as a property value, Whiteness can be understood as the right to ownership—of land, self, and country. Race can thus be understood as "colonialism speaking," a technology invented to ensure the externality of racialized subjects from the national body politic and their geographic separation and containment.[39]

---

[33] Id. at 3.

[34] EQUAL JUSTICE INITIATIVE, LYNCHING IN AMERICA: CONFRONTING THE LEGACY OF RACIAL TERROR (3d ed. 2017), https://lynchinginamerica.eji.org/report/.

[35] Joint Statement, Am. Civil Liberties Union, to the Forty-Third Session of the Human Rights Council, Urgent Debate on "The Current Racially Inspired Human Rights Violations, Systemic Racism, Police Brutality and the Violence Against Peaceful Protest" (June 17, 2020), https://www.aclu.org/hearing-statement/joint-statement-urgent-debate-current-racially-inspired-human-rights-violations.

[36] CIVIL RIGHTS CONGRESS, WE CHARGE GENOCIDE: THE HISTORIC PETITION TO THE UNITED NATIONS FOR RELIEF FROM A CRIME OF THE UNITED STATES GOVERNMENT AGAINST THE NEGRO PEOPLE 8 (1951).

[37] Id. at 60.

[38] Cheryl I. Harris, Whiteness as Property, 106 HARV. L. REV. 1710, 1792 (1993).

[39] PATRICK WOLFE, TRACES OF HISTORY: ELEMENTARY STRUCTURES OF RACE 117 (2016).

In its turn to the United Nations demanding accountability for genocide, the Civil Rights Congress furthered the understanding of White supremacy as "a matter of concern for mankind everywhere" and continued the Black internationalist tradition.[40] Black internationalists in the United States conceive of themselves as an "internal colony"[41] whose conditions and futures mirrored other colonized peoples.[42] These conditions, aimed at limiting Black life in the United States, include ghettoization, exclusion from gainful employment, medical experimentation, forced sterilization, exclusion from quality housing, lack of access to quality healthcare, education, and credit, and the systematic taking of life with impunity. The criminal legal system— featuring over-policing, racial profiling, selective enforcement, mass incarceration, disproportionate sentencing, lack of adequate representation, and hypersurveillance—works both to make Black people vulnerable to exploitative deprivation as well as to protect those takings for the enrichment of a White racial class in the United States. Similar to historic slave patrols, police and policing today is merely the enforcement arm of a settler-colonial political economy.

As explained by James Baldwin in 1966, "the police are simply the hired enemies of this population. They are present to keep the Negro in his place and to protect [W]hite business interests, and they have no other function."[43] Baldwin's understanding of the police as an exogenous enemy apparatus also explains their systematic and disproportionate use of force against Black protesters. "Occupied territory is occupied territory," he writes, "and it is axiomatic, in occupied territory, that any act of resistance, even though it be executed by a child, be answered at once, and with the full weight of the occupying forces." Indeed, Black protest in the United States has historically been treated like an insurgency and reflects the steady militarization of police in the 20th century.[44]

---

[40] CIVIL RIGHTS CONGRESS, *supra* note 36, at xii; ROBIN D.G. KELLEY, FREEDOM DREAMS: THE BLACK RADICAL IMAGINATION (2003).

[41] Joan Goldsworthy, *Baraka, Amiri 1934–*, ENCYCLOPEDIA.CÓM, https://www.encyclopedia.com/education/news-wires-white-papers-and-books/baraka-amiri-1934 (last visited May 3, 2022) (entry reproduced from CONTEMPORARY BLACK BIOGRAPHY (Ashyia N. Henderson ed., 2016) (noting that Baraka ridiculed the notion of a separate Black society in his essay "Black Is a Country").

[42] NIKHIL PAL SINGH, BLACK IS A COUNTRY: RACE AND THE UNFINISHED STRUGGLE FOR DEMOCRACY (2005).

[43] James Baldwin, *A Report from Occupied Territory*, THE NATION (July 11, 1966), https://www.thenation.com/article/culture/report-occupied-territory/.

[44] Dia Kayyali, *The History of Surveillance and the Black Community*, EFF.ORG (Feb. 13, 2014), https://www.eff.org/deeplinks/2014/02/history-surveillance-and-black-community; Gene Demby, *I'm From Philly. 30 Years Later, I'm Still Trying to Make Sense of the MOVE Bombing*, NPR CODE

Pointing to the historical fact that U. S. nationalism was born in the crucible of "state aggression" against rebellious slaves and Indigenous nations, professor and prison abolitionist Ruthie Wilson Gilmore connects the broad acceptance of punitive carceral regimes today to an American national identity rooted in military culture.[45] "Indian Wars," thousands of battles against Native American tribes along the western frontier, constituted the majority of U.S. military activity in the late 19th century.[46] K-Sue Park has shown that it was not just the formal military but that the U.S. government recruited "informal civilian forces . . . to assume the risks of frontier conflict [against Indigenous peoples] with promises of property."[47] For the United States, imperial expansion began within its borders, rather than across blue waters, which significantly shaped its national identity and state formation.[48]

Boomerang Effect: U.S. Law Enforcement Training in Israel Continues Legacies of Police Militarization

As authors in this volume and in the Racing National Security online symposium that preceded it,[49] as well as many other contributions from scholars[50] have shown, militarized regimes of repressive power have historically circulated between the colony and the metropole. There is no stark demarcation between the domestic and foreign sphere among colonial powers, rather their metropole is constituted by their peripheral regimes. In *Discourse on*

SWITCH (May 13, 2015), https://www.npr.org/sections/codeswitch/2015/05/13/406243272/im-from-philly-30-years-later-im-still-trying-to-make-sense-of-the-move-bombing.

[45] Ruth Wilson Gilmore, *Fatal Couplings of Power and Difference: Notes on Racism and Geography*, 54 PRO. GEOGRAPHER 15, 24 (2002).

[46] Julian Go, *The Imperial Origins of American Policing: Militarization and Imperial Feedback in the Early 20th Century*, 125 AM. J. SOC. 1200 (2020); *see also* Moses A. Dirk, *Empire, Resistance, and Security: International Law and the Transformative Occupation of Palestine*, 8(2) HUMANITY: AN INT'L J, HUM. RTS., HUMANITARIANISM, & DEV. 379–409 (2017) (the United States applied the Lieber Code to regulate its treatment of soldiers and deliberately excluded natives from the scope of its protections thus facilitating the massacre of Native tribes with impunity).

[47] K-Sue Park, *Who Are the Insurgents and Counterinsurgents?*, JADALIYYA (Aug. 25, 2014), https://www.jadaliyya.com/Details/31134.

[48] *See* AZIZ RANA, THE TWO FACES OF AMERICAN FREEDOM (2010); *see also* J. Kehaulani Kauanui, *Decolonial Self-Determination and No-State Solutions*, HUMAN. BLOG (July 2, 2019), http://humanity journal.org/blog/decolonial-self-determination-and-no-state-solutions/ (for a discussion of the Blue Water Thesis, which the United States ushered in order to protect itself against self-determination claims among Native American nations).

[49] *Racing National Security*, JUST SEC., https://www.justsecurity.org/tag/racing-national-security/ (last visited May 3, 2022).

[50] LALEH KHALILI, TIME IN THE SHADOWS: CONFINEMENT IN COUNTERINSURGENCIES (2012).

Colonialism, Martinican poet and revolutionary Aimé Césaire described this phenomenon as the "boomerang effect." Savage violence inflicted in the colony works to "decivilize the colonizer, to brutalize him in the true sense of the word, to degrade him, to awaken him to buried instincts, to covetousness, violence, race hatred, and moral relativism . . ." Ultimately, that violence manifests in the colonial metropole, be it in the Gestapos and the prisons and even in the racialized violence of Nazism, the antecedents of which lie in Europe's colonial geography.[51]

Julian Go draws on this analytical model to demonstrate how the exigencies of U.S. imperial expansion and domination in the late 19th century constituted the formation, and militarization, of U.S. law enforcement. In doing so, Go challenges much of the pertinent literature that traces development of U.S. police militarization to the Vietnam War, wherefrom flowed novel counterinsurgency methods to U.S. streets. After the U.S. military solidified the western frontier, it continued its expansion and occupied Hawai'i in 1893. After defeating the Spanish in the Spanish-American War in 1898, it became the colonial power in the Philippines, Guam, and Puerto Rico, and for a short time in Cuba, Haiti, Nicaragua, and the Dominican Republic. In what is described as its first guerilla war against Filipinos in the Philippine-American War, the U.S. Department of War oriented the military toward "the need of colonial conquest and counterinsurgency" and developed a "military-imperial regime."[52]

Go traces how the police reformers of the early 20th century drew on the military-imperial regime as a significant source of inspiration. This included an organizational structure that created a hierarchical chain of command, professionalization of law enforcement featuring training academies and entry tests, as well as operational and tactical methods including surveillance, mapping, anticipatory policing, weapons training, and mounted police units. Between 1890 and 1915, nearly forty percent of a sample of 114 police departments had at least one military veteran who served as police chief. Go demonstrates that this "imperial feedback" effectively transformed U.S. law enforcement from a body that regulated public disorder and, at times, offered social services to the modern police organization we know today aimed at preventing and suppressing crime.[53]

---

[51] Aimé Césaire, Discourse on Colonialism 36 (Joan Pinkham trans., 1955).
[52] Go, *supra* note 48, at 1202–03.
[53] *Id.* at 1196–97.

The Vietnam War, and Third World Revolt more generally, during the 1960s marked another significant juncture of imperial feedback and police militarization. Seeing themselves as an "internal colony" and inspired by anticolonial national liberation movements, over one hundred thousand American Blacks participated in uprisings, labeled "riots," in opposition to White supremacist structural and physical violence during this time.[54] Elizabeth Hinton notes that in the five summers of the Lyndon B. Johnson administration, there occurred no less than 250 "incidents of urban disorder" constituting "the greatest period of domestic bloodshed the nation has witnessed since the Civil War."[55] In response, the Johnson administration merged its anti-poverty and anti-crime policy efforts in legislation that laid the foundation for contemporary mass incarceration.

While initially intended to rout out violence by targeting the socioeconomic sources of discontent, President Johnson's Great Society programs ultimately abandoned anti-poverty initiatives and expanded surveillance and punishment as the primary modes of social welfare.[56] These transformations occurred in the context of, and response to, Black rebellion. Hinton notes that only two days after the 1965 Watts riot, Congress unanimously passed the Law Enforcement Assistant Act, which established direct federal funding for local law enforcement. Lawmakers, as well as Johnson himself, saw urban police serving low-income communities as the primary beneficiaries of these funds. Johnson believed that these officers were "fighting a war within [U. S.] boundaries" and were risking their lives much like the soldiers "in the rice paddies of Vietnam."[57] In 1968, still in the throes of the Vietnam War and the apex of Black rebellion, the Omnibus Crime Control and Safe Streets Act significantly expanded these initiatives.[58] The Safe Streets Act incentivized greater surveillance of Black communities and allocated surplus weapons from Vietnam, like army tanks, M-1 military carbines, and bulletproof vests, to U.S. cities to quash rebellions.[59]

The development of Special Weapons and Tactics (SWAT) units were among new law enforcement technologies transferred from Vietnamese theaters of war. As described by Radley Balko, SWAT teams are trained in

---

[54] Elizabeth Hinton, "A War within Our Own Boundaries": Lyndon Johnson's Great Society and the Rise of the Carceral State, 102 J. Am. Hist. 100 (2015).
[55] Id. at 100.
[56] Id. at 111.
[57] Id. at 103.
[58] Omnibus Crime Control and Safe Streets Act of 1968, Pub. L. No. 90-351, 82 Stat. 197 (1968).
[59] Hinton, supra note 56, at 110.

military methods and "learn to break into homes with battering rams and to use incendiary devices called flashbang grenades, which are designed to blind and deafen anyone nearby. Their usual aim is to 'clear' a building—that is, to remove any threats and distractions (including pets) and to subdue the occupants as quickly as possible."[60] While framed as necessary in the "war on drugs," the first SWAT team was deployed in December 1969 to attack the Los Angeles chapter of the Black Panther Party, a Black revolutionary organization committed to internationalism and self-determination.[61] While initially brandished on the backs of Black rebellions, SWAT teams have become a common feature of U.S. policing. As of 2008, seventy-five percent of populations of under 50,000 have a SWAT unit, while nearly ninety percent of cities with more than 50,000 have such a feature.[62]

The early 1990s marked yet another iterative development in police militarization. The National Defense Authorization Act for Fiscal years 1990 and 1991 formally established the 1033 program, which facilitates the transfer of excess military equipment to local law enforcement. In 1996, Congress made the 1033 program a permanent feature and consecrated the military's direct role in policing.[63] Initially meant to aid in the "war on drugs," the program has overseen the transfer of military grade weapons to local police units. However, it has also transferred more mundane items like office supplies and cameras indicating that, far more than a transactional relationship between police and military, the 1033 program represents the imbrication of the two institutions.

In continuation of police militarization, U.S. law enforcement began training with the Israeli police, military, and secret service following al-Qaeda's attacks on September 11, 2001. Israel touts itself as a leader in national security and has increased the selling power for its weapons technologies by

---

[60] Radley Balko, *Rise of the Warrior Cop*, WALL ST. J. (Aug. 7, 2013, 4:44 PM), https://www.wsj.com/articles/rise-of-the-warrior-cop-1375908008.

[61] Famma Gamal, *The Racial Politics of Protection: A Critical Race Examination of Police Militarization*, 104 CAL. L. REV., 979, 995 (2016). (The "war on drugs" refers to a racialized policy of selective enforcement, racial profiling and surveillance, and harsh and disproportionate sentencing that targeted Black communities under the auspices of eradicating drug use and trade. The policy, in fact, has legitimated the expansion of police power, and stat violence more broadly, to further subjugate Black communities.).

[62] Christopher J. Kincaid, *From Warfighters to Crimefighters: The Origins of Domestic Police Militarization* (2015) (Western Political Science Association: The Politics of People in Motion Conference Paper, 2015), http://www.wpsanet.org/papers/docs/From%20Warfighters%20to%20Crimefighters_The%20Origins%20of%20Domestic%20Police%20Militarization%20.pdf.

[63] Steven M. Radil, Raymond J. Dezzani & Lanny D. McAden, *Geographies of U.S. Police Militarization and the Role of the 1033 Program*, 69 PRO. GEOGRAPHER, 203, 207 (2017).

boasting that they are "battle-tested"—primarily on Palestinians.[64] In 2017, Israel sold $9.2 billion worth of weapons globally, 31 percent of which were drones and drone missiles.[65] In 2003, the Department of Homeland Security established an office in Israel to consecrate the police exchanges and, in 2012, the New York Police Department (NYPD) opened its own branch in an Israeli District Police Headquarters.[66] Organized by official Israeli and U.S. government agencies as well as private security firms and NGOs like the Anti-Defamation League, thousands of U.S. police officers have traveled to Israel for training in counterterrorism methods.[67] While the United States needs no training in achieving totalizing force, the police exchanges have transported several Israeli counterinsurgency technologies to U.S. cities.[68]

Perhaps of greatest significance is the fact that Israeli officers are training U.S. law enforcement officers—responsible for peacetime order—in methods that Israel applies to Palestinians, whom it considers a foreign and enemy population. This irony was not lost on Black activists who have borne the brunt of militarized law enforcement and have been explicitly called "terrorists" by President Donald Trump.[69] Trump's pronouncements are an example of casting Black protest as a national insurgency—whether to a White supremacist social order or as a conduit for external threats like communism—thus justifying state violence to quell them.

The racialization of Black communities as national security threats is imbricated in the history of police militarization. In his work on imperial feedback, Julian Go highlights how the racialization of colonized subjects shaped the perceptions of military veterans who—now police chiefs and officers upon return to the United States—imported and applied this racial framework to internal colonies, spaces featuring "large or rising numbers of minorities."[70] Fanna Gamal highlights that even the Posse Comitatus

[64] Ayelett Shani, *Israel Would Be Embarrassed If It Were Known It's Selling Arms to These Countries*, HAARETZ (Aug. 7, 2015), https://www.haaretz.com/.premium-turning-blood-into-money-1.5383840.

[65] Assaf Uni, *Germany Set to Sign €1b Israel Aerospace UAV Deal*, GLOBES (Apr. 8, 2018, 9:11 PM), https://en.globes.co.il/en/article-germany-set-to-sign-1b-israel-aerospace-uav-deal-1001230794.

[66] Margaret Hartmann, *NYPD Now Has an Israel Branch*, NEW YORKER MAG. (Sept. 6, 2012), https://nymag.com/intelligencer/2012/09/nypd-now-has-an-israel-branch.html.

[67] *Frequently Asked Questions About the Deadly Exchange*, DEADLY EXCHANGE, https://deadlyexchange.org/frequently-asked-questions-deadly-exchange/ (last visited May 3, 2022).

[68] DEADLY EXCHANGE, THE DANGEROUS CONSEQUENCES OF AMERICAN LAW ENFORCEMENT TRAININGS IN ISRAEL (Sept. 2018), https://deadlyexchange.org/wp-content/uploads/2019/07/Deadly-Exchange-Report.pdf.

[69] Angela Dewan, *Trump Is Calling Protesters Who Disagree with Him Terrorists, That Puts Him in the Company of the World's Autocrats*, CNN (July 26, 2020), https://www.cnn.com/2020/07/25/politics/us-protests-trump-terrorists-intl/index.html.

[70] Go, *supra* note 48, at 1211–12.

Act (1878) intended to prevent the military from serving police functions, circumscribed the role of the military in particular deference to White sensibilities. Military interventions never ceased against Native tribes as well as rebellious laborers.[71] Militarized responses to recent Black uprisings reflect the historic securitization of Black communities.

During the heavily militarized occupation of Ferguson in 2014, featuring Kevlar vests, armored tanks, and tear gas, activists noted that the St. Louis County Police Chief had traveled to Israel for a week-long counterterrorism training only three years before.[72] This fact became more acute considering Israel's ongoing aerial and ground offensive against the besieged Palestinian population in Gaza. In this context, Palestinian and Black activists began drawing vivid connections between U.S. and Israeli state violence. Rachel Gilmer, co-director of the Dream Defenders, recalls that moment as 'ma[king] clear what the state was about and the level it would go to, to repress revolutionary uprising from Black people.' She continues that seeing tweets from Palestinians providing advice on how to respond to tear gas following the events in Ferguson '[made clear] that borders mean everything and mean nothing because they're using the same tactics on people all over the world and profiting weapons corporations globally that sustain the supremacy of a ruling class.'[73]

Accordingly, since at least 2014, Black and Palestinian activists have increasingly engaged in campaigns targeting these links between U.S. and Israeli militarized law enforcement. Activists have challenged technologies used by U.S. prison systems and the Israeli military, like G4S surveillance systems,[74] the police exchange program,[75] and organized campaigns to end U.S. military support to Israel.[76] In doing so, activists have demonstrated how a vision aimed at global decolonization can be operationalized in local projects.

---

[71] Gamal, *supra* note 63, at 982.
[72] *The Ferguson/Palestine Connection*, EBONY (Aug. 19, 2014), https://www.ebony.com/news/the-fergusonpalestine-connection-403/.
[73] Erakat, *supra* note 9, at 472.
[74] *Stop G4S*, BDS: PALESTINIAN BDS NAT'L COMM., https://www.bdsmovement.net/stop-g4s (last visited May 3, 2022).
[75] Ali Younes, *Durham First US City to Ban Police Training with Israeli Military*, AL JAZEERA (Apr. 19, 2018), https://www.aljazeera.com/news/2018/4/19/durham-first-us-city-to-ban-police-training-with-israeli-military.
[76] JTA, *Black Lives Matter Endorses BDS: Israel Is "Apartheid State,"* HAARETZ (Aug. 4, 2016), https://www.haaretz.com/israel-news/black-lives-matter-endorses-bds-israel-is-apartheid-state-1.5420685.

Conclusion

Black Palestinian solidarity has helped build analytical bridges between the fight for Palestinian existence under apartheid[77] and the struggle for liberation from the "internal colony" of Black existence in the United States—and beyond, to the U.S. occupation of Hawai'i and Puerto Rico, to ongoing settler-colonial expansion on Standing Rock Sioux lands, as well as interventions in Venezuela and Bolivia. The emphasis on profitable military technologies spanning the globe reflects a concern not merely with Black and Palestinian lives but a broader concern with U.S. imperialism. The contemporary movement harkens back to an earlier period when the prevailing colonial condition made clear the relationship between domestic and international state violence. Anti-imperialist activism today is even more profound because it has crystallized in the absence of a Third World revolt, which historically connected the United States to other colonial geographies.[78]

Asli Bâli aptly describes this phenomenon in chapter eight, as the "military-industrial-policing complex," which has gained increasing attention during recent Black uprisings. Activists have connected the abolitionist demand to defund the police with a more robust social welfare program that makes prisons obsolete. They have insisted that the United States can afford these programs by reducing its military budget; hence, the emergent social media hashtags to #DefundPolice and #DefundMilitary.

The movement has yielded incremental success as well as significant pushback. For example, in 2020, the Minneapolis City Council proposed disbanding its police department only to be rejected by a voter referendum in 2021.[79] More broadly, a right-wing movement has only grown, attempted a coup, banned books, defamed Critical Race Theory, and insisted that anti-police violence is, in fact, the U.S.'s discrimination problem.[80] In Congress, the effort to shrink the U.S. military budget—which the Trump administration increased by twenty percent—imploded as the Joe Biden administration

[77] For a more thorough discussion of the applicability of the apartheid framework in Palestine, *see, e.g.*, Noura Erakat & John Reynolds, *We Charge Apartheid?: Palestine and the International Criminal Court*, TWAIL Rev. (Apr. 20, 2021), https://twailr.com/we-charge-apartheid-palestine-and-the-international-criminal-court/.

[78] *See* Erakat, *supra* note 9.

[79] N'dea Yancey-Bragg, *Push to Disband Minneapolis Police Fails Despite Calls for Reform after George Floyd Death*, USA Today (Nov. 3, 2021, 7:36 AM), https://www.usatoday.com/story/news/nation/2021/11/02/minneapolis-police-proposal-dismantle-department-fails/8564868002/.

[80] Blue Lives Matter, Facebook, https://www.facebook.com/bluematters/ (last visited May 3, 2022).

topped Trump's budget by nearly $37 billion.[81] One promising development is that, in response to grassroots efforts, the Anti-Defamation League (ADL) suspended its law enforcement training program in Israel. The leaked ADL memo admits:

> [I]n light of the very real police brutality at the hands of militarized police forces in the U. S., we must ask ourselves difficult questions like whether we are contributing to the problem. That is, we must ask ourselves why is it necessary for American police, enforcing American laws, would need to meet with members of the Israeli military. We must ask ourselves if, upon returning home, those we train are more likely to use force.[82]

It was precisely grassroots coalitions informed by anti-imperialist politics and solidarity principles that raised these questions and shed light on the entwinements of domestic and international state violence. While admittedly daunting, what is clear is that within these demands and praxes of transnational solidarity are seeds for a decolonial future. One in which young men like Ahmad can attend their sister's wedding and dance all night, where fathers like George Floyd can watch their daughters flourish, and young women like Breonna Taylor can live to realize their dreams. These are among the most generative offerings of Black-Palestinian solidarity.

---

[81] *Biden Signs Enormous Military Budget into Law*, AL JAZEERA (Dec. 27, 2021), https://www.aljaze era.com/news/2021/12/27/biden-signs-enormous-us-military-budget-into-law.

[82] Memorandum from George Selim, SVP of Programs and Greg Ehrie, VP for Law Enforcement and Analysis, Anti-Defamation League to CEO Jonathan Greenblatt (June 20, 2020) (on file with *Jewish Currents* magazine).

V

COMPARATIVE AND INTERNATIONAL PERSPECTIVES ON RACE AND NATIONAL SECURITY

10

Racial Transitional Justice in the United States

Yuvraj Joshi[*]

Introduction

Transitional justice is a field that aims to help societies overcome conflict and oppression.[1] Its goals include promoting accountability for wrongdoings, redressing, and ensuring the non-repetition of injustices, opening political and social space to marginalized people, and facilitating societal reconciliation. Societies pursue these goals through measures such as truth and reconciliation commissions, criminal prosecutions, reparations programs, and institutional reforms.[2]

For years, the U.S. government has endorsed transitional justice approaches abroad, such as in Colombia, Congo, and Sri Lanka,[3] while ignoring the need for transitional justice at home. Internationally, the United States has been exempted from the political and legal considerations applied

[*] I am grateful first and foremost for the efforts and engagement of Matiangai Sirleaf, including through the "Racing National Security" series and the Race and National Security workshop that she organized. All authors and readers of this volume are the beneficiaries of her brilliance. I am also grateful for the generative feedback of Fasika Delessa, David Gray, Lucas Janes, Rachel López, Zina Miller, and Victoria Roman and for the excellent research and editorial support of Merran Hergert, Thea Udwadia, and Liana Wang.
[1] *See generally* RUTI G. TEITEL, TRANSITIONAL JUSTICE (2000); Pablo de Greiff, *Theorizing Transitional Justice*, 51 NOMOS 31 (2012); COLLEEN MURPHY, THE CONCEPTUAL FOUNDATIONS OF TRANSITIONAL JUSTICE (2017); Laurel E. Fletcher & Harvey M. Weinstein, *Writing Transitional Justice: An Empirical Evaluation of Transitional Justice Scholarship in Academic Journals*, 7 J. HUM. RTS. PRAC. 177 (2015).
[2] Not all processes labeled as "transitional justice" are designed to achieve these goals. Rodrigo Uprimny & Maria Paula Saffon, *Uses and Abuses of Transitional Justice Discourse in Colombia*, 6 PRIO POL'Y BRIEF 1 (2007) (distinguishing between "manipulative" and "democratic" transitional justice). Furthermore, critical scholars question whether transitional justice can advance all its goals simultaneously and to an equal extent. Bronwyn Anne Leebaw, *The Irreconcilable Goals of Transitional Justice*, 30 HUM. RTS. Q. 95 (2008).
[3] U.S. DEPT. STATE, 2015–16 ADVANCING FREEDOM AND DEMOCRACY REPORT, https://2017-2021.state.gov/2015-16-advancing-freedom-and-democracy-report/index.html#_edn60 (last visited May 1, 2022).

Yuvraj Joshi, *Racial Transitional Justice in the United States* In: *Race and National Security*. Edited by: Matiangai V.S. Sirleaf, Oxford University Press. © Oxford University Press 2023. DOI: 10.1093/oso/9780197754641.003.0011

to other transitional societies, despite this country's frayed democracy and centuries-long imposition of state-sponsored racial violence.

Certainly, there have been attempts to challenge this inertia. For example, from 1989 until his retirement in 2017, Rep. John Conyers Jr. introduced a bill (H.R. 40) in every Congress to study reparations for slavery.[4] Civil rights leader Sherrilyn Ifill's 2007 book, *On the Courthouse Lawn*, elaborated transitional justice principles for American struggles with racism.[5] Journalist and author Ta-Nehisi Coates's 2014 article, "The Case for Reparations," reminded Americans that broader reparations are still pending more than two centuries after freedwoman Belinda Sutton successfully petitioned for a pension from her former enslaver's estate.[6] Religion professor Anthony Bradley's 2018 essay applied the "Chicago Principles of Post-conflict Justice" to individual American states.[7] Yet, despite these efforts, the U.S. government has proceeded as if transitional justice does not belong "here."

However, two recent and interrelated events, each emerging out of this country's struggles with White supremacy, have highlighted the relevance of transitional justice approaches in the United States.

In January 2021, President Donald Trump's attempts to overturn the results of a democratic election culminated in a violent insurrection at the U.S. Capitol. Americans debated whether to hold Trump and his enablers accountable or whether to "move on" from the four years of his presidency in the interest of social stability. This tension between the pursuit of stability and accountability can be understood as a transitional justice dilemma that arises as societies seek to surmount conflict, known internationally as the "peace versus justice dilemma."[8]

In addition to a violent insurrection, the United States recently saw the largest racial justice demonstrations in its history. These protests reissued demands to address policing and other state violence, implement truth and reconciliation processes to confront historical and ongoing injustices, and obtain reparations for decades and centuries of racist oppression. Such

---

[4] *See* Commission to Study and Develop Reparation Proposals for African Americans Act, H.R. 40, 115th Cong. (2017).

[5] SHERRILYN A. IFILL, ON THE COURTHOUSE LAWN: CONFRONTING THE LEGACY OF LYNCHING IN THE TWENTY-FIRST CENTURY, at xv (rev. ed. 2018).

[6] Ta-Nehisi Coates, *The Case for Reparations*, ATLANTIC (June 2014), https://www.theatlantic.com/magazine/archive/2014/06/the-case-for-reparations/361631.

[7] Anthony Bradley, *Finally Healing the Wounds of Jim Crow*, FATHOM MAG. (July 11, 2018), https://www.fathommag.com/stories/finally-healing-the-wounds-of-jim-crow.

[8] *See infra* text accompanying notes 55–65 (discussing the peace versus justice dilemma in the American context).

demands fundamentally call for transitional justice processes that deal with the legacy and threat of White supremacy in the United States.

While Americans increasingly speak of truth commissions and reparations, they typically do so without engaging with the broader field of transitional justice either as practiced or in theory. When transitional justice does enter American political discourse, it is seldom by name and most often by reference to the work of individual countries, particularly South Africa and Canada. Yet the international field of transitional justice offers broader insights for the United States to consider.

For example, transitional justice has provided a useful vocabulary and normative framework for other societies to center the values of accountability, redress, non-repetition, and reconciliation in their recoveries from conflict and oppression. American legal and political decision-making could benefit from a transitional justice perspective, since the failure to prioritize these values may be an important reason why the United States has struggled to surmount its racist history.

Furthermore, transitional justice is a holistic notion that has been used to connect individual laws and policies as elements of an integrated transition process.[9] The United States struggles with racism in part because government agencies and institutions such as the Supreme Court pretend that the brief implementation of discrete measures has resolved centuries of racial subordination, when transitional justice is a complex, intergenerational process.

This chapter examines America's struggles with anti-Black racism through an international transitional justice lens. Building on the author's earlier work,[10] it draws upon both transitional justice *practice*, which involves developing and implementing processes to overcome systematic human rights abuses, and transitional justice *theory*, which identifies the promises and

---

[9] Alexander L. Boraine, *Transitional Justice: A Holistic Interpretation*, 60 J. Int'l Affs. 17, 19 (2006); de Greiff, *supra* note 1, at 34; Tricia D. Olsen, Leigh A. Payne & Andrew G. Reiter, *The Justice Balance: When Transitional Justice Improves Human Rights and Democracy*, 32 Hum. Rts. Q. 980, 982 (2010).

[10] *See generally* Yuvraj Joshi, *Racial Equality Compromises*, 111 Calif. L. Rev. 529 (2023); Yuvraj Joshi, *Racial Time*, 90 U. Chi. L. Rev. (2023); Yuvraj Joshi, *Weaponizing Peace*, 123 Colum. L. Rev. (2023); Yuvraj Joshi, *Racial Justice and Peace*, 110 Geo. L.J. 1325 (2022); Yuvraj Joshi, *Racial Transition*, 98 Wash. U. L. Rev. 1181 (2021); Yuvraj Joshi, *Affirmative Action as Transitional Justice*, 2020 Wis. L. Rev. 1; Yuvraj Joshi, *Racial Indirection*, 52 U.C. Davis L. Rev. 2495 (2019); Yuvraj Joshi, *Does Transitional Justice Belong in the United States?*, Just Sec. (July 13, 2020), https://www.justsecurity.org/71372/does-transitional-justice-belong-in-the-united-states/; Yuvraj Joshi, *MLK Believed "No Justice, No Peace,"* Just Sec. (Jan. 18, 2021), https://www.justsecurity.org/74235/mlk-believed-no-justice-no-peace/.

limitations of transitional approaches and distinguishes between desirable and undesirable forms of transitional justice.

The chapter begins by discussing the phenomenon of American exceptionalism that has allowed the United States to evade transitional justice scrutiny. It then presents historical, legal, and comparative perspectives that situate the United States in a racial transitional justice context. In so doing, this chapter offers a vision for how the transitional justice experiences of other countries could inform the United States struggles with anti-Black racism.

While this chapter focuses on anti-Black racism, the United States is a settler-colonial society in which the dispossession and erasure of Indigenous peoples on their own lands underpin logics of White supremacy.[11] U.S. histories of anti-Blackness, settler colonialism, racial and ethnic exclusion, and xenophobia are entwined in ways that require focused attention.[12] Future research may more fully engage these histories and bodies of law such as the *Cherokee Cases*, the *Chinese Exclusion Cases*, and the *Insular Cases* to understand the structural dynamics of racism in the United States, as well as transitional justice's responses to them.[13]

American Exceptionalism in Transitional Justice

The United States is a country like many others struggling to leave conflict and oppression behind. The United States has sought to move beyond a racial past marked by overt structures of racial domination. And it is experiencing

[11] On the relationship between settler colonialism and White supremacy, *see* Iyko Day, *Being or Nothingness: Indigeneity, Antiblackness, and Settler Colonial Critique*, 1 CRIT. ETHNIC STUD. 112 (2015); Andrea Smith, *Indigeneity, Settler Colonialism, White Supremacy*, in RACIAL FORMATION IN THE TWENTY-FIRST CENTURY 66 (Daniel Martinez HoSang, Oneka LaBennett & Laura Pulido eds., 2012); NATSU TAYLOR SAITO, SETTLER COLONIALISM, RACE, AND THE LAW (2020); Speed Shannon, *The Persistence of White Supremacy: Indigenous Women Migrants and the Structures of Settler Capitalism*, 122 AM. ANTHROPOLOGY 77 (2020).

[12] *See* Justin Leroy, *Black History in Occupied Territory: On the Entanglements of Slavery and Settler Colonialism*, 19 THEORY & EVENT (2016); Juan F. Perea, *The Black/White Binary Paradigm of Race: The "Normal Science" of American Racial Thought*, 85 CALIF. L. REV. 1213 (1997); Maggie Blackhawk, *Federal Indian Law as Paradigm Within Public Law*, 132 HARV. L. REV. 1787 (2019).

[13] Blackhawk, *supra* note 12, at 1820–25 (discussing the *Cherokee Cases*); Natsu Taylor Saito, *The Enduring Effect of the Chinese Exclusion Cases: The "Plenary Power" Justification for On-Going Abuses of Human Rights*, 10 ASIAN L.J. 13 (2003) (discussing the *Chinese Exclusion Cases*); Aziz Rana, *How We Study the Constitution: Rethinking the Insular Cases and Modern American Empire*, 130 YALE L.J.F. 312 (2020) (discussing the *Insular Cases*).

a period of transition that is neither exactly the past, nor yet the desired racially just future.

Yet although the U.S. government has sought a *transition* from slavery and Jim Crow, it has eschewed *transitional justice* in response to racist human rights violations. This section describes certain beliefs about American society that have prevented the widespread application of a transitional justice framework to the United States.

The United States as an "Established" Democracy

Since its inception, the field of transitional justice has been more concerned with transitions to democracy—such as in Argentina and Chile as they emerged from dictatorships—than with transformations within "established" democracies. According to a standard account, transitional justice is inapposite to the United States because the United States is assumed to be an "established" democracy.

However, this posture rests on both an overestimation of American democracy and an underestimation of the transition process: democracy in the United States is not as "established" as commonly assumed, democratization is a continual rather than one-time process, and transition requires more than achieving a formal democratic regime.

Claims that emphasize the United States' status as an "established" democracy ignore the denial of basic political rights and representation from the onset of colonialism and slavery to the present day.[14] Generations of writers have shown how American democracy has been—and remains—incomplete, given the nation's lack of racial justice.[15]

In a 2004 article, political scientists Francisco González and Desmond King drew the distinction between "restricted" and "full" democracy and characterized the United States as a "restricted" democracy prior to the implementation of the 1964 Civil Rights Act and the 1965 Voting Rights Act.[16]

---

[14] Dana Hedgpeth, *"Jim Crow, Indian Style": How Native Americans Were Denied the Right to Vote for Decades*, Wash. Post (Nov. 1, 2020), https://www.washingtonpost.com/history/2020/11/01/native-americans-right-to-vote-history/.

[15] W.E.B. Du Bois, Black Reconstruction in America, 1860–1880 (1935); Nikole Hannah-Jones, *The 1619 Project*, N.Y. Times Mag. (Aug. 14, 2019), https://www.nytimes.com/interactive/2019/08/14/magazine/1619-america-slavery.html.

[16] Francisco E. González & Desmond King, *The State and Democratization: The United States in Comparative Perspective*, 34 Brit. J. Pol. Sci. 193, 194 (2004).

This distinction rested on the fact that certain groups were denied civil rights protections and excluded from the voting process. Yet, these landmark civil rights laws have been progressively eroded by the courts, rendering the United States something still less than a full democracy today.[17]

An enduring feature of Black oppression in the United States has been a backsliding away from democracy.[18] Transition is thus better conceptualized as the progressive realization of democracy and non-regression rather than the mere attainment of a formal democratic regime. For example, the "preclearance" requirement of the Voting Rights Act, which scrutinizes proposed voting laws in states with a history of discriminatory voting practices, supports democratic transition by sustaining democratic inclusion. But the Supreme Court's 2013 decision in *Shelby County v. Holder* struck down the coverage formula used to determine which states would be subject to this preclearance requirement, effectively nullifying the requirement pending new legislation.[19] In the wake of *Shelby County*, voter suppression laws have been enacted in several jurisdictions previously covered by the preclearance provision, as well as in other states where minority votes present a threat to White supremacy.[20]

Transition is not only a move toward democracy and the rule of law but also charts a path toward peace and justice. In his "Letter from a Birmingham Jail" in 1963, Dr. Martin Luther King Jr. made the distinction between a negative peace, characterized by an absence of violence, and a positive peace, characterized by the presence of justice.[21] King expressly called for "transition from an obnoxious negative peace . . . to a substantive and positive peace, in which all men will respect the dignity and worth of human personality."[22] Recurring protests against police violence and structural racism in the United States indict the government's failures to secure

---

[17] CAROL ANDERSON, ONE PERSON, NO VOTE: HOW VOTER SUPPRESSION IS DESTROYING OUR DEMOCRACY (2018); Vesla M. Weaver & Gwen Prowse, *Racial Authoritarianism in U.S. Democracy*, SCI. MAG. (Sep. 4, 2020), https://science.sciencemag.org/content/369/6508/1176.

[18] DOUGLAS A. BLACKMON, SLAVERY BY ANOTHER NAME: THE RE-ENSLAVEMENT OF BLACK AMERICANS FROM THE CIVIL WAR TO WORLD WAR II (2008).

[19] Shelby Cnty. v. Holder, 570 U.S. 529 (2013).

[20] Sherrilyn Ifill, *Before 2020: Upgrade Voting Systems, Restore Voting Rights Act, End Voter Suppression*, USA TODAY (Nov. 12, 2018, 3:15 AM), https://www.usatoday.com/story/opinion/2018/11/12/end-voter-suppression-restore-voting-rights-act-update-machines-column/1965522002/.

[21] The distinction between negative and positive peace has roots in both transitional justice theory and Black political thought, which points to the benefits of placing them into conversation. *See* Joshi, *Racial Justice and Peace*, *supra* note 10.

[22] Martin Luther King Jr., *Letter from Birmingham Jail*, 26 U.C. DAVIS. L. REV. 835, 842 (1993).

such a substantive and positive peace. They remind the United States of the need to focus its transitional efforts towards achieving a true multiracial democracy.

"Too Much" or "Too Little" Change Since Racial Apartheid

The notion that either "too much" or "too little" has changed since America's formal racial apartheid has inhibited transitional justice analyses from being adopted in the United States.

Those who claim "too much has changed" claim that slavery, Jim Crow, and the present should not be understood as a single transition. For them, the racial challenges the United States faces today are long removed from the past. This perspective risks overstating the changes and understating the continuities between the past and present. Undoubtedly, the United States of today is not exactly the same as the antebellum or Jim Crow United States. But this does not preclude legacies of the wrongful past from being present in today's society, nor the evolution of past racist practices into new forms. The passage of significant time and intervening events since slavery and Jim Crow have not rendered questions of racial transition obsolete.

For those believing "too little has changed," the language of transition or progress obscures continuities with the past and implies structural change where it does not truly exist. For them, calling the United States "transitional" is a misnomer because it suggests that American society is overcoming, rather than reconfiguring and continuing, its racist past. This perspective reminds us that progress is not linear or guaranteed. Therefore, any transitional analysis of the United States must account for discontinuity and continuity, steps both forward and back, and not simply the former.

American Exceptionalist Ideology

American exceptionalist ideology depicts the United States as the leader in the global struggle for liberty. This ideology forms part of the reason why the United States has been willing to champion abroad but not domesticate a transitional justice framework. In 1963, James Baldwin wrote about "the collection of myths to which [W]hite Americans cling: that their ancestors were all freedom-loving heroes, that they were born in the greatest country the world has ever seen."[23] Today, those same myths impede a collective recognition of the United States' violence at home and abroad.[24]

American exceptionalism presents the U.S. as a society founded on liberty and equality rather than settler colonialism and White supremacy. It treats centuries of dispossession and oppression as aberrational rather than foundational parts of American history. And it posits that any racial inequality problems were resolved with the civil rights era and its landmark cases and laws. The former United Nations Special Rapporteur on racism, E. Tendayi Achiume, explains in *Just Security* that this exceptionalism "implicitly treats existing domestic law as a high watermark for achieving justice and equality, when this law falls short even of global human rights anti-racism standards."[25] While the United States has been exempted from transitional justice scrutiny based in part on this exceptionalism, the enduring—and increasingly international[26]—criticisms of the United States' failures to address racism should lead us to consider this country alongside others with oppressive histories.

Racial Transitional Justice in the American Context

A transitional perspective is needed to make sense of racial justice and injustice in the United States. A polity committed to ridding itself of the vestiges of oppression *requires* an account of the past out of which it is emerging, the future it ought to pursue, the transition pathway between them, and the present stage of transition. Such a general theory is needed to make decisions about the legitimacy of various practices (what aspects of the past cannot be tolerated in the present?), to develop strategies (what is necessary to create a future distinct from the past?), and to determine progress (what of the past is behind and what is still present?).

Such transitional theories underpin American legal and political decision-making, yet the transitional bases of decisions are rarely acknowledged and

---

[23] James Baldwin, The Fire Next Time 101 (First Vintage Int'l ed. 1993) (1963).

[24] Aziz Rana, *Race and the American Creed: Recovering Black Radicalism*, 24 N + 1 (2016), https://nplusonemag.com/issue-24/ politics/race-and-the-american-creed/.

[25] E. Tendayi Achiume, *The United States' Racial Justice Problem Is Also an International Human Rights Law Problem*, Just Sec. (June 5, 2020), https://www.justsecurity.org/70589/the-united-states-racial-justice-problem-is-also-an-international-human-rights-law-problem/.

[26] *UN Experts Condemn Modern-day Racial Terror Lynchings in US and Call for Systemic Reform and Justice*, UN News Ctr. (June 5, 2020), https://www.ohchr.org/EN/NewsEvents/Pages/DisplayNews.aspx?NewsID=25933.

sometimes even denied. Transitional justice can serve as a framework to examine the existing approaches to democratic transition in the United States in light of a more global theory. This section presents historical, legal, and comparative perspectives that situate the United States in a racial transitional justice context, thereby developing a U.S.-specific account of transitional justice.

Historical Transition

Colonialism and slavery were America's original sins that still haunt the nation.[27] Colonialism is a historical and ongoing project that erases Indigenous peoples from their lands and replaces them with settlers.[28] Slavery survived under the Constitution of 1789 and its underlying ideology of innate Black inferiority and difference permeated American life.[29]

Following the Civil War, Reconstruction attempted to remedy slavery's wrongs. In addition to adopting three constitutional amendments, Congress enacted the nation's first federal civil rights law in 1866, and the Freedmen's Bureau Acts, which opened schools and provided funding, land, and other assistance to help create colleges for the education of Black students. Because they aimed to redress harms and set the stage for reconciliation, such Reconstruction era policies would today be recognized as types of transitional justice reforms.[30]

But Reconstruction lasted for only twelve years and left emancipated people with very limited rights, even fewer resources, and the pain of unfulfilled promises. A loophole in the Thirteenth Amendment's abolition of slavery permitted the forced labor of those convicted of a crime. This enabled southern states to tie recently emancipated people to their former enslavers through "Black Codes" that criminalized such "offenses" as loitering and vagrancy. Adding insult to injury, Congress voted to close the Freedmen's

---

[27] On the significance of colonialism and slavery in American racial formation, *see* CLAUDIO SAUNT, BLACK, WHITE, AND INDIAN: RACE AND THE UNMAKING OF AN AMERICAN FAMILY (2005); TIYA MILES, THE TIES THAT BIND: THE STORY OF AN AFRO-CHEROKEE FAMILY IN SLAVERY AND FREEDOM (2005).

[28] Patrick Wolfe, *Settler Colonialism and the Elimination of the Native*, 8 J. GENOCIDE RES. 387, 388 (2006) (describing this "logic of elimination").

[29] DAVID WALDSTREICHER, SLAVERY'S CONSTITUTION: FROM REVOLUTION TO RATIFICATION (2009).

[30] Bernadette Atuahene, *Property and Transitional Justice*, 58 UCLA L. REV. DISCOURSE 65, 86 (2010).

Bureau in 1872, after which most of its schools closed down. Five years later, Rutherford B. Hayes gained the presidency by agreeing to withdraw federal troops from the South, bringing Reconstruction to a close.

With the end of Reconstruction came a new wave of White supremacist practices. Although Jim Crow laws and policies were concentrated in the South, racism and segregation were rooted nationwide. In its 1896 decision *Plessy v. Ferguson*, the Supreme Court ratified racial segregation under the "separate but equal" principle.[31] Throughout the Jim Crow era, a wide array of state laws and practices, including ostensibly "race-neutral" ones such as poll taxes, disenfranchised Black people and other racial minorities. Lynching, rape, and other forms of violence were inflicted with impunity to assert White supremacy.

The Second Reconstruction attempted to complete the unfinished work of the First Reconstruction. In 1954, *Brown v. Board of Education* declared racial segregation in public education unconstitutional. Although segregationists responded to *Brown* with "massive resistance," a decade later Congress enacted the 1964 Civil Rights Act (passed following racial justice protests throughout the South), which barred discrimination in federally supported programs; the 1965 Voting Rights Act (passed after the historic marches from Selma to Montgomery), which aimed to remove barriers to voting; and the 1968 Fair Housing Act (passed amid protests following Dr. King's assassination), which prohibited discrimination in the housing market.

In addition to landmark cases and laws, this civil rights era featured deliberative processes that might today be labeled as transitional justice. For example, the 1966 White House Conference on Civil Rights brought together over 2,400 participants and proposed reforms relating to economic security and welfare, education, housing, and administration of justice.[32] In 1968, the Kerner Commission similarly recommended reforms to employment, education, the welfare system, housing, and policing.[33] These reports proposed holistic approaches to societal transition that find support in contemporary transitional justice theory.[34] But President Lyndon B. Johnson shelved the

---

[31] Plessy v. Ferguson, 163 U.S. 537 (1896).

[32] "To Fulfill These Rights," White House Conference on Civil Rights (1966), https://eric. ed.gov/?id=ED032354.

[33] Nat'l Advisory Comm'n on Civ. Disorders, Report of the National Advisory Commission on Civil Disorders (1968).

[34] de Greiff, *supra* note 1, at 34 (transitional justice measures "are not elements of a random list" but "[r]ather, they are parts of a whole").

Kerner Report's recommendations, avoiding a systematic racial reckoning and furthering racial subordination.

Ultimately, the Second Reconstruction yielded to racial retrenchment, as courts and other actors abandoned previous efforts to secure racial justice. The "Southern strategy" used to attract southern White Democrats to the Republican party helped elect Richard Nixon in 1968 and 1972 and Ronald Reagan in 1980. Their policies and appointments to the Supreme Court halted and reversed many of the gains made during the civil rights era. This backtrack on racial equity took various forms, from the resegregation of public schools to the development of punitive crime policies that "both responded to and moved the agenda on civil rights."[35]

In the face of a long period of racial retrenchment, the pursuit of racial justice continues. Following the mid-2020 uprisings, Rep. Barbara Lee called for a U.S. Commission on Truth, Racial Healing, and Transformation.[36] U.S. cities and states have initiated truth, justice, and reconciliation processes, as well as reparations programs.[37] Universities and theological seminaries have offered limited reparations to the descendants of enslaved people from whom they profited.[38] But attempts to secure broader reparations

[35] Vesla M. Weaver, *Frontlash: Race and the Development of Punitive Crime Policy*, 21 STUD. AM. POL. DEV. 230, 265 (2007).

[36] *See* Press Release, Rep. Barbara Lee, In the Wake of COVID-19 and Murder of George Floyd, Congresswoman Barbara Lee Calls for Formation of Truth, Racial Healing, and Transformation Commission (June 1, 2020), https://lee.house.gov/news/press-releases/in-the-wake-of-covid-19-and-murder-of-george-floyd-congresswoman-barbara-lee-calls-for-formation-of-truth-racial-healing-and-transformation-commission.

[37] *See, e.g.*, GREENSBORO TRUTH & RECONCILIATION COMM'N, GREENSBORO TRUTH & RECONCILIATION COMMISSION REPORT: EXECUTIVE SUMMARY 2 (May 25, 2006), http://www.greensborotrc.org/exec_summary.pdf; *TIRC Decisions*, ILL.: TORTURE INQUIRY & RELIEF COMM'N, https://tirc.illinois.gov/tirc-decisions.html; Nicholas Creary, Opinion, *Md. Lynching Commission Offers Chance to Investigate, Atone*, BALT. SUN (Apr. 29, 2019, 10:55 AM), https://www.baltimoresun.com/opinion/op-ed/bs-ed-op-0430-lynching-commission-20190429-story.html; Andy Fies, *Evanston, Illinois, Finds Innovative Solution to Funding Reparations: Marijuana Sales Taxes*, ABC NEWS (July 19, 2020, 11:03 AM), https://abcnews.go.com/US/evanston-illinois-finds-innovative-solution-funding-reparations-marijuana/story?id=71826707; Ovetta Wiggins, *Landmark Commission Begins Tackling "Unconfronted Truth" of Racially Motivated Lynchings in Md.*, WASH. POST (Sept. 18, 2020), https://www.washingtonpost.com/local/md-politics/maryland-lynching-report/2020/09/18/ba8655e8-f8fa-11ea-a275-1a2c2d36e1f1_story.html; Neil Vigdor, *North Carolina City Approves Reparations for Black Residents*, N.Y. TIMES (July 16, 2020), https://www.nytimes.com/2020/07/16/us/reparations-asheville-nc.html; Soumya Karlamangla, *Who Should Get Reparations in California?*, N.Y. TIMES (Mar. 4, 2022), https://www.nytimes.com/2022/03/04/us/reparations-california.html.

[38] *See* Jesús A. Rodríguez, *This Could Be the First Slavery Reparations Policy in America*, POLITICO MAG. (Apr. 9, 2019), http://politi.co/2UsZjo7; Collin Binkley, *Harvard Pledges $100 Million to Atone for Role in Slavery*, NBC BOSTON (Apr. 26, 2022, updated Apr. 26, 2022, at 3:21 pm), https://www.nbcboston.com/news/local/harvard-pledges-100-million-to-atone-for-role-in-slavery/2703907/.

for slavery, Jim Crow practices, and ongoing discrimination have often stalled.[39]

The U.S.' centuries of racist violence and multiple attempts at transition do not lend themselves to easy analysis. Throughout American history, some people have sought and supported transition to a multiracial democracy, while others have deliberately worked against it. Today, supporters of multiracial democracy highlight the ongoing legacies and practices of racism, while opponents contend that racial injustice has long disappeared and that any further attempt at transition constitutes a race-based injustice against White people. Recognizing America's racial history—including how the Reconstruction and civil rights periods of relative improvement employed transitional justice-type measures—is a vital step toward understanding the United States within a transitional context.

Legal Opinions

No special courts were established to steer the United States away from slavery and segregation. Instead, the U.S. Supreme Court has been a forum where transitional justice issues are consistently raised. Court opinions concerning racial equality are both illustrative and constitutive of America's racial transition: they offer a window into how transitional concerns shape the law and how law shapes the transition process. Studying these opinions can therefore help us to better understand and address the real-world dynamics of transition.

Transitional Discourses: Reckoning versus Distancing

For much of its history, the Supreme Court's decisions openly enshrined White supremacy. But particularly since its 1954 decision in *Brown v. Board of Education*, transitional perspectives have shaped the Court's race jurisprudence. The Supreme Court's pursuit of racial transition can be characterized into two approaches: *reckoning with* and *distancing from* the past.[40]

In the civil rights era, the Supreme Court mandated remedies designed to reckon with past and present racism. For example, under a "freedom of

---

[39] *See* Juana Summers, *A Bill to Study Reparations for Slavery Had Momentum in Congress, but Still No Vote*, NPR (Nov. 12, 2021, 5:00 AM), https://www.npr.org/2021/11/12/1054889820/a-bill-to-study-reparations-for-slavery-had-momentum-in-congress-but-still-no-vo.

[40] Joshi, *Racial Transition, supra* note 10, at 1202–34 (developing this distinction).

choice plan" that allowed all students in a deeply segregated county to choose their school, no White students had chosen a historically Black school, while only a few Black students had chosen a historically White school. In 1968, a unanimous Court in *Green v. County School Board of New Kent County* said that the freedom of choice plan was insufficient for "transition to a unitary, nonracial system of public education. . . ."[41] New Kent County had not satisfied its "affirmative duty" to eliminate racial discrimination "root and branch,"[42] and needed to propose "a plan that promises realistically to work, and promises realistically to work now."[43] In so holding, *Green* highlighted the need for transitional measures to be both effective and timely in order to meet judicial standards.[44]

But with the racial retrenchment and conservative appointments starting in the late 1960s, the Court's decisions shifted from reckoning with the past toward distancing from the past. The Court denied continuities between blatant racism from the antebellum and Jim Crow past, which it denounced, and racism in the present, which it discounted.[45] It also became preoccupied with identifying a discrete endpoint of the transition process—the point at which America's links to its racist past would be deemed severed once and for all and "extraordinary" policies such as voter protections and affirmative action would no longer be required.[46]

In 1991, for instance, *Board of Education of Oklahoma v. Dowell* held that court-ordered desegregation decrees were not to operate "in perpetuity," regardless of whether they were needed.[47] Chief Justice Rehnquist interpreted references to "transition" in *Green* to suggest "a temporary measure to remedy past discrimination" rather than something more enduring.[48] Justice Marshall's dissent rejected *Dowell's* preoccupation with "temporariness and permanence" because "the continued need for a [desegregation] decree will turn on whether the underlying purpose of the decree has been achieved."[49] For Marshall, that purpose was not achieved "so long as conditions likely to inflict the stigmatic injury condemned in *Brown I* persist."[50]

---

[41] 391 U.S. 430, 436 (1968).

[42] *Id.* at 437–38.

[43] *Id.* at 439.

[44] *See also* Swann v. Charlotte-Mecklenburg Bd. of Educ., 402 U.S. 1, 28 (1971) (recognizing that transitional measures did not have to be ideal in order to be valuable and worthwhile).

[45] Joshi, *Racial Transition, supra* note 10, at 5–6.

[46] *Id.*

[47] 498 U.S. 237, 248 (1991).

[48] *Id.* at 247.

[49] *Id.* at 267 n.11 (Marshall, J., dissenting).

[50] *Id.* at 252.

Such insistence on endpoints for transition was mirrored in affirmative action and voting rights cases.[51] With the shift from reckoning to distancing, civil rights measures that were once deemed necessary and urgent were declared inappropriate and outdated—and even antithetical to the project of ensuring a racially just society. Thus, while striking down voter protections in *Shelby County v. Holder* in 2013, Chief Justice John Roberts proclaimed that "[n]early 50 years later, things have changed dramatically."[52]

Such a distancing jurisprudence limits not just what the Court sees as constitutionally required but what it sees as constitutionally permissible in the pursuit of transition. By painting slavery and segregation as exceptional periods that were successfully overcome, a distancing approach rejects that settler colonialism and White supremacy have been the nation's governing doctrines from the beginning and are still with us. By casting civil rights measures aside as obsolete and even detrimental, this jurisprudence maintains America's systemic racism as well as Americans' misperceptions regarding racial equality, impeding possibilities for transition.

In contemplating transitional approaches, American courts have been faced with a series of transitional dilemmas. These dilemmas include a reconciliation between moving away from pervasive and pernicious use of race and continuing to use race to remedy historical wrongs, between looking forward and looking backward, between the individual and the collective, and (as discussed next) between peace and justice.[53]

Transitional Dilemmas: Peace versus Justice

One of the central discussions in transitional justice is the peace versus justice dilemma, characterized as the challenge to "reconcile legitimate claims for justice with equally legitimate claims for stability and social peace."[54] Transitional justice scholarship on this dilemma grapples with questions such as: What is "peace" and what is "justice"? Are peace and justice competing goals or are they compatible and even complementary? Are peace and justice of similar normative and practical importance or should one

---

[51] Grutter v. Bollinger, 539 U.S. 306, 342 (2003); Shelby Cnty. v. Holder, 570 U.S. 529, 546 (2013).

[52] *Shelby Cnty.*, 570 U.S. at 547, 552.

[53] Joshi, *Affirmative Action as Transitional Justice, supra* note 10, at 17–25 (outlining these dilemmas).

[54] Paige Arthur, *How "Transitions" Reshaped Human Rights: A Conceptual History of Transitional Justice*, 31 Hum. Rts. Q. 321, 323 (2009). Importantly, not all claims to "stability and social peace" are equally legitimate. *See* Joshi, *Weaponizing Peace, supra* note 10.

take priority over the other? Is the relationship between peace and justice inherent or is it contingent on particular circumstances?

Transitional justice scholars and practitioners have examined these questions with respect to countries other than the United States.[55] Yet the peace versus justice dilemma also animates America's attempted transition from slavery, segregation, and White supremacy, as it seeks to balance pursuing racial equality with ensuring social stability and harmony. When Americans have disagreed about how that balance should be struck, some have called upon the courts to settle their disputes.

American courts have thus long faced versions of the peace versus justice dilemma without recognizing them as such. Courts have been asked to decide: Does the advancement of racial equality facilitate or impede the achievement of racial harmony?[56] Is the potential for social unrest and disharmony a legitimate basis for limiting equality?[57] If racial justice and peace come into tension, which should prevail?[58]

The Supreme Court's 1958 decision in *Cooper v. Aaron* illustrates this dilemma. *Cooper* held that Arkansas state officials, who had refused to abide by *Brown v. Board of Education*, must begin desegregating the state's public schools.[59] Rejecting a school board's proposal to delay integration by two-and-a-half years in order to maintain "public peace," the Court concluded that "law and order are not here to be preserved by depriving the Negro children of their constitutional rights."[60]

Although the field of transitional justice emerged decades after *Cooper v. Aaron*, its insights deepen our understanding of this landmark civil rights case. In *Cooper*, the Supreme Court heard arguments that can be viewed as competing transitional justice claims. For example, with respect to a peace-justice balance, the school board insisted that the justice-related interests of Black children had to be weighed against (and ultimately give way to) the justice-related interests of other students in having an operational

<hr>

[55] *See* PEACE VERSUS JUSTICE? THE DILEMMA OF TRANSITIONAL JUSTICE IN AFRICA (Chandra Lekha Sriram & Suren Pillay eds., 2009); AFR. UNION, TRANSITIONAL JUSTICE POLICY (2019), https://au.int/sites/default/files/documents/36541-doc-au_tj_policy_eng_web.pdf.

[56] *See, e.g.*, Regents of the University of California v. Bakke, 438 U.S. 265 (1978); Parents Involved in Cmty. Schs. v. Seattle Sch. Dist. No. 1, 551 U.S. 701 (2007).

[57] *See, e.g.*, Brown v. Bd. of Educ., 349 U.S. 294 (1955); Cooper v. Aaron, 358 U.S. 1 (1958).

[58] *See* Joshi, *Racial Justice and Peace, supra* note 10.

[59] Cooper v. Aaron, 358 U.S. 1 (1958).

[60] *Id.* at 16.

education system as well as the peace-related interests of local communities.[61] Meanwhile, the National Association for the Advancement of Colored People (NAACP) emphasized the importance of a justice-based peace which protects the education rights of all children.[62] With respect to timing and sequencing, the school board claimed that postponing integration by two-and-a-half years was not a case of justice denied, but merely justice delayed for the sake of immediate peace.[63] In contrast, the NAACP responded that further delays both denied justice to Black people and rendered enduring peace more difficult to achieve.[64] A transitional justice analysis invites us to consider the peace-justice logics that are operative in *Cooper* and other racial equality cases.[65]

Transitional justice theory provides a basis not only for evaluating America's ongoing transition but also for improving how courts and other segments of society pursue democratic values. At the same time, court opinions serve as valuable case studies for thinking about the racial transition project, including the different transitional paths available and the values at stake.

Comparative Experience

Comparative experience reveals that the centuries-long oppression of Black Americans is precisely the kind of massive human rights violation that necessitates a systematic transitional justice response. The United States is most clearly comparable with South Africa, one of the paradigmatic sites of transitional justice.[66] Both the United States and South Africa have deep histories of state-enforced and enabled racial subordination.[67] The pre–civil

---

[61] *Brief for the Petitioners: Cooper v. Aaron, in* 54 LANDMARK BRIEFS AND ARGUMENTS OF THE SUPREME COURT OF THE UNITED STATES: CONSTITUTIONAL LAW 553 (Philip B. Kurland & Gerhard Casper eds., 1975).

[62] *Brief for Respondents: Cooper v. Aaron, in* 54 LANDMARK BRIEFS AND ARGUMENTS OF THE SUPREME COURT OF THE UNITED STATES: CONSTITUTIONAL LAW 595 (Philip B. Kurland & Gerhard Casper eds., 1975).

[63] *Brief for the Petitioners, supra* note 61.

[64] *Brief for Respondents, supra* note 62.

[65] Joshi, *Racial Justice and Peace, supra* note 10 (undertaking this analysis).

[66] Joshi, *Affirmative Action as Transitional Justice, supra* note 10 (comparing these countries as transitional contexts).

[67] Whereas the South African transition is widely conceptualized as a transition from the apartheid system, the parameters of the American transition are not as well-theorized. To be clear, racism in South Africa predates the apartheid system, even if (as some have argued) the racist logic of colonial rule differed from that of apartheid. DAVID THEO GOLDBERG, RACIST CULTURE: PHILOSOPHY AND THE POLITICS OF MEANING 185–96 (1993).

rights United States was arguably no more an "established" democracy than apartheid South Africa. Deeper understanding of the history and legacies of America's racial apartheid only bolsters such comparisons.

Comparative experience also discredits claims that it is "too late" to address America's legacies of slavery, segregation, and White supremacy.[68] Countries spanning from Canada to the Philippines have taken centuries to grapple with the legacies of their past. For example, Canada's 2008 Truth and Reconciliation Commission reached back to the Residential Schools started in the 1860s, established to "aggressively assimilate" Indigenous children into Euro-Canadian culture; the mandate of Burundi's 2014 Truth and Reconciliation Commission extended to cover crimes since 1885; Mauritius's 2009 Truth and Justice Commission went back to the start of colonialism in 1638; the Commission on the Truth of Black Slavery in Brazil reached back to the Atlantic slave trade era in the 1500s; and the Philippines' Framework Agreement on the Bangsamoro and Transitional Justice and Reconciliation Commission reached back to pre-1521 colonization.[69]

The transitional justice canon demonstrates that governments need to address historic injustices and their legacies, even within democracies and even without regime change. If Canada could be compelled to establish a truth commission to begin grappling with racist wrongs,[70] nothing exempts the United States from doing the same.

Comparative insights further suggest that the United States is struggling with an "unmastered past."[71] Historian Gavriel Rosenfeld describes an unmastered past as "a historical legacy that has acquired an exceptional,

---

[68] Joshi, *Racial Time, supra* note 10.

[69] Truth & Reconciliation Comm'n of Can., *Our Mandate*, https://web.archive.org/web/202 00507215137/http://www.trc.ca/about-us/our-mandate.html (last visited May 1, 2022) (Canada) (the Truth and Reconciliation Commission's website is archived through the Wayback Machine; the original web address was http://www.trc.ca/about-us/our-mandate.html); Beatrice Tesconi, *Burundi Extends the Mandate of the Truth and Reconciliation Commission to Cover Crimes Since 1885*, ICL MEDIA REV. (Oct. 31, 2018), http://www.iclmediareview.com/31-october-2018-buru ndi-extends-the-mandate-of-the-truth-and reconciliation-commission-to-cover-crimes-since-1885 (Burundi); TRUTH & JUST. COMM'N, REPORT OF THE TRUTH AND JUSTICE COMMISSION (2011), https://perma.cc/R6GY-PGQH (Mauritius); Márcia Leitão Pinheiro, *A Truth Commission in Brazil: Slavery, Multiculturalism, History and Memory*, 18 CIVITAS-REVISTA DE CIÊNCIAS SOCIAIS 683 (2018) (Brazil); KRISTIAN HERBOLZHEIMER, THE PEACE PROCESS IN MINDANAO, THE PHILIPPINES: EVOLUTION AND LESSONS LEARNED, NOREF: NORWEGIAN PEACEBUILDING RESOURCE CTR. REP. (Dec. 2015) (Philippines).

[70] The Canadian Truth and Reconciliation Commission emerged from the advocacy of Indigenous peoples, which culminated in the Indian Residential School Settlement Agreement between Residential School survivors, the Assembly of First Nations, Church bodies, and the Government of Canada. *Settlement Agreement*, RESIDENTIAL SCHS. SETTLEMENT, https://www.residentialschoolset tlement.ca/settlement.html (last visited May 1, 2022).

[71] Joshi, *Racial Transition, supra* note 10, at 1247–48.

abnormal, or otherwise unsettled status in the collective memory of a given society."[72] Given the denialism of American racism prevalent in the moral panic over critical race theory and the challenges to voting rights, affirmative action, and public education,[73] a national truth commission with widely disseminated findings may be necessary to establish an accurate and authoritative historical record. Such a historical record is important for countering denial of systemic violence, addressing patterns of violence in reform efforts, and achieving societal reconciliation in the long term. Until the United States takes such preliminary steps to address its past, its transition to a multiracial democracy will be imperiled as harms compound and past progress is erased.

While the United States has been involved in transitional justice responses elsewhere, insights gained from other contexts could also be applied to the United States today. For example, the implementation of truth commissions and reparations in the United States should learn from foreign examples such as South Africa and Sierra Leone, which are studied in depth in the transitional justice literature.[74] Additionally, countries such as Northern Ireland have considered demilitarization and reduction of the police force in light of sustained civil strife.[75] Their experiences may serve as case studies for the United States to engage with.

Of course, the United States should not uncritically adopt transitional justice approaches from elsewhere. Other countries (including South Africa and Canada) offer both positive and cautionary lessons for the United States to consider.[76] Transitional justice also has more fundamental limitations and needs to be considered with careful attention to specific contexts and local demands.[77] At the same time, beliefs about the United States' democracy,

---

[72] Gavriel D. Rosenfeld, *A Looming Crash or a Soft Landing? Forecasting the Future of the Memory "Industry,"* 88 J. Mod. Hist. 122, 126–27 (2009).

[73] *Welcome to the #TruthBeTold Campaign*, Afr. Am. Pol'y F., https://www.aapf.org/truthbetold (last visited May 1, 2022).

[74] Matiangai V.S. Sirleaf, *The Truth About Truth Commissions: Why They Do Not Function Optimally in Post-Conflict Societies*, 35 Cardozo L. Rev. 2263 (2013); Kelebogile Zvobgo, *Demanding Truth: The Global Transitional Justice Network and the Creation of Truth Commissions*, 64 Int'l Stud. Q. 609 (2020).

[75] Fionnuala Ní Aoláin, *Women, Security, and the Patriarchy of Internationalized Transitional Justice*, 31 Hum. Rts. Q. 1055 (2009).

[76] Mahmood Mamdani, *Amnesty or Impunity? A Preliminary Critique of the Report of the Truth and Reconciliation Commission of South Africa (TRC)*, 32 Diacritics 33 (2002); Rosemary L. Nagy, *The Scope and Bounds of Transitional Justice and the Canadian Truth and Reconciliation Commission*, 7 Int'l J. Trans. Just. 52 (2013).

[77] Zinaida Miller, *Transitional Justice, Race, and the United States*, Just Sec. (June 30, 2020), https://www.justsecurity.org/71040/transitional-justice-race-and-the-united-states/.

progress, and exceptionalism should not place it beyond the reach of transitional justice. Americans should recognize that their nation has much to learn from the experiences of others. If transitional justice belongs "there," it belongs "here" too.

Conclusion

This chapter has advanced a racial transitional justice analysis of the United States for three key reasons.

First, a transitional justice lens reveals different American theories of transition and offers a way to compare these *internal* accounts of racial change in the United States. Whereas Supreme Court decisions since the 1970s have promoted a narrow transition from racial apartheid to "colorblindness,"[78] racial justice advocates such as Dr. King have offered far more expansive and emancipatory understandings of "transition from an obnoxious negative peace . . . to a substantive and positive peace."[79] Engagement with transitional justice opens new avenues for making these more critical perspectives throughout American history cognizable by law.

Second, transitional justice offers an independent *external* perspective to assess America's local theories of transition and a framework for aligning local approaches with international human rights norms. E. Tendayi Achiume counsels looking beyond the United States for guidance because "international human rights norms require and offer the foundation for a better system than the one currently in place in this country."[80] Seriously considering the external perspective of transitional justice can help reorient American law toward a better internal approach, one that learns from other countries' experiences of transition and supports transnational racial justice struggles.

---

[78] "The way to stop discrimination on the basis of race is to stop discriminating on the basis of race." Parents Involved in Cmty. Sch. v. Seattle Sch. Dist. No. 1, 551 U.S. 701, 748 (2007).

[79] King, *supra* note 22. Enduring transitional justice measures may be necessary to manage what Derrick Bell termed "the permanence of racism." DERRICK BELL, FACES AT THE BOTTOM OF THE WELL: THE PERMANENCE OF RACISM (1993); Derrick Bell, *Racism Is Here to Stay: Now What?*, 35 How. L.J. 79 (1991). Robert Meister similarly describes "transitional time" as a time "of indefinite duration, potentially permanent. . . ." ROBERT MEISTER, AFTER EVIL: A POLITICS OF HUMAN RIGHTS 85 (2010). Monica Bell proposes "a perpetual governance process" to address racialized policing given "the phoenix-like resilience of institutional racism. . . ." Monica C. Bell, *Anti-Segregation Policing*, 95 N.Y.U. L. REV. 650, 744, 763 (2020).

[80] Achiume, *supra* note 25.

Third, transitional justice not only recommends broader remedies than American civil rights law but may be necessary for the kinds of *structural* changes that the Black Lives Matter movement is demanding.[81] Protesters today are not demanding discrete remedies for discrete harms. Instead, they are calling for a comprehensive and coordinated transition process that deals with the legacy and threat of White supremacy in the United States. Within a transitional justice framework, redirecting resources from policing could be a way of funding reparations for slavery, Jim Crow, and ongoing racism. It could also be a way of redressing the harms of policing. Thus, "defunding the police" may be both a means to reparations and a form of repair.

Ultimately, the United States needs an integrated justice strategy—one that pursues reparations and policing reform alongside affirmative action, voting rights, political and judicial reform, and other structural changes. None of these changes alone can overcome White supremacy, yet all of them working in tandem can place the United States on a more democratic path. Transitional justice can help guide this effort.

---

[81] *Vision for Black Lives*, MOVEMENT FOR BLACK LIVES, https://m4bl.org/policy-platforms/ (last visited May 1, 2022).

11

Black Guilt, White Guilt at the International Criminal Court

Rachel López[*]

Introduction

All but one defendant convicted at the International Criminal Court (ICC) has been a Black man. This is not a coincidence. This chapter elucidates how the jurisdictional and substantive law that governs the ICC systematically results in Black guilt [1] being heightened while White guilt is minimized. With these convictions, the ICC builds on a long history of criminalizing Blackness, but there is something particularly invidious about this in the context of international criminal law that this chapter seeks to expose. Since the ICC supposedly prosecutes only "the most serious crimes of international concern," these convictions express the not-so-subtle suggestion that the "worst of the worst" criminals on the planet are Black men. More troubling still, given the long-standing characterization of international crimes as evil, it perpetuates well-documented stereotypes of darker skin being associated with wickedness, thereby building on a pernicious narrative of the "evil Black body."

Proponents of the ICC have defended the racialized nature of these prosecutions as simply a consequence of the court following its own rules, but as this chapter illustrates, it is precisely these rules that embed systemic racism within the structural design of the court, making the near exclusive conviction of Black men inevitable. Moreover, often these rules are justified

[*] This chapter was greatly enriched by feedback from José Enrique Alvarez, Haley Anderson, Randle DeFalco, Meg deGuzman, Fasika Delessa, James Gathii, Rebecca Hamilton, Brandon Hasbrouck, Marissa Jackson Sow, Yuvraj Joshi, Alexis Lovings, Zinaida Miller, Tamia Morris, Jaya Ramji-Nogales, Victoria Roman, Matiangai Sirleaf, and Ronald Slye.
[1] Throughout this chapter, when I use the phrase "Black guilt" or "White guilt," I seek to express in the plainest of terms how culpability (or guilt) at the ICC is racialized because what is criminalized is often race dependent.

Rachel López, *Black Guilt, White Guilt at the International Criminal Court* In: *Race and National Security*. Edited by: Matiangai V.S. Sirleaf, Oxford University Press. © Oxford University Press 2023.
DOI: 10.1093/oso/9780197754641.003.0012

as being in the service of peace and security, but a closer look reveals a contradiction. By shifting the focus away from the broader forces that set the stage for violence and toward the inherent wickedness of the defendant, the ICC promotes a shallow understanding of the root causes of atrocity, thereby undermining international criminal law's potential for contributing to collective peace and security. This chapter thus argues that in order to reach its full potential, the ICC should break from its nominally race-neutral stance and instead adopt an explicitly antiracist orientation to international criminal punishment.

Institutionalizing Black Guilt

Many have reflected on the African bias at the ICC, arguing that the selective prosecution of the court reflects a bias against the African continent.[2] The numbers support such accusations. All those charged as well as all those convicted by the ICC, have been from African countries. But the geographic focus of such analyses obfuscates a starker, uncomfortable truth: all those charged and convicted by the court have been Black or Brown and not one has been White.[3]

Proponents of the ICC have defended these prosecutorial choices by pointing to the fact that the ICC is just following its own rules, acting upon self-referrals from African nations or referrals from the United Nations Security Council.[4] Yet, building off the work of others, particularly Kamari

---

[2] Rebecca J. Hamilton, *Africa, the Court, and the Council*, in ELGAR COMPANION TO THE INTERNATIONAL CRIMINAL COURT 261 (2019) ("One of the defining narratives of the Court's first 15 years of operation has been that it has an anti-Africa bias.").

[3] Randle C. DeFalco & Frédéric Mégret, *The Invisibility of Race at the ICC: Lessons from the US Criminal Justice System*, 7 LONDON REV. INT'L L. 55, 59 (2019); Kamari Clarke, *Negotiating Racial Injustice: How International Criminal Law Helps Entrench Structural Inequality*, JUST SEC. (July 24, 2020), https://www.justsecurity.org/71614/negotiating-racial-injustice-how-intern ational-criminal-law-helps-entrench-structural-inequality/. For a list of all ICC defendants, *see Filter by Case*, INT'L CRIM. CT., https://www.icc-cpi.int/Pages/defendants-wip.aspx#Default= %7B%22k%22%3A%22%22%7D (last visited May 3, 2022).

[4] Hamilton, *supra* note 2, at 270 ("At every opportunity, Court officials drew on the vision of the Court, present since its inception, as an a-political institution, stressing that an anti-Africa bias could not follow from decisions based on the law."). *See, e.g.*, Max du Plessis, *Confronting Myths About the International Criminal Court and Its Work in Africa*, in PROTECTING HUMANITY: ESSAYS IN INTERNATIONAL LAW AND POLICY IN HONOUR OF NAVANETHEM PILLAY 437 (2010); W. Chadwick Austin & Michale Thieme, *Is the International Criminal Court Anti-African?*, 28 PEACE REV. 342, 345 (2016) ("It seems somewhat disingenuous to complain of racial targeting when it is African governments themselves asking for the court to intervene."); Sanji Mmasenono Monageng, *Africa and the International Criminal Court: Then and Now*, in AFRICA AND THE INTERNATIONAL CRIMINAL COURT 13, 19 ("Hundreds of African legal practitioners have made the [ICC] what it is. Frankly, it is absolutely ridiculous to accuse the Court of being racist."); Alex Whiting, *South Africa's ICC*

Clarke, Randle DeFalco, Rebecca Hamilton, Frédéric Mégret, John Reynolds, and Sujith Xavier, this section demonstrates why such justifications are inadequate to allay concerns about racial bias at the ICC. They do not explain, for instance, why none of the defendants have been White. Rather, this section outlines how the institutional design and jurisdictional rules of the court heighten Black guilt, while minimizing White guilt, often under the guise of promoting peace and security. While this invidious process has different instantiations throughout international criminal law, here I focus narrowly on how seemingly technical, "neutral" rules and procedures implicate the ICC in the reproduction of structural racism. In particular, I focus on (1) the outsized role of the United Nations Security Council in creating levers of power for non-member states to amplify Black guilt while immunizing White violence; (2) the limited temporal and definitional focus of the ICC on certain international crimes to the exclusion of harms that most concern the Global South—especially those involving White guilt; and (3) the general selectivity and the other forms of discretion built into the system which in practice manifest anti-Black bias.

As a starting point, the outsized role of the United Nations Security Council in the matters handled by the court is partly to blame. The Rome Statute, the treaty which established the court, empowers the Security Council both to refer and defer ICC investigations, with the Security Council being the sole entity with the power to confer jurisdiction onto the territory of non-ICC members.[5] These rules, and how they have been instrumentalized to date, are an example of how the work of the ICC helps cement the racial hierarchy and power imbalances already present within the international legal order into the ICC legal regime.[6] Notably, five permanent members, more than half of which are majority White nations, control most of the decision-making at the Council. Each has veto power over nonprocedural decisions, including

Withdrawal: Why? And What Now?, JUST SEC. (Oct. 22, 2016), https://www.justsecurity.org/33765/south-africas-icc-withdrawal-why-now/ ("The claim of bias is misplaced and obscures the real issue. The notion that the ICC Prosecutor targets Africa out of some kind of bias against the continent is both ludicrous and pernicious. . . . In truth, the Prosecutor has decided to investigate where the Court has jurisdiction, serious crimes are being committed, and there exists a reasonable prospect that investigations will be fruitful.").

[5] Rome Statute of the International Criminal Court art. 13(b), July 17, 1998, 2187 U.N.T.S. 3 (entered into force July 1, 2002). The Rome Statute refers to these investigations as situations, but for ease of understanding, I will call them investigations through this chapter.
[6] John Reynolds & Sujith Xavier, *The Dark Corners of the World: TWAIL and International Criminal Justice*, 14 J. INT'L CRIM. JUST. 959, 964 (2016).

whether to refer cases to the ICC or delay them.[7] More troubling still, three of the permanent members are not even parties to the Rome Statute, meaning that international crimes committed in their territories are not subject to ICC jurisdiction. Thus, despite opting out of the ICC, those nations have the power to obstruct or push ICC investigations.[8] Specifically, acting through the Security Council, they have the power to grant ICC jurisdiction over other nations which, like them, have not joined the court, while, at the same time, blocking investigations into their own nationals or crimes committed in their territory.[9] Through these rules, the power and privilege of majority White nations have become embedded in the Court's structure and thereby, its decision-making.[10]

And the results are predictable. The Security Council has only asked the ICC to investigate crimes in two African nations, Sudan and Libya, but issued no referrals for documented torture and war crimes by the United States and United Kingdom in Iraq and Afghanistan.[11] While Article 16 of the Rome Statute was meant to allow the Security Council to step in and delay prosecutions if doing so is in the interest of maintaining peace and security, so far, it has only been used to immunize White guilt, shielding the citizens of majority White nations from the court's reach. In fact, the first evocation of the Security Council's deferral power was only made after the United States. threatened to veto a resolution renewing the United Nations peacekeeping mission in Bosnia (as well as all other future peacekeeping operations) unless a provision immunizing its troops from criminal liability was included.[12] Since then, the Security Council has invoked Article 16 two additional times, each time at the United States' behest to immunize soldiers from any criminal liability resulting from military operations authorized by the Security Council.[13]

While the Security Council has used Article 16 to minimize the guilt of White majority nations, it refused to use this power to defer investigations

[7] U.N. Charter art. 27(3).
[8] Rome Statute of the International Criminal Court arts. 13(b) & 16, July 17, 1998, 2187 U.N.T.S. 3 (entered into force July 1, 2002).
[9] Hamilton, *supra* note 2, at 266.
[10] *Id.* at 265.
[11] *Id.* at 264, 277.
[12] *See* S.C. Res. 1422 (July 12, 2002); S.C. Res. 1487 (June 12, 2003); S.C. Res. 1497 (Aug. 1, 2003); Hamilton, *supra* note 2, at 266–67; Charles C. Jalloh, Dapo Akandeb & Max du Plessisc, *Assessing the African Union Concerns about Article 16 of the Rome Statute of the International Criminal Court*, 4 AFR. J. LEGAL STUD. 5, 17 (2011).
[13] *See* ROBERT CRYER ET AL., AN INTRODUCTION TO INTERNATIONAL CRIMINAL LAW AND PROCEDURE 142–44 (4th ed. 2007).

in two African nations, Sudan and Kenya, despite repeated requests from the African Union to do so.[14] Functionally, this has meant that White leaders who authorized torture, like George W. Bush and Donald Rumsfeld, have evaded criminal liability before the ICC, while Black and Arab-African heads of state like Uhuru Muigai Kenyatta and Omar al-Bashir faced charges.[15]

In addition to these jurisdictional rules, the temporal and definitional limitations on what counts as a prosecutable crime before the ICC renders White violence less visible and consequential. Like other tribunals that have tried international crimes, such as the International Criminal Tribunal for the Former Yugoslavia (ICTY), International Criminal Tribunal for Rwanda (ICTR), and the Extraordinary Chambers in the Courts of Cambodia, the ambit of the ICC's prosecutorial reach is time limited.[16] Specifically, the crimes committed before the Rome Statute entered into force on July 1, 2002, are off the table.[17] As will be discussed further in the third section of this chapter, this narrow temporal gaze often obfuscates the role of colonial powers in the violence under investigation by the ICC and shields them from prosecution for their past empire-building crimes, most notably slavery and genocide. In a broader sense, these rules have criminalized the processes by which the Global North became wealthy, at the same time as effectively granting them de facto amnesty for those same acts.

The impunity for colonial era crimes of the Global North is compounded by the fact that the type of violence currently perpetrated by these majority White nations also tends to be untouched by international criminal law, while those crimes which typify Western stereotypes of Black men have been vigorously pursued.[18] First, as Kamari Clarke illuminated in her groundbreaking book, *Fictions of Justice*, the choice of acts considered to be the "most serious crimes of international concern" under the Rome Statute and therefore prosecutable by the ICC exacerbates Black guilt, while mitigating White guilt. Omitted from actionable crimes are those most likely to be committed by majority White nations, such as colonial domination, economic aggression,

---

[14] Hamilton, *supra* note 2, at 273.

[15] *Id.* at 263.

[16] Clarke, *supra* note 3; *see also* Randle C. DeFalco, *Time and the Visibility of Slow Atrocity Violence*, 21 INT'L CRIM. L. REV. 905, 930 (2021).

[17] *See* Rome Statute of the International Criminal Court art. 11, July 17, 1998, 2187 U.N.T.S. 3 (entered into force July 1, 2002).

[18] DeFalco & Mégret, *supra* note 3, at 81–82. Christine Schwöbel-Patel has also described how racialized and gendered tropes of victimization also play into international criminalization. *See generally* Christine Schwöbel-Patel, *Spectacle in International Criminal Law: The Fundraising Image of Victimhood*, 4 LONDON REV. INT'L L. 247 (2016).

the use of nuclear weapons, the recruitment, use, financing, and training of mercenaries, and environmental atrocities.[19] These crimes were all dropped during the negotiation of the Rome Statute because they were considered to "devalu[e] the concept of crimes against the peace and security of mankind."[20] Implicitly, they were not seen as unquestionably undermining peace and security. Instead, the ICC only has jurisdiction over four crimes: war crimes, crimes against humanity, genocide, and the crime of aggression.[21] Of these crimes, the crime of aggression is the only one that is most often perpetrated by majority White states, and it was left inoperable until 2018 largely due to pushback from the United States.[22] Even now, the crime of aggression is not prosecutable against the nationals of those countries most likely to engage in military action, like the United Kingdom, the United States, France, and Russia, because these states have not acceded to the ICC's jurisdiction, either generally or specifically when it comes to this crime.[23] This paradox came to a head recently, as due to this rule, the ICC has been unable to prosecute any Russian nationals for the crime of aggression after Russia's invasion of Ukraine despite widespread consensus that it constituted aggressive war.[24]

[19] KAMARI CLARKE, FICTIONS OF JUSTICE: THE INTERNATIONAL CRIMINAL COURT AND THE CHALLENGE OF LEGAL PLURALISM IN SUB-SAHARAN AFRICA 56–58 (2009); *see also Summaries of the Work of the International Law Commission: Draft Code of Crimes Against the Peace and Security of Mankind (Part II)*, INT'L L COMM'N, https://legal.un.org/ilc/summaries/7_4.shtml (last visited Dec. 4, 2017).

[20] CLARKE, *supra* note 19, at 57 (quoting Report of the International Law Commission on the Work of the Its Forty-Seventh Session (1995), at 10 § 28.); *see also* Antony Anghie & B.S. Chimni, *Third World Approaches to International Law and Individual Responsibility in Internal Conflicts*, 2 CHINESE J. INT'L L. 77, 95 (2003) ("Thus the ICC Statute does not outlaw the use of nuclear weapons, in a situation where this issue is surely fundamental to the goal of the ICC, to prevent the acts harming innocent civilians.").

[21] Rome Statute of the International Criminal Court art. 5, July 17, 1998, 2187 U.N.T.S. 3 (entered into force July 1, 2002).

[22] Celestine Nchekwube Ezennia, *The Modus Operandi of the International Criminal Court System: An Impartial or a Selective Justice Regime?*, 16 INT'L CRIM. L. REV. 448, 471–72 (2016). For further discussion on the negotiations regarding the definition of the crime of aggression, *see generally* Dire Tladi, *Kampala, the International Criminal Court and the Adoption of a Definition of the Crime of Aggression: A Dream Deferred*, 35 S. AFR. Y.B. INT'L L. 80 (2010).

[23] International Criminal Court Res. ICC-ASP/16/Res.5, Activation of the Jurisdiction of the Court over the Crime of Aggression (Dec. 14, 2017), https://asp.icc-cpi.int/iccdocs/asp_docs/Reso lutions/ASP16/ICC-ASP-16-Res5-eng.pdf (confirming "that in the case of a State referral or proprio motu investigation the Court shall not exercise its jurisdiction regarding a crime of aggression when committed by a national or on the territory of a State Party that has not ratified or accepted these amendments . . ."); *see also Status of Treaties Amendments on the Crime of Aggression to the Rome Statute of the International Criminal Court*, U.N. TREATY COLLECTION, https://treaties.un.org/Pages/ ViewDetails.aspx?src=TREATY&mtdsg_no=XVIII-10-b&chapter=18&clang=_en (last visited May 3, 2022) (listing states that have accepted or ratified the amendments on the crime of aggression to the Rome Statute). While the Security Council could still refer such cases to the ICC, because these countries have veto power at the Security Council, the political reality of that is near impossible.

[24] Jennifer Trahan, *Revisiting the History of the Crime of Aggression in Light of Russia's Invasion of Ukraine*, 26 ASIL INSIGHTS 1 (Apr. 19, 2022), https://www.asil.org/insights/volume/26/issue/2#_

While the ICC is pursuing charges of war crimes against Russian President Vladimir Putin and another Russian official for their involvement in the unlawful deportation of Ukrainian children to Russia, these same officials are essentially untouchable for their involvement in the crime of aggression.[25] Yet, as Dr. Gaiane Nuridzhanian, a Ukrainian law professor with expertise in international criminal law, has noted, Russia's aggression has done more damage to her country than all their war crimes taken together.[26]

In addition, when majority White nations have been involved in other crimes that fall within the four corners of the Rome Statute, they are often dismissed by the ICC, usually for being insufficiently grave, a threshold requirement at the court.[27] This has been the case with international crimes, such as war crimes and torture, committed by Israel, the United States, Australia, and the United Kingdom.[28] Most recently, the new ICC prosecutor justified his decision to "deprioritise" the investigation into atrocities committed by American forces in Afghanistan and instead focus on the Taliban and affiliates of the Islamic State, on the basis of the "gravity, scale and continuing nature of alleged crimes."[29] In addition, powerful nations frequently facilitate the international crimes of other less powerful nations from behind the scenes by providing weapons, technical support, or intelligence.[30] By

ednref16. However, in a notable departure from the usual immunity afforded to powerful states, the ICC has opened investigations into war crimes and crimes against humanity genocide committed in Ukraine, since Ukraine assented to its jurisdiction via a declaration in 2015, pursuant to Article 12(3) of the Rome Statute. *See* Statements of ICC Prosecutor, Karim A.A. Khan QC, on the Situation in Ukraine (Feb. 28, 2022), https://www.icc-cpi.int/news/statement-icc-prosecutor-karim-aa-khan-qc-situation-ukraine-i-have-decided-proceed-opening.

[25] Press Release, Int'l Crim. Ct., Situation in Ukraine: ICC Judges Issue Arrest Warrants Against Vladimir Vladimirovich Putin and Maria Alekseyevna Lvova-Belova (Mar. 17, 2023), https://www.icc-cpi.int/news/situation-ukraine-icc-judges-issue-arrest-warrants-against-vladimir-vladimirovich-putin-and.

[26] Gaiane Nuridzhanian, *Justice for the Crime of Aggression Today, Deterrence for the Aggressive Wars of Tomorrow: A Ukrainian Perspective*, JUST SEC. (Aug. 24, 2022), https://www.justsecurity.org/82780/justice-for-the-crime-of-aggression-a-ukrainian-perspective/.

[27] Margaret M. deGuzman, *Gravity Rhetoric: The Good, the Bad, and the "Political,"* 107 PROC. ASIL ANN. MEETING 421, 422–23 (2013). *Cf.* Michael Mandel, *Politics and Human Rights in International Criminal Law: Our Case Against NATO and the Lessons to Be Learned from It*, 25 FORDHAM INT'L L.J. 95, 97 (describing the ICTY as being "far more concerned with legitimating NATO's war on Yugoslavia than with doing justice").

[28] Rachel López, *The Law of Gravity*, 58 COLUM. J. TRANSNAT'L L. 565, 589–90 (2020); *see, e.g.*, Kevin Jon Heller, *The OTP Lets Australia Off the Hook*, OPINIO JURIS (Feb. 2, 2021), http://opiniojuris.org/2020/02/17/the-otp-lets-australia-off-the-hook/.

[29] Statement of the Prosecutor of the International Criminal Court, Karim A.A. Khan QC, Following the Application for an Expedited Order Under Article 18(2) Seeking Authorisation to Resume Investigations in the Situation in Afghanistan (Sept. 27, 2021), https://www.icc-cpi.int/Pages/item.aspx?name=2021-09-27-otp-statement-afghanistan.

[30] Rachel López, *The Duty to Refrain: A Theory of State Accomplice Liability for Grave Crimes*, 97 NEB. L. REV. 101, 120–21 (2018); *see also* Rebecca J. Hamilton, *State-Enabled Crimes*, 41 YALE J. INT'L

acting through proxies, these nations advance their national interest and entrench their power without getting their hands dirty. Their crimes of aiding and abetting others' grave crimes are likely to escape punishment because they are less visible and perhaps less likely to be considered serious enough to warrant investigation by the ICC.[31]

Prosecuting Evil

In response to allegations of anti-African bias, supporters of the ICC have claimed that the focus on Africa is not racially motivated, but rather is just the unfortunate result of following the rules.[32] For example, former ICC prosecutor, Luis Moreno Ocampo, repudiated the accusations of bias in his selection of cases, asserting that his job was "to apply the law without political considerations."[33] To this end, he has characterized allegations of African bias as "hypocrisy," saying, "[W]e are in Africa for two reasons: the most serious crimes under ICC jurisdiction are in Africa . . . and African leaders requested the court's intervention."[34] In essence, his argument, much like those of other proponents of the ICC, is that we should not be concerned with racism at the court, because the exclusive prosecution of African defendants resulted from a race-neutral application of the law.

Somewhat ironically, given Ocampo's insistence on rule-following, this persistent focus on deliberate racism breaks the ICC's own antidiscrimination rules. Namely, the Rome Statute itself requires the ICC to follow and apply the law "consistent with internationally recognized human rights and be without any adverse distinction founded on grounds such as [inter alia] race."[35] This

---

L. 102 (2016) (critiquing the way that international criminal law, in the post-Nuremberg period, has focused on individual accountability at the expense of considering the enabling role that states play in the commission of atrocities).

[31] *See generally* RANDLE DEFALCO, INVISIBLE ATROCITIES: THE AESTHETIC BIASES OF INTERNATIONAL CRIMINAL JUSTICE (2022). *Cf.* Zinaida Miller, *Effects of Invisibility: In Search of the "Economic" in Transitional Justice*, 2 J. INT'L TRANSITIONAL JUST. 266 (2008).

[32] *See* Austin & Thieme, *supra* note 4.

[33] Statement from L. Moreno-Ocampo, Prosecutor, ICC, at ISS Symposium on "The ICC that Africa Wants," Working with Africa: The View from the ICC Prosecutor's Office (Nov. 9. 2009); SYMPOSIUM ON "THE ICC THAT AFRICA WANTS": KEY OUTCOMES AND RECOMMENDATIONS 3 (2010), https://www.files.ethz.ch/isn/139879/10%20November%202009.pdf.

[34] *Arena: Is the ICC Biased Against African Countries?*, AL JAZEERA (Mar. 12, 2016), https://www.youtube.com/watch?v=1XHyJYOYZDk.

[35] Rome Statute of the International Criminal Court art. 21(3), July 17, 1998, 2187 U.N.T.S. 3 (entered into force July 1, 2002).

nod to human rights law is noteworthy. Under the International Convention on the Elimination of All Forms of Racial Discrimination (CERD), the primary international human rights treaty to address racism, a violation of its antidiscrimination principles does not require a showing of discriminatory intent. Instead, a policy or practice that appears racially neutral, but has a discriminatory effect is still considered to be discrimination under CERD.[36] CERD also requires the ICC to take measures to amend, rescind, or nullify any laws or regulations, such as those described in this chapter, that have the effect of *perpetuating* racial discrimination.[37]

Additionally, as Kamari Clarke, Randle DeFalco, and Frédéric Mégret have all pointed out, such repudiations reveal a rather thin understanding of racism.[38] By definition, structural racism can be entrenched in institutional design and embedded in rules, even when individual actors in a system harbor no racial animus.[39] Yet, as this section elaborates, the effects of such "unconscious racism" are no less harmful. Particularly in the context of international criminal law, the ICC's trained focus on Black men reinforces racialized stereotypes, thereby perpetuating White supremacist ideologies. Indeed, recent empirical evidence has shown that people often associate dark skin with immorality and wickedness.[40] Specifically, dubbed the "bad is black" effect, psychologists have found that when people learn about "evil acts," they are more likely to believe that they were committed by someone with dark skin.[41] More problematic still, the darker your complexion, the more likely society is to support extreme punishment of you.[42]

---

[36] Theodor Meron, *The Meaning and Reach of the International Convention on the Elimination of All Forms of Racial Discrimination*, 79 AM. J. INT'L L. 283, 289 (1985) ("Because the objective of the Convention is the attainment of equality, facially neutral policies or practices that have a disparate impact on some racial groups should be prohibited, despite the absence of discriminatory motive.").

[37] *See* Rome Statute of the International Criminal Court art. 2, July 17, 1998, 2187 U.N.T.S. 3 (entered into force July 1, 2002).

[38] Clarke, *supra* note 3; DeFalco & Mégret, *supra* note 3, at 57, 64–65.

[39] DeFalco & Mégret, *supra* note 3, at 57.

[40] Adam A. Alter et al., *The "Bad Is Black" Effect: Why People Believe Evildoers Have Darker Skin Than Do-Gooders*, 42 PERSONALITY & SOC. PSYCH. BULL. 1653 (2016); Calvin John Smiley & David Fakunle, *From "Brute" to "Thug": The Demonization and Criminalization of Unarmed Black Male Victims in America*, 26 J. HUM. BEHAV. SOC. ENV'T 350 (2016); Kelly Welch, *Black Criminal Stereotypes and Racial Profiling*, 23 J. CONTEMP. CRIM. JUST. 276 (2007); Cynthia J. Najdowski, Bette L. Bottoms & Phillip Atiba Goff, *Stereotype Threat and Racial Differences in Citizens' Experiences of Police Encounters*, 39 L. & HUM. BEHAV. 463 (2015). Granted, these studies focused on the United States, but the stereotypes of the African continent in other Western countries have been no less racialized, informed by the understanding of Africa as the "Heart of Darkness." Reynolds & Xavier, *supra* note 6, at 968.

[41] Daisy Grewal, *The "Bad Is Black" Effect*, SCI. AM. (Jan. 17, 2017), https://www.scientificamerican.com/article/the-bad-is-black-effect/.

[42] NAZGOL GHANDNOOSH, THE SENTENCING PROJECT, RACE AND PUNISHMENT: RACIAL PERCEPTIONS OF CRIME AND SUPPORT FOR PUNITIVE POLICIES 18–19 (2014), https://www.senten

The operationalizing of these stereotypes in the context of international criminal law is particularly noxious. Since international crimes are often portrayed as inherently evil, the ICC's narrow focus on the criminal acts of Black men reinforces these racial stereotypes.[43] Implicit in such characterization is a lack of reason.[44] These crimes are not committed for a specific purpose or under certain conditions, but rather attributed to the inherent wickedness or lust for power or violence.[45] Such stereotypes have not been absent from the courtrooms of international criminal law, with prosecutors at times evoking themes of darkness and hell in an effort to secure convictions.[46] Cast under such light, international criminal law could be portrayed as replicating the modalities of the civilizing mission of international law of the 19th century, which relied on stereotypes regarding the inherent violence and inferiority of "Blackness" to justify slavery and colonialization.[47] Subtly embedded in the race neutral defenses of the ICC is the notion that international criminal law is needed to civilize Africa or as Ocampo's preceding remarks imply, that the ICC has been forced to train its eye on Africa because that's where the most serious violence occurs.

Further to this point, when defendants are exclusively dark-skinned, as they are at the ICC, international criminal justice becomes a tool for confirmation bias—an expression of our racialized understanding of wrongdoing.

cingproject.org/publications/race-and-punishment-racial-perceptions-of-crime-and-support-for-punitive-policies/.

[43] Miriam J. Aukerman, *Extraordinary Evil, Ordinary Crime: A Framework for Understanding Transitional Justice*, 15 HARV. HUM. RTS. J. 39 (2002); ROBERT MEISTER, AFTER EVIL: A POLITICS OF HUMAN RIGHTS (2011); CARLOS SANTIAGO NINO, RADICAL EVIL ON TRIAL (1996); HANNAH ARENDT, EICHMANN IN JERUSALEM: A REPORT ON THE BANALITY OF EVIL (1963); Diane Orentlicher, *Settling Accounts: The Duty to Prosecute Human Rights Violations of a Prior Regime*, 100 YALE L.J. 2537, 2537 (1991) (beginning her article with the following quote from A. SOLZHENITSYN, THE GULAG ARCHIPELAGO 178 (1974): "When we neither punish nor reproach evildoers, we are not simply protecting their trivial old age, we are thereby ripping the foundations of justice from beneath new generations.").

[44] An empirical study by Sofia Stolk of opening statements in international criminal tribunals revealed a paradox: "[V]iolence is described as a rational plan that is devoid of reason at the same time." Sofia Stolk, *A Sophisticated Beast? On the Construction of an "Ideal" Perpetrator in the Opening Statements of International Criminal Trials*, 29 EUR. J. INT'L L. 677, 685 (2018).

[45] *Id.* at 684–87.

[46] *Id.* at 688–92; *see also* Reynolds & Xavier, *supra* note 6, at 966 (citing Transcript, Sesay, Kallon, and Gbao (SCSL-04-15-T), Trial Chamber, 5 July 2004, at 19) ("This idealized rule of law stands in marked contrast to the state of nature depicted by Crane in his Prosecution statements during the trials of the Revolutionary United Front leaders, whereby Sierra Leone is the setting for 'a tale of horror, beyond the gothic into the realm of Dante's inferno', populated by 'dark shadows' and 'hounds from hell'.").

[47] DeFalco & Mégret, *supra* note 3, at 75–76; Anghie & Chimni, *supra* note 20, at 85. NTINA TZOUVALA, CAPITALISM AS CIVILISATION: A HISTORY OF INTERNATIONAL LAW 45 (2020).

Indeed, the construction of certain rules at the ICC create a feedback loop reaffirming preexisting implicit bias. For example, the ICC can dismiss or move ahead with cases based on how grave the crime is perceived to be. As I have explored in past work, research has shown that an individual's determination of what constitutes the worst acts is highly dependent on their own demographic characteristics, including their race, class, political orientation, and gender—to name a few.[48] Since approximately 69 percent of all professional staff at the ICC and 68 percent of those in higher ranks are European (as compared to only 16.5 percent and 19.8 percent, respectively, who are African), gravity determinations are more likely than not to reflect Eurocentric understandings of criminality.[49] And in the court's decisions, we can see such implicit biases at work. For instance, the ICC has deemed torture by U.S. forces in Iraq not grave enough to merit prosecution, while the recruitment of child soldiers in the Congo and destruction of cultural property in Mali are.[50]

Such racialized understandings of international crimes are particularly concerning given the current rationales leveled in support of international criminal law on the whole. As the deterrent effect of international criminal punishment remains unclear, the proponents of international criminal law are increasingly turning to expressive theories of punishment as justifications for the ICC's work.[51] For example, David Luban has argued that, through international criminal punishment, the international community engages in both norm affirmation and norm projection (i.e., the articulation of new codes of behavior).[52] In sum, international criminal punishment has value

---

[48] López, *supra* note 28, at 620–21.

[49] *See* Int'l Crim. Ct., Report of the Committee on Budget and Finance on the Work of Its Thirty-Sixth Session, annex V (2021), https://asp.icc-cpi.int/sites/asp/files/asp_docs/ASP20/ICC-ASP-20-5-ENG-CBF36%20Report-10ago21.1300.pdf (Annex V: Geographical Representation). Figure 2 in Annex V references "Western Europeans and other states." Since the only continent not otherwise represented in the figure is North America, these other states are likely in that continent. For that reason, these statistics are just an approximation.

[50] Int'l Criminal Court Office of the Chief Prosecutor, OTP Response to Communications Received Concerning Iraq 8 (Feb. 9, 2006), https://www.icc-cpi.int/news/otp-response-communications-received-concerning-iraq [https://perma.cc/QMA4-M37V]; *see also* INT'L CRIM. CT., CASE INFORMATION SHEET: SITUATION IN THE DEMOCRATIC REPUBLIC OF THE CONGO, THE PROSECUTOR V. THOMAS LUBANGA DYILO, Int'l Criminal Court, ICC-01/04–01/06 (July 2021), https://www.icc-cpi.int/CaseInformationSheets/lubangaEng.pdf; *Al Mahdi Case: The Prosecutor v. Ahmad Al Faqi Al Mahdi*, INT'L CRIM. CT., https://www.icc-cpi.int/mali/al-mahdi (last visited May 4, 2022).

[51] Padraig McAuliffe, *Suspended Disbelief: The Curious Endurance of the Deterrence Rationale in International Criminal Law*, 10 N.Z. J. PUB. & INT'L L. 227, 254–61 (2012) (critiquing the empirical research showing that a deterrence effect exists in international criminal law); CARSTEN STAHN, JUSTICE AS MESSAGE: EXPRESSIVIST FOUNDATIONS OF INTERNATIONAL CRIMINAL JUSTICE 6 (2021).

[52] STAHN, *supra* note 51, at 58.

because it reflects our current beliefs and future aspirations. Understanding the purpose of international criminal law through this lens, it is imperative to ask whether the ICC's near exclusive focus on Black men is sending the right message. Or given the current structural racism embedded in the ICC's design, are we merely affirming the racial biases of the Global North and cementing the current global power structures under the guise of law?

Alternatively, if the international community seeks to express what it values most through international criminal punishment, it should adopt an *antiracist expressive orientation*, rather than the nominally race-neutral approach articulated by ICC officials and other proponents.[53] Antiracism is a framework developed by Ibram X. Kendi. According to Professor Kendi, striving to be antiracist means more than just being "not racist."[54] Being "not racist" is akin to being "color-blind" or in a state of denial—that is, failing to see or denying the effects of racism.[55] Rather, being antiracist requires playing an active role in identifying and dismantling the systemic racism embedded in the regular practices and rules of institutions.[56] To adopt an *antiracist expressive orientation*, the ICC would have to openly commit itself to antiracism in its administration of international criminal law. It must then take a hard look at itself, identifying and rescinding those policies that reproduce racism and instituting new antiracist policies that eliminate racial inequity.[57] This process will take time and be ongoing, but at a minimum, adopting an antiracist approach would necessitate nullifying rules like Article 16 that reproduce the structural racism embedded in the international legal order, allowing for evolving definitions of crimes that account for the harms of most concern to the Global South, including those involving environmental atrocities that are often perpetrated by majority White states, limiting the power of states that are not parties to the Rome Statute to influence proceedings at the ICC, and hiring staff in numbers that statistically reflect the racial and national diversity of its state parties. Through adopting such an expressly

---

[53] Gratitude is in order to Randle DeFalco for suggesting this framing in this chapter. A similar approach was also proposed by Rebecca Hamilton in her discussion of a communication alleging international crimes perpetrated by Australia against the asylum seekers held in Australia's offshore detention facilities on the islands of Nauru and Manus. Rebecca Hamilton, *Australia's Refugee Policy an Opportunity for the ICC to Combat Image of Bias*, JUST SEC. (Mar. 6, 2017), https://www.justsecurity.org/38326/australias-refugee-policy-opportunity-icc-combat-perception-bias/.

[54] For a general explanation of antiracist approaches, *see* IBRAM X. KENDI, HOW TO BE AN ANTIRACIST (2019).

[55] *Id.* at 10, 226.

[56] *Id.* at 19.

[57] *Id.* at 232.

antiracist approach to international criminal punishment, the international community can express its outrage at both atrocity and racism by prioritizing the punishment of pernicious uses of power that harm marginalized people regardless of nationality and race.

Decontextualizing Harm

An antiracist approach to criminal punishment is also needed, because, as this section explains, the racialized nature of international prosecution undermines peace and security by shallowing our understanding of why violence occurs. Instead of trying to analyze and understand what causes violence, this racialized version of "justice" permits atrocity to be written off as "evil," lacking in reason or purpose.[58] Put another way, the othering effect that racism facilitates hides the causes and conditions that foment violence and thereby impedes the international community (or in some cases, regional authorities) from advancing measures that are more likely to arrest violence in the future.[59] In the course of demonstrating this point, this section also documents how the ICC rules related to promoting peace and security have been used by powerful majority White nations to racialize criminal punishment at the ICC in ways that have the potential to undercut collective security.

For example, the narrow gaze of the ICTR on the Black Rwandan perpetrators cast the genocide as part of an internal conflict between two tribes, the Hutu and Tutsi. This trained focus averted eyes from the role of the colonial powers like Belgium that created and propagated these racial categories, fomenting the animosity between these two imagined tribes

---

[58] *See, e.g.*, the statement of David Crane, the first prosecutor of the Special Court for Sierra Leone, in David Crane, *Dancing with the Devil: Prosecuting West Africa's Warlords: Building Initial Prosecutorial Strategy for an International Tribunal after Third World Armed Conflicts*, 37 Case W. Rsrv. J. Int'l L. 1, 3–4 (2005) ("Fertilized by greed and corruption, what grows out of these regions of the world are terror, war crimes, and crimes against humanity. Conflicts in these dark corners are evolving into uncivilized events. They appear to be less political and are more criminal in origin and scope.").

[59] Clarke, *supra* note 19, at 3 ("This reclassification of responsibility has had the effect of subliminating root causes of violence, reassigning accountability to those few high-ranking leaders in sub-Saharan Africa who are seen as responsible for mass violations."); *see also id.* at 2–3 (describing how the defense attorney for Thomas Lubanga pointed to the root causes of violence in Ituri, such as challenges of poverty and sovereign control of the wealth of the land, but the prosecution focused narrowly on the guilt of one Black man).

for their own gain.[60] This, too, minimized the appearance of White guilt as a contributor to violence, while also assuaging White guilt by making the superpowers in the Security Council feel like they had done something, even if they had done very little to stop the genocide in real time.[61] This dynamic is not unique to Rwanda. As Antony Anghie and B.S. Chimni explain, "[c]ontemporary ethnic conflict is not simply the latest expression of primordial forces. Its nature, its conduct, its shape are all inextricably linked both with colonialism and with the very modern forces of globalization that inevitably involve North-South economic relations."[62]

Additionally, the institutional design and jurisdictional rules described in the first section of this chapter have subjected decisions about peace and security to the racial politics of the world stage with destabilizing effects. One of the most enduring dilemmas for nations grappling with the aftermath of atrocity is whether to pursue punishment in the name of "justice" or to forgo prosecutions in the name of "peace."[63] At the ICC, Article 16 was designed to mediate this tension between the search for peace and demands for criminal justice.[64] This sensitive role was entrusted to the Security Council, which has the power to delay prosecutions if they might undermine peace and security.[65] In practice, however, the consequence has been that the judgment of Black African nations closest and most affected by violence in the region has been supplanted with that of the majority White superpowers on issues of peace and security. Inevitably, this has meant that there is little recourse when powerful majority White nations engage in acts that threaten peace and security, at the same time that prosecutions of African leaders are pursued even if they might derail ongoing peace processes.

The Security Council's involvement in the investigation into atrocities in Sudan is a prime example. Upon determining that "the situation in Sudan continues to constitute a threat to international peace and security," the Security Council asked the ICC to investigate the ongoing violations of

---

[60] Jose Alvarez, *Crimes of States/Crimes of Hate: Lessons from Rwanda*, 24 YALE J. INT'L L. 365 (1999).

[61] A. CASSESE, INTERNATIONAL CRIMINAL LAW 339 (2003) ("[S]ensitive to the criticisms that the establishment of the ICTY represented yet another illustration of the disproportionate attention paid to the problems of Europe vis-à-vis the developing world, the international community was also anxious to establish a Tribunal for Rwanda so as to assuage its conscience and shield itself from accusations of double standards.").

[62] Anghie & Chimni, *supra* note 20, at 96.

[63] Rachel López, *Post-Conflict Pluralism*, 39 U. PA. J. INT'L L. 749, 757–67 (2018).

[64] Jalloh, Akandeb & Plessisc, *supra* note 12, at 11.

[65] U.N. Charter art. 24; Jalloh, Akandeb & Plessisc, *supra* note 12, at 11.

human rights and humanitarian law in Darfur.[66] In order to exercise its referral power under the Rome Statute, the Security Council must have thought that criminal trials of those responsible in Sudan would help to maintain or restore international peace and security in the region.[67] While the African Union (AU) initially supported the investigation, once the ICC charged the sitting Sudanese President Omar al-Bashir, it vehemently opposed it.[68] This decision pitted the United Nations Security Council, which has "primary responsibility for the maintenance of international peace and security" under the United Nations Charter, against the Peace and Security Council of the AU, which has "primary responsibility for promoting peace, security[,] and stability in Africa."[69] Instead of promoting peace and security, the AU feared that the pursuit of criminal punishment of the incumbent Sudanese president would derail ongoing efforts at a peaceful resolution to the Darfur crisis.[70] On this basis, the AU requested that the Security Council defer the investigation, a request that was supported by a super majority of the international community.[71] However, this request was met with silence from the Security Council, which never officially affirmed or denied it.[72]

If anything, in this context, the Security Council's use of Article 16 deferral power jeopardized peace and security. At the time, many commentators saw the Security Council's referral of the situation in Sudan as a sign of the ICC's growing credence on the world stage, as it signified an acceptance of the court by many of its detractors, especially the United States, which did not veto the referral to the ICC. A closer look reveals a much more complicated picture in which Black guilt is aggravated and White guilt is immunized in ways that ultimately undercut collective security. First, the U.S.' decision to abstain from the resolution, rather than veto it, must be understood in context. At the time, U.S. relations with its European allies were strained as support for the Iraq War waned due to emerging evidence of its own international crimes, namely, the torture of detainees at Guantanamo and Abu Ghraib.[73]

---

[66] S.C. Res. 1593 (Mar. 31, 2005).

[67] Jalloh, Akandeb & Plessisc, *supra* note 12, at 6, 15.

[68] Hamilton, *supra* note 2, at 270.

[69] U.N. Charter art. 24; U.N. Charter art. 16; Protocol Relating to the Establishment of the Peace and Security Council of the African Union (adopted July 9, 2022, entered into force Dec. 26, 2003).

[70] Jalloh, Akandeb & Plessisc, *supra* note 12, at 8.

[71] *Id.* at 23; Hamilton, *supra* note 2, at 273.

[72] Hamilton, *supra* note 2, at 273.

[73] REBECCA HAMILTON, FIGHTING FOR DARFUR: PUBLIC ACTION AND THE STRUGGLE TO STOP GENOCIDE 54–69 (2011) (detailing the central role of securing ongoing European support for the U.S. invasion of Iraq in the U.S. government's decision to abstain from vetoing the U.N. Security Council referral of Darfur to the ICC).

This political reality made it too costly to expressly oppose a referral of the situation in Darfur to the ICC.[74]

Second, embedded in the resolution referring the situation in Darfur to the ICC was an escape clause for the United States. Much like in the resolution authorizing peacekeeping in Bosnia described in the first section of this chapter, this resolution evoked Article 16 as authority for granting non-parties to the Rome Statute exclusive jurisdiction over any criminal acts by their nationals in Sudan.[75] This resolution went a step further than prior Article 16 clauses, offering even greater protection to U.S. troops and leaders. Instead of giving the Security Council the power to authorize criminal proceedings as was the case in prior resolutions, it left it to the states contributing military personnel to waive their exclusive right to jurisdiction. Because this Article 16 clause discriminated between the peacekeepers that are party to the Rome Statute and those that are not, U.S. peacekeeping forces were immunized, while other peacekeepers, mostly from Africa, the continent with the most membership in ICC, were not.[76] The fact that this provision was designed to protect the United States in exchange for waiving its veto power was no secret. The United States ambassador to the United Nations at the time commented, "[t]his resolution provides clear protections for United States persons. No United States persons supporting the operations in the Sudan will be subjected to investigation or prosecution because of this resolution."[77] In effect, the resolution made the wrongdoing of troops from participating African nations international crimes and that of mostly White U.S. troops matters of domestic affairs.[78] Given the very low chance of prosecution of U.S. troops in U.S. domestic courts, in effect, it became an exchange of Black criminalization for White impunity.

---

[74] Id.

[75] S.C. Res. 1593, ¶ 6 (Mar. 31, 2005) (providing "that nationals, current or former officials or personnel from a contributing State outside Sudan which is not a party to the Rome Statute of the International Criminal Court shall be subject to the exclusive jurisdiction of that contributing State for all alleged acts or omissions arising out of or related to operations in Sudan established or authorized by the Council or the African Union, unless such exclusive jurisdiction has been expressly waived by that contributing State").

[76] Thirty-three African countries are part to the Rome Statute, the most of any continent. See list, The State Parties to the Rome Statute: African States, INT'L CRIM. CT., https://asp.icc-cpi.int/en_me nus/asp/states%20parties/african%20states/Pages/african%20states.aspx (last visited May 4, 2022).

[77] Jalloh, Akandeb & Plessisc, supra note 12, at 20.

[78] U.N. Security Council, 60th Sess., 5158th meeting, U.N. Doc. S/PV.5158 at 4 (Mar. 31, 2005); Demographics of the U.S. Military, COUNCIL ON FOREIGN REL. (July 13, 2020, 9:00 AM), https://www. cfr.org/backgrounder/demographics-us-military.

Many members of the United Nations as well as numerous commentators questioned how the use of Article 16 deferral power to immunize troops of non-parties to the ICC concerned matters of peace and security.[79] Judging from the drafting history, legal scholar Carsten Stahn has concluded that "Article 16 was certainly not meant to provide a basis for the immunity of a whole group of actors in advance and irrespective of any concrete risk of indictment or prosecution."[80] In fact, a provision of blanket immunity for peacekeepers was proposed but expressly excluded from the Rome Statute after "widespread doubts" surfaced about its content.[81] Rather, Article 16 was meant to be a case-by-case determination of when peace and security interests cautioned against speedy prosecutions, not an anticipatory blanket amnesty.[82] Indeed, it would seem difficult to know in advance whether prosecution would threaten peace and security without knowing the circumstances of the act. To the contrary, it is possible that not holding soldiers accountable for committing mass atrocities against a civilian population could undermine the legitimacy of the ICC and impede its ability to promote collective security.

Conclusion

In short, the racialized nature of prosecutions cannot be justified as the unfortunate consequence of following the rules. As this chapter and the work of other legal scholars have illuminated, the near exclusive focus on Black defendants is the result of rules that systemically heighten Black guilt while minimizing White guilt. The broader effect of such systemic bias at the ICC is particularly invidious because it reinforces well-documented racialized associations of dark skin with evil. A deeper reckoning with the rules that yield such consistently racially discriminatory results is imperative especially given the increased prominence of expressive theories of punishment in international criminal law, which justify criminal prosecutions for their role in communicating the international community's sense of right and wrong.[83] If not, international criminal law risks being not much more than

[79] CRYER ET AL., *supra* note 13, at 142–44; Carsten Stahn, *The Ambiguities of Security Council Resolution 1422*, 14 EUR. J. INT'L L. 85 (2003).
[80] Stahn, *supra* note 79, at 90.
[81] *Id.* at 95.
[82] *Id.* at 89.
[83] STAHN, *supra* note 51, at 29–30.

an expression of racialized perceptions of wrongdoing. Indeed, cast under such light, international criminal law could easily be portrayed as an extension of international law's civilizing mission, which relied on stereotypes regarding the inherent violence and inferiority of "Blackness" to justify slavery and colonialization.[84] Instead, the ICC should adopt an antiracist orientation to its work, identifying how structural racism is embedded in its institutional design and recognizing the role that race and racism might be playing in its decisions.

---

[84] DeFalco & Mégret, *supra* note 3, at 75–76; Anghie & Chimni, *supra* note 20, at 85.

12

The United Nations Cannot Rest on Past Laurels

The Time for Courageous Leadership on Anti-Black Racism Is Now

*Adelle Blackett**

Introduction: The Links between Peace, Security, and Racial Justice

Linking arms with the Reverend Dr. Martin Luther King Jr. in the 1965 march for civil rights and racial justice from Selma to Montgomery, Alabama, was Nobel Peace Prize–winner, Ralph Bunche. Bunche was a high-ranking African American United Nations official. He assured the marchers, who had pressed on in the face of state violence and hate crimes, to assert their fundamental rights, that "[i]n the UN we have known from the beginnings that secure foundations for peace in the world can be built only upon the principles and practices of equal rights and status for all peoples, respect and dignity for all men. The world, I can assure you, is overwhelmingly with us."[1] Can the same assertion confidently be made today?

The Charter of the United Nations links international peace with security,[2] while the Constitution of the International Labour Organization (ILO)—the

* This chapter is part of an ongoing research project funded by a Social Sciences and Humanities Research Council of Canada Insight Grant for a project entitled "Slavery is Not a Metaphor," 2021. I am grateful to Matiangai Sirleaf and her editorial support team as well as reader Fionnuala Ni Aoláin for their valuable insights. I also thankfully acknowledge the excellent research assistance provided by Austin McDougall and Audrey Parent, McGill J.D. & B.C.L. candidates, enabling me to finalize this chapter.

[1] Ralph Bunche, Nobel Laureate, Speech, March on Montgomery from Selma (Mar. 25, 1965), https://oac.cdlib.org/view?docId=hb2g5005m3&query=&brand=oac4.
[2] U.N. Charter art. 1, ¶ 1. International peace and security are linked repeatedly throughout the whole document, which exclusively mentions "international peace" alongside "security."

Adelle Blackett, *The United Nations Cannot Rest on Past Laurels* In: *Race and National Security*. Edited by: Matiangai V.S. Sirleaf, Oxford University Press. © Oxford University Press 2023. DOI: 10.1093/oso/9780197754641.003.0013

United Nations specialized agency[3] founded alongside the League of Nations in 1919, which survived to win a Nobel Peace Prize for its fiftieth birthday in 1969[4]—affirms that universal and lasting peace requires social justice.[5] Social justice was conceived as encompassing economic justice and racial justice.[6] At the 2022 World Trade Organization's Inaugural Presidential Lecture, the Right Honourable Mia Amor Mottley, prime minister of Barbados, echoed these United Nations and ILO starting points when she challenged the global community to move beyond formal affirmations of equality, by redressing substantive inequities. She affirmed that "there is no national security without international security"[7] and that peace must be understood "both in terms of security and economic justice."[8] "We know," she argued, "that a transformative agenda is required."[9]

I argue that any transformative agenda that understands justice as a prerequisite to world peace must be transnational and must entail courageous United Nations leadership aimed at acknowledging and redressing the legacies of the four-centuries-long global institution of the transatlantic enslavement of over 17 million Africans. For decades, however, the United Nations seemed to rest on past laurels on the issue of racial injustice, and in particular on anti-Black racism. It took the unspeakable eight-minute, forty-six-second video of the murder of George Floyd on May 25, 2020, in the thick of the global COVID-19 pandemic, for the United Nations once again to foreground racial injustice, name the multifaceted "inequality pandemic" within and beyond global institutions, and commit in Secretary-General António Guterres's 2020 Nelson Mandela Lecture to a New Social Contract.[10]

---

[3] Convention on the Privileges and Immunities of the Specialized Agencies, Annex I, International Labour Organization (ILO), July 12, 1948, 33 U.N.T.S. 290.

[4] *The Nobel Peace Prize 1969*, NOBEL PRIZE, https://www.nobelprize.org/prizes/peace/1969/ summary/ (last visited May 4, 2022).

[5] Int'l Labour Org. [ILO], *Constitution of the International Labour Organization*, pmbl. (Apr. 20, 1948) ("Whereas universal and lasting peace can be established only if it is based upon social justice").

[6] *Id.*

[7] World Trade Org., *Presidential Lecture Series with Mia Mottley, Prime Minister of Barbados*, YOUTUBE, at 50:05 (Mar. 23, 2022), https://www.youtube.com/watch?v=2IDy3KlRZFc; *see also* Julie Carrington, *WTO in the Vanguard of International Trade*, BARBADOS INFO. SERV. (Mar. 23, 2022), https://gisbarbados.gov.bb/blog/wto-in-the-vanguard-of-international-trade/.

[8] World Trade Org., *Presidential Lecture Series with Mia Mottley, supra* note 7, at 15:35.

[9] *Id.* at 15:55.

[10] António Guterres, *18th Nelson Mandela Annual Lecture—Tackling the Inequality Pandemic: A New Social Contract for a New Era*, U.N. WEB TV (July 18, 2020), https://media.un.org/en/asset/k18/ k18oruy0cd (transcript available online at *Secretary-General's Nelson Mandela Lecture: "Tackling the Inequality Pandemic: A New Social Contract for a New Era" [as Delivered]*, U.N. SEC'Y GEN. (July 18, 2020), https://www.un.org/sg/en/content/sg/statement/2020-07-18/secretary-generals-nel

The 2020 racial reckoning did not emerge spontaneously. Far from it: it was the ardently compelling work of transnational social movements for Black lives[11] that enabled new spaces within the United Nations' human rights framework to emerge alongside existing antiracism mechanisms under the full or partial purview of the Office of the High Commissioner for Human Rights (OHCHR). These emergent spaces have the tall task of addressing the global security challenge that is the persistence of anti-Black racism.

The human rights framework, however, is a stunningly small part of the United Nations; it struggles to penetrate the organization's broader inner workings. This chapter contends that emergent spaces to address anti-Black racism can only be sustained with deliberate, honest engagement with racial justice throughout the United Nations system and must encompass issues of staff representation. It calls specifically for the establishment of a Special Representative to the United Nations Secretary-General on People of African Descent and compatible structures in United Nations specialized agencies such as the ILO.

Resting on Past Laurels

Recall that in early June 2020, United Nations officials, anxious to show their solidarity in the massive, worldwide demonstrations seeking #JusticeforGeorgeFloyd and affirming the urgency of movements for Black lives, were deterred from doing so by an internal circular sent by a United Nations ethics board, which labeled participation in those antiracist demonstrations as not "impartial." United Nations special rapporteurs on freedom of assembly, past (Maina Kiai) and present (Clément Voule), sounded the alarm, the former tweeting that the conflation of the right to protest for racial justice with political partisanship was a "grotesque & dangerous distortion."[12]

Secretary-General Guterres quickly recalibrated to allow "personal expressions of solidarity or acts of peaceful civic engagement" in the face of

son-mandela-lecture-%E2%80%9Ctackling-the-inequality-pandemic-new-social-contract-for-new-era%E2%80%9D-delivered).

[11] *See* Tendayi Achiume, *Transnational Racial (In)justice in Liberal Democratic Empire*, 134 HARV. L. REV. F. 378, 381–82 (2021).
[12] Maina Kiai (@Maina_Kiai), TWITTER (June 5, 2020, 2:51 AM), https://twitter.com/maina_kiai/status/1268797645864173568.

the "murderous act of police brutality." He added that "[t]he position of the United Nations on racism is crystal clear: this scourge violates the United Nations Charter and debases our core values."[13] In doing so, Guterres invoked the United Nations' proud history at the forefront of the anti-apartheid and civil rights movements.

Invoking the United Nations' Past

In their quest for racial justice, a range of Pan-Africanist leaders from within the continent and throughout its diaspora, including many prominent African Americans, have repeatedly turned to the United Nations for support. There are defining[14] past United Nations moments on anti-Black racism, including at the ILO.

Allusions to the United Nations' past should particularly acknowledge the strength of newly decolonized states provided within the United Nations and the ILO. I focus on the ILO because of the latent if largely forgotten promise that might have emerged—and could still emerge—from a positive labor vision required to redress the legacies of slavery and articulate a vision of working and living in freedom.[15] For instance, newly independent members of the tripartite ILO (governments, employers, and workers) led much of the international condemnation of apartheid resulting in South Africa's withdrawal from the ILO in 1964 for thirty years.[16] This followed South Africa's

[13] António Guterres, *Note to Correspondents: Secretary-General's Letter to Staff on the Plague of Racism and Secretary-General's Remarks at Town Hall*, U.N. Sec'y Gen. (June 9, 2020), https://www. un.org/sg/en/content/sg/note-correspondents/2020-06-09/note-correspondents-secretary-gener als-letter-staff-the-plague-of-racism-and-secretary-generals-remarks-town-hall.

[14] *African Leaders Highlight UN's Ability to Support Countries and Rid World of Fear and Violence*, U.N. News (Sept. 29, 2015), https://news.un.org/en/story/2015/09/510452-african-leaders-highli ght-uns-ability-support-countries-and-rid-world-fear-and.

[15] *See* Adelle Blackett & Alice Duquesnoy, *Slavery Is Not a Metaphor: U.S. Prison Labor & Racial Subordination through the Lens of the ILO's Abolition of Forced Labor Convention*, 67 UCLA L. Rev. 1504 (2021); *see also* Michael Banton, International Action against Racial Discrimination 26, 57 (1996); Gay McDougall, *Toward a Meaningful International Regime: The Domestic Relevance of International Efforts to Eliminate All Forms of Racial Discrimination*, 40 How. L.J. 571, 582 (1997) (recalling that CERD's core definition of racial discrimination was drawn in part from the ILO). For discussions by U.S. legal historians adopting a positive labor vision through the reading of the U.S. Thirteenth Constitutional Amendment, *see* Lea VanderVelde, *Labor Vision of the Thirteenth Amendment*, 138 U. Penn L. Rev. 437 (1989); James Gray Pope, *What's Different about the U.S. Thirteenth Amendment and Why Does It Matter?*, 71 Md. L. Rev. 189 (2011); Rebecca Zietlow, The Forgotten Emancipator: James Mitchell Ashley and the Ideological Origins of Reconstruction (2018).

[16] Int'l Labour Org. [ILO], *1964 Declaration Concerning the Policy of "Apartheid" of the Republic of South Africa* (July 8, 1964), https://www.ilo.org/century/history/iloandyou/WCMS_217915/lang-- en/index.htm.

previous withdrawal from the United Nations Economic, Social and Cultural Organization in 1955.[17] The nonaligned movement of states from the Global South was also influential in pushing for international sanctions against apartheid-era South Africa,[18] all the while engendering a movement for an alternative vision of international economic relations, the New International Economic Order.[19]

When he accepted the ILO's Nobel Peace Prize in 1969, the United States lawyer David Morse, who was then its director-general, foregrounded the institution's early transnational action. He argued that given its tripartite governance structure, combining fulsome representation of workers, employers, and governments, "[t]he ILO has provided the nations of the world with a meeting ground, an instrument for cooperation and for dialogue among very different interests."[20] While Morse acknowledged that the ILO has "of course lived and operated in a world of sovereign states, it has nevertheless gradually extended the scope and possibilities of transnational action."[21] For Morse, this ILO vision constitutes a growing transnationalism that is part of how the ILO "patiently, undramatically, but not unsuccessfully, worked to build an infrastructure of peace."[22]

As I recall elsewhere,[23] Morse received the prize on behalf of the ILO five years after Reverend Dr. Martin Luther King Jr. accepted the Nobel Peace Prize, and soon after Dr. King's assassination on April 4, 1968. Though Morse did not mention Dr. King's work or legacy, he must have recognized the need to acknowledge the "South of the North," that is, those within industrialized

[17] UNESCO General Conference, *Consequences of the Withdrawal of a Member State: Report by the Director-General*, 23 C/INF. 21, 4 X/EX/2 (Oct. 14, 1985), https://unesdoc.unesco.org/ark:/48223/pf0000066890.
[18] Hari Sharan Chhabra (U.N. Centre Against Apartheid), *Non-Aligned Movement and the Struggle Against Apartheid*, U.N. Doc. No. 18/84 (1984), https://digitallibrary.un.org/record/81231.
[19] G.A. Res. 3201 (S-VI), Declaration on the Establishment of a New International Economic Order (May 1, 1974); *see also* James Thuo Gathii, *Third World Approaches to International Economic Governance*, in INTERNATIONAL LAW AND THE THIRD WORLD 255 (Richard Falk, Balakrishnan Rajagopal & Jacqualine Stevens eds., 2008); Margot E. Salomon, *From NIEO to Now and the Unfinished Story of Economic Justice*, 62 INT'L. & COMPAR. L.Q. 31 (2013); Nils Gilman, *The New International Economic Order: A Reintroduction*, HUMAN. J. (Mar. 19, 2015), http://humanityjournal.org/issue6-1/the-new-international-economic-order-a-reintroduction/.
[20] David A. Morse, *International Labour Organization Nobel Lecture: ILO and the Social Infrastructure of Peace* (Dec. 11, 1969), https://www.nobelprize.org/prizes/peace/1969/labour/lecture/ (text of David A. Morse's, Director General of ILO, lecture in behalf of the ILO).
[21] *Id.*
[22] *Id.*
[23] Adelle Blackett, *On the Presence of the Past in the Future of International Labour Law*, 43 DALHOUSIE L.J. 947 (2020).

societies who live at the margins and face ongoing dispossession.[24] Morse referenced racialized and religious minorities, migrant workers, and workers who receive low pay. He contended that it was both necessary and feasible to redress racial discrimination and eliminate poverty in the Global North. According to Morse, that action would become a basis for a deepened "international solidarity" with the Global South.[25] Unfortunately, institutionally, the ILO did not consistently retain this course.

While it is highly symbolic that in 1990, soon-to-be South African president Nelson Mandela addressed the 77th session of the ILO to "salute the ILO for its enormous contribution to our common struggle,"[26] there are not only high points in the United Nations' past when it comes to racial justice. W.E.B. Du Bois and other leading Pan-Africanists interacted with both the League of Nations and the ILO in the early 1920s.[27] Du Bois encouraged the ILO's first director-general, Albert Thomas, to address the issue of "native" labor, and in particular Black labor. In internal memos, Thomas called for the unit to be staffed by a Black man, but Du Bois's gently penned offer to the ILO to consider his candidacy to head that unit was met with inaction.[28] Instead, the ILO embroiled itself in the process of building a "Native labour code" that

[24] *See, e.g.,* Adelle Blackett, *Situated Reflections on International Labour Law, Capabilities, and Decent Work: The Case of Centre Maraîcher Eugène Guinois,* Revue Québécoise de Droit Int'l 223 (2007) (explaining the relationship between racialized status and migrant status in the segregation and structural racial injustice faced by Black agricultural workers in the contemporary global economy in the Global North); *see also* Adrian A. Smith, *Temporary Labour Migration and the "Ceremony of Innocence" of Postwar Labour Law: Confronting "the South of the North,"* 33 Canadian J.L. Soc'y 261 (2018) (critiquing the limited engagement with the South of the North in much emergent transnational labor law scholarship); Eve Tuck & K. Wayne Yang, *Decolonization Is Not a Metaphor,* 1 Decolonization: Indigeneity, Ed. & Soc'y 1 (2012) (on the ongoing character of the dispossession of Indigenous peoples in the context of settler colonialism); Tapji Garba & Sara-Maria Sorentino, *Slavery Is a Metaphor: A Critical Commentary on Eve Tuck and K. Wayne Yang's "Decolonization Is Not a Metaphor,"* 52 Antipode 764 (2020) (engaging with dispossession and land in its relationship to slavery); Adelle Blackett, *Slavery Is Not a Metaphor,* 66 Am. J. Compar. L. 927 (2018) (explaining the importance of engaging with the legacies of slavery in any credible account of contemporary slavery and the law); Neil Roberts, Freedom as Marronage (2015) (affirming that slavery is more than a metaphor).

[25] Morse, *supra* note 20.

[26] *Address by Mr. Nelson Mandela at the 77th International Labour Conference,* Int'l Labour Org. (June 8, 1990), https://www.ilo.org/global/about-the-ilo/newsroom/statements-and-speec hes/WCMS_215611/lang--en/index.htm); *see also* Int'l Labour Org., *Highlights of Nelson Mandela's 1990 Address to the ILO,* YouTube (Dec. 6, 2013), https://www.youtube.com/watch?v=uGBiaa25 SyM (recording of highlights from Nelson Mandela's June 8, 1990, address at the Seventy-Seventh International Labour Conference).

[27] *See* McDougall, *supra* note 16, at 571–72; *see also* David Levering Lewis, W.E.B. Du Bois: The Fight for Equality and the American Century, 1919–1963 (2000).

[28] Selected, digitized archival documents are being made available through the Labour Law and Development Research Database (LLDRD) at McGill University, to which the author has access. *See How We Collaborate: Labour Law and Development Research Database,* McGill Labour L. & Dev. Res. Lab'y, https://www.mcgill.ca/lldrl/how-we-collab (last visited May 4, 2022).

was shaped largely by colonial administrators whose focus was decidedly not addressing transatlantic slavery's legacy of racial injustice.

It follows that invocations of the United Nations' past must be careful, balanced accounts that show the importance of at once consistently deepening the understanding of the persistence of racial subordination and simultaneously developing transformative action to move the institution, and its quest for racial justice, forward. This moment of racial reckoning has, remarkably, provided both within the United Nations.

The Urgent Debate and Beyond

In 2020, United Nations Human Rights Commissioner Michelle Bachelet swiftly issued a strong statement situating George Floyd's killing alongside "a long line of killings of unarmed African Americans by US police officers and members of the public."[29] Shortly after Bachelet's statement, the United Nations Human Rights Council held an "urgent debate" on "current racially inspired human rights violations, systemic racism, police brutality and violence against peaceful protests."[30] The families of George Floyd, Breonna Taylor, Philando Castile, and Michael Brown, accompanied by the American Civil Liberties Union, sought more than a single debate and requested a special session of the United Nations Human Rights Council to address police use of excessive force, as a breach of the United States' international obligations.

The response to the families' request illustrates where so much of the United Nations leadership on antiracism has come from recently: mechanisms linked to the OHCHR, and in particular the United Nations special procedures mandate holders, led by then United Nations Special Rapporteur on Contemporary forms of racism, racial discrimination, xenophobia and related intolerance, legal scholar Tendayi Achiume, and the Working Group of Experts on Peoples of African Descent. During

---

[29] Press Release, U.N. Office of the High Commissioner for Human Rights, UN Human Rights Chief Urges "Serious Action" to Halt US Police Killings of Unarmed African Americans (May 28, 2020), https://www.ohchr.org/en/press-releases/2020/05/un-human-rights-chief-urges-serious-action-halt-us-police-killings-unarmed.

[30] U.N. Human Rights Council Statement, Human Rights Council Holds an Urgent Debate on Current Racially Inspired Human Rights Violations, Systemic Racism, Police Brutality and Violence Against Peaceful Protests (June 17, 2020), https://www.ohchr.org/en/statements/2020/06/human-rights-council-holds-urgent-debate-current-racially-inspired-human-rights?sub-site=HRC.

the urgent debate, the special procedures mandate holders issued an urgent call for commissions of inquiry into systemic racism in law enforcement both in the United States and globally.[31] As Achiume chronicles, the request of the Africa Group of states at the United Nations,[32] authored by Ambassador Dieudonné W. Désiré Sougouri of Burkina Faso, was ultimately accepted.[33] It signaled the "remarkable success of United States and transnational racial justice advocates in defining and placing systemic racism in law enforcement on the agenda of the global human rights system and simultaneously shifting the global conversation on racial justice in ways that were inconceivable"[34]

---

[31] Statement from Independent Experts of the Special Procedures of the U.N. Human Rights Council, Statement on the Human Rights Council Urgent Debate Resolution (June 19, 2020), https://www.ohchr.org/en/news/2020/06/statement-human-rights-council-urgent-debate-resolution; *see also* Achiume, *supra* note 11 (chronicling the difficult movement toward addressing the racial justice claims).

[32] Human Rights Council Draft Res. 43/ . . . , The Promotion and Protection of the Human Rights and Fundamental Freedoms of Africans and of People of African Descent Against Police Brutality and Other Violations of Human Rights, U.N. Doc. A/HRC/43/L.50 (June 17, 2020).

[33] Human Rights Council Res. 43/1, Promotion and Protection of the Human Rights and Fundamental Freedoms of Africans and of people of African Descent Against Excessive Use of Force and Other Human Rights Violations by Law Enforcement Officers, U.N. Doc. A/HRC/RES/43/1 (June 19, 2020).

[34] Achiume, *supra* note 11, at 386. Achiume is sanguine, however, about the failure to shift away from business as usual as concerns mandating an independent commission of inquiry focusing on the United States. *Id.* at 387. By the conclusion of the Urgent Debate, reports Achiume:

> Human Rights Council adopted a consensus resolution that was a shadow of the Africa Group's strong proposal. Rather than authorizing an independent commission of inquiry for the United States, the Human Rights Council directed the High Commissioner of Human Rights to prepare a thematic report on systemic anti-Black racism in law enforcement. The progression from an unpublished draft of the resolution to the introduced Draft Resolution, to the finalized Human Rights Council Resolution illustrates the gradual erosion of accountability for the United States driven by the WEOG.

Id. at 388.

This prompted the National Conference of Black Lawyers, the International Association of Democratic Lawyers, and the National Lawyers Guild to set up the International Commission of Inquiry on Systemic Racist Police Violence Against People of African Descent in the United States. The inquiry was led by twelve international Commissioners and conducted hearings into the cases of 44 Black people, all but one of whom were killed by police between 2000 and 2021. The resulting report, published in March 2021, "find[s] a pattern and practice of racist police violence in the U.S. in the context of a history of oppression dating back to the extermination of First Nations peoples, the enslavement of Africans, the militarization of U.S. society, and the continued perpetuation of structural racism." It describes the Human Rights Council "succumbing to enormous pressure by the U.S. and its allies" as it "directed the Office of the High Commissioner of Human Rights to prepare a report on systemic racism [. . .] throughout the world," in lieu of a U.N. Commission of Inquiry grounded in the United States. The first of its numerous recommendations are addressed to the Human Rights Council and to the OHCHR and include the constitution of an independent Commission of Inquiry mandated to conduct full investigation into incidents of police violence against people of African descent in the U.S. and the appointment of an Independent Expert of Systemic Racist Police Violence in the United States. NAT'L CONFERENCE OF BLACK LAWYERS ET AL., REPORT OF THE INTERNATIONAL COMMISSION OF INQUIRY ON SYSTEMIC RACIST POLICE VIOLENCE AGAINST PEOPLE OF AFRICAN DESCENT IN THE UNITED STATES 13 (Mar. 2021), https://inquirycommission.org/website/wp-content/uploads/2021/04/Commission-Report-15-April.pdf.

until that time. Due to the significant mobilizing and call to reckoning of social movements from across the African diaspora, the United Nations was galvanized to respond. The Human Rights Council established a new, international, independent mechanism focused on criminal justice, comprising three experts with law enforcement and human rights expertise.[35]

But special rapporteurs are not United Nations officials. They are unpaid and act independently, sounding the alarm on critical thematic issues (alongside country mandates) that require individual or structural action, including action by the United Nations funding supports country visits, studies, and expert consultations, but that funding is severely limited.[36] Relying on the pivotal independent initiative of special rapporteurs is not enough.

The work across special rapporteurs is also understandably, inherently uneven. It is telling that no descendant of transatlantic slavery has ever held the special rapporteurship on contemporary forms of slavery. United Nations acknowledgment that slavery was a centuries-long global institution in which a wide range of states—whether or not they had large slave-holding populations—participated and profited[37] should permeate the mandate. The mandate should foster long-overdue conversations that honor the experiences of the descendants of transatlantic slavery around the globe who live its brutal legacies. And of course, the United Nations' work on the legacies of slavery should extend beyond the special rapporteurship and other United Nations special procedure mandate holders to reach the United Nations' core operations.

Finally, and pragmatically, although the Human Rights Council has been the situs for the overwhelming majority of the work to redress anti-Black racism, barely three percent of the United Nations' regular budget goes to human rights. The United Nations' work on human rights remains heavily reliant on voluntary contributions.[38] Reckoning with anti-Black racism

[35] Human Rights Council Res. 47/21, Promotion and Protection of the Human Rights and Fundamental Freedoms of Africans and of People of African Descent Against Excessive Use of Force and Other Human Rights Violations by Law Enforcement Officers Through Transformative Change for Racial Justice and Equality, U.N. Doc. A/HRC/Res/47/21 (July 13, 2021).
[36] See, e.g., Joanna Naples-Mitchell, Perspectives of UN Special Rapporteurs on their Roles: Inherent Tensions and Unique Contributions to Human Rights, INT'L J. HUM. RTS. 232, 241–45 (2011) (arguing that "[t]he most urgently needed reforms in the rapporteur scheme, then, are not structural but budgetary").
[37] ERIC WILLIAMS, CAPITALISM AND SLAVERY (1944); see also SLAVERY'S CAPITALISM: A NEW HISTORY OF AMERICAN ECONOMIC DEVELOPMENT (Sven Beckert & Seth Rockman eds., 2016).
[38] See OHCHR's Funding and Budget, U.N. HUM. RTS. OFF. OF THE HIGH COMM'R, https:// www.ohchr.org/en/about-us/funding-and-budget#:~:text=Human%20rights%20gets%20a%20t iny,including%20the%20Human%20Rights%20Council (last visited May 4, 2022); see also General Assembly Meeting Coverage, Fifth Committee Approves Secretary-General's Proposed $3.12 Billion

needs to permeate the United Nations' broader structure. Representation of people of African descent within the United Nations should be counted and prioritized.

Certainly, the United Nations treaty bodies have a distinct role to play. The Committee on the Elimination of Racial Discrimination (CERD) implements the International Convention on the Elimination of Racial Discrimination (ICERD) that emerged at the height of the civil rights movement. CERD responded rapidly to police brutality and other extrajudicial anti-Black violence in the United States, issuing a statement on the Prevention of Racial Discrimination that underscored the "systemic and structural discrimination" that "disproportionally promotes racial disparities against African Americans."[39] Other treaty bodies—from the Human Rights Committee, to the Committee on the Elimination of Discrimination against Women, to the Committee on Migrant Workers—should integrate an understanding of anti-Black racism, including from an intersectional lens,[40] into their human rights monitoring to build cohesive interpretations and recommendations. Other actors, notably the appointment in 2003 by the secretary-general of five independent eminent experts with a mandate to follow up on the implementation of the provisions of the Durban Declaration and Programme of Action,[41] can buttress the work and shape directions.

Program and Budget for 2022, Concluding Main Part of Seventy-Sixth Session, U.N. Doc. GA/AB/4378 (Dec. 23, 2021), https://www.un.org/press/en/2021/gaab4378.doc.htm.

[39] U.N. Committee on the Elimination of Racial Discrimination, Statement on the Prevention of Racial Discrimination, Including Early Warning and Urgent Action Procedures (June 12, 2020). Statements of the Committee on the Elimination of Racial Discrimination are available to download at, Decisions, Statements, and Letters, U.N. HUM. RTS. OFF. OF THE HIGH COMM'R, https://www.ohchr.org/en/treaty-bodies/cerd/decisions-statements-and-letters#b (last visited May 4, 2022).

[40] Kimberlé Crenshaw, Demarginalizing the Intersection of Race and Sex: A Black Feminist Critique of Antidiscrimination Doctrine, Feminist Theory and Antiracist Politics, 1 U. CHI. LEGAL F. 139 (1989); Kimberlé Crenshaw, Mapping the Margins: Intersectionality, Identity Politics, and Violence against Women of Color, 43 STAN. L. REV. 1241 (1991); see also Devon Carbado, Colorblind Intersectionality, 38 SIGNS 1 (2013); Sirma Bilge, Intersectionality Undone, 10 DU BOIS REV.: SOC. SCI. RSCH. 405 (2013).

[41] G.A. Res. 56/266, Comprehensive Implementation of and Follow-up to the World Conference Against Racism, Racial Discrimination, Xenophobia and Related Intolerance, U.N. Doc. A/RES/56/266 (Mar. 27, 2003); see also Report of the Group of Independent Eminent Experts on the Implementation of the Durban Declaration and Programme of Action on its Sixth Session, U.N. Doc. A/74/173 (July 19, 2019).

The Persisting Racial Contract in the Inequality Pandemic

In the midst of the current International Decade for People of African Descent (2015–2024), is the current United Nations able to provide the leadership on anti-Black racism the United States and the world urgently need now?

Secretary-General Guterres's call for a new social contract must challenge the racial contract, undergirded by the understanding that "White supremacy is the unnamed political system that has made the modern world what it is today."[42] For the late philosopher Charles Mills, the racial contract has not only been "invisibilized" but rendered illegible by those who have constituted it, enabling an "epistemology of ignorance."[43] If the racial reckoning of 2020 broke through this illegibility and challenged claims that the depth of the persistence of anti-Black racism was unknown, the challenge remains to acknowledge a global theoretical framework that recognizes racism to be "*itself* a political system, a particular power structure of formal or informal rule, socioeconomic privilege, and norms for the differential distribution of material wealth and opportunities, benefits and burdens, rights and duties."[44] Racism was not an anomaly to Western humanism, but rather constitutive of it.[45] The purpose was to enable economic subordination.

The implications for a United Nations called upon to provide courageous leadership within and beyond the United Nations system are significant. In particular, the legacy of slavery must be the root of United Nations action on anti-Black racism. Yet the United Nations' work on contemporary forms of slavery is largely divorced from what historian Saidiya Hartman refers to as the "afterlife of slavery," leaving Black lives imperiled by "skewed life chances, limited access to health and education, premature death, incarceration and impoverishment."[46] The intervening centuries become exceptions to the "epoch of *non*racial slavery of antiquity,"[47] and a subsequent postracial

---

[42] CHARLES W. MILLS, THE RACIAL CONTRACT 1 (25th anniversary ed. 2014).

[43] *Id.* at 18. Mills added that "*white misunderstanding, misrepresentation, evasion and self-deception on matters related to race* are among the most pervasive mental phenomena of the past few hundred years, a cognitive and moral economy psychically required for conquest, colonization, and enslavement. And these phenomena are in no way *accidental*, but *prescribed* by the terms of the Racial Contract." *Id.* at 19 (emphasis in original).

[44] *Id.* at 3 (emphasis in original).

[45] *Id.* at 26–27.

[46] SAIDIYA HARTMAN, LOSE YOUR MOTHER: A JOURNEY ALONG THE ATLANTIC SLAVE ROUTE 6 (2006); *see also* Matiangai Sirleaf, *Racial Valuation of Diseases*, 67 UCLA L. REV. 1820 (2021) (offering a racial valuation framework of health and disease, which captures the impact of slavery, colonialism, and neocolonialism on Black, Indigenous, and racialized bodies).

[47] MILLS, *supra* note 42, at 54.

framing of contemporary forms of slavery has re-emerged. But in a postcolonial context in which racial subordination is enacted on the very body of the "[B]lack Other,"[48] there is no return to the nonracial. Approaches to contemporary slavery must acknowledge the persistence of racial subordination.[49]

Secretary-General Guterres's powerful acknowledgment that the COVID-19 pandemic shines a spotlight on racial injustice should galvanize operational units and specialized agencies to act. Even accounting for the many factors that may predispose historically marginalized communities to adverse health consequences—such as housing conditions and inadequate, discriminatory access to healthcare—available data confirm that the disparities are linked to occupations, according to the late AFL-CIO economist and Howard University Professor William Spriggs.[50] Spriggs underscored what COVID-19 has made acutely visible: African Americans are overrepresented among the "essential workers" who put their lives on the line to provide services and cannot shelter in place or socially distance.[51] They are consequently overexposed to the coronavirus and death.

Racialized COVID-19 disparities extend far beyond the United States.[52] They affect most pluralist societies, which is to say, most societies. Legacies of slavery and servitude remain in the racialized bodies of those who do the work. Yet there is precious little comparative and international guidance on this topic. Consider Canada, which has yet to reckon fully with its own history of slavery and shared legacy of anti-Black racism in education, employment, and the criminal justice system.[53] Amid the pandemic, several Canadian jurisdictions have refused community requests to collect data on the racial

[48] *Id.* at 52.
[49] *See* Adelle Blackett, *Racial Capitalism and the Contemporary International Law on Slavery: Re-Membering Hacienda Brasil Verde*, 25 J. INT'L ECON. L. 334 (2022); *see also* Blackett, *Slavery Is Not a Metaphor, supra* note 24.
[50] *See generally The Disproportionate Impact of COVID-19 on African American Workers, D.C. Labor & Employment Relations Association Webinar*, DC LAB. & EMP. RELS. ASS'N (May 27, 2020), https://lerachapter.org/dclera/events/disproportionate-impact-of-covid-19-on-african-american-workers/ (announcing webinar with William Spriggs, Chief Economist, AFL-CIO, and Professor of Economics, Howard University); The Urgency of Now to Speed the Recovery: Hearing Before the US House of Representatives Committee on Financial Services, 117 Cong. 1 (2021) (Statement by William Spriggs).
[51] *The Disproportionate Impact of COVID-19, supra* note 50.
[52] Elizabeth J. Williamson et al., *Factors Associated with COVID-19–related Death Using OpenSAFELY*, 584 NATURE 430 (2020).
[53] *See, e.g.,* OFF. OF THE CORRECTIONAL INVESTIGATOR (CANADA), 2018–2019 ANNUAL REPORT 79 (June 25, 2019), https://www.oci-bec.gc.ca/cnt/rpt/pdf/annrpt/annrpt20182019-eng.pdf (on the overrepresentation of Black and Indigenous peoples in Canadian prisons); *see also* OFF. OF THE CORRECTIONAL INVESTIGATOR (CANADA), 2020–2021 ANNUAL REPORT (June 30, 2021), https://www.oci-bec.gc.ca/cnt/rpt/pdf/annrpt/annrpt20202021-eng.pdf (on the disproportionate use of force against Black and Indigenous inmates).

distribution of COVID-19 in Canada. United Nations technical cooperation with member states—on race-based data collection, appropriate human
rights use of that data, and, in turn, data-driven, human rights–inspired policies to address COVID-19—is one example of the kind of urgently-needed
international support the United Nations should provide.

A Distinct Role for the ILO

The ILO has a distinct role to play in addressing both the COVID-19 and inequality pandemics that perpetuate racial injustice. Work on social protection
and labor market policies is crucial, but as Secretary-General Guterres has
affirmed in his 2020 Mandela Lecture, that work is insufficient to "tackle entrenched inequalities." Targeted policies on race are needed: key constituents
in the ILO's July 2020 Global Summit acknowledged as much.[54] Yet ILO
advice on addressing COVID-19 in the workplace has been largely devoid
of attention to racial disparities. And while the ILO's 1944 constitutional
annex—the Declaration of Philadelphia[55]—offers an early international link
of antiracism to material well-being and "spiritual development in conditions
of freedom and dignity, of economic security and equal opportunity," the
ILO's 2019 Centenary Declaration[56] does not even mention race or racism.

In 2019, the ILO's Committee of Experts on the Application of Conventions
and Recommendations issued a general observation on racial discrimination.[57] It mentioned "afro-descendants" and the International Decade for
People of African Descent in passing, but encouraged disaggregated data
gathering respectful of confidentiality, proactive measures, and tripartite
consultations with "interested groups."[58] The Committee of Experts has,
for years, called on the United States to account for its mass incarceration

[54] *ILO Constituents' Day, ILO Global Summit: COVID-19 and the World of Work*, INT'L LABOUR
ORG. (July 9, 2020), https://global-summit.ilo.org/en/event/constituents-day/.

[55] Int'l Labour Org. [ILO], Declaration Concerning the Aims and Purposes of the International
Labour Organization (May 10, 1944), https://www.ilo.org/legacy/english/inwork/cb-policy-guide/
declarationofPhiladelphia1944.pdf.

[56] Int'l Labour Org. [ILO], ILO Centenary Declaration for the Future of Work (June 21, 2019),
https://www.ilo.org/wcmsp5/groups/public/@ed_norm/@relconf/documents/meetingdocument/
wcms_711674.pdf.

[57] ILO COMMITTEE OF EXPERTS ON THE APPLICATION OF CONVENTIONS AND RECOMMENDATIONS,
GENERAL OBSERVATION ON THE APPLICATION OF THE DISCRIMINATION (EMPLOYMENT AND
OCCUPATION) CONVENTION, 1958 (No. 111) (2019), https://www.ilo.org/wcmsp5/groups/public/---
ed_norm/---normes/documents/publication/wcms_717510.pdf.

[58] *Id.* at 2–3, 7–8.

of African Americans, under the United States-ratified Abolition of Forced Labour Convention of 1957 (No. 105).[59] In the midst of a pandemic that puts all those whose households cannot shelter in place at risk, the words of Albert Thomas are as relevant now as they were in 1921 as he echoed W.E.B. Du Bois's work: "[T]here will be no true protection of labour if we do not concern ourselves with the conditions of Black labour."[60]

The jury is out on whether the United Nations' specialized agency for labor, potentially so central to any meaningful engagement with redressing the historical legacies of slavery, will be able to engage with a transformative agenda that recognizes the urgency of Du Bois's centenary affirmation about how deeply linked the conditions of Black labor are to all labor protection. Despite past omissions on racialization, since 2022 the ILO has been led for the first time since its founding in 1919, by an African national, former Prime Minister of Togo, the Hon. Gilbert Houngbo.[61] As this new chapter begins, a reimagining of the "whole of the UN" approach to redressing anti-Black racism should be prioritized.

A Transformative Agenda

In July 2021, the United Nations through the Human Rights Council released a historic, four-point Agenda Towards Transformative Change for Racial

---

[59] Convention (No. 105) Concerning the Abolition of Forced Labour, June 25, 1957, T.I.A.S. 96–303, 320 U.N.T.S. 291.

[60] ILO archival materials are available through the Labour Law and Development Research Database (LLDRD) at McGill University. *See How We Collaborate: Labour Law and Development Research Database*, McGILL LABOUR L. & DEV. RES. LAB'Y, https://www.mcgill.ca/lldrl/how-we-col lab (last visited May 4, 2022).

It is not without interest to note that, in the very beginning of this movement, the second Pan-African Congress, assembled at Paris, London, and Brussels from August 28 to September 6 in 1921 last adopted the following address to the League of Nations: "The second Pan-African Congress requests that a special section should be established in the International Labour Office for the detailed consideration of the conditions and needs of native workers in Africa and elsewhere. This Congress is seriously of opinion that the labour problems of the world can neither be understood nor solved while the work of those belonging to all coloured races, particularly the [B]lack races, is enslaved and neglected; the Congress is further of opinion that the first step towards the world emancipation of labour will have been taken when a serious enquiry into native labour has been organised."

ALBERT THOMAS, ILO DIRECTOR-GENERAL, REPORT OF THE DIRECTOR, THIRD INTERNATIONAL LABOUR CONFERENCE 68 (Oct. 23, 1921); *see also* Adelle Blackett, *Theorizing Emancipatory Transnational Futures of International Labor Law*, 113 AM. J. INT'L L. 390 (2019).

[61] Press Release, Int'l Labour Org., New Director-General of the International Labour Organization Elected: The ILO Governing Body has Elected Gilbert F. Houngbo as the Organization's 11th Director-General, Who Will Take Office in October 2022 (Mar. 25, 2022), https://www.ilo.org/glo bal/about-the-ilo/newsroom/news/WCMS_840324/lang--en/index.htm.

Justice and Equality.[62] Its agenda was framed in a report from the OHCHR that acknowledged the historical significance of the legacy of slavery to the racism faced by Africans and people of African descent and the resulting "dehumanization of people of African descent."[63]

The report was careful first to contextualize systemic anti-Black racism, acknowledging:

> [R]acism and racial discrimination against Africans and people of African descent are often rooted in policies and practices grounded in the debasement of the status of individuals in society. Their impact is particularly apparent in, although not limited to, States with a legacy of or with significant links to enslavement, the transatlantic trade in enslaved Africans and/or colonialism resulting in sizeable communities of people of African descent.[64]

The report then offered a comprehensive definition of the concept of systemic racism against Africans and people of African descent, including as it relates to structural and institutional racism:

> [T]he operation of a complex, interrelated system of laws, policies, practices and attitudes in State institutions, the private sector and societal structures that, combined, result in direct or indirect, intentional or unintentional, de jure or de facto discrimination, distinction, exclusion, restriction or preference on the basis of race, colour, descent or national or ethnic origin. Systemic racism often manifests itself in pervasive racial stereotypes, prejudice and bias and is frequently rooted in histories and legacies of enslavement, the transatlantic trade in enslaved Africans and colonialism.[65]

In acknowledging the intersectional and compounded[66] forms of marginalization and exclusion, the message is one of confronting legacies, through both accountability and redress, with the full participation of peoples and communities concerned.

---

[62] U.N. High Commissioner for Human Rights, *Annual Report of the United Nations High Commissioner for Human Rights and Reports of the Office of the High Commissioner and the Secretary-General, Promotion and Protection of the Human Rights and Fundamental Freedoms of Africans and of People of African Descent Against Excessive Use of Force and Other Human Rights Violations by Law Enforcement*, U.N. Doc. A/HRC/47/53 (July 9, 2021).

[63] *Id.* at ¶ 15.

[64] *Id.* at ¶ 8.

[65] *Id.* at ¶ 9.

[66] *Id.* at ¶ 10.

The four-part agenda calls first for member states to "step up," stop denying and start dismantling systemic racism, and accelerate the pace of action. Second, it calls for actors to "pursue justice," that is to end impunity for human rights violations by law enforcement officials and close trust deficits. Third, it expresses concern to ensure that actors "listen up" by centering the voices of people of African descent, alongside those who stand up against racism. It calls for their concerns not only to be heard but also to be acted upon. And fourth, it centers the critical importance of "redress," by acknowledging and confronting legacies. This includes accountability measures, special measures, and reparative justice.[67] It underscores that "reparations are essential for transforming relationships," affirming that "measures taken to address the past—which extend beyond financial compensation to include guarantees of non-repetition and institutional and educational reform—should seek to transform the future."[68]

In keeping with this transformative agenda, but following some initial reluctance from Western states, the General Assembly unanimously created the Permanent Forum of People of African Descent, comprising five experts selected by the General Assembly and five experts selected by the Human Rights Council on July 28, 2021.[69] Appointments to the Permanent Forum were shrouded in transparency deficits that strained the perception that representatives of Black communities were in fact being heard, and reflected a statist, regional distribution logic that has tended to underserve people of African descent living as racially subordinated minorities in many Western states.[70] The Permanent Forum was designed as a "consultative mechanism for people of African descent and other relevant stakeholders" and a platform to improve the "safety and quality of life and livelihoods of people of African descent, as well as an advisory body of the Human Rights Council." Its mandate is extensive, and it includes providing expert advice and recommendations to the Human Rights Council, the Main Committees of the General Assembly, and organs, programs, funds, and agencies of the United Nations.[71] It is of no small import that it is expected to "consider the

---

[67] *Id.* at ¶ 68.

[68] *Id.* at ¶ 64.

[69] G.A. Res. 75/314, Establishment of the Permanent Forum of People of African Descent (July 28, 2021).

[70] Consider in contrast that the United Nations Permanent Forum on Indigenous Issues (UNPFII), constituted as a high-level advisory body to the Economic and Social Council, has sixteen members.

[71] G.A. Res. 75/314, Establishment of the Permanent Forum of People of African Descent ¶ 1 (July 28, 2021).

elaboration of a United Nations declaration on the promotion, protection and full respect of the human rights of people of African descent."[72] The first two sessions of the forum have enables crucial claiming of United Nations space by representatives of Black communities. Drafters of the monumental declaration with the potential to transform the global narrative on Blackness would do well to build a sustained comprehensive strategy beyond the sessions, and to reckon in particular with the meaning of work in dignity, economic prosperity, mutuality, and Black flourishing for Black communities.

A Call for Deeply Deliberate Action, Within and Across the United Nations System

The United Nations Transformative Agenda must be linked to transformative action to redress anti-Black racism that pervades the entire United Nations system, much as contemporary work on gender has done. It must capture a consciousness of the global character of anti-Black racism in the way that it permeates the differential treatment of Africans and people of African descent, irrespective of nationality, as reports of the discriminatory treatment at the border and in neighboring states of Ukrainians of African descent and foreign students fleeing the Russian invasion of Ukraine have starkly shown.[73] This treatment has underscored the depths of the persisting racial contract, its rootedness in the dehumanization that the history of enslavement and colonialism underscores, and the need for concerted responses that understand the global and transversal character of the harm. As the United Nations has come to understand through its engagement with Indigeneity, nationality is simply not a sufficient filter to ensure that historically marginalized descendants of transatlantic slavery are represented and heard. Indeed, it may compound the underrepresentation and mask persisting subordinated presence.

The weight of history adds to the urgency of this moment and requires the United Nations to "do more than condemn expressions and acts of racism," as high-ranking United Nations officials of African and African descent publicly urged in 2020.[74] For we allow the past to be erased and its legacies to

---

[72] *Id.* at ¶ 1(a)–(c).

[73] *UNHCR Chief Condemns "Discrimination, Violence and Racism" Against Some Fleeing Ukraine,* U.N. NEWS (Mar. 21, 2022), https://news.un.org/en/story/2022/03/1114282.

[74] *Citing "Weight of History", Senior Officials of African Descent Issue Call to "Go Beyond and Do More" to End Racism,* U.N. NEWS (June 14, 2020), https://news.un.org/en/story/2020/06/1066

persist unless and until we redress the structural anti-Black violence that is exacted on people of African descent. In this fraught moment—with the deep discontent that surrounds it—there is an unmistakable opportunity to shift course and be deeply deliberate about redressing anti-Black racism in transformative ways.

A Special Representative to the Secretary-General

Transformation will not happen unless initiatives are comprehensive, coherently structured, and complete. In 2020, Secretary-General Guterres invited the United Nations to turn inward, for a "deep and sincere discussion among colleagues about racism, including at the United Nations."[75] High-ranking officials echo that call: "To initiate and sustain real change, we also must have an honest assessment of how we uphold the United Nations Charter within our institution."[76] The assessment and implementation cannot simply be an internal affair—the stakes for people of African descent, the descendants of transatlantic slavery, are simply too high and representation within the United Nations too diffuse.

A fitting place to initiate necessary internal, transversal work across the whole of the United Nations would be to name a Special Representative to the United Nations Secretary-General on People of African Descent. The Special Representative should receive a mandate to look closely and carefully at the United Nations' past, present, and future role in addressing anti-Black racism, to support and accompany proactive measures to ensure critical representation of people of African descent throughout the United Nations and its specialized agencies, and to have a specific focus on turning the United Nations inquiry inward. This is a remaining piece of the United Nations' architectural puzzle, and its absence is both glaring and counterproductive to

242 (including the full text of the letter by U.N. Senior African Officials, On the Black Lives Matter Protests and Other Mass Demonstrations Against Systemic Racism and Police Brutality) [hereinafter *Open Letter*].

[75] Guterres, *supra* note 13.
[76] *Open Letter*, *supra* note 74. An internal United Nations working group on addressing racism in the workplace has been developing recommendations on equity in employment applicable to UN officials.

the aims of transformative action. It is pivotal to ensuring overall coherence and prioritization of issues affecting people of African descent.

Madiba, the "global inspiration" for Secretary-General Guterres's "New Social Contract" lecture, cautioned us to "use time wisely and forever realize that the time is always ripe to do right." The time for the United Nations to act to redress anti-Black racism within and beyond the United Nations is now.

VI
CONCLUSION

Reforming, Transforming, and Radically Imagining National Security

Matiangai V.S. Sirleaf

Introduction

It is worth returning to W.E.B. Du Bois's provocation in the early 1900s that begins this volume: "The problem of the 20th century is the problem of the color-line."[1] Du Bois's insights help to draw attention to how the world order is socially constructed and contested along racial lines. Rendering race visible in this volume helps to shift sites of analysis in generative ways for national security. While the contributions in *Race and National Security* take place several decades after Du Bois's writings, certainly "questions concerning the extent to which race and racism continue to subliminally structure contemporary world politics, in both material and ideological ways remain as significant as ever."[2]

Yet once national security is forced to confront the racial hierarchy that underpins its origins and its ongoing legacy of racial subordination as the pieces in this volume rightfully admonish us to do, what is the path forward? The contributors to this volume present us with tremendous possibilities and provide numerous theoretical and policy insights ranging from reforming to transforming national security. This reflection surfaces the threads in this volume and unearths the tension between reforming and perfecting national security and the security state. It ruminates on more transformative agendas aimed at reimagining national security and reducing the reach of the security state. Using key insights from abolition theory, this chapter problematizes many of the core assumptions in national security. It concludes that if scholars

---

[1] W.E.B. Du Bois, *To the Nations of the World*, *in* Lift Every Voice: African American Oratory, 1787–1900, at 905, 906 (Philip S. Foner & Robert James Branham eds., 1998) (1900).

[2] Race and Racism in International Relations: Confronting the Global Colour Line 3 (Alexander Anievas, Nivi Manchanda & Robbie Shilliam eds., 2015).

Matiangai V.S. Sirleaf, *Reforming, Transforming, and Radically Imagining National Security* In: *Race and National Security*. Edited by: Matiangai V.S. Sirleaf, Oxford University Press. © Oxford University Press 2023.
DOI: 10.1093/oso/9780197754641.003.0014

and policymakers are truly committed to addressing race and racism in national security, in theory and in practice, and to centering the experiences of those terminally on the receiving end of racialized state violence, radical imagination may very well be the only meaningful path forward for national security.

Engaging with Race

Several pieces in this volume identify increasing discussions of race as a necessary development in the field of national security. For example, James Thuo Gathii argues in chapter one that engaging in discussions about race is productive for those who study national security from a critical lens and who incorporate race as an important element of their scholarship, and for those who do not consider race at all in their work, scholarly, policy, or otherwise. One clear advantage of advancing racial analyses is the ability to see what might otherwise be obscured. Indeed, several chapters in this book clarify the racialized relationship between domestic and international state violence. Margaret Hu's work in chapter seven especially helps us to understand why and how justifications for the increased militarized surveillance of communities of color in the United States proliferate and run parallel with similar rationales for the adoption of biometric surveillance abroad in occupied and racialized nations.

Moreover, Adelle Blackett's chapter makes clear the importance of raising consciousness of the global character of anti-Black racism and the way that it permeates the differential treatment of Africans and people of African descent, irrespective of nationality. In chapter twelve, she unearths how this treatment underscored the depths of the persisting racial contract, its rootedness in the dehumanization that the history of enslavement and colonialism underpins, and the need for concerted responses that understand the global and transversal character of the harm. She observes that the United Nations has come to understand through its engagement with Indigeneity that nationality is simply not a sufficient filter to ensure that historically marginalized descendants of transatlantic slavery are represented and heard. Blackett cautions us that, instead, nationality may compound the underrepresentation and mask persisting subordination.

Furthermore, James Thuo Gathii maintains in chapter one that taking race into account is especially important for policymakers who provide advice to the political branches on foreign affairs. He asserts that providing color-blind advice that is decontextualized from considerations and implications relating to race and identity does not advance national security goals effectively. Similarly, in chapter eleven, Rachel López suggests that adopting an antiracist orientation, identifying how structural racism is embedded in institutional design and recognizing the role that race and racism is playing in decisions could make for better policymaking at the institutional level. Presumably, the security state could stand to benefit from reforms aimed at bolstering engagement with race in several ways. The tension here, especially given the lived experience of historically subordinated groups, is whether perfecting the security state in this way would further subordination or antisubordination in national security.

Changing Pedagogy

Du Bois once wrote that since lions have no historians, "lion hunts are thrilling and satisfactory human reading," and since Black people purportedly "had no bards . . . it has been widely told how American philanthropy freed the slave."[3] His commentary highlights the ways in which those who have the power and privilege of storytelling can deny the agency, lived experiences, and resistance of those othered and racialized. Drawing on these insights, Jaya Ramji-Nogales, in chapter six, argues that this book provides a history that is rarely imparted in law or other graduate or professional schools, let alone grade or high schools. Accordingly, Ramji-Nogales identifies reforming pedagogy as an important first step in dismantling the harmful legacy of "foreignness" in national security. She maintains that dismantling the social norms that have constructed racialized national security threats requires an understanding of the virulent racism and terroristic violence perpetrated against migrants of color throughout history. She asserts that both traditional and social media have an important reparative role to play. Ramji-Nogales eloquently argues that it is only through recognition of this history of White supremacist violence, and the role of immigration law in codifying hatred, that popular discourse can move in an antiracist direction.

---

[3] W.E.B. Du Bois, *Darkwater: Voices from Within the Veil, in* THE OXFORD W.E.B. Du Bois READER 481, 551 (Eric J. Sundquist ed., 1996) (1920).

Ramji-Nogales recognizes that the contemporary attacks on the teaching of antiracist values in schools show that this will be an uphill battle. Accordingly, developing a critical national security teaching agenda and curriculum, which explicitly centers the role of race and empire in the discipline, could be a meaningful intervention. Yet, as this book and prior scholarship from Du Bois and others indicate, this work has been hidden in plain sight for quite some time.

Certainly, the dominant theoretical approaches to national security— balance of power, collective security, democratic peace theory, and other frameworks that are usually taught—do not account for race as structuring national security as Du Bois and some contemporary scholars today recommend. Conventional frameworks in national security necessarily engage with race shallowly, if at all, in their attempts at explaining the international order. The result could be a misdiagnosis of problems and ineffectual solutions and interventions. By centering race in the training of would-be national security experts and practitioners, conceivably this could have a trickle-down effect on how national security is experienced. It is also possible that changes to norms, syllabi, theoretical frameworks, curriculum, academic fields, and the like may not necessarily translate to substantive policy changes creating dissonance between theory and praxis.

Diversifying National Security

One of the policy implications emanating from the insights in this volume could be focused on diversifying national security by ensuring that scholars and practitioners in national security are demographically representative of historically subordinated groups and places.[4] In chapter one, James Thuo Gathii notes that there were fewer Black individuals working in the U.S. State Department during the Trump administration than at any time in its history. However, he goes on to insist that the responsibility for antiracism should not rest on the small cadre of people of color in government. In chapter twelve, Adelle Blackett also stresses the need to build proactive measures to ensure critical representation of people of African descent throughout the United Nations and its specialized agencies. Relatedly, in Jaya Ramji-Nogales's

---

[4] See also Maryam Jamshidi, A Critical National Security Agenda (unpublished manuscript) (abstract on file with author).

analysis in chapter six, she queries what it would take to transform "foreign-ness" from a national security threat into an asset. She maintains that diversity is a strength and that we should celebrate and recognize racial, religious, and linguistic diversity.

Yet, if the experience with policing is any guidance, simply changing the faces of repression does not address the function, logic, and underlying culture of policing. Indeed, hiring more Black police officers in Memphis, Tennessee, did not stop these officers from brutalizing Tyre Nichols to death for alleged reckless driving, which there was no evidence to even support.[5] Likewise, it is no comfort to those tortured under the CIA's euphemistically named "enhanced interrogation program"[6] that Gina Haspell was appointed as the agency's first female leader. Her being a "Girl Boss" did not provide any solace or substantive change in policy. Indeed, she is notoriously on record for supporting the destruction of videographic evidence of torture.[7] These and many other cases make it evident that representation alone will not save us.

Toward Transformation

Recognizing this, many contributions in this book push for transform-ative change. Some offer reforms for specific areas of law such as Jaya Ramji-Nogales's intervention in chapter six on undoing the codification of "anti-foreignness" in immigration law. Ramji-Nogales maintains that an immigration system grounded in fairness and equality would require radical transformation of current laws and policies, with an eye to both undoing historical harms and injecting humanity, dignity, and compassion throughout. While Andrea Armstrong, in chapter five, provides recommendations aimed at the carceral state and at disrupting carceral secrecy as one avenue toward embracing a more just form of security. Further, Catherine Powell argues in chapter two for a more expansive understanding of "security," which in turn

---

[5] Rick Jervis & Jessica Guynn, *When the Officers Are Black: Tyre Nichols' Death Raises Tough Questions About Race in Policing*, USA TODAY (Jan. 30, 2023), https://www.usatoday.com/story/news/nation/2023/01/28/tyre-nichols-death-black-police-officers/11136520002/.

[6] *See, e.g.*, Douglas A. Johnson, Alberto Mora & Averell Schmidt, *The Strategic Costs of Torture: How "Enhanced Interrogation" Hurt America*, 95 FOREIGN AFFS. 121 (2016).

[7] Glenn Kessler, *CIA Director Nominee Haspel and the Destruction of Interrogation Tapes: Contradictions and Question*, WASH. POST (May 11, 2018), https://www.washingtonpost.com/news/fact-checker/wp/2018/05/11/cia-director-nominee-haspel-and-destruction-of-interrogation-tapes-contradictions-and-questions/.

calls for transformative change, beyond incremental reform, with respect to policing, poverty, and racism. Additionally, Yuvraj Joshi in chapter ten, maintains that the United States needs an integrated justice strategy—one that pursues reparations and policing reform alongside affirmative action, voting rights, political and judicial reform, and other structural changes. Joshi insists that none of these changes alone can overcome White supremacy, yet all of them working in tandem can place the United States on a more democratic path, with transitional justice helping to guide this effort.

While the preceding interventions are focused domestically, Adelle Blackett in chapter twelve stresses the need for transformative action to redress anti-Black racism at the international level. Blackett emphasizes that a transformative agenda at the United Nations requires the United Nations to "do more than condemn expressions and acts of racism," as high-ranking officials of African and African descent publicly urged in 2020.[8] She admonishes us that we allow the past to be erased and its legacies to persist unless and until we redress the structural anti-Black violence that is exacted on people of African descent. Blackett writes with the fierce urgency of now and identifies this time, as fraught as it is, as an unmistakable opportunity to shift course and to be deeply deliberate and transformative. Blackett cautions us in her chapter that transformation will not happen unless initiatives are comprehensive and complete. But what would such transformation entail in national security?

Insights from Abolition

Abolitionist theory has valuable insights. To invoke Mariame Kaba's words here, we must abolish the security state because "liberal reforms . . . have failed for nearly a century."[9] Kaba argues that "more rules" will not "mean less violence."[10] The implications of several, though not all, contributions in this volume lead toward a form and a vision of abolition—that the security state has deleterious consequences for communities internally and externally and

---

[8] Citing "Weight of History," Senior Officials of African Descent Issue Call to "Go Beyond and Do More" to End Racism, U.N. NEWS (June 14, 2020), https://news.un.org/en/story/2020/06/1066 242 (including the full text of the letter by U.N. Senior African Officials, On the Black Lives Matter Protests and Other Mass Demonstrations Against Systemic Racism and Police Brutality).

[9] Mariame Kaba, Yes, We Mean Literally Abolish the Police, N.Y. TIMES (June 12, 2020), https://www.nytimes.com/2020/06/12/opinion/sunday/floyd-abolish-defund-police.html.

[10] Id.

must be abolished as currently constituted. Numerous contributions articulate the ways in which the national security state has a racially disparate impact both internally and externally. Certainly, there is not a single era in the history of national security in which the security state was not used as a force of violence against people of color. Du Bois identified the problem of the color line in the 1900s, and its effect is still felt everywhere. The impact and reach of the security state is one wherein marginalized people are suppressed and racial hierarchies and the status quo are upheld. The problems identified in this volume are so profound and integral that it should leave us skeptical that reforms that tinker around the edges with the apparatus of national security will be productive. Undoubtedly, reforms which leave problematic structures in place will not achieve the transformation needed for national security and the security state.

A fundamental abolitionist understanding is that the carceral state as a form of social control is unacceptable. The security state overlaps with the carceral state and is similarly immoral, cruel, and unjust. At its core, it is a dehumanizing institution. One consequence of this view is that none of the theories of national security from older models and approaches, like the balance of power or collective security, to newer frameworks and conceptualizations like the democratic peace theory or the incentive theory, justify the role of national security in the world order. Further, because states have persistently violated rights, excluded persons and groups, and subordinated peoples internally, transnationally, and internationally, they do not have the moral standing to act in ways that call people to account for purported national security transgressions. This is more than a functionalist argument that national security as practiced does not work, or about effectiveness, deterrence, violence prevention, rehabilitation and reform, and the like. Certainly, functionalist arguments can and have been advanced in this book and elsewhere that the security state exacerbates the problems that it seeks to solve. Instead, this is a deeper critique that the vast impacts of the security state on human beings are fundamentally harmful and morally wrong. The operating principles and systems that would need to take the place of the security state are so qualitatively different that the concept of abolition may best describe and pave the way for this approach.

Abolitionist visions are certainly far afield from the topics that usually consume national security experts. As Aziz Rana notes in chapter three, these conversations tend to focus more on technical legal debates about the means used to project force and power. Rana astutely observes in his chapter, that the very narrowness of the discussions—when is targeted killing acceptable; where and for how long can detainees be held—reflects essential and pervasive limitations of the field. Rana demonstrates how national security discussions that center around conventional trade-offs—how to balance liberty and security—even when critical of particular security excesses, rarely confront what it would mean to properly remove from government officials their largely unchecked and continuous capacity to exercise discretionary violence. Rana argues that national security as a field infrequently considers how today's modes of coercion replicate historic settler and racial assumptions of inferiority.

A common response to abolitionist positions is what to do about the "worst of the worst" offenders. In the realm of national security, the worst of the worst actors are often deemed terrorists. Yet an abolitionist framework provides a lens to question the ability of the current approach to deal with the "worst of the worst." Scholars like Gil Gott aptly note that the demonization of "enemy groups" is racialized in national security law and policy.[11] Indeed, Jaya Ramji-Nogales in chapter six clarifies how this demonization is evidenced in the intersection between immigration law and policy, and national security claims to safeguard White majoritarian interests from the racialized other. Additionally, the work of scholars such as Wadie E. Said demonstrates how the construction of the terrorist, the criminal, and the illegal immigrant as "foreign" facilitates the migration of "war on terror" practices from the global arena to the domestic, while in other instances police practices are brought to bear in the context of external wars.[12] Similarly, commentators like Sahar Aziz and Khaled E. Beydoun have made explicit connections between the targeting of Black and Brown populations as "terrorists" for dissident activity, in "Fear of a Black and Brown Internet: Policing Online Activism."[13] While others like Darryl Li have scrutinized the consequences of policing transnational Muslim populations and the concomitant placement of some people outside the law and others above it.[14] None of this renders us anymore

[11] Gil Gott, *The Devil We Know: Racial Subordination and National Security*, 50 VILL. L. REV. 1073, 1075 (2005).

[12] Wadie E. Said, *Law Enforcement and the American Security State*, 4 WIS. L. REV. 819, 835–48 (2019).

[13] Sahar F. Aziz & Khaled A. Beydoun, *Fear of a Black and Brown Internet: Policing Online Activism*, 100 B.U. L. REV. 1151 (2020).

[14] Darryl Li, *A Universal Enemy?: "Foreign Fighters" and Legal Regimes of Exclusion and Exemption Under the "Global War on Terror,"* 41 COLUM. HUM. RTS. L. REV. 355 (2010).

secure, and it certainly does not render targeted groups, peoples, and nations any more secure.

An abolitionist vision of security is not a world in which the security state keeps Black, Brown, and other marginalized peoples in check through threats of and actual arrest, detention, torture, incarceration, violence, and death. Monica C. Bell clarifies in chapter four that "thick safety" demands social, economic, and physical conditions that produce the ability to protect self, family, and community from threats, including the threat of state violence. Bell notes that the distinction between "thin safety and thick safety" is not merely a domestic challenge but that this bifurcation also appears in external and global conversations about national security. Moreover, Andrea Armstrong, in chapter five, pertinently exhibits how claims of security are often pretextual for expanding governmental authority and heightened secrecy. Furthermore, a major abolitionist insight is interrogating the role of institutions, as opposed to individualizing and decontextualizing acts of violence. Indeed, Aslı Bâli's contribution in chapter eight clarifies that activists are informed by the knowledge that the causes of racial violence cannot be explained by abuses or excesses committed by individuals alone, that instead there is a need to look structurally at the institution of policing itself and the criminal legal system. Notably, Tracey L. Meares, a professor and member of the Obama administration's President's Task Force on 21st Century Policing, recognized before the uprising that "policing as we know it must be abolished before it can be transformed."[15]

Thus, another important insight of abolition theory is the acknowledgment that a toxic system cannot be reformed. In chapter ten, Yuvraj Joshi articulates how protesters were not demanding discrete remedies for discrete harms. Instead, they were calling for a comprehensive and coordinated transition process that deals with the legacy and threat of White supremacy in the United States. Joshi maintains that within a transitional justice framework, redirecting resources from policing could be a way of funding reparations for slavery, Jim Crow, and ongoing racism. He postulates that it could also be a way of redressing the harms of policing. Joshi observes that "defunding the police" may be both a means to reparations and a form of repair. In chapter nine, Noura Erakat observes that activists have connected the abolitionist demand to "defund the police" with a more robust social welfare program that

---

[15] Tracey L. Meares, *Policing: A Public Good Gone Bad*, Bos. Rev. (Aug. 1, 2017), https://www.bostonreview.net/articles/tracey-l-meares-public-good-gone-bad/.

makes prisons obsolete. Erakat points out that protestors have insisted that the United States can afford these programs by reducing its military budget; hence, the social media hashtags to #DefundPolice and #DefundMilitary.

Significantly, Aslı Bâli in chapter eight connects how calls for the military to intervene to suppress protests in American cities inadvertently illustrated how institutions and practices of racialized violence at home are connected to the aerial bombardment campaigns, extrajudicial (drone) killings, and indefinite detentions that are the hallmarks of the overseas military engagements of the American security state. Bâli educates us on how policing at home and America's military engagements abroad are two faces of the same coin. She contends that the protests against police violence drew attention to the coercive apparatus of the state and illuminated how the tactics, weapons, and training employed to suppress resistance abroad can also be deployed against protesters in America's cities.

A further proposition for national security informed by abolitionist theory is that the only way to limit the excesses of the security state is to reduce its footprint in the world. In other words, if there is less contact between the public and the security state apparatus, then there are fewer opportunities for the security state to brutalize and enact violence. Yet fundamentally re-envisioning national security requires more than just reducing the size and scope of the security state. Bâli movingly argues that dismantling the structures of racist policing at home requires recognizing this continuum of security state violence that connects domestic policing, border enforcement, and America's ever-expanding military footprint abroad. She convincingly displays how national debates about divestment from militarized policing must connect arguments about "defunding the police" to a transformative vision for the sprawling security state, one that disrupts practices of racialized violence and advances a vision of racial justice at home and abroad.

Undoubtedly, an advocacy strategy that connects investment in communities at home to global reparative justice is a formidable political vision that must confront the economic drivers at play. Indeed, challenging the role of "racial capitalism," a term coined by Cedric Robinson, which refers to the centrality of race in structuring social and labor hierarchies in capitalist economies,[16] will be key for any transformative change of the security state.

---

[16] *See generally* CEDRIC ROBINSON, *Racial Capitalism: The Nonobjective Character of Capitalist Development, in* BLACK MARXISM: THE MAKING OF THE BLACK RADICAL TRADITION 9 (3d ed. 2020) (1983).

Du Bois in 1915 recognized this connection when he intimated that "we gain industrial peace at home at the mightier cost of war abroad."[17] He queried:

> What do nations care about the cost of war, if by spending a few hundred millions in steel and gunpowder they can gain a thousand millions in diamonds and cocoa? How can love of humanity appeal as a motive to nations whose love of luxury is built on the inhuman exploitation of human beings, and who, especially in recent years, have been taught to regard these human beings as inhuman?[18]

Writing many decades later, Noura Erakat, in chapter nine touches on the continued salience of the political economy of the security state. Erakat notes that instead of shrinking the U.S.s military budget, which the Trump administration had increased by twenty percent, the Biden administration increased the budget by nearly $37 billion dollars. Yet, as Bâli contends, in chapter eight, so long as America's security state comprises forms of racialized violence that connect the local to the global, opposition strategies must also address the deep connections between policing, border enforcement, and military deployments to do justice to the eloquent demands that radiated across the globe during the uprising.

Revisiting these demands is especially necessary now, given the ongoing backlash to substantial racial reckoning and transformation. Yet, as Catherine Powell notes in chapter two, we have faced retrenchment before and must equip ourselves for a longer battle. Powell argues that we will continue to experience periods of progress and retrenchment, and that a human rights paradigm has the potential to develop broader, more robust movements to challenge periods of retrenchment. Both Erakat in chapter nine and Powell in chapter two, emphasize the important role of social movements. Powell sees encouragement in the way that activists are increasingly returning to the language and substance of human rights to draw interconnections between various movements at home and abroad. For Erakat, grassroots coalitions, structured by anti-imperialist politics and solidarity principles, can raise crucial questions, and shed light on the entwinements of domestic and

---

[17] W.E.B. Du Bois, *The African Roots of War*, ATLANTIC (May 1915) https://www.theatlantic.com/magazine/archive/1915/05/the-african-roots-of-war/528897/.
[18] *Id.*

international state violence. The perilousness of the present moment requires the bold vision that many of the contributors in this volume seek to advance.

Radical Imagination

Abolitionists encourage us to use radical imagination to envision another world. Monica C. Bell, in chapter four, clarifies that "radical imagination" means that ideas are radical in a Left political sense and radical in their boldness and expansiveness. Mariame Kaba notes that domestically, "when people, especially [W]hite people, consider a world without the police, they envision a society as violent as our current one, merely without law enforcement — and they shudder. As a society, we have been so indoctrinated with the idea that we solve problems by policing and caging people that many cannot imagine anything other than prisons and the police as solutions to violence and harm."[19] Bell cautions us that the language of radical imagination, though motivating to some advocates and activists, might seem frightening or unrealistic to others. However, Bell advises that it is important to remember that there is magical thinking on all sides. Bell asserts that it takes imagination to envision a world without police and prisons, but that it also takes a very bold imagination to believe that it is possible to stop unjustified, extrajudicial, and racialized police killings with mere training and resources.

Quite a few of the contributions in this volume offer different guidance on what radical imagination means as applied to national security. For Aziz Rana, in chapter three, the field of national security must reckon with foreign interventionism as only one expression of a broader colonial imagination and infrastructure, present since the framing and never adequately uprooted. Rana encourages us to adopt the same anticolonial imagination that circulated during the global era of decolonization and to direct it at the American security project itself. Radical imagination, according to Rana, necessitates rejecting the presumptive legitimacy of the state's international police power. For Rana, radical imagination includes ending the colonial status of all the existing territorial dependencies—in line with the genuine political desires of local and self-determining communities. Rana also suggests that such radical imagination encompasses everything from sharing sovereignty with Native peoples and land return to reparations,

---

[19] Kaba, *supra* note 9.

decriminalizing the border, transformative and structural reforms to intelligence and policing apparatuses, and providing judicial avenues for the remedy of past colonial crimes as well as contemporary national security ones. Rana's and other offerings in this book certainly provide a platform for us to think more deeply and critically about what decolonizing national security and disentangling the discipline from race and empire require.

Abolition provides a unique framework through which to question the core assumptions of national security—its purpose, its function, and its impact, and to take seriously the scale of human devastation wrought by interventions done in its name. An abolitionist framework pushes us to consider an end to the security state as a catch-all solution for societal problems. What would the world look like with billions of extra dollars freed from the security state? Abolitionist theory forces us to consider: Why national security? What does security mean to historically subordinated groups? Are there other less dehumanizing and brutalizing alternatives? What would it mean to build other means and methods of security? How might modest reforms perpetuate the worst features of the current system? In the end, if scholars and policymakers are earnestly committed to addressing these issues in theory and in practice, and to centering the experience of those who have long been on the receiving end of racialized state violence, radical imagination may well be the only meaningful path forward for national security.

Index